FINALE POWER!

Mark Johnson

Finale Power!

Copyright ©2002 Muska & Lipman Publishing, a division of Course Technology

Credits: Senior Editor, Mark Garvey; Production Editor, Rodney A. Wilson; Proofreader, Don Prues; Copyeditor, Martin Sterpka; Technical Editors, Allen Fisher, Michael Johnson, Kami Miller; Cover Design and Interior Design and Layout, Chad Planner, *Pop Design Works*; Indexer, Kevin Broccoli, *Broccoli Information Management*.

Publisher: Andy Shafran

Third-Party Software Developers: TGTools Plug-in Collection, Tobias Giesen; Patterson Plug-in Collection, Robert Patterson; JW Plug-ins, Jari Williamsson; Dolet for Finale, Recordare LLC; SharpEye, Visiv.

Library of Congress Catalog Number: 2002113690

ISBN 1-929685-62-9

5   4   3   2   1

Muska & Lipman Publishing
2645 Erie Avenue, Suite 41
Cincinnati, Ohio 45208
www.muskalipman.com
publisher@muskalipman.com

About the Author

Mark Johnson is an employee at MakeMusic!, who has worked as a technical support representative and quality assurance technician for Finale, and other notation products. He is an alumnus of St. Olaf College, where he attained a degree in music theory and composition. He continues to work as a composer, technical writer, and freelance engraver.

Dedication

I dedicate this book to my parents and family who have always been encouraging and supportive in all of my endeavors.

Acknowledgments

I would like to thank the following people for their expertise, guidance and encouragement: everyone in the Technical Support and Quality Assurance departments at MakeMusic!, the music faculty at St. Olaf College, and the many inquisitive Finale users who contacted me during my time in technical support. Your contributions made this book possible.

Contents

vi

3 Basic Note Entry, Articulations, and Expressions 49

6 Slurs, Hairpins, Other Smart Shapes, and Repeats 131

7 Creating and Working With Multiple Staff Scores 157

Introduction

Welcome to the world of Finale. You are about to embark on a journey through the most powerful music notation software in existence, and have plenty of fun along the way.

In this book, you'll learn about creating professional-quality sheet music with Finale, and if you already know how to do this, you'll learn how to do it faster. We'll start by establishing a solid understanding of Finale's framework and then master the everyday shortcuts and tricks that make Finale a breeze to use. We'll then take you through every step of the score creation process, from starting a new document, to entering and spacing your music, to layout, extracting parts, and, finally, printing the score.

Finale has always had a notorious reputation for difficulty, often described as having a "high learning curve." Leave all of that behind. Nowadays, Finale is as easy to learn and use as any professional publishing program. The complexity of music notation itself is the main demon here, and Finale is the ultimate tool for conquering it. That's where this book comes in. You will be presented with a musical topic, and then given a tutorial explaining the many ways to create and customize the musical element using one or several of Finale's tools or options. In other words, you don't need to start with knowledge of Finale to get the most out of this book, just a basic knowledge of music theory and terminology.

If you are a regular Finale user now, you will learn how to quicken your pace using special tricks, little-known features, and supplemental third-party plug-ins. If you have used older versions of Finale, you may be astounded to discover the time-saving improvements built into Finale in the last few versions. Many tasks that involved complicated workarounds in the past can now be done with just a few simple commands.

Over the past several years, Finale has evolved into a program with more power than ever before, and you can harness it. This book will show you how.

What You'll Find in This Book

The goal of this book is to teach you the necessary skills to get the most out of Finale. This book is neither a quick startup guide (like the Finale Installation and Tutorials manual), nor a detailed explanation of menu items and dialog boxes (Like the Finale User Manual). Finale Power! bridges the gap, and integrates the simplicity of a tutorial with virtually all of Finale's tools, including advanced features and plug-ins that you might have overlooked, or never thought you had a reason to use.

After reading this book, you will know how to:

- Begin and set up a new score with any number of staves, each defined for any instrument or transposition you wish.
- Quickly enter music into your score using Finale's entry methods, both with and without a MIDI keyboard.

- Add and/or define articulations, dynamic markings, rehearsal letters, slurs, and other markings to your music.
- Change clefs, key signatures, and time signatures at any point in your score, as well as customize these items in every way.
- Easily define repeat markings for display and playback.
- Create staff groups, edit barlines, and work efficiently with multiple staff scores overall.
- Edit any element of your score, including beams, music spacing, noteheads, tuplets, and measure numbers, both individually and throughout your document.
- Lay out your measures, systems, and pages for printing.
- Extract parts from a score, and even explode a multipart staff into two or more parts.
- Compose with Finale, and learn how to create specific types of scores such as lead sheets, guitar TAB, and chant.
- Open scanned sheet music in Finale, post your music on the Web, and integrate Finale with other programs such as MIDI sequencers and SmartMusic Studio. Even open files in earlier Finale versions.
- Use Finale's plug-ins and plug-ins created by third-party developers to boost efficiency.
- Customize playback.
- Use Finale as an educational tool. Quickly create custom, technique-building exercises as well as musical examples and worksheets.
- Use the many subtle features that make your time spent in Finale efficient, productive, and fun.

Who This Book Is For

This book is for anyone who wants to get the most out of Finale. If you have never used Finale before, this book is a great introduction to the program. You will be taken step-by-step through the basics, establishing a solid foundation that will prepare you for the more advanced techniques you will learn in later chapters. If you use Finale now, prepare to revolutionize your Finale experience with innovative procedures, tips, and tricks, using everything Finale has to offer in addition to third-party plug-ins and even external programs. Whether you are just becoming familiar with this program, or want to become a Finale power user, this book is for you.

How This Book is Organized

This book contains fifteen chapters:

- Chapter 1: "Getting Started." You'll be introduced to Finale's framework, how it is organized, and how it works. Here, you will become acquainted with fundamental tricks and terminology that will prepare you for the chapters to come.

- Chapter 2: "Beginning a New Score." You'll learn the variety of ways to begin a new project, and how to choose the right one. We'll cover how to create a new score from scratch or easily generate a new custom document with the Setup Wizard. You'll learn how to customize all of the elements generated by the Setup Wizard from within the document, and you'll learn the basics for editing any new score.

- Chapter 3: "Basic Note Entry, Articulations, and Expressions." We'll cover the two most common note entry methods—Simple Entry and Speedy Entry—and how to use a MIDI keyboard for note entry. Also, you'll learn how to enter articulations and expressions. By the end of this chapter, you will be prepared to score an instrumental solo with dynamic markings and articulations.

- Chapter 4: "Advanced Note Entry, Chords, and Lyrics." You'll learn more ways to enter music into your score, including real-time entry with a MIDI keyboard (HyperScribe). We'll also describe how to add lyrics and chord symbols. By the end of this chapter, you will be prepared to create a lead sheet with chord symbols and lyrics.

- Chapter 5: "Clefs, Key Signatures, and Time Signatures." Here, you'll learn how to add clef, meter, and time changes at any point in your score. We'll also move into more advanced techniques for manipulating the appearance of clefs, key signatures, and time signatures.

- Chapter 6: "Slurs, Hairpins, Other Smart Shapes, and Repeats." You'll learn how to create and customize all of these items. Highlights of this chapter include how to tell Finale to adjust slurs for you automatically and how to most easily define repeat barlines and text.

- Chapter 7: "Creating and Working With Multiple Staff Scores." Here, you'll learn how to handle scores with many staves For example, you'll learn to create and edit staff groups and barlines, and even select certain staves for viewing. We'll cover how to eliminate empty staves in systems (optimize), and even how to make changes to all staves in your score at once.

- Chapter 8: "Alternate Notation, Staff Styles, and Guitar Tablature." You'll learn how to create staves with alternate notation styles, such as slash, rhythmic, and tablature notation, and then learn how to apply these styles, or any staff attribute, to any region of a staff. At the end of this chapter, use the skills you have learned to create a guitar part with TAB.

- Chapter 9: "Editing Your Music." Here, we'll cover the many ways to edit your score en masse. Copy, paste, transpose, or choose from many other options to edit any region of your score. Here, you'll also learn how to fine-tune the music spacing and manage fonts.

- Chapter 10: "Fine Tuning: the Details." You'll learn how to align and position just about any item in your score with great precision, as well as how to make fine adjustments to beams, stems, noteheads, accidentals, augmentation dots, and ties.

- Chapter 11: "Measure Numbers, Graphics, Part Extraction, and Printing." You'll learn how to finalize your score by defining the measure numbering, inserting graphics, creating parts from the score, and printing.

- Chapter 12: "Tricks for Specific Projects and Composing With Finale." Here, we'll focus on techniques for creating particular types of notation, including chant, figured bass, and cross staff notation. You'll also become acquainted with Finale's orchestration and compositional utilities such as the Piano Reduction and Composer Assistant plug-ins.

- Chapter 13: "Customizing Finale, Scanning, and Tricks for Music Educators." You'll learn how to customize the Finale program to fit your personal working style by managing Finale's Program Options. You'll also learn the best ways to open a scanned score into Finale and how to use Finale as an educational tool.

- Chapter 14: "Playback and the MIDI Tool." You'll learn how to quickly spot-check your music for accuracy using the many built-in tricks for defining playback of staves and regions. You'll also learn how to generate an accurate MIDI performance of your score using the MIDI Tool and other features and plug-ins designed to edit playback.

- Chapter 15: "Integrating Finale With the Web and Other Programs." You'll learn how to share files online, post your music to a website and transfer Finale files to other programs. You'll also learn how to expand Finale's capabilities using the many available third-party plug-ins.

About the Accompanying CD-ROM

Included with your Finale Power! book package is a companion CD-ROM containing supplemental third-party plug-ins, music examples, and links to informational Finale websites. You will be directed to the Finale Power! CD-ROM at certain points throughout the book. To use the material on this CD, simply place the disk into your CD-ROM drive. An HTML page will auto-launch with links to several websites and a Read Me file containing complete installation instructions for the included material. If you do not see the "Finale Power! Utilities" title page appear upon inserting the accompanying CD-ROM, in Windows, open the Windows Explorer (Window-E), select your CD-ROM drive, and double-click the file "FP.htm." On Macintosh, simply double-click the Finale Power! CD-ROM icon, and then double-click FP.htm. Links to resources included on the CD-ROM can also be found online at www.finalepower.com.

1
Getting Started

OK, it's time to start the journey to Finale proficiency! If you are familiar with programs similar to Finale, some of the basics might come easy for you. If not, this chapter will be extremely useful for understanding how Finale is organized and how it works. If you consider yourself an experienced Finale user, there are tricks and procedures here that will help boost your productivity on a program-wide level. If you haven't had much experience with Finale, don't worry. This chapter is particularly important for the individual who has never used Finale. In any case, the terminology and general concepts described in this chapter will lay the groundwork for topics we'll be discussing later.

Here's a summary of what you will learn in this chapter:

> ▶ How to register your copy of Finale.
> ▶ How to install Finale, and set up for use with MIDI.
> ▶ How to get around in Finale.
> ▶ Finale file types.

Before You Begin

I am going to assume you already own Finale, and preferably the most recent version. This book is written to be consistent with Finale 2003, so if you own an earlier version, some of the instructions will not apply. If you are considering an upgrade, install the Finale 2003 demo available at www.makemusic.com. The Finale demo is a fully functional copy of the latest Finale version, but without the ability to save, and it limits printing to one page. Feel free to use the Finale demo in conjunction with this book to decide whether an upgrade is right for you.

Register Finale

Register your copy of Finale. There are many benefits that come along with becoming a registered owner. For example, you become eligible for free technical support via phone or e-mail. If you decide to call tech support, you may be subject to the long distance charges, but no one will ask for your credit card number. As a registered owner, you can also upgrade your copy of Finale as new versions become available. These upgrades are much less costly than buying Finale outright. Also, with the new features and bug fixes, owning the most recent upgrade is key to getting the most out of Finale. MakeMusic! Coda Music Technologies, referred to throughout the rest of the book as Coda, traditionally releases a new version of Finale each summer. In addition, registered owners benefit from free maintenance updates as they become available.

Your Version of Finale

There are many versions of Finale scattered about. In the late 1980s, Coda released Finale 1.0; since then, there have been over ten large-scale product upgrades. Each upgrade contains useful new features, bug fixes and interface improvements. In the last few years particularly, Finale has become much easier to learn, and it has become far better at handling many of the complex tasks that required awkward workarounds in the past. Actually, to explain how to do everything described in this book would take twice as many pages for an older version of Finale. To make the most of Finale and this book, I strongly recommend upgrading to the most recent version of Finale. Again, this book is written to be consistent with Finale 2003, and some major reorganization has been done, especially since Finale 2002.

In addition to owning the most recent Finale version, it is also important to get the latest product update. After each upgrade release, Coda continues to add new features and fix bugs that crop up. Registered owners can either download the latest update from Coda's website (www.makemusic.com) or contact their customer service department for an update CD. This update is free, and you should consider it part of the software you purchased. Check Coda's website periodically to be sure you have the most recent update.

Each time a new version of Finale comes out, all changes and bug fixes are documented in the Read Me file. To make sure you are up to date with the most recent changes, I recommend reading through this file whenever you upgrade or update Finale. The Read Me file is located in your Finale folder.

Your Finale Package

Whether or not you are new to Finale, it is a good idea to become familiar with the resources that came with your Finale package. These include the Installation and Tutorials manual, Quick Start Video Tips, Quick Reference Card, and User Manual. Below is a brief description of these resources and how to use them most effectively as you work with Finale.

Installation and Tutorials

Though I will cover the fundamentals of Finale in this book, you will find the Installation and Tutorials that come with Finale a valuable resource, especially if you are new to Finale. Use the manual for help with installation and MIDI setup, as there are step-by-step instructions for these at the beginning. Run through the tutorials to get a good feel for many of the basic features. This is especially beneficial for learning how to use the most common tools in the context of real-world situations.

Quick Start Video Tips

Once you have installed Finale, you may also want to take a look at the Quick Start Video Tips. These are short video clips that introduce several key features, describing their purpose and how to use them. You will be prompted to watch these the first time you start the program.

Quick Reference Card

The Quick Reference Card is a small pamphlet-like book containing information that you may want to access quickly instead of hunting through the User Manual. In it, you will find all the keyboard shortcuts, font characters and a visual index of the tools you will need to use for a variety of musical figures. Keep your Quick Reference Card near your computer any time you are working with Finale. It can save you a lot of time.

The User Manual

The Finale User Manual (formally known as the On-Line Documentation) is in PDF format and available from the Help menu. Veteran Finale users will discover that this is the replacement to those three bulky volumes that used to accompany the software. You will find this electronic format very convenient as you jump between chapters easily while investigating any topic right from your computer screen. It is heavy in content, describing the functionality of each dialog box in great detail, and is a valuable resource for the beginner and expert user alike.

You will benefit most from the User Manual by treating it as a reference to a specific subject. For instance, say you want to modify your measure numbers. Click the Help menu and choose Index from the User Manual submenu. Find Measure Numbers from the alphabetical list and click it to get directly to the chapter describing measure numbers. Do not attempt to read through the User Manual as you would the tutorial (or this book). You may not need to know all the information given on a certain topic to complete the task at hand. Also, there may be other valuable time-saving methods and tricks from other areas of the program you might be missing. To make the most of Finale, you will need to develop an approach to each individual project and incorporate many of Finale's tools. There is even a small description for how to use the User Manual in the User Manual itself. Once you have the program started, click the Help menu and choose How to Use the User Manual from the User Manual submenu.

The Companion CD-ROM

Included with Finale Power! is a CD-ROM containing the JW plug-ins, Patterson Plug-in Collection, TGTools plug-ins, Dolet for Finale, and SharpEye. These are all supplemental plug-ins that have been designed to give your Finale package even more power. They make many complicated tasks easy, and include shortcuts for playback, spacing, part extraction and many other tasks. The JW plug-ins are yours for free. TGTools, the Patterson Collection, Dolet, and SharpEye are full-featured demo versions you can use at no cost for a limited time. Throughout the book, you will be referenced to these plug-ins where appropriate, so you won't have to do things the long way when you don't have to. Here is a short description of the supplemental plug-ins included in the Finale Power! companion CD-ROM.

TGTools

TGTools, created by Tobias Giesen, is a set of third party plug-ins you can use to enhance your Finale software. After installing TGTools, you will see a new item in the menu bar at the top of your screen—TGTools—which contains over sixty additional features. This plug-in set includes utilities for expression management, music spacing, playback, part extraction and much more. It has become a staple for many professional Finale users, and I highly recommend incorporating it into your Finale repertoire. Throughout this book, you will be directed to the TGTools plug-ins where appropriate.

To install the TGTools demo, insert the Finale Power! companion CD-ROM. Then, if you are connected to the Internet, click the TGTools link to go to the TGTools download page, where you can download a demo version. Follow instructions on the site to download and install

TGTools. If you do not have an Internet connection, click the Read Me link for instructions on installing TGTools from the companion CD-ROM.

The TGTools plug-in set available for download, and included on the companion CD-ROM, is a full-featured 30-day trial version. After 30 days, you can use only one TGTools dialog per Finale session. You can extend your evaluation period by requesting a registration code from developer Tobias Giesen. To do this, or to purchase a registered version of TGTools, visit www.tgtools.de. Also, these plug-ins are improved regularly, so be sure to check the site periodically to make sure you have the most recent version. The version included on the companion CD is v2.04b.

Patterson Plug-in Collection

The Patterson Plug-in Collection, created by Robert Patterson, contains many helpful utilities. Here is a short description of a few of them:

▶ Beam Over Barlines: Use this plug-in to easily extend beams across barlines (otherwise a lengthy procedure).

▶ Mass Copy: Use the Mass Copy plug-in to copy items attached to notes without having to copy the notes themselves. With this plug-in, it is possible to mass copy entry-attached items with Select Partial Measures checked under the Edit menu.

▶ Staff Sets: This plug-in enhances the functionality of staff sets, which allow you to isolate selected staves for viewing in Scroll View (described further in chapter 7). With this plug-in, you can define a view percentage for each staff set, and also define as many staff sets as you like (instead of just the eight offered by Finale).

There are many other plug-ins included with the Patterson Plug-in collection. A fully functional thirty-day trial of this set can be downloaded from www.robertgpatterson.com.

JW Plug-ins

The JW plug-ins are developed and distributed for free by third-party plug-in developer Jari Williamsson. Among them are:

▶ JW Tempo: Define accelerandos and ritardandos for easy playback. All you need to do is select a region, set the beginning and ending tempo, and click OK.

▶ JW Search and Replace: Search for any type of text (text blocks, expressions, staff names, etc.), and replace all occurrences quickly and easily.

▶ JW Playback: Tell Finale to play back any number of staves, groups, or a measure region without having to go into the Instrument List.

These are just a few of the plug-ins available. You can download all of the freeware JW plug-ins at www.jwmusic.nu/freeplugins/index.html. You will find complete installation instructions for the JW plug-ins on the Finale Power! companion CD-ROM.

Dolet

Dolet is a utility you can use to export and import files in MusicXML format on the Windows platform only. If you own Finale 2003, you already have access to the Dolet Lite plug-in, which, too, can be used to export or import MusicXML files. The full version of Dolet is compatible with Finale 2000, 2001 and 2002, and therefore offers a method of compatibility among these Finale versions. By exporting a file from Finale 2003 in MusicXML format and importing it in Finale 2000, for example, you have essentially achieved backwards compatibility with a good deal of accuracy.

You can also use the MusicXML import feature to open files created in any other program that supports the MusicXML format. One program that supports the MusicXML file format is the SharpEye scanning utility.

SharpEye

On Windows, you can use SharpEye to open scanned sheet music and convert it to MusicXML for import into Finale. Many have found this process offers the most accurate solution for converting sheet music into a Finale file. A fully functional trial version of SharpEye is available at their website (www.visiv.co.uk/dload.htm), as well as on the Finale Power! companion CD-ROM. You can find instructions for converting scanned sheet music into a Finale file using SharpEye in chapter 13.

Other Resources

If you are ever curious about the functionality of one of the dialog boxes, simply click the Help button. There is a Help button in just about every dialog box. On Windows, it's usually to the right of the Cancel button; on a Macintosh, the Help button looks like a square box with a question mark. Clicking the Help button will open a window containing a description of the dialog box and links to related material. Click the Find tab in the upper left to search though the help topics.

TIP

On Windows, press the F1 key to open the context help at any time. On a Macintosh, click the Help button in any dialog box to open the context help.

I will do my best to cover all the common troubleshooting tips, but if you run into something and can't find the solution here, go to www.makemusic.com and search the Finale Knowledge Base. The articles in this searchable database were compiled by Coda technical support and cover all of the common problems they are used to hearing. If you can't find the answer there, you can contact Coda technical support at macsupport@makemusic.com (Macintosh users), or winsupport@makemusic.com (Windows users). Or, you can reach them by phone—check the Finale About Box for specific contact information. In Windows, go to the Help menu and select About Finale. On a Mac, go to the Apple menu and select About Finale. To be eligible for technical support, you will need to own a registered copy of Finale. You can also go to the www.codamusic.com website and log on to the user forum to discuss Finale with other Finale users.

Installation and MIDI Setup

There are good installation and MIDI setup instructions available at the beginning of the Installation and Tutorials manual. I recommend using these instructions to get started. Instead of hashing through the same detailed step-by-step procedure, this section will focus on common problems people encounter during the installation and MIDI setup process.

Installation

Nine times out of ten, installation will be a breeze. Pop the CD in and just keep clicking Next, OK or Accept and everything should work like a charm. Unfortunately, when something goes wrong things can get a little complicated. Here are some helpful tips to avoid or to solve potential installation problems. Since many of the common problems are platform specific, we'll cover Windows and Macintosh installation separately.

Installation on Windows

Here are some tricks to a smooth installation on the Windows platform:

1. If you plan to install a new version of Finale, first remove all older versions of Finale from your system. When you do this, make sure you spare any files you have created and saved in the Finale folder. Your new version of Finale will be able to open all files saved from any earlier version.

2. Before installation, close all programs running on your computer. This includes any programs running in the background, such as antivirus software. For Windows 98 or ME, press Ctrl-Alt-Del once to bring up the Close Program/Task Manager dialog box. This lists every process that is running on the system. Explorer and Systray are always running, so leave them alone. If you see anything other than those two, click on any one of the others and click End Task. When that goes away, press Ctrl-Alt-Del again and End Task on another one in the list. (If a program remains on the list after you have tried to End Task on it, click on it. Click and hold on End Task for ten seconds, then release it. If a "This program is not responding ..." message box appears, click the End Task button in the message box). Repeat the process until only Explorer and Systray are left. Then, begin the installation. For Windows 2000 or XP, Press Ctrl-Alt-Del once and click Task Manager. Click the Applications tab and End Task on all of the items there. Click on the Processes tab. This lists every process that is running on the system. Click on User Name or User Group to reorganize the list. Start at the top, highlight a process and click the End Process button. There are some processes that Windows will not let you shut down, so when you reach one of these, you may exit the Task Manager.

3. While installing on a machine running Windows, you may get an error message that complains about a missing DLL (dynamic-link library) file. The error message will say something like "The dynamic link library MSVCP60.DLL could not be found in the specified path." To resolve this problem, either update your copy of MS Windows or run a search online and download the missing DLL file. Generally, you will want the most recent DLL updates available.

4. After installation, restart your computer. Though you may not be prompted to do this, it is still a good idea. By doing this, you also restart all of the tasks you closed down before installation.

5. If, following installation, you open Finale and see a bunch of strange characters on the screen, you may be missing your Finale music fonts. To reinstall them, run the Finale installation again and when you see a window for Install Type, choose Custom and click Next. Put a checkmark on all items that have "TrueType," or "PostScript" in their names. Click Next until the installation is completed. Then, restart your computer.

Installation on Macintosh

The number of common installation problems is fewer on Macintosh computers than on Windows. However, there are a few things to know that might be helpful while getting started.

If you are running OSX, Finale should run in Classic Mode, but you will need to run the installer in OS 9. Apple recommends doing this for all classic software not yet compliant with OSX. In OSX, click the Apple menu, choose System Preferences and then Startup Disk. Choose your OS 9 System Folder and close out of the System Preferences. When you restart, you will be running in OS 9. Install Finale as you would normally. If you plan to use OMS (Open Music System) or FreeMIDI, these will also need to be installed and configured while operating in OS 9. You can then boot back into OSX and run Finale in Classic Mode: Go to the Apple menu and choose Control Panels, then Startup Disk. Select your OS X System folder and click Restart.

If you have plenty of RAM and want to increase Finale's speed, or if you have plenty of RAM and are getting Memory Errors (Type 1, 2 and 3), you may want to increase the memory allotted to Finale. To do this, close Finale, then go to the Finder and Open the Finale folder. Click once on the Finale icon so it is highlighted. Click the File menu, choose Get Info, and then select Memory from the submenu. Here, you will see a Memory Requirements section. If you do not see the Memory Requirements section, find the pop-up menu called "General Information," then click on it and change it to "Memory." Increase the values for Preferred Size and the Minimum Size. The new memory allocations will take effect next time you start Finale.

MIDI Setup

Again, use the Finale Installation and Tutorials for basic MIDI setup instructions. If you are having problems, here are some things to try. First, make sure your MIDI cables are connected properly:

Hooking Up the MIDI Cables

If you want to use an external MIDI instrument (like a MIDI keyboard) with Finale, make sure the MIDI input device is properly connected to the computer. As simple as it sounds, incorrectly connecting the MIDI cables is a common mistake. If you have a Windows computer and are using a MIDI cable connected to the fifteen-pin jack at the back of your computer, you should connect the MIDI Out cable to the MIDI In port on your keyboard, and the MIDI In cable to the MIDI Out port on your keyboard. If you are using a MIDI interface (this includes most Mac users), one cable should connect to the MIDI Out on the interface and MIDI In on the keyboard. Likewise, the other cable should connect the MIDI In on the interface and the MIDI Out on the keyboard. In other words, the MIDI that comes out of the MIDI input device should go in to the computer or interface.

Some synthesizers have several modes, so if you are having trouble playing a file, make sure your synthesizer is set to receive and transmit MIDI data. Consult the synthesizer manual if you do not know how to do this.

MIDI Setup on Windows

After you have checked the cables, you will need to tell Finale to use the drivers for MIDI In and MIDI Out. MIDI input refers to the information coming into the computer from the MIDI keyboard (note entry into Finale), and MIDI output refers to information sent to the keyboard from the computer (playback from Finale). In Finale, click the MIDI menu and choose MIDI Setup. On the left, select the MIDI driver for your MIDI In device. To see what choices you have available, click the drop-down arrow to see various drivers that are installed. If you have a Sound Blaster card, for example, you might select the driver in that list that says "SB16 MIDI In." On the right side of the MIDI Setup dialog box, choose the driver for your MIDI output. If you want your music to play through a synthesizer, look for an option with "MPU" or "MIDI Out" in its name. If you are using your soundcard (internal sounds) for output, look for an option with "Synth" or "FM" in its name.

If you do not see these drivers in the MIDI Setup window, they have not been installed on your machine or there is a problem with them. You may need to reinstall the drivers for your soundcard or MIDI interface. Contact the manufacturer of your soundcard or interface for more information on reinstalling the device drivers. Once your soundcard is set up properly with your computer, it will work in Finale.

MIDI Setup on Macintosh

To set up MIDI in Finale on a Mac, click the MIDI menu and choose MIDI Setup. For MIDI System, choose one of the available options. If you are using a serial MIDI interface, choose the Finale MIDI driver option. Then, for the Output and Input device settings, after channels 1-16, choose the serial port you are using for your MIDI interface.

If you are using a newer Mac with USB ports, you can use a USB MIDI interface to connect your computer to an external MIDI device. Install the drivers that came along with your USB MIDI interface first. There will be driver installation instructions included with your USB interface. After you have done this, you will need to install a MIDI driver, either FreeMIDI or OMS (Open Music System). You can find the installers for FreeMIDI and OMS on your Finale CD, and they are likely included with your interface. The most recent version of FreeMIDI or OMS can be found on your interface manufacturer's website. OMS and FreeMIDI are not Coda products, so if you are having trouble installing or configuring FreeMIDI or OMS, contact the manufacturer of your USB MIDI interface. They should be able to help.

After you have installed FreeMIDI or OMS, open Finale, click the MIDI menu and choose MIDI Setup. For MIDI System, choose either FreeMIDI or Open Music System. Then, for the top dropdown under Output Device, choose the device name that represents your keyboard. Do the same for the Input Device. You should now be able to use your external MIDI device for input and playback with Finale. (If a device name is italicized, that means it is no longer a part of your active FreeMIDI or OMS configuration and will not work. Most often, you will be able to select the same device name in the menu that is not italicized).

Getting Around in Finale

Let's get acquainted with the outlying structure of Finale and general navigation skills required to use the program. Many instructions throughout this book make the assumption that you are familiar with the following subjects, so it is important to learn about them in preparation for other chapters. Some of this information may seem rudimentary at first, but there are also some pleasant surprises at this level that could have easily slipped by a regular Finale user.

To prepare for this section, launch Finale. Close any dialog boxes that appear. Then, click the File menu, choose New, and then Default Document. This will open a single staff document that you can use to experiment with the following subjects.

A Tool-Based Program

At the core of Finale lies the Main Tool Palette (Figure 1.1). Just about everything you do in Finale is in the context of one of these twenty-seven Main Tools (on Windows, this palette is split into the Main and Advanced Tools Palette). For example, to enter an articulation, first click the Articulation tool. To add a staff, first click the Staff tool. As you work on your score, you can usually make a good guess as to which tool you will need to use, but sometimes it isn't completely clear. For example, you may want to enter a tempo marking at the beginning of your piece. To do this, click the Mass Mover tool, choose a plug-in from the Plug-ins menu, then edit the tempo marking with the Expression tool. The new Finale user then asks, "So what's the Tempo tool for?" thus beginning the downward spiral of frustration that has accompanied the novice Finale user for years. Don't worry, that's what this book is for. The chapters are organized by musical subject, so we will often jump around to different tools to complete similar notation tasks.

Figure 1.1
The Main Tool Palette

When you click a tool in the Main Tool Palette, as many as two things can change on your screen. You may see another tool palette appear that you can use to specify a certain task. For instance, when you click the Simple Entry tool, the Simple Entry Palette appears. You can choose a tool in the Simple Entry Palette to specify a rhythmic value to click into your staff. When you click a tool in the Main Tool Palette, you may also see a new menu item appear at the top of your screen. From this menu, you can customize the way the tool works or you can customize items related to the tool. Click the Staff tool to see the Staff menu appear at the top of your screen, as shown in Figure 1.2.

Figure 1.2
Some Main tools, like
the Staff tool, are
accompanied by a
corresponding menu.

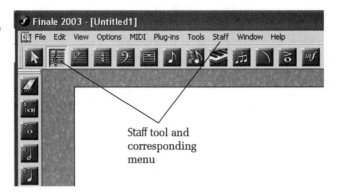

Staff tool and
corresponding
menu

Working with Palettes

You can show or hide any palette with the Window menu. Click the Window menu. The
palettes currently visible have a checkbox to the left of them. Click a checked palette name to
hide it from the screen, or click one of the unchecked palettes to display it. In many cases, you
won't have to worry about manually turning these palettes on or off because Finale
automatically displays them when appropriate.

TIP
In Windows, right-click on the area surrounding a docked palette (the blank
area), or a scroll bar, to easily choose the tool palettes you want to display.

Instead of hiding a palette, you may simply want to move it out of the way. On Mac, the tool
palettes are "floating." These palettes can be repositioned and reshaped by dragging them with
your mouse. On Windows, when you first launch Finale, the tool palettes are located near the
top of your screen. In this state, they are said to be "docked." You can tear each one off
individually (undock it) by dragging the small vertical bar located at the left edge of each palette.
You will now notice a title bar at the top of the palette bearing its name. To change its shape,
move your cursor to the edge of the palette so you can see a small line with two arrows pointing
in opposite directions. Now click and drag to change the shape you prefer. To hide it, simply
click the "X" in the upper right corner. If you drag the palette back to the top of the screen, it
will become docked wherever you decide to place it. To return any undocked palette back to its
most recent docked position, just double-click it. You can also dock palettes at the bottom or at
either side of your screen. Just drag the palette to the edge of your screen until the gray outline
changes shape. Release the mouse button and the palette will dock into place.

TIP
Windows users can remove rarely used tools from a palette to save space. On Windows, click the View menu, choose Customize Palettes, and then select the palette you want to customize.

Message Bar/Status Bar

On Windows, any time you move your cursor over any Finale icon, you will see a brief description of the icon in the Message Bar (Mac) or Status Bar (Windows). To see a description of the tool in the Message Bar on Mac, click on the tool. On Windows, the Status Bar is located at the bottom of your screen (Figure 1.3). On Macintosh, the Message Bar is directly above your score (Figure 1.4). The short description can be especially handy for keyboard shortcut reminders. Click one of the tools now to see the name of the active tool and its description in the Status/Message bars.

Figure 1.3
On Windows, notice the Status Bar in the lower left corner of your screen.

Figure 1.4
On Macintosh, notice the Message Bar located just above your score.

Tool Tips

If you are using Windows, move the cursor over a tool and leave it stationary for a moment. A small box will appear containing the name of the tool. These small boxes are called "Tool Tips" and are available on all tools in any tool palette. These sometimes contain keyboard shortcuts you can use to access the tool more easily.

TIP

As you work, you will find yourself switching between tools a lot. On Windows, to easily select tools you use often, program them to function keys. To do this, simply click the tool you desire to program, hold down Shift and press a function key (F2-F12). On Mac, hold down Control and Option and press a key between F and the comma key. Highlight the tool you wish to be associated with that key and click OK. To access the tool, press Control and the key you programmed (F-comma.) This information is saved with the document, so it will be usable any time you open the document in the future (later, you will learn to customize your default files or templates so that new documents will contain your settings).

The Menus

Notice the menu items at the top of the screen (Figure 1.5). Each of these is a set of controls that governs the document, the program, or the tool selected. The Help menu, which provides informative resources, is the only exception. Nine of these menus will always be visible. These include the File, Edit, View, Options, MIDI, Plug-ins, Tools, Window, and Help menus. The other menu(s) will only appear if the corresponding tool is chosen (Click the Staff tool, for instance, and the Staff menu appears). Like the Main tools, we'll direct you to a menu item when describing a subject that calls for it.

Figure 1.5
The menus

File   Edit   View   Options   MIDI   Plug-ins   Tools   Staff   Window   Help

Many menu items can be accessed easily with keyboard shortcuts. There are certain menu items you might find yourself using frequently (in my case, Undo is a usual one). Click the Edit menu and look to the right of the Undo command. You will see the keystroke Ctrl-Z (Cmd-Z on Mac). Instead of clicking the menu item every time you want to undo, simply use this keyboard shortcut. Refer to the menus for other keyboard shortcuts to save you time as you work.

TIP

On Windows, you can program any menu item to a keyboard shortcut. To do this, click the Plug-ins menu, choose TGTools and click Menu Shortcuts.

TIP

On Windows, you can use keystrokes to open any menu item. Hold down the Alt key and type the underlined letter in the menu name (i.e. Alt-T to open the Tools menu). Then use the underlined letter of the menu item to select it. This is an alternative to clicking the item with your mouse cursor.

Basic Finale Vocabulary

There is some general terminology you need to know. Some of the following terms are unique to Finale, and some are common to other software programs, but all will be used repeatedly throughout this book.

Handles

Handles are small boxes that appear near items in your score that are available for editing (Figure 1.6). Anytime you want to edit an articulation, text block, or expression, for example, click the corresponding tool, or double-click the item with the Selection tool, to see this box appear. You will then be able to click and drag or nudge (with the arrow buttons) the handle to move the item.

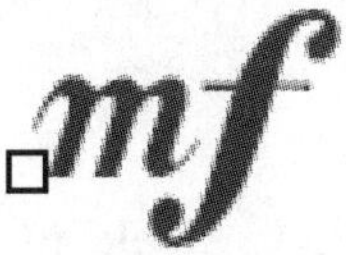

Figure 1.6
Notice the handle to the lower left of this expression.

Often, handles can be double-clicked to open a dialog box for more editing options, or context-clicked (Windows: right-click; Mac: Ctrl-click) to open a context menu containing options specific to that item. You will become more familiar with these procedures as we apply them for certain tasks.

The Cursor

You will find that the state of the cursor can be an informative tool. It can tell you which staff or note an item will be attached to, the exact item that will be entered, or if Finale is processing something. As you work through the program, take note of when the cursor changes and use it to your advantage. There will be descriptions of these cursor changes throughout this book.

The Scroll Bars

On the bottom and right side of your Finale window, you will see vertical and horizontal scroll bars. Click and drag the box within the scroll bars in Page or Scroll view to adjust the viewable area of the page.

Scroll View

There are two ways to view your score in Finale, Scroll View and Page View. When you first open a document, it appears in Page View. From the View menu, choose Scroll View. In this view, you will see one system extending horizontally all the way to the last measure without interruption. This view is great for entering and editing your music without having to flip through pages. Many Finale users prefer to use Scroll View exclusively while entering music, and do not even visit Page View until it's time to lay out the score for printing. Use the scroll bar at the bottom of your screen to navigate through your score, or type a number in the entry field to the left of the scroll bar to move to a specific measure.

Page View

Now click the View menu and choose Page View. Page View is a representation of how the document will look if printed. Items specific to pages, such as the title, page numbers and staff systems are now visible. Use the arrows located at the bottom of the screen to move forward or backward through pages. You can also move to a specific page by typing the page number in the entry field. To easily switch between Scroll and Page view, press Ctrl-E (Command-` on Mac).

TIP

If you want to set up measures you can access quickly in Scroll or Page view, set up Bookmarks. Click the View menu, choose Bookmarks, and then select Add Bookmark (or press Ctrl/Command-B).

Display Colors

You may already have noticed the array of colored items in Finale. In addition to contributing to aesthetic appeal, these actually do serve a purpose. The color of an item allows one to see, at a glance, what tool created it. As you work in Finale, note the color of items and which type of item relates to which color. To see a breakdown of all the colors associated with each element in your score, click the View menu and choose Select Display Colors. You can also use this dialog box to modify the display colors as you wish.

TIP

You can easily edit any item on your screen with the Selection tool. In older Finale versions, to edit any item, you first had to find and click the item's corresponding tool. Now, you can move or delete most items in your score by simply clicking the Selection tool and then clicking the item. There is even a keyboard shortcut for the Selection tool: Ctrl-Shift-A on Windows; Command-Shift-A on Macintosh.

Navigation Tools

Quickly navigating around your score is key to working efficiently within Finale. You can easily adjust the viewable area of your score, zoom in and out, move quickly to a specific measure, or even set up bookmarks to common locations. Changing the viewable area of your screen has no effect on the printout.

Zooming

While working on your document, you may want to zoom in to make fine adjustments or zoom out to see more of your score. While in Page or Scroll view, click the View menu, open the Scale View To submenu and choose a different view percentage; try 200%. Notice the staves become larger. Instead of going all the way to the view menu, you can also use keyboard shortcuts to change your view percentage:

▶ Crtl/Cmd-1 = 100%

▶ Crtl/Cmd-2 = 200%

▶ Crtl/Cmd-4 = 400%

▶ Crtl/Cmd-5 = 50%

▶ Crtl/Cmd-0 = Other (to enter a different percentage)

For more control over viewing various sections of your score, use the Zoom tool. Click the Zoom tool and then click a section of your score to zoom in or Ctrl/Option click to zoom out. In Page View, to specify an area to enlarge, click and drag your cursor diagonally. Notice a dashed box appears. When you release the mouse button, the enclosed area will enlarge to fit the entire viewable area.

TIP

On Windows, click the middle mouse button at any time to zoom in. Ctrl-click the middle mouse button to zoom out. On Mac, Shift-Control-Command-click to zoom in and Shift-Control-Option-Command-click to zoom out.

The Hand Grabber Tool

In addition to zooming in and out, you also need a way to move the viewable region. This is the purpose of the Hand Grabber tool. Click the Hand Grabber tool. Now click and drag to move the page or systems around.

TIP

On Windows, the Hand Grabber tool can be used at almost any time by right-clicking and dragging. On Mac, Option-Command-click and drag.

CAUTION:

In Scroll View, only use the Hand Grabber to move the viewable area vertically. Use the scroll bar exclusively to move around horizontally. You will always want to see the left edge of your staves in Scroll View.

Redrawing Your Screen

While editing your score, you may find that portions of your screen are whited out, or artifacts of items remain on the screen after you delete them. This is a common nuisance that has been around in Finale for ages. When this happens, simply hold down the Ctrl/Command key and press D. This key command will redraw your screen and restore the integrity of the viewable area.

Measurement Units

There are many cases where you might be asked to enter a value to specify a certain distance. For example, you may want to place your title an inch, centimeter or number of EVPUs (ENIGMA Virtual Page Units) from the top page margin. To choose your unit of measurement, click the Options menu, choose Measurement Units, and click one of the available options. Table 1.1 shows an explanation of the relationship between all of the available measurement units.

Table 1.1
Measurement Units Comparison Table

EVPUs	Spaces	Inches	Centimeters	Millimeters	Points	Picas
24	1	.083	.212	2.12	6	.667
1	.042	.0035	.009	.09	.25	.042
288	12	1	2.54	25.4	72	6
113	4.708	.392	1 (.997)	10	28.25	2.3622
11	.458	.038	.1 (.097)	1	2.75	.2362
4	.167	.014	.035	.35	1	.083
48	2	.167	.423	4.23	12	1

In addition to spatial units of measurement, Finale also uses a system of rhythmic or durational measurement. All rhythmic durations (quarter note, eighth note, etc.) can also be expressed in EDUs (ENIGMA Durational Units). Table 1.2 describes the EDU equivalent for each rhythmic duration.

Table 1.2
EDU to Rhythmic Value Equivalents Table

Rhythmic Value	EDU	Rhythmic Value	EDU	Rhythmic Value	EDU
double whole	8192	quarter	1024	dotted 32nd	192
dotted whole	6144	dotted eighth	768	triplet sixteenth	171
whole	4096	triplet quarter	683	32nd	128
dotted half	3072	eighth	512	dotted 64th	96
half	2048	dotted sixteenth	384	64th	64
dotted quarter	1536	triplet eighth	341	dotted 128th	48
half note triplet	1365	sixteenth	256	128th	32

Document and Program Options

There are two general types of settings in Finale: Document Options and Program Options. Document Options are saved with the document and affect only the document on which you are working. They are designed for global changes to your music or layout. Click the Options menu and choose Document Options. Here you will be able to set up a variety of document-wide specifications relating to music spacing, beaming, page format, and many others. We will be covering many of these Document Options throughout this book.

Program Options affect the general operation of the program and will not have any effect on the music in a document. Click the Options menu and choose Program Options (Figure 1.7). Here you can customize how Finale behaves based on your own preferences. Here are some helpful Program Options that are good to know. You can also find more ways to customize the Finale program using the Program Options in chapter 13.

Figure 1.7
Make all program-wide settings in the Program Options dialog box.

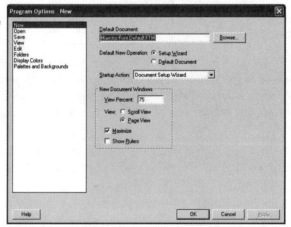

Auto Save

Though you will want to get into the habit of saving often, if you want, you can tell Finale to save your document automatically at regular intervals. This feature adds some insurance in case of a crash, freeze, power outage, etc. In the Program Options dialog box, click the Save option on the left side. Check Auto Save Files(s) and then enter the number of minutes. I like to set this to ten minutes, but you might prefer to save more or less frequently, based on the reliability of your computer.

After you have activated Auto Save, you should then specify a folder into which to put the files that are saved automatically. Click the Folders section of the Program Options dialog box and find the Auto Save option. Click the Browse or Select button to the right and specify a folder. If you ever need to find your Auto Save files, you can look here to find the path. The files saved by Auto Save are not standard Finale files. They will have the extension .ASV. To open them, launch Finale, click the File menu, choose Open and navigate to the folder you have chosen for Auto Save. In the Open dialog box, be sure to display all file types. Then double-click the .ASV file to open it.

CHAPTER 1

Make Backups When Saving Files

Each time you save a file, Finale also creates a backup copy of your file. This backup file is the last saved version of the file you were working on (not including auto saves). If you save a file, and then find that you have saved undesirable changes, you can rely on your backup file to go back to the previously saved version. Note that you will only have one backup file per Finale file. This file is continually being overwritten per each save command, making Backups when Saving Files is turned on by default. If you would like to turn it off, click Save in the left side of the Program Options dialog box and uncheck Make Backups when Saving Files.

If you have Make Backups when Saving Files turned on, you should specify a folder for your backup files. Look in the Folders section of the Program Options dialog box and find the Backup option. Click the Browse or Select button to the right and specify a folder. If you ever need to find your Backup files, you can look here to find the path. The backup files you save are not standard Finale files. They will have the extension .BAK. To open them, launch Finale, click the File menu, choose Open and navigate to the folder you have chosen for Auto Save. In the Open dialog box, be sure to display all file types. Then double-click the .BAK file to open it.

Startup Action

Finale automatically starts the Document Setup Wizard each time you launch Finale. Though this is the most effective way to create new custom documents, you may want Finale to open a template or default document at startup instead. To change the behavior of Finale during startup, click New on the left side of the Program Options dialog box, then click the drop-down arrow after Startup Action.

To quickly open the type of new document you have selected for Default New Operation, hold down the Ctrl/Command key and press N to begin either the Setup Wizard or a New Default Document.

TIP
To set the initial type of view (Scroll/Page View) and the view percentage for any new document, click New in the Program Options dialog box.

Your Default Music Folder

By default, each time you choose to save a new file, Finale automatically prompts you to save in the Finale folder. You are also prompted to choose a file from the Finale folder every time you want to open an existing file. If you want to save and open all of your files from a folder other than the Finale folder, in the Program Options, select Folders. Click the Browse or Select button to the right of the Music field and select the desired folder. Now, every time you choose Save or Open from the File menu, Finale will automatically take you to the music folder you specified.

Save Preferences at Exit

When this box is checked, any changes you make in the Program Options will also apply after you close and reopen Finale. If you only want the Program Options to apply to a single Finale session, uncheck this checkbox.

Preferences and the Finale.Ini File

All of the settings you make in Program Options are saved to a file on your computer. On Mac, this is the Finale Preferences file, which is located in your System Preferences folder. If you want to restore your Finale program back to the way it was when you first installed, simply navigate to the Preferences folder and drag the Finale Preferences file into the Trash.

On Windows, all of your preferences are saved to the Finale.ini file (sometimes it will just say Finale and have a text file icon), which is basically a text file located in your Finale folder. If you want to restore your Finale program back to the way it was when you first installed, navigate to your Finale Folder and delete the Finale.ini.

CAUTION

On Windows, if you decide to delete the Finale.ini file, make sure you take note of your product serial number. All registration information is stored in the Finale.ini; so the next time you start Finale you will be asked to provide this information. Before deleting the Finale.ini, click the Help menu and choose About Finale to record your serial number. On Macintosh, the registration info is not saved in the Finale Preferences file, but is saved to a separate file in the Preferences folder called Finale Registration. There is little, if ever, any need to delete the Finale Registration file.

File Types

Several types of files can be saved from and/or opened in Finale. Each type is represented with a different icon on your operating system. In addition, in Windows, each individual file type will conclude with its own three-letter extension. You may want to become familiar with these file types and what they are used for. For information on Finale's ability to import files in formats other than the ones described here, see chapter 13.

Finale Files (.MUS)

Files saved normally from Finale are in Coda Notation File format. Any Finale file can be opened in the version of Finale with which it was created or any newer version. Finale files are not backwards compatible, so you won't be able to open a new file in an older version of Finale. However, Finale files will open cross-platform (Windows to Macintosh or Macintosh to Windows). Also, since Finale 2001, the file size has decreased considerably from files saved in earlier versions due to automatic file compression while saving.

TIP

If you are saving a file on Macintosh that you intend to open on Windows, be sure that the ".MUS" extension appears at the end of the file name. This allows Windows to associate the file with Finale. In the Save As dialog box, make sure Append File Extensions is checked. In versions of Finale before version 2002, simply type .MUS at the end of the file name.

TIP

If you want to share a Finale file with someone who does not have a version of Finale as current as yours, have them download Finale NotePad from www.makemusic.com. NotePad is a free, simplified notation program that can open any Finale file because it is based on the newest Finale version. You will be able to play files, make minor edits, transpose, save, start new files, and even print using this software. Oh, and did I mention it's free!

Enigma Transportable Files (.ETF)

This type of file was originally designed for opening files cross-platform (from Macintosh to Windows and vice versa). In current versions of Finale, it is no longer necessary to save ETF files for the purpose of cross-platform file sharing. ETF files are much larger in size than Finale Binary files because they are not compressed. They are basically Finale documents in the form of a text file, so they are somewhat less prone to corruption if sent as an e-mail attachment. If you plan on e-mailing your files to friends, I recommend using WinZip (Windows) or Stuffit (Mac) to compress a Coda Notation file (.MUS) to guard against file corruption, as opposed to saving an ETF, though sending a zipped or stuffed ETF is another option to try if all else fails. To save a file in ETF format, click the File menu and choose Save As. For Files of Type, choose ENIGMA Transportable File, then enter a file name and click Save.

NOTE

In Finale, the acronym "ENIGMA" stands for Environment for Notation utilizing Intelligent Graphic Music Algorithms (in case you were wondering).

Coda Template Files (.FTM)

Finale comes with about fifty template files, each containing a default setup for certain types of projects. For instance, if you want to start a piece for concert band, you can save time by opening the Full Concert Band template file that contains a blank concert band score. These preset documents are located in the Templates folder (within the Finale folder). On Windows, these files have the extension FTM. Template files are handled differently on Windows than they are on Macintosh. On Windows, template files are different than regular Coda Notation files. They always open as Untitled documents in Finale, so you will not be prompted to overwrite them when you save. In this way, the original template file is preserved. On Macintosh, a template file is the same kind of file as a Coda Notation file, but can be opened as an Untitled document by choosing New > Document from Template from the File menu. On Macintosh, any file can be opened as an Untitled document by using the Document from Template command. In these ways, template files can be used over and over again.

On Windows, to save your own template, click the File menu and choose Save As. For files of type, choose Coda Template file, then enter a file name and click Save. On Mac, choose Save As, give your template a name and save your template in the Coda Notation File format. Then, choose File > New > Document from Template to open it.

MIDI Files (.MID)

Files in MIDI format are basically standard music files that are transferable among almost all music software. They are very small in size and will open cross-platform. In the context of Finale, they are generally a representation of the playback. When you save a MIDI file from Finale, only the playback information will be retained in the file. When you open a MIDI file in Finale, you will see a translation of the playback information in the form of notation, but all information (page formatting, text, etc.) will be lost. See chapter 15 for more information on saving and opening MIDI files in Finale.

TIP

On Windows, you might want to associate .ETF, .FTM or maybe even .MID files with Finale. Once Finale is associated to a file type, any time you double-click the file's icon, it will open in Finale automatically (typically, *.ETF and *.FTM are automatically assigned to Finale when you install). To create an association, open Windows Explorer (double-click the My Computer icon on your desktop) and find a file type you would like to associate with Finale. Then right-click the file icon. In the Context menu, choose Open With. When you see a list of applications, choose Finale and click OK. Now you can open that file type simply by double-clicking it while working in Windows.

Web Files (.HTM)

You can post Finale files on the Web. To do this, simply choose the File menu, choose Save Special and then Save as Web Page. Select a destination, enter a file name and click Save. When you do this, two files will be saved to the specified location, an MUS file and an HTM file. If you are referencing the HTM file from a website, you will also need to place the corresponding MUS file in the same folder. To save a Finale file for compatibility with the Web, choose the File menu, Save Special, and then Save as Web Page. You will then see the Web Page Options dialog box, as shown in Figure 1.8.

Figure 1.8
Web Page Options
dialog box

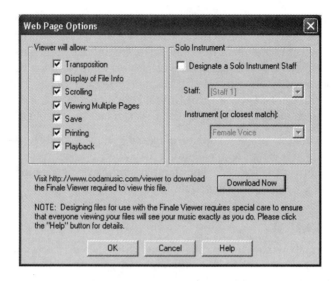

In this dialog box, choose the options that will be available to someone who views the file (print, playback, etc.). Click OK and save the file to a desired location.

When someone opens the link to your Finale file from a website, the file will open in the Finale Viewer. The Finale Viewer can be downloaded from Coda's website at http://www.codamusic.com/coda/fin_viewer.asp. There will be more information on sharing files over the Web in chapter 15.

Library Files (.lib)

Virtually all elements of a document you can define yourself—such as articulations, expressions, shapes, and many others—are organized into libraries. When you open a new default document, Finale offers a collection of default libraries that contain common markings that you can access from various places in Finale. When you select an articulation from the Articulation Selection dialog box, for example, you are choosing a character that exists in the document's Articulation library. When you define a new articulation, Finale saves the new articulation in the document's Articulation library so it will always be available while working with the document. You can use libraries to transfer elements you have defined in one document to any other document. Throughout the book, you will learn how to do this for a wide variety of items.

SmartMusic Accompaniment Files (.SMP)

You will be able to save files that are compatible with SmartMusic Studio in Finale. SmartMusic Studio is another software program developed by Coda that features intelligent accompaniment that will listen to and follow your spontaneous tempo changes as you play your wind instrument or sing. To save a SmartMusic accompaniment, choose the File menu, Save as Special and then Save as SmartMusic Accompaniment. There will be more information on saving SmartMusic accompaniments in chapter 15.

Other File Types

Other than Auto Save and Backup files (ASV and BAK), which were described earlier in this chapter, there is another little-known file type that can be saved from Finale that has the extension *.NOT. *.NOT files can be saved and opened in the Transcription Mode of HyperScribe. Transcription Mode is basically a Finale MIDI sequencing utility that allows you to record a piece first, and enter the notation information (barlines, quantization, etc.) later. There will be more information on Transcription Mode in chapter 4.

2
Beginning a New Score

Now that you have a feel for how Finale works, let's move ahead into the first step for any project: starting a new document. There are several ways to begin your score in Finale. The one you choose will depend on the type of project and how much customization you want control over from the start. Do you want to add and define your staves manually, or have Finale do it for you? In most cases, the Document Setup Wizard will suit your needs just fine, though you might also find one of the existing templates ideal for your project. If you want more control over your score from the start, you could use Finale's default document or a document without libraries. In this chapter, you will learn how to decide which method to use for the type of project you want to start, as well as other helpful tips that apply to almost any new document.

Here's a summary of what you will learn in this chapter:

▶ How to start a score with the Document Setup Wizard.

▶ How to customize your staves.

▶ How to enter and modify text (title, page number, copyright).

▶ The fundamentals of working with the Mass Edit Tool.

▶ The basics of page layout.

Opening a New Document

If you are new to Finale, I recommend using the Document Setup Wizard to begin a new document. You will find this method the easiest for defining all elements critical to a new score—including title, instrument(s), key signature, time signature, and tempo.

Starting a Score with the Document Setup Wizard

The Setup Wizard is perhaps the most common and versatile way to begin a new document. When you first launch Finale, the Setup Wizard opens by default. While in Finale, to start the Setup Wizard at any time, click the File menu, and choose New and then Document With Setup Wizard. You can also hold down the Ctrl/Command key and press N to begin the Setup Wizard. Let's start the Setup Wizard now. If you haven't changed any of your Program Options, simply launch Finale and you will see page 1 of the Document Setup Wizard. If you already have Finale open, hold down Ctrl/command and press N.

Page 1: Title, Composer, Copyright, and Page Size

Any time you start the Setup Wizard, you will see this page (Figure 2.1). Here, enter the title, composer, and copyright of your piece. To move between fields, you can either click on them or press the TAB key.

Figure 2.1
On page 1 of the Setup Wizard, enter the title, composer, copyright, and page size.

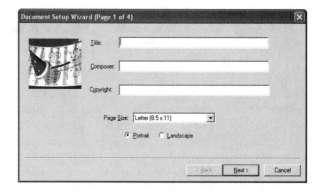

If you haven't thought of a title yet, don't worry; you can leave any of these fields blank if you like. In the Copyright field, you may want to enter a copyright symbol (©). To do this on Windows, hold down the Alt key and type 0169 in the number keypad (with Num Lock on). On Macintosh, hold down the Option key and press the letter G. When you are ready to move ahead, click the Next button.

Page 2: Choose Your Parts

Now choose the instruments you want in your piece. In the left column, choose the instrument family, then double click the instrument you want to add in the second column. You will see the instrument appear in the third column in orchestral score order, regardless of the order you choose them (Figure 2.2). Each instrument you add will become one staff in your Finale score (except in the case of keyboard instruments), so if you want four Trumpet staves, add four trumpets.

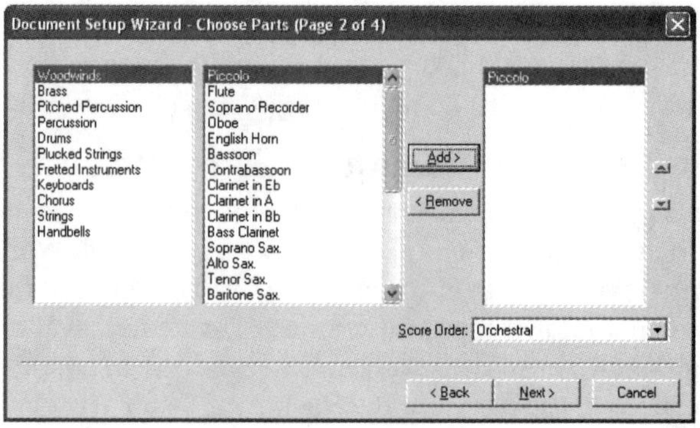

Figure 2.2
On page 2 of the Setup Wizard, add the parts.

To change the order of your instruments, click the Score Order dropdown arrow beneath the third column and choose from the available options. To manually change the order of your instruments, highlight the instrument you would like to move (in the third column), then click the up or down arrows on the right to change their positioning. Double-click any instrument in the third column to remove it. Finale will automatically group staves of similar instrumental sections (with group brackets) in the score upon completing the Setup Wizard. Finale will even incrementally number like instruments, so you need not worry about adding a 1, 2, 3, or 4 to the trumpet names, for example. When you have chosen all of your instruments and placed them in the order you like, click the Next button to continue to the next page. Feel free to click the Back button at any time to make any changes to the previous page. The Setup Wizard will retain all of your settings.

Page 3: Specify Time and Key Signature

Here you can specify the Time and Key signatures of your piece (Figure 2.3).

Figure 2.3
On page 3 of the Setup Wizard, choose the Time Signature and Key Signature.

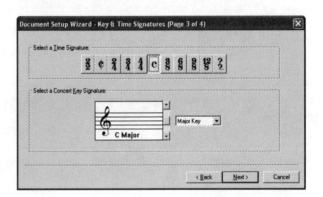

To select a Key Signature, click the up or down arrows of the vertical scroll bar to the right of the Key Signature display in the lower portion of this dialog box. Clicking the up arrow will add a sharp to your Key Signature (or take away a flat), and clicking the down arrow will add a flat to your Key Signature (or take away a sharp). Then choose Major or Minor from the dropdown menu to the right of the Key Signature display. Don't worry about instrument transposition here, just select the concert key of your piece.

To select a Time Signature, click one of the available Time Signature buttons in the upper portion. If the Time Signature you want to use is not available, click the far right button (with the question marks) to specify a custom Key Signature. You will see a dialog box, as seen in Figure 2.4

CHAPTER 2

Figure 2.4
In the Time Signature dialog box, specify a meter for your piece.

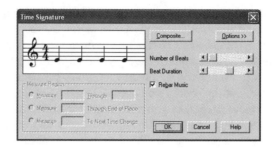

For Number of Beats, click the left or right arrow to increase or decrease the number of beats per measure in your Time Signature. For Beat Duration, click the left or right arrow to increase or decrease the rhythmic value of each beat. Click OK to choose your custom Time Signature. There will be information on more advanced Time Signature options in chapter 5.

Once you have chosen a Key and Time signature, click the Next button to continue.

Page 4: Define Tempo Marking, Pickup, and Music Font

Finalize your customized score on page 4 by specifying an initial tempo marking, pickup measure and default music font for your score (Figure 2.5).

Figure 2.5
On page 4 of the Setup Wizard, specify a tempo marking, pickup measure, and music font.

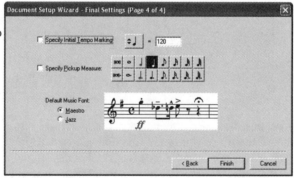

If you have a specific tempo marking in mind, check Specify Initial Tempo Marking, then enter the number of quarter note beats per minute in the entry field to the right. If you would like to specify a different rhythmic value for your tempo indication, click the quarter note and choose a different note value from the dropdown menu (Figure 2.6).

Figure 2.6
Choose the duration of
the pickup measure
from the
dropdown/popup
menu.

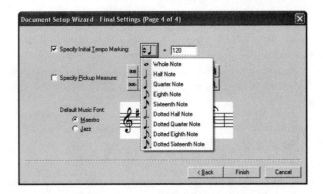

If you would like a pickup measure before the first measure of your piece, check Specify Pickup Measure. Then choose the value of your pickup measure from one of the boxes to the right.

Finally, you may want to change the general appearance of your music. Finale allows you to choose between two default music fonts. In the preview window, you currently see a representation of the standard Maestro font. If you would like your music to appear as though it were handwritten, you may want to use the Jazz font. Under Default Music Font, click the Jazz radio button to see a representation of the Jazz font in the preview window. Once you have selected the default music font, click Finish. Finale will open a document using all of the information you provided in the Setup Wizard.

New Default Document

You can begin a new, basic, single staff document by choosing File > New > Default Document. This will open a treble clef staff in the key of C, and in common time. This might be an attractive option for a lead sheet or solo document. Or, if you are composing and haven't yet figured out what kind of instrument or key you might be using, a new default document might be the way to go.

TIP
If you find yourself making the same changes to the default document every time you open it, customize it to save yourself time. Open a new document, make your changes, and then choose Save As... from the File menu. Name the file "Maestro Font Default.FTM" (on Mac, just "Maestro Font Default"), then save the file to your Finale folder and replace the existing default file. Now, these settings will apply any time you open a new default document.

Document from Template

As mentioned in chapter 1, Finale comes with over thirty preset templates you can use to get a head start while starting a new project. If the score you are working on has a common instrumentation (brass quintet, piano grand staff, etc.), try starting with a template. To open a template, click File > New > Document from Template. Then browse through the folders to see the available options.

Document without Libraries

If you want to start a completely empty document without any presets or libraries, click File > New > Document Without Libraries. You will see a document with a single measure and no text at all. You will also find that there are no articulations or expressions from which to choose. Use this option to start a document only if you feel comfortable setting up your score and loading all libraries from scratch. For information on loading articulation and expression libraries, see chapter 3.

Exercise Wizard

This feature, new to Finale 2002, was built specifically to allow music educators to create customized, technique-building exercises quickly and easily (for a rehearsal warm-up, for example). This wizard will ask you to specify from a variety of scales, twisters, keys and articulations for each exercise. Then, you can print the exercise (or number of exercises) for any ensemble while Finale takes care of the transposition and articulation placement. The whole process takes about ten minutes or so—depending on the speed of your printer—and can be a great utility for any conductor in an educational setting. You can find more specific information on creating exercises with the Exercise Wizard in chapter 13.

Customize Your Document

Regardless of the method you used to begin your document, you may find that you want to change your Key Signature, Time Signature, or other element. The following section covers how to safely change these settings at any point while working on your score, as well as other techniques you should know for any document.

Add, Remove, or Insert Measures

After opening a new document with the Setup Wizard or a default document, you will have twenty-one measures. Your piece will probably be either longer or shorter than this. To add a measure to the end of your score at any time, simply double-click the Measure Tool. To add a specific number of measures, click the Measure Tool and then click the Measure menu and choose Add (or Ctrl/Option click the Measure Tool). You will see the Add Measure dialog box (Figure 2.7). Enter the number of measures you would like to add here and click OK. The number of measures you specify will be added to the end of your score.

Figure 2.7
Enter the number of
measures you would
like to add to the end of
the score in the Add
Measure dialog box.

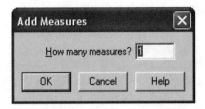

There are a couple of ways to delete measures. With the Measure Tool selected, highlight the measures you want to delete. Choose the Measure menu and then Delete. You can also delete measures using the Mass Edit tool. Click the Mass Edit tool, highlight the measures you want to delete and then press the Delete key on your keyboard. We will cover more Mass Edit options, such as clearing or copying measures at the end of this chapter.

To insert new measures at the beginning or in the middle of your score, click the Measure tool and click a measure to highlight it. From the Measure menu, choose Insert. Type the number of measures and click OK. The number of measures you specify will appear, inserted to the left of the highlighted measure.

Changing the Key Signature

To change the opening Key Signature, click the Key Signature tool. Doubleclick the first measure of your score to open the Key Signature dialog box. Use the scroll bars to specify the number of sharps or flats in the Key Signature and click OK. This will change the Key Signature at measure one for all staves proportionally. In other words, Finale will consider transposing staves and assign the appropriate Key Signature to each staff. We'll explain how to change the pitch of a transposing instrument staff soon.

TIP
To change the staff attributes for all of your staves at once, use the Global Staff Attributes plug-in. Click the Plug-ins menu and choose Global Staff Attributes. Now make any settings that you want to apply to all your staves and click OK.

Changing or Hiding the Time Signature

To change the Time Signature of your piece, click the Time Signature tool. Now, doubleclick the first measure of your piece. This opens the Time Signature dialog box. For Number of Beats, click the left or right arrow to increase or decrease the number of beats per measure in your Time Signature. For Beat Duration, click the left or right arrow to increase or decrease the rhythmic value of each beat. Click OK to return to your score and see the new Time Signature. There will be information on more advanced Time Signature options in chapter 5.

To hide the Time Signature completely, click the Staff tool and doubleclick a measure in a staff. The Staff Attributes dialog box opens. In the Items to Display section, uncheck Time Signature. Click OK to return to your score. Do this for any other staves as necessary.

CHAPTER 2

Changing or Entering a Staff Name

After you have created a document with the Setup Wizard, you will notice a staff name to the left of each of your staves. To change this name, or enter a new one, click the Staff tool and double-click the staff to open the Staff Attributes dialog box. To change the full staff name, click the Edit button to the right of Full Staff Name. The Edit Text dialog box opens. Change or delete the staff name here. Click OK to return to Staff Attributes. To change the abbreviated staff name (the one that appears at the beginning of all subsequent systems), click the Edit button to the right of Abb. Staff Name. The Edit Text dialog box opens. Change or delete the abbreviated staff name here. Click OK to return to Staff Attributes, then click OK to return to your score.

To enter a sharp, flat or other accidental character in the staff name, use a text insert. While in the Edit Text dialog box, move the cursor to the place you want to enter the accidental. Then, from the Text menu, choose Inserts > Sharp, Flat or Natural.

Configuring a Staff for a Transposing Instrument

Since not all instruments are in the key of C, Finale allows you to set up staves for transposing instruments, such as a Bb Clarinet or an Eb Alto Sax. If you used the Document Setup Wizard to start your score, then all of the staff transpositions are already defined for you. However, if you started your score from a New Default Document, you will have to set up the staff transpositions for the appropriate staves. To specify a transposition for a staff, click the Staff tool and doubleclick the staff. Click the Select button to the right of Transposition. To the right of Key Signature, click the dropdown arrow and choose the pitch of the transposing instrument. Click OK twice to return to your score. Now, any notes in your staff will display according to the transposition you chose.

After specifying a transposition for a staff, Finale automatically calculates the appropriate Key Signature based on the concert key. For instance, if the concert Key Signature of your piece is C major, any staff set to a French horn transposition (up a perfect fifth, add one sharp), will automatically display in the key of G (one sharp) and the pitches will be displayed up a perfect fifth. Note that the staff transposition only affects the displayed pitches of the music and never the sounding pitches. Finale will always play back any notes in a transposed staff in concert pitch. In the case of a French horn, the sounding notes are a perfect fifth down from the written pitch, as it would sound if played by a French horn. To view all of your staves back in concert pitch, check Display in Concert Pitch from the Options menu. For information on regional staff transpositions (i.e. instrument doubling, etc.), see chapter 8 under Staff Styles.

Changing the Clef

You can change the opening clef of any staff with the Staff tool. Click the Staff tool and doubleclick a staff to open the Staff Attributes dialog box. In the upper left portion, click the Select button to the left of the clef display. You can now choose one of the eighteen clefs. Click OK twice to return to your score and see the new clef. For information on adding a clef change within a staff, see chapter 5.

Changing the Tempo Marking

Changing the tempo marking is slightly more involved than many of the other topics in this section. However, it's far easier now than it used to be in earlier Finale versions. First, if there is a tempo marking in your score, delete it. Click the Selection tool, click on the tempo marking and press the Delete key.

To enter a new tempo marking, click the Mass Edit tool. Highlight the first measure, click the Plug-ins menu and choose Create Tempo Marking. This will open the Create Tempo Marking dialog box, as seen in Figure 2.8.

Figure 2.8
Use the Create Tempo Marking plug-in to specify a tempo marking to place in the score.

Now, choose the rhythmic duration and type a value for the desired number of beats per minute. If you want your piece to play back at the specified tempo, check Define Expression for Playback. Click OK to return to your score. You should notice the tempo marking above the first measure.

If you have multiple staves in your score, you will see the tempo marking above all of your staves. To set the tempo marking to show on the top staff only, do this:

1. Click the Expression tool.
2. Right/Ctrl-click one of the tempo marking handles to bring up a context menu.
3. Choose Edit Measure Expression Assignment.
4. In the Show On section, choose Staff List and click the Edit button.
5. In the Always Show On section, check Top Staff Score and Top Staff Parts.
6. Click OK twice to return to your score.

You should now see your tempo marking above the first measure on the top staff only.

Adding or Removing a Pickup Measure

To add a pickup measure to your score, click the Options menu and choose Pickup Measure. You should now see the Pickup Measure dialog box (Figure 2.9).

Figure 2.9
Define a pickup in the
Pickup Measure dialog
box.

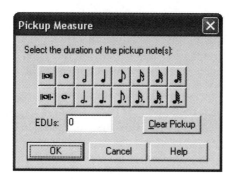

Click the box representing the duration of your pickup measure, and then click OK to return to
your score. Now, Finale will treat the first measure of your score as a pickup measure of the
values specified. Measure number 1 will be redefined to the measure after the pickup.

Showing or Hiding Measure Numbers

By default, Finale will display measure numbers at the beginning of each system. To show
measure numbers on each measure, first click the Measure tool. Then click the Measure menu >
Measure Numbers > Edit Regions (or right/Ctrl-click the Measure tool and choose Edit Measure
Number Region). The Measure Number dialog box will appear. In the Positioning & Display
section, choose Show Every.... Then, in the fields to the right, enter "1" and "1" to tell Finale to
show measure numbers every measure starting with measure 1. Click OK to return to your score.
You can now click and drag the measure number handles to position them, or click a handle
and press the Delete key to delete it.

To hide all measure numbers on a staff, click the Staff tool and doubleclick the staff. The Staff
Attributes dialog box opens. In the Items to Display section, uncheck Measure Numbers and
click OK. There will be more information on changing the font, style and enclosure of measure
numbers, as well as on how to program several measure number regions, in chapter 11.

Define a Staff for Playback With the Instrument List

If you changed the name and transposition of a staff, you may also want to change the
playback instrument. To change the instrument of any staff for playback, click the Window
menu and choose Instrument List. The Instrument List dialog box should appear on your
screen (Figure 2.10).

Figure 2.10
Use the Instrument List
to assign playback
sounds to staves.

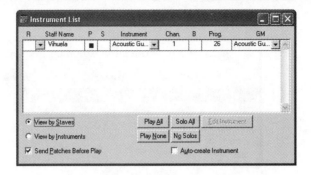

Now, under the Instrument Column, click the drop-down arrow in the row of the staff you want to change. In this drop-down menu, choose the new instrument for your staff.

If the instrument you want to use is not there, choose New Instrument (at the top of the drop-down menu). This will open the Instrument Definition dialog box. Name your new instrument, choose an unused channel (a channel that is not being used for any other staff or instrument). Then click the drop-down arrow to the right of General MIDI and choose the instrument sound you want to use. Click OK, then close out of the Instrument List to return to your score. Repeat this process for any other staves as needed.

For more information on configuring a staff for playback using a non-General MIDI instrument, such as an external sound module, see chapter 14.

TIP

For more control over playback, Windows users can try the JW Playback plug-in available on the companion CD-ROM. With this plug-in, you can easily define any number of staves, groups, or measures for playback. Also, see chapter 14 for more playback techniques you can use to review your score.

Enter and Modify Text (Title, Composer, Copyright)

When you open a new score, you will see three text blocks on your page by default: title, composer, and copyright. These items are Page-Assigned Text Blocks, and their placement will remain fixed according to the page margins (or page edge). In other words, as you edit and move measures around, these items will stay in the same place on the page. Page-Attached text will always appear green on your screen by default. The use of text blocks should generally be restricted to text that has nothing to do with the performance of the music. This includes the title, composer, copyright, and page numbers. For this section, you will need the Text tool selected throughout.

CHAPTER 2

Entering Text Blocks

The best way to enter or modify the title, composer, or copyright text of any piece is to use the File Info dialog box (Figure 2.11). To get there, click the File menu and choose File Info.

Figure 2.11
Store the title, composer, description, and other information about the document in the File Info dialog box.

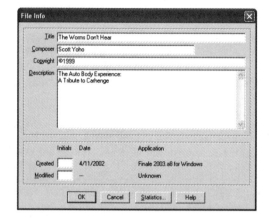

Enter a new title, composer, and copyright in this dialog box, then click OK. You will probably see the new text already appear in your score in the appropriate place. If not, double-click where you want to place the title. A dashed box will appear on your score. Click the Text menu > Inserts > Title. Now, the title appears in the specified location. You can also insert any of the other File Info this way by choosing Composer, Copyright, etc. from the Inserts submenu.

To enter any page-assigned text directly into the score, first make sure you are in Page View (View menu > Page View). Then, click the Text tool, and doubleclick in the score. You will see a dashed box enclosing a cursor. Type your text here. The box will expand as you type. Then, click anywhere in the score when you are finished typing to remove the dashed editing frame.

Text blocks can also be assigned to a specific measure. If your measure layout changes, the text block will move with its assigned measure. Any text block entered while working in Scroll View will automatically be measure-assigned. Measure-assigned text blocks are always red by default. In general, if you want to assign text consisting of only a single word or just a couple of words to a measure, you will probably want to use a measure-attached expression instead of a measure-assigned text block. You can find more information on measure-attached expressions in chapters 3 and 7.

If you want to enter a measure-assigned text block in Page View, first click anywhere in the score so none of the text block handles are selected. Then click the Text menu and choose Assign to Measure. Now, any text you enter will be measure-assigned. To revert back to entering page assigned text, make sure no handle is selected and choose Assign to Page from the Text menu. Page-assigned text can only be entered in Page View.

Editing a Text Block

You can easily reposition or delete any text block. To move text, click the Text tool, then click the text block's handle. Drag it anywhere on the page or use the arrow keys to nudge it for fine adjustments. To delete it, click the text block handle and press the Delete key. Remember, you can use the Selection tool to select any item, move it, edit it, or delete it.

Changing the Font, Size, or Style

To change the font, size, or style, doubleclick a text block handle, so a dashed box surrounds the text. Hold down the Ctrl/Command key and press A. All of the text should be highlighted. Click the Text menu and choose Font. This opens the Font dialog box. Select a new font, size or style for the text block here. Click OK to return to your score.

Alignment and Positioning

If simply dragging text into place isn't consistent enough, you can specify the precise location of any text block relative to the page margin, page edge, or assigned measure. Rightclick (on Mac, Control-click) the title, for instance, and choose Edit Frame Attributes. This will open the Frame Attributes Dialog box (Figure 2.12).

Figure 2.12
Use the Frame
Attributes dialog box for
precise positioning of
text blocks.

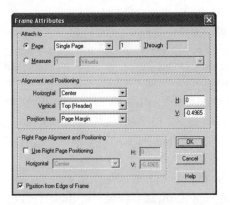

In this box, specify the placement of the text block. On the left side of the Alignment and Positioning section, choose the general location of the chosen text block from the drop-down menus. For instance, for the title, you would probably choose Center for Horizontal and Top (header) for Vertical. Then, you can fine-tune the placement in the H: (horizontal) and V: (vertical) fields to the right. These values indicate any adjustment from your settings in the left side of this section. In this case, to move the title a half inch below the top page margin, enter "-.5" in the V: field. Click OK to return to your score and review the placement. Use this method to position any page-assigned text block.

You can also adjust the positioning of measure-assigned text blocks in the Frame Attributes dialog box. Right click the handle on a measure-assigned text block and choose Edit Frame. Now, use the H: and V: fields to specify the distance from the beginning of the measure in the H: field and the distance above or below the top staff line in the V: field. The beginning of a measure in this case relates to the default position of the first note or rest (after the Time or Key Signature). Click OK to return to your score and review the placement.

Page Numbers

If you started your document with the Setup Wizard, Default Document, or a Template, there will already be page numbers at the top of each page starting with page 2. To enter new page numbers into your score, double-click where you would like to place the page number. Then choose the Text menu > Inserts > Page Numbers (or press Ctrl/Command-Shift-P). You can specify the positioning of your page numbers exactly like page-assigned text blocks (as described above).

Left and Right Pages

You may want to place your page numbers on alternating sides of each page if you intend your music to end up on left and right pages of a book, for instance. If you are already using the Maestro Font Default file, this may be set up for you. Otherwise, to do this, first move into Page View (View menu > Page View), and then follow these steps:

1. Right/Control-click the handle on a page number and click Frame Attributes.
2. In the Alignment and Positioning section, choose Left for Horizontal and Top for Vertical.
3. In the Attach To section, after Page, choose Left Pages.
4. Enter a Page Range in the field to the right. For instance "1 through 0", where "0" indicates to the end of the piece (odd numbers are always right pages and even numbers are always left pages).
5. Click OK to return to your score. Now, you will see page numbers on every other page. We'll then number the remaining pages.
6. Move to a right page (page without a page number).
7. Doubleclick anywhere on the page in the score to open a new text block.
8. Choose the Text menu > Inserts > Page Numbers (or press Ctrl/Command-Shift-P). A page number will appear in the score.
9. Right/Control-click the handle on the page number and click Frame Attributes.
10. In the Alignment and Positioning section, choose Right for Horizontal and Top for Vertical.
11. In the Attach To section, after Page, choose Right Pages.
12. Enter a Page Range in the field to the right. For instance, "2 through 0" so the first page will not be numbered.
13. Click OK to return to your score.

Other Text Tool Tricks

In this section, we have covered the very basics of the Text tool. There are many other ways to modify text blocks. You can change the tracking, line spacing, baseline, and several other parameters. Many of these other features resemble functionality you may have seen before in word processing programs. In order to maintain focus on music notation (and avoid redundancy with the User Manual), we won't go into every one of these features here. There may, however, be a few Text tool tricks you might want to know about.

Entering Musical Symbols (Sharp, Flat, etc.) in a Text Block

To enter accidentals in a text block, move the cursor to the desired location within a text block. Then click the Text menu, and open the Inserts submenu. Choose one of the accidentals in this submenu. The accidental will appear in your score.

If you want to add other music characters, such as rhythmic durations, you can change the font of a portion of your text block. Highlight a region of a text block, then click the Text menu and choose Font. Choose one of the music fonts (Maestro, Petrucci, etc.) and click OK. The characters will change to their corresponding music symbol. You will find a chart showing the keystrokes for all characters for every Finale music font under the Help menu (on Windows, refer to the User Manual submenu of the Help menu). For more control over editing text, you might consider using Finale's built-in text editor.

Finale's Text Editor

If you want to create a large amount of text, or perform more advanced tasks like mixing fonts within a text block, use Finale's text editor. Click the Text menu and choose Edit Text. You can use this window to enter a large amount of text at once. Use the Text menu in this window to change the font, size, style, or any other attribute of a highlighted region of text.

Display a Text Block On-Screen Only

If you want a text block to display on your screen, but not in the printout, choose a text block by clicking its handle. Then, click the Text menu and choose Show Only on Screen. Now, the text block will not appear when the document is printed.

TIP

In large documents, you may want to search and change every occurrence of a text block, or other text (expression, staff name, etc.). To do this, use the JW Search and Replace plug-in available on the companion CD-ROM. See chapter 15 for more details.

Introduction to the Mass Edit Tool

Formally known as the Mass Mover tool, the Mass Edit tool is fundamental to working with Finale efficiently. This workhorse eliminates a great deal of redundancy, offering many powerful editing features that can be applied to any portion of your score. You will be using this tool to copy music, transpose, move measures around, change beaming, tweak music spacing, and perform a variety of other tasks. For now, we'll get into the most common uses of the Mass Edit tool, and how to use it most effectively. There will be more information on applying advanced Mass Mover operations in chapter 9. Click the Mass Edit tool now. For this section, we'll assume you already have the Mass Edit tool selected.

CHAPTER 2

Selecting Regions

The first step to editing with the Mass Edit tool is selecting a region of music. First, click the Edit menu and make sure Select Partial Measures is not checked (or make sure the icon to the left of this option is not surrounded in white). Now, click the first measure in your score. It should become highlighted, indicating it is selected. Click above measure 1 and drag below measure 2 (you'll see a dashed box appear). Release the mouse button and measures 1 and 2 will be selected. Click and drag over any region of your score to easily select multiple measures. Now, let's say you want to select measures 1 through 5. Hold down the Shift key and click measure 5. Notice the first five measures are highlighted. Hold down the Shift key and press the right arrow key. Now, the selected area extends to the end of the piece. You can also use the left arrow to highlight any region to the beginning of the piece. Click anywhere outside the highlighted area to clear the selection. Hold down Ctrl/Command and press A to select the entire document (or choose Select All from the Edit menu).

TIP

At any point while working in the Mass Edit tool, you can right-click (Windows)/Command-Option (Macintosh) and drag to move the viewable area of the page.

Selecting Partial Measures

You may want to edit or copy a portion of a measure, or a region that doesn't begin and end on a barline. To do this, click the Edit menu and check Select Partial Measures (the menu item should now have a checkmark next to it). Click and drag over the first half of the first measure to highlight the beginning of the measure. When there are notes or rests in a staff, you will be able to highlight any region starting with even the smallest subdivision. Doubleclick a measure to quickly highlight the entire measure. Also, with a partial measure selected, hold down Shift and press the right arrow to select to the end of the measure, or the left arrow to select to the beginning of the measure. Press the left or right arrow again to select to the end or beginning of the piece.

The Select Regions Dialog Box

For more control over selection, you may want to specify the exact beat or EDU to start and end your region (remember, EDUs are Finale's unit of rhythmic duration—there are 1,024 EDUs in a quarter note, 512 in an eighth note, etc.). To do this, choose Select Region from the Edit menu. This will open the Select Region dialog box (Figure 2.13).

Figure 2.13
Use the Select Region
dialog box for precision
in selecting a region of
measures.

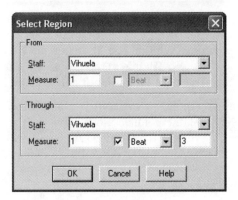

In this dialog box, choose the beginning and end of your region down to the precise subdivision.
Leave the checkbox empty if you want to select from the beginning of the specified measure.
Click OK to return to your score with the region selected.

Copy and Clear Music

Of course, one of the great beauties of music notation with a computer is the ability to copy
large sections of music from one place to another. In Finale, this is quite simple to do. Let's start
by entering a few notes in the first measure of your document. Click the Simple Entry tool. Click
the Quarter Note tool in the Simple Entry Palette and click four quarter notes on any pitch in the
first measure. Now, select the Mass Edit tool. Click the Edit menu and uncheck Select Partial
Measures (if it is checked). Click the first measure so it is highlighted. Now, click on the
highlighted area and drag to measure 2. When you see a black boarder surround measure 2,
release the mouse button. You should now see the Copy Measures dialog box (Figure 2.14). For
now, just click OK and you will see your music copied to measure 2.

Figure 2.14
Choose the number of
times you want to copy
a selected region in the
Copy Measures dialog
box.

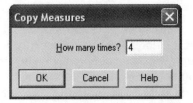

Now, let's say we want the same one bar pattern throughout the first ten measures. Click and
drag around the first two measures so they are highlighted. Now, click on the highlighted area and
drag to the right so measures 3 and 4 are surrounded with a black boarder. Release the
mouse button. Now, for How Many Times?, enter 4 and click OK. You should now see the two
measures copied four times each, filling the first ten measures of your staff.

You may need to copy music to a location that is not visible on the screen. This makes drag-
copying impossible. To copy a section of music to any measure in your score, first highlight the

section you wish to copy, using the scroll bars at the bottom and right side of your screen so that the destination measure is showing. On Windows, hold down Ctrl and Shift, and click in the destination measure. On Mac, hold down Option and Shift, and click the destination measure. Choose the number of times and click OK. Try this in the document you have been working on. Highlight a measure of music, then Ctrl-Shift/Option-Shift and click on any empty measure.

You may want to remove the original music as you copy it to a new location. To do this, highlight a measure or any region containing music. Hold down the Ctrl/Command key and press X (or choose Cut from the Edit menu). On Windows, this will open the Cut Measures dialog box, as seen in Figure 2.15. On Macintosh, you will see a dialog box with identical functionality.

Figure 2.15
Choose whether to delete or clear the selected region in the Cut Measures dialog box.

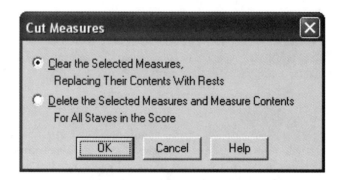

Leave Clear Measures, Replacing their Contents with Rests selected and click OK. On Macintosh, click Clear. The measure should now be filled with a whole rest. Highlight an empty measure. Hold down the Ctrl/Command key and press V (or choose Replace Entries from the Edit menu). The music will appear in the highlighted measure. To completely delete the original measure while copying, follow these same steps, but choose Delete the Selected Measure and Measure Contents for All Staves in the Score in the Cut Measures dialog box.

If you want to insert music between two measures, without replacing any entries, click the Mass Edit menu and choose Copy and Insert. By doing this, it will actually add measure to your document, inserted before the selected region. Now, simply highlight a region and drag-copy it into place. The original music will shift to the right of the inserted music. If you cut the original music, highlight the destination measure and choose Insert from the Edit menu.

Clear any highlighted region of note or rest entries by pressing the Backspace key on Windows, or the Clear key on Macintosh. To completely delete a measure (for example, to remove extra measures at the end of a score), highlight the measures and press the Delete key.

Introduction to Page Layout

In general, most Finale users agree that page layout should be the last stage in editing a score before printing. There are, however, a few basic principals you should be aware of as you continue to develop a working knowledge of Finale. These concepts should be adequate for finalizing small projects, particularly single staff documents such as lead sheets. We'll cover more advanced page layout topics in chapter 11.

Page Layout Icons and Margins

Whenever the Page Layout tool is chosen, you will see system margins, page margins, and perhaps Page Layout icons appearing on your page (Figure 2.16).

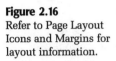

Figure 2.16
Refer to Page Layout Icons and Margins for layout information.

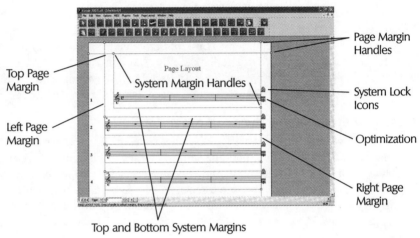

Top Page Margin

Left Page Margin

System Margin Handles

Top and Bottom System Margins

Page Margin Handles

System Lock Icons

Optimization

Right Page Margin

CHAPTER 2

If you have entered music into your score in Page View, you may have noticed measures moving from system to system automatically. This is Finale's way of maintaining consistent music spacing as you enter. Any time you specify a number of measures on a system (by using Fit Music, or even manually moving measures between systems), Finale will lock the system, preventing Automatic Music Spacing from ever shifting the measures. Systems that are locked will be tagged with a System Lock Icon that looks like a padlock (Figure 2.16). To lock any system, highlight the measures in the system with the Mass Edit tool and choose Lock Systems from the Mass Edit menu (to unlock systems, choose Unlock from the Mass Edit menu). Instead of choosing Lock Systems and Unlock Systems from the Mass Edit menu, try using the L key on Windows or Command-L on Macintosh.

The icon with two miniature staves (shown in blue) indicates a system has been optimized (Figure 2.16). Optimization is used for hiding empty staves in a system, adjusting staves independently within a system and making other system-specific changes. There will be a description of optimization, as well as when to use it, in chapters 7 and 11. In case you care to experiment a bit with optimization (or remove it from an existing score), here's how to apply it and remove it. Click a system handle and choose Optimize Staff Systems from the Page Layout menu (or right/Control-click anywhere within a system). Choose Optimize Staff Systems and click OK to apply Optimization. Click Remove Staff System Optimization and click OK to remove it.

The System Lock and Optimization icons will not appear in your printout; only on-screen. To show or hide these icons on your screen display, use the Show Page Layout Icons command under the View menu.

Editing Staff and System Spacing

Now, it's time to learn the basics for editing the layout of staves and systems. Here, we'll cover how to space staves and systems, and other techniques that come into play. First, it is important to make the distinction between staves and systems.

When you look at your score in Scroll View (View menu > Scroll View), you will see the total number of staves in your document. Think of Scroll View as one really long system that can stretch into eternity. Only when you look at your score in Page View (View menu > Page View) will you be able to see your staff systems. In Page View, a system is one or more staves extending across the page that are intended to be played at the same time.

Changing the Distance Between Staves

There are a few ways to adjust staff and system spacing. To demonstrate how to space staves and systems, we'll first need more than one staff in our score. First, move to Scroll View. Click the Staff tool, then click the Staff menu and choose New Staves. In the New Staves dialog box, enter 2 and click OK. You should now see three staves in your score. Each staff will have a handle on the upper left corner. Click this handle to drag any staff up or down. These spacing changes will also apply in Page View.

You may want to increase or decrease the amount of space between each staff in a system. To do this, click the Staff menu and choose Respace Staves. You will see the Respace Staves dialog box (Figure 2.17).

Figure 2.17
Choose the space between each staff, or scale the distance between staves, in the Respace Staves dialog box.

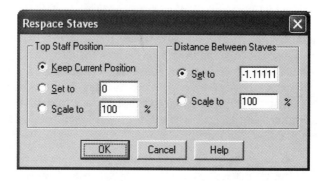

Enter a negative value after Set To and click OK to space all your staves a specific distance apart. Choose Respace Staves from the Staff menu and choose a percentage for Scale To if you want to reduce or increase the distance between each staff proportionally, but not necessarily have the staves evenly spaced.

Changing the Distance Between Systems by Dragging

You may want to manually adjust the staff systems in your score. Click the Page Layout tool to see the dashed margins around each system. Then, simply click within any system and drag. When you drag a system, all systems beneath the one you are dragging will adjust respectively. To drag a system independently (so that systems below are not influenced), hold down the Ctrl/Option key, then click and drag. You will only be able to move a system until the margin collides with an adjacent system margin or a page margin. To move systems closer together, or closer to the top or bottom page margin, you will need to edit their margins.

You will see a handle on the upper left and lower right corner of each system (Figure 2.16). Use these handles to adjust system margins. For instance, you may want to move the top staff system closer to the top page margin. To do this, click the handle on the upper left corner of the top system margin and drag it down. Now, click on the staff lines of the top system and drag it up to the top of the page (the distance between systems below it will not change). If you want to move the second system closer to the top system, try dragging the handle on the lower right corner of the top system up. All systems will move up toward the top system margin.

To move all systems closer together or farther apart, click a handle on the lower right of one of your systems and press Ctrl/Command - A to Select All (or choose Select All from the Edit menu). Now, all bottom system margin handles should be highlighted. Drag one down to increase the distance between all systems or drag one up to decrease the distance. For more control, you can also use the arrow keys to nudge system handles.

Space Systems Evenly

You can easily space all systems evenly on a page so the top and bottom systems lie against the top and bottom page margins. To do this, choose Space Systems Evenly from the Page Layout menu. In the Space Systems Evenly dialog box, choose the page, or a page range, and click OK. All systems will be spaced evenly and more closely resemble a standard engraving layout (Figure 2.18).

Figure 2.18
Notice the system margins line up with the top and bottom page margins in Space Systems Evenly.

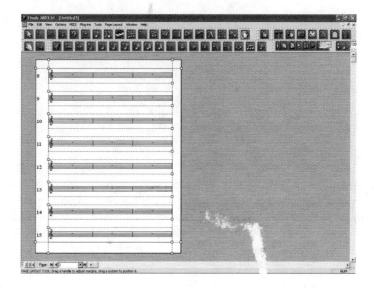

CHAPTER 2

Moving Measures Across Systems

You can easily move measures between systems with the Mass Edit tool. Highlight the last measure in a system and press the down arrow to move it to the next system. Also, highlight the first measure in a system and press the up arrow to move it to the prior system. You can also do this for several measures at once.

Fitting Selected Measures to a System

You can easily fit any number of measures to a single system. First, make sure you are in Page View (Edit menu > Page View). Highlight the measures you want to fit on one system. Click the Mass Edit menu and choose Fit Music. Choose Lock Selected Measures into One System and click OK. The highlighted measures now all appear on one system.

Specifying Number of Measures per System for a Selected Region

To specify a certain number of measures per system for a selected region, highlight the region you want to change (Ctrl/Command-A to Select all). Then, click the Mass Edit menu and choose Fit Music. Choose Lock Layout with _ Measure(s) per System and enter a number. Click OK. Your selected region will now contain the number of measures per system you specified.

Resizing a Page

If you find all of your music is too large or small on the page, you can use the Resize tool to change the page reduction. This will change the size of all the music on your page without changing the margins or page size. Click the Resize tool and click an empty area of your page (outside any staves or systems). You will see the Resize Page dialog box (Figure 2.19).

Figure 2.19
Reduce or enlarge all elements on a page by choosing a percentage in the Resize Page dialog box.

Enter a percentage (less than 100% will reduce the music on the page; greater than 100% will enlarge the music on the page) and choose a page range. You will probably want to keep Page 1 Through End of Piece chosen so all of your pages appear at the same reduction. Click OK to return to your score and review the new sizing. You can also resize individual systems, staves, and even notes with the Resize tool. There will be a more on the Resize tool in chapter 11.

Redefining Pages and Page Format for Score

If you want to revert to Finale's default page format, click the Page Layout menu and choose Redefine Pages. Choose the pages you want to redefine from the Redefine Pages submenu. You will see a message warning that all page layout information will be lost. Click OK to return to the default page layout settings. Any time you choose to redefine your pages, Finale will draw settings from the Page Format for Score dialog box found in the Options menu > Page Format > For Score. (Figure 2.20.)

Figure 2.20
Configure settings in this dialog box to specify a default page format to revert to any time you choose Redefine Pages from the Page Layout menu. There will more information on this dialog box in chapter 11.

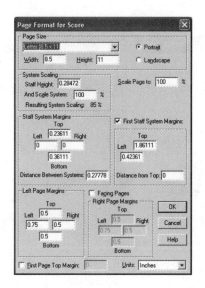

Page Size, Orientation, and Printing

When you start a score with the Setup Wizard, a Default Document or a template, Finale will use a standard 8 × 11 page size in portrait orientation. To change the size and orientation of your page, click the Page Layout menu and choose Page Size. This will open the Page Size dialog box (Figure 2.21).

Figure 2.21
Use the Page Size dialog box to specify page size and orientation.

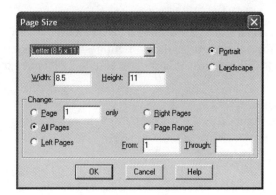

CHAPTER 2

In this dialog box, choose a new height and width for your page. You can also change the orientation of the page by choosing Landscape or Portrait on the right. Choose the page range to which you want to apply the changes. Then, choose All Pages to apply these changes to all pages. Click OK to return to the score. You should now see the new page size on your screen.

Now that you have set a new page size in Finale, before you print the document you will need to modify your print settings so this information corresponds to the page size and orientation of your document. Click the File menu and choose Page Setup. You will now see the Page Setup dialog box (Figure 2.22).

Figure 2.22
In the Page Setup dialog box, choose the page size and orientation for the printed page.

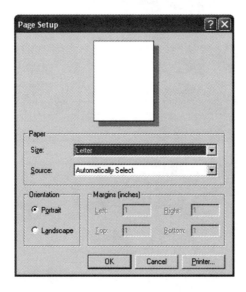

Here, choose the same orientation and page size you indicated in the Page Size dialog box. Then, click the printer driver to open the settings for your print driver. Set up your printer to print the specified page size here. Consult your printer's instruction manual for specific information on how to specify a new page size. Once you have made print settings, click OK in the Page Setup dialog box. Then, choose Print from the file menu to open the Print dialog box. Click Print to send your score to the printer.

The above instructions are just the basics to setting up a score for printing. A variety of other options are available in Finale, including left and right pages, tiled pages, and placing many "Finale pages" on a single printed page. Information on more advanced page layout topics can be found in chapter 11.

3

Basic Note Entry, Articulations, and Expressions

So far, we have focused on the concepts and methods common to the first stages of any new project. Now, it's time to expand our focus to the more diverse practice of entering notes, articulations, and expressions.

There are differing opinions about the best way to enter these items. Some find entering all the notes first, followed by articulations and then expressions, works best. Others prefer entering all these items at the same time, while progressing from measure to measure. The method you adopt should depend on the size of the project you are working with, as well as the materials you have available to you. If you are composing a work from scratch, you may want to include these markings immediately to help you remember a specific phrase or musical idea. If you are copying from an existing score, entering all of your notes and then going back to enter articulations or expressions may be a faster method for you.

Finale offers many ways to enter notes into a staff. In this chapter, we will be covering the two most common: Simple Entry and Speedy Entry. Let's first discuss some terminology we will be using in this chapter. An "entry" in Finale is essentially any note or rest. Also, notes stacked vertically (as in a chord) are also defined as an "entry." An "articulation" is a marking attached to a single entry. As you reposition an entry, its articulation(s) will move with it respectively. These include, but are not limited to, standard articulations such as accents and staccatos. You may also find the Articulation tool useful for fingerings and other items. Finally, an "expression" is generally an item that affects a region of music and can be attached to a note or measure. Examples of items you will be entering with the Expression tool are dynamic markings, tempo indications and rehearsal letters.

Here's a summary of what you will learn in this chapter:

▶ How to enter notes and rests with the mouse and keyboard: Simple Entry.

▶ How to enter notes and rests faster: Speedy Entry.

▶ How to enter articulations (accents, staccato markings).

▶ How to enter expressions (dynamics, tempo indications, rehearsal letters).

▶ How to create a simple arrangement.

The Simple Entry Tool

This tool has recently been renovated and is now more intuitive and powerful than ever. You can use the Simple Entry tool for entering notes, rests, chords, grace notes, tuplets, and ties. It is also a powerful editing tool. You can modify the pitch of any note, add accidentals and augmentation dots, as well as flip stems, break/join beams, and even hide notes. Though this is the simplest and most intuitive form of note entry, even advanced users find it crucial to every stage in working with a score. Users of any skill level will greatly benefit by learning how to harness the full potential of this tool. We'll start by getting acquainted with entering notes. Note that these instructions apply only to Finale version 2002 and later.

Entering Notes in Simple Entry

To prepare for this chapter, let's begin a new document. Click the File menu, choose New, and select Default Document. This provides a good canvas for us to experiment with basic note entry. The first time you launch Finale, the Simple Entry tool is already selected by default. Click the Simple Entry tool now if it isn't chosen already. Click the eighth note in the Simple Entry Palette. Notice that when you position your mouse over the staff, your cursor now looks like an eighth note. Now, click the half note and the cursor changes to a half note. Your cursor will always reflect the duration chosen in the Simple Entry Palette. Click the quarter note icon, move the cursor to the middle staff line in the first measure, and click to enter a quarter note on middle line B. You can use this method to enter notes of any duration into your staff. Notice your cursor jump between the staff lines and spaces as you slowly drag over a staff. Click to place the note on the desired staff line or space.

Figure 3.1
Choose a rhythmic value, pitch alteration, grace note, triplet, tie or a combination of these tools from the Simple Entry Palette for entry into the score.

TIP
Finale is set by default to play back notes as you enter them and change their pitch. To turn this feature off, click the Simple menu and uncheck Playback.

You can specify a great deal of information before entering a note by choosing several items in the Simple Entry Palette at once. There are six categories in the Simple Entry Palette separated with a small vertical bar. These consist of independent elements that could exist on any entry. They include note duration, alteration (sharp/flat/natural), tie, tuplet and grace note. You can choose one item from any number of these six categories before clicking into the score. Let's say you wanted to enter a sharp dotted eighth note with a tie. From the Simple Entry Palette, doubleclick the Eighth Note tool (to deselect everything but the eighth note), then click the Dot tool and the Tie tool. You can now see all of these items on your cursor. Click in the score and you will see a dotted eighth with a tie on whatever pitch you click on. To select any one tool independently, doubleclick it and all other Simple Entry tools will deactivate.

Now, let's say you have just entered a note, but it ended up on the wrong pitch. Press the left arrow button and the note becomes highlighted in purple. This note is now selected (we'll get into this more later on). Press the up and down arrows to change its pitch. You can also click the note, hold down the mouse button, and drag the note to the desired location. These techniques will come in handy any time you misplace a note or want to change the pitch right away. To deselect a note or rest, press the Escape or Backspace key on Windows, or the Clear key on Macintosh.

To enter a chord, simply click notes above or below an existing entry. You can stack up to twelve notes vertically to create thick chords. You will be able to edit the pitches of each note in a chord independently.

Select the Eraser icon and click any note to delete it. Click the stem of a chord with the Eraser tool to delete the entire chord; click directly on a note head in a chord to remove a note from a chord. Press Ctrl/Cmd-Z to undo the most recent edit.

Entering Rests

There are a few ways to enter rests into your score with Simple Entry. You may already have noticed rests added to measures in your score. By default, Simple Entry automatically fills incomplete measures with rests after clicking into a different measure or changing tools in the Main Tool Palette. To see this for yourself, enter a quarter note into an empty measure. Then click a note into a different measure. The first measure fills with rests. If you want to disable this feature and enter all rests manually, click the Simple menu and uncheck Fill With Rests. If you turn it off, you will still be able to go back and fill measures with rests later on with the Mass Mover Fill with Rest feature (we'll cover this later in chapter 9).

To enter rests manually, start by opening the Simple Entry Rests Palette if you don't see it on your screen already. Click the Window menu and choose "Simple Entry Rests Palette." Notice the appearance of the new palette filled with rests of various durations.

Figure 3.2
Specify the rhythmic
duration of a rest for
entry into the score
from the Simple Entry
Rests Palette.

You can treat this palette the same as the Simple Entry Palette to enter rests. However, there is a better way. Use keyboard shortcuts! This is one aspect of Simple Entry that changed notably in Finale 2002. To quickly choose a rest, simply hold down the Shift key (or Enter key in the num pad) and press a duration number. Your cursor will change to a rest of that duration. You can also press the R key to toggle between notes and rests of the same duration in your cursor. Click

CHAPTER 3

in a measure to enter the rest, or on existing notes to change them into rests of the duration you have chosen. To change any note in your score to a rest of the same duration, Ctrl/Option click it (it will change color) and press the R key. There will be a complete explanation of selection later in this chapter.

Accidentals

If you enter a note without specifying an accidental, Finale will always assume you want the note entered on the diatonic pitch, regardless of what key you are in. Any divergence from the Key Signature will need to be specified with one of the five alteration tools: Sharp, Flat, Natural, Half Step Up and Half Step Down. To enter a note with an accidental, click the desired note duration, then click the Sharp, Flat or Natural icon in the Simple Palette. Now, your cursor tells you the duration and the alteration (sharp/flat/natural) that will be entered after you click into the score. Click somewhere in the staff to see how this works. Choose the Half Step Up or Half Step Down tool and click a note to raise or lower its pitch in half steps. You can add double sharps or double flats this way as well. To remove the accidental from the cursor, either click its icon again or doubleclick the desired note duration.

NOTE

The Sharp, Flat and Natural tools are said to be absolute, meaning independent from the Key Signature. Clicking an F# into a staff with the Sharp tool will always result in an F#. If the alteration is already implied in the Key Signature (an F# in the key of G major, for instance), Finale will automatically hide the accidental since it is already part of the diatonic scale. If you want to ensure that any note you enter will appear one half step above or below the diatonic pitch in any key, choose the Half Step Up or Half Step Down tool. For example, in the key of G major, clicking an F into your staff with the Half Step Up tool will result in an F double sharp (since F# is already part of the diatonic scale). To be clear, the only time the Sharp tool will act differently than the Half Step Up tool is while entering or editing notes already altered by the key signature.

Tuplets

The Simple Entry Tuplet tool is a bit different than the others. This tool was added in Finale 2002 in response to many customer requests for an easier method of tuplet entry. In one click, you can add an entire triplet, quintuplet or any other type by specifying a custom tuplet. Let's start by entering an eighth note triplet. Click the Eighth Note icon, then the Tuplet icon. Click into an empty measure. Notice there is now an eighth note, followed by two rests, all within a tuplet bracket. You can leave both tools selected and simply click over the next two rests to finish entering your triplet. To change this figure a quarter note-eighth note triplet, delete the middle note and change the first entry to a quarter note. You can also change three existing notes into a triplet by clicking on the first of the three with just the Simple Tuplet tool selected. To specify a tuplet definition other than a triplet (quintuplet, sextuplet, etc.), choose the Simple Tuplet tool, hold down the Shift key and click in the score. In the Simple Entry Tuplet Definition dialog box, enter your settings (i.e. 6 in the place of 4 for a sextuplet, etc.) and click OK. If you will be entering many custom tuplets, check Save as Default Simple Entry Tuplet

Definition in the Simple Entry Tuplet Definition dialog box to save your settings. There will be more on defining and editing tuplets in chapter 9.

Keyboard Shortcuts

By now you may be wondering: "Am I really going to have to click all these icons before entering each note?" The answer is no. We've covered the concepts of how Simple Entry works, now let's learn how to do the same stuff faster. The engineers at Coda implemented keystrokes you can use to quickly select or deselect any simple tool. Using these keystrokes will greatly improve the speed of entering notes in Simple Entry. Notice the number on each note duration icon. Press one of these numbers to select its corresponding note duration. Now, press the S key and the period key (.) to add a sharp and an augmentation dot. Click your mouse on any Simple Entry tool to see its keyboard shortcut in the message/status bar. On some of the tools, you will notice that two keystrokes are available. This is because you will find all of the keystrokes on both the number keypad (num lock on) and the QWERTY keyboard. You can use either, but many users find the number keypad faster, since all of the keys are closer together.

TIP

To select any single tool in the Simple Palette and deselect all others, double-press any keyboard shortcut (much like a doubleclick).

Editing Notes in Simple Entry

You may have already noticed that it is possible to select any Simple Entry icon by itself. This comes in handy when editing existing notes. Doubleclick the Tie icon (or double press the letter T), for instance, and then click on any note to add or remove a tie. You can edit notes with any Simple tool by simply selecting the appropriate item and clicking the entry. Keep in mind that all Simple tools selected will affect the entry you click. For instance, if you have both the Sharp and Half Note icons selected, any note you click will become a half note as well as sharp note. Like entering notes, editing would be far more difficult if there weren't timesaving keyboard shortcuts to make your life easier. In this case, Finale does more than just offer tool selection keystrokes. You can use many keyboard commands to edit any note by selecting it!

Selecting Notes

Note selection is an integral part to making the most of the Simple Entry tool, and one of the most revolutionary changes that came about in Finale 2002. The same keyboard shortcuts you used to choose note durations, accidentals and the like from the Simple Palette can also be used to modify any selected note. Click a series of quarter notes into a measure. Now, press the left arrow key. Notice the last note you entered is now highlighted in purple. Press the 4 key to change it to an eighth note, or the S key to add a sharp. Experiment with the other shortcuts. Use the left and right arrows to move between entries. You can also select any note in your score easily by holding down Ctrl/Option and clicking an entry. To remove the selection from the note (so that keyboard shortcuts can be used for tool selection again), press the Esc or Backspace/Clear key.

Selecting Notes in Chords

You can move the selection between notes in a chord and even select several notes within an entry at once. Enter a chord of seven notes in a measure. Press the left arrow to select the previous note entered. Now, hold down Ctrl/Option and use the up and down arrows to highlight any one note in the chord for editing. To select multiple notes within a chord, hold down Ctrl-Shift/Option-Shift and click all of the notes in the chord you want to select.

Figure 3.3
Ctrl/Option-click to
select noncontiguous
notes in a chord.

To select all notes in a chord, select one of the notes and press Ctrl/Cmd-A or Ctrl/Option-click above or below it. Any keystroke will now affect all highlighted notes. If you change the pitch or duration with any one note of the chord selected, all notes in the chord will change. To see all of the available keystrokes for note selection, click the Simple menu and choose Simple Navigation Commands.

Selecting Notes Automatically During Entry

While entering notes, you may want to edit them immediately with one or more of the many keystrokes. To do this, click the Simple menu and choose Select Notes on Entry. Now, any note you enter will be selected automatically and ready for you to edit. To temporarily remove all selections, press Escape or Backspace/Clear.

If you choose to use this feature, you may find it frustrating to change note durations without affecting the selected note (since you will need to clear the selection first). To avoid this, program your function keys (F2-F8) to note durations using the TGTools, Menu Shortcuts plug-in. You will find all of the Simple Entry note durations under the Tools menu. This way, you can change the duration of the next note you want to enter without affecting the selected note. Note that this will override any Tool metatool you have already programmed with these function keys.

Other Editing Commands for Selected Notes

In addition to note durations, accidentals and the other commands similar to Tool Selection and Selected Note editing, there are several other commands that were built in specifically for selected notes. Select a note and press the L key to flip its stem, the R key to change it to a rest, and the H key to hide an entry. You can also break/join the beam between a note and the previous entry (B) or show/hide an accidental (A). To see a full list of the possibilities, click the Simple menu and choose Simple Edit Commands. A full list of the keyboard shortcuts can be found in your Quick Reference Card.

Figure 3.4
Choose Simple Edit
Commands from the
Simple menu to see a
list of keyboard
shortcuts.

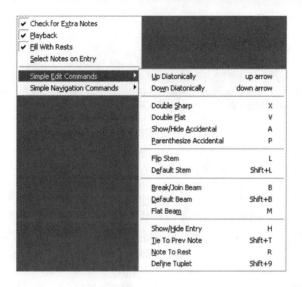

✔ Check for E__x__tra Notes		
✔ __P__layback		
✔ __F__ill With Rests		
Select Notes on Entry		
Simple __E__dit Commands ►	__U__p Diatonically	up arrow
Simple Na__v__igation Commands ►	Do__w__n Diatonically	down arrow
	Double __S__harp	X
	Double __F__lat	V
	Show/Hide __A__ccidental	A
	__P__arenthesize Accidental	P
	Fl__i__p Stem	L
	D__e__fault Stem	Shift+L
	__B__reak/Join Beam	B
	De__f__ault Beam	Shift+B
	Flat Bea__m__	M
	Show/__H__ide Entry	H
	__T__ie To Prev Note	Shift+T
	Note To Rest	R
	De__fi__ne Tuplet	Shift+9

Entering More Than One Voice, Layers

It is common to see more than one melodic line, or voice, entered in the same staff. With layers, you can enter up to four independent voices in any measure. Notice the four boxes (or pop-up menu on Mac) in the lower left corner of the screen labeled 1, 2, 3, and 4. These are the layer selection controls. Make sure Layer 1 is selected and click four quarter notes on the top staff line. Now select layer 2. Click the Eighth Note tool, or press the 4 key, and click eighth notes into the same measure on the middle line. They are red, so you will always know these notes are in layer 2 in case you want to edit them later.

Figure 3.5
Enter multiple voices in
your score using layers.

The stems on your notes in layer 2 automatically flip down in accordance with standard notation practice. You can flip the stems by selecting them and pressing the L key, or you can change the default stem direction for each layer of your document in the Layer Options dialog box (we'll cover this later). You can use the remaining layers to enter up to two more independent voices in this measure. They will each have their own color so you can distinguish between them (layer 3 green, and 4 blue). You will only be able to edit one layer at a time in Simple Entry. For example, if you want to add or edit notes in layer 1, select layer 1 in the lower left corner of your screen first.

TIP

You can also use keyboard shortcuts to switch between layers. On Windows, hold down Alt-Shift and press the number of the layer you would like to select. On Macintosh, hold down Cmd-Option and press the number of the layer you would like to select.

You may want to begin entering notes in a new layer somewhere within the measure instead of the first beat. To do this, enter notes at the beginning of the measure and hide them with the H key. Try this: Select layer 1 and enter two half notes in an empty measure on the top staff line. Now, let's say you want to enter quarter notes only on beats three and four. Click layer 2 and enter a half note on beat one, then two quarter notes on beats three and four. Now, Ctrl/Option-click the half note and press the H key to hide it.

If you want stems extending in both directions on a single note (to indicate two voices in unison), you could enter overlapping notes in layer 1 and layer 2. Do this if you need to enter more than one layer in the measure anyway. To apply beams in both directions in a single layer, use the Double-Split Stem special tool. We will cover more on special tools in chapter 10.

Entering Notes and Rests Faster: Speedy Entry

Though the Simple Entry tool is very powerful and intuitive, it doesn't come close to the agility of the Speedy Entry tool. Speedy Entry is the preferred note entry method for many experienced Finale users due to its speed, navigation abilities, and MIDI compatibility. In this chapter, we will cover the various methods of note entry within this tool, both with and without a MIDI keyboard. Click the Speedy Entry tool and notice the Speedy menu that appears at the top of your screen. You will be using the many features in this menu to customize the way Speedy Entry works. These features will be explained throughout this chapter as we cover the methods and tricks to which they apply.

If you are using a MIDI keyboard for input, note that the first part of this chapter applies to editing in Speedy Entry both with or without a MIDI keyboard. In other words, even in Speedy's MIDI entry mode, all of the non-MIDI features (besides actual note-entry) are available. You may find these techniques useful for editing after entering notes with your MIDI keyboard. If you are unfamiliar with Speedy Entry, I recommend reading through the entire Speedy Entry section.

NOTE

If you are using a German or Swiss-German keyboard, consult the Finale User Manual to learn how to customize the Speedy key map.

To prepare for this section, let's open Finale's piano grand staff template. Click the File menu, choose New, and then Document from Template. Doubleclick the General Templates folder, then doubleclick the file "Pianograndstaff.FTM". You should now see an empty grand staff score.

Navigation in Speedy Entry

While using Speedy Entry, you will be entering notes within the context of the Speedy Frame.

Figure 3.6
Enter notes quickly
using the Speedy
Frame.

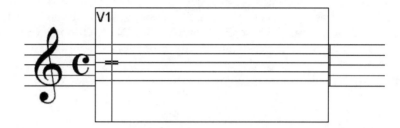

Click any measure to activate the Speedy Frame. You can also show or hide the Speedy Entry Frame by pressing the number 0. When you show it this way, it will appear on the most recently active measure. There are several ways to move the Speedy Entry Frame around your score. Click any measure to activate the Speedy Frame. Move the cursor horizontally by pressing the left and right arrow keys. You can also move from measure to measure this way. Move the frame horizontally among measures by pressing the left and right bracket keys ([and]) on your computer keyboard. Move the frame to between staves in a system (from the top to bottom staff in your piano score): Windows—hold down Shift and use the up and down arrows; Macintosh—press the Return key to move down a staff, Shift-Return to move up.

Until Finale 2002, the Speedy Frame's size was fixed. Increasing the view percentage of your file did not increase the Speedy Frame size. Now the Speedy Frame's size will adjust automatically based on your view percentage. To select a fixed size of the frame or to allow for a greater frame size at high view percentages, click the Speedy menu and choose Speedy Options. You will find these settings in the Frame section.

Speedy Entry Without a MIDI Keyboard

The most basic way to use Speedy Entry is with the computer keyboard. Click the Speedy menu and uncheck Use MIDI Keyboard for Input (if there is not a check to the left of this item, just click the Speedy menu again to return focus to your score). You are now ready to use your computer keyboard for note entry.

Press the up and down arrows on your keyboard and notice the small horizontal bar move up and down between the staff lines and spaces. We will refer to this horizontal bar as the Speedy Entry cursor. Use this cursor to specify the pitch of the note you want to enter. Move the cursor to the third space C and press the 5 key to enter a quarter note. Use the same keystrokes for note durations (1-8) you used in Simple Entry. After you enter each note, the cursor automatically advances to the right. Now, press the down arrow twice to move the cursor down to the second space A and press the 4 key twice to enter two eighth notes. Now, press the 6 key to enter a half note. Once you have filled a measure, the Speedy Frame automatically jumps to the next measure.

Using the QWERTY Keyboard to Specify Pitch

There is a faster way to move the cursor between pitches in Speedy Entry without using the arrow keys or a MIDI keyboard. If you engage Caps Lock, all of the letters on your computer keyboard will act differently. Click an empty measure with the Speedy Entry tool chosen. Press Caps Lock and press the A key to move the cursor down to middle C. Each letter to the right corresponds to the next highest staff location: S=D, D=E, F=E, and so on. Press the Q key to start from the third space or Z to begin below the staff. Use each adjacent letters to move up or down to different pitches. This can be an effective way to quickly enter notes if you spend some time getting used to the keystrokes. Remember, to access the Speedy Entry keyboard shortcuts, Caps Lock must be disengaged.

Entering Rests

After entering any note, simply press the Backspace/Clear key to change it to a rest. To change any chord to a rest, position the cursor so that it is not on a note or pitch present in the chord (otherwise, pressing Backspace/Clear will remove an individual note). Any time the Speedy Frame leaves a measure, Finale will automatically fill any space at the end with rests. To avoid this, and enter all of your rests manually, click the Speedy menu and choose Speedy Options. In the Frame section, uncheck Fill With Rests When Leaving Measure.

Edit as You Enter

Unlike Simple Entry, in this form of Speedy Entry, you will always add accidentals, dots, ties, etc., after entering the note. There is no "selection" necessary other than placing the cursor on, or adjacent to, the note. Press 5 to enter a quarter note in an empty measure, then press the + key to add a sharp, press period (.) to add an augmentation dot, or T for a tie. Now, enter three more quarter notes (the frame will move to the next measure). Press the S key. Finale will look back across the barline and add the sharp to the last note of the previous measure. Press the T key to begin a tie on the last note of the previous measure. Also use keystrokes during entry to flip stems, break/join beams, change enharmonic spelling, etc. You will be able to use all of the Simple Entry keystrokes for editing in the Speedy Frame. For a complete list of keystrokes, click the Speedy menu and choose Speedy Edit Commands.

Figure 3.7
Choose Speedy edit commands from the Speedy menu to see a list of keyboard commands for Speedy Entry.

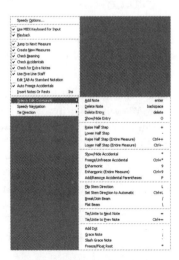

You may want to insert a note between existing entries. To do this, click the Speedy menu and choose Insert Notes or Rests (on Windows, press the Insert key; Macintosh, press Shift-I). Next, click an empty measure. You will notice black triangles at the top and bottom of the vertical insertion bar within the Speedy Frame. Enter two quarter notes in the measure. Press the left arrow so the cursor is covering the second quarter note. Your measure should look like this:

Figure 3.8
Speedy Entry in Insert
mode

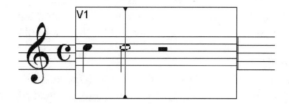

Press the 6 key to insert a half note between the two quarter notes. To activate or deactivate Insert Notes or Rests, you can also press the Insert key in Windows or Shift-I on Mac.

NOTE
If you are familiar with the Speedy edit commands as they were before Finale 2002, don't worry, they will also work. Just make sure Caps Lock is on (and Use MIDI Keyboard is deactivated under the Speedy menu).

Accidentals

After you have entered a note, use the + or – keys to raise or lower notes incrementally (by half steps). For instance, to change a G to a G#, place the cursor over it and press +. To change it back to a G, press -. The plus and minus keys act the same as the Half Step Up and Half Step Down keys in Simple Entry. To show an accidental on any note, use the A key. To hide any accidental, press the * key (you can use these two keystrokes interchangeably in most occasions, though the A key won't hide "real" accidentals, just courtesy accidentals). Again, you can also use any of the Simple Entry commands (S, F, N, etc.) to enter accidentals as you would on a selected note in Simple Entry.

Chords

To enter a chord, simply move the cursor directly above or below a note and press the Enter key. Finale will automatically enter a note of the same duration as the existing one. To remove a single note from a chord, move the cursor directly on top of it and press Backspace/Clear. To delete an entire chord, use the Delete key. To change the chord to a rest, move the cursor over the stem (not on top of a notehead), and press the Backspace/Clear or R key.

Tuplets

Entering tuplets of any kind is easy in Speedy Entry. With the Speedy Frame active, hold down the Ctrl/Option key and press the number corresponding to the number of notes you would like to enter in the tuplet (3 for triplet, 6 for sextuplet, etc.). You will see the number appear in the upper right corner of the Speedy Entry Window. Next, enter these notes (of the same duration for now) and Finale will automatically place them within a tuplet definition. The first note you enter in the series will contain the information that tells Finale the value of the tuplet. For instance, if you press Ctl/Option-3, then enter a quarter note, Finale will assume you want a quarter note triplet. Therefore, always begin the tuplet with the value that represents the crucial subdivision. If you wish to enter a tuplet whose first note does not begin on the crucial subdivision, press Ctrl/Option-1 to open the Tuplet Definition dialog box for more advanced tuplet settings. There will be more on defining and editing tuplets in chapter 9.

Layers in Speedy Entry

The basic concept of layers in Speedy Entry is exactly the same as in Simple. If you need to enter multiple voices or melody lines in the same staff, you will need to use multiple layers. On Windows, click the layer selection boxes in the lower left of your screen to specify a layer; on Macintosh, click and select Layer from the popup menu. To move between layers on Windows, hold down Shift and press the ' (apostrophe) key; on Macintosh, hold down Shift and use the Up and Down arrows. In the Speedy Frame, nonactive layers are grayed out in the background. To hide notes in any layer, use the H or O key. You will also be able to specify multiple note durations on the same beat in Speedy Entry using voices.

Voices

To enter multiple melodic lines, I recommend always using layers. However, when working with Speedy Entry, you have the option of using up to two voices in each layer. With voices and layers combined, you can have up to eight independent passages simultaneously in one staff! You may already have noticed the "V1" located in the upper left of the Speedy Frame. This indicates the voice with which you are currently working. At any time, while working in Speedy Entry, press the ' (apostrophe) key to move to voice 2 or back to voice 1. After entering a note in voice 1, press the ' key (notice V1 change to V2), move your cursor to the desired pitch and enter a note of any duration. Since notes in voice 2 can be entered anywhere over an existing note in voice 1, they can come in handy for independent lines that begin somewhere other than the first beat (so you don't have to go back and hide notes in different layers).

Speedy Entry with a MIDI Keyboard

You can improve the speed of Speedy Entry dramatically with the aid of a MIDI keyboard. In this mode of Speedy, you can use your MIDI keyboard to specify all pitches and use the computer keyboard for durations, ties, etc. You will also have the option to abandon the computer keyboard almost entirely by programming MIDI pitches to durations, ties and navigation controls. Again, it is important to note that all of the information that pertains to editing existing notes without a MIDI keyboard is still valid and may be useful for adjusting your notes once they have been entered, without changing back to non-MIDI mode.

To use a MIDI keyboard (or any external MIDI device) for input, you will need to ensure it is properly connected to the computer and set up in Finale. For complete instructions on MIDI setup, consult the Finale Installation and Tutorials manual.

TIP

To test if your MIDI keyboard is set up properly, hold down a pitch and press one of the duration numbers while the Speedy Frame is active (make sure Use MIDI Keyboard for Input is checked under the Speedy menu). If you get a note, Finale is receiving the MIDI information from your keyboard. If you get a rest, this information is not getting through. If this is the case, consult chapter 1 of this book for troubleshooting solutions or the Finale Installation and Tutorials manual for instructions on MIDI setup.

To configure Speedy Entry to use a MIDI keyboard, click the Speedy menu, and check Use MIDI Keyboard for Input. Now, click a measure to activate the Speedy Frame. Hold down middle C on your MIDI keyboard and press the 5 key. Finale will place a quarter note into your staff on middle C. While holding down any pitch, use the standard duration keystrokes (1-8) to enter any note duration on that pitch. Finale will add accidentals automatically.

TIP

To change the enharmonic spelling of any note, use the 9 key.

Next, without pressing any notes down on your MIDI keyboard, press the 5 key. You will see a quarter rest. Any time you press a number without holding down one of the keys on your MIDI keyboard, a rest of the corresponding duration will appear in your score.

You can enter several notes at once from your MIDI keyboard. Hold down as many notes as you want (up to 12) and press one of the duration keys to enter a chord into your score.

Entering tuplets into your score works almost the same way as in Speedy Entry without MIDI. With a Speedy Frame open, hold down Ctrl/Option and press the 3 key. You will see the number 3 appear in the upper right corner of the Speedy Frame. Hold down the first pitch and press a number for the duration of the first note of the triplet. Enter the following two notes as you would normally. Note that triplet duration information is contained in the first note.

Entering Many Notes of the Same Duration

Let's say you want to enter a passage of eighth notes without having to press the 4 key for each note. Press the Caps Lock key. Press the 4 key, and you will see the number 4 appear in the lower left corner of the Speedy Frame. Now, every time you play a note or chord on your MIDI keyboard, Finale will enter an eighth note into your score. To start entering quarter notes, press the 5 key and begin entering notes with your MIDI keyboard. To enter a rest, simply strike three consecutive notes, half steps apart; for instance, C, C# and D. Many Finale users endorse this method as the fastest way to use Speedy Entry, especially in scores containing long strands of notes of similar duration.

Using Caps Lock mode of Speedy Entry with MIDI also makes entering long strands of tuplets easy. Invoke the Speedy Frame on an empty measure and press Caps Lock. Press the 4 key to specify an eighth note duration. Now, hold down the Ctrl/Option key and press 3 on your computer keyboard. The number 3 appears in the upper right corner of the Speedy Frame indicating a triplet. Enter several notes using your MIDI keyboard. Each new set of three notes will be defined as a triplet.

Figure 3.9
Entering a strand of
triplets in Speedy Entry

To stop entering tuplets, press the number of the note duration (then the number in the upper right corner of the Speedy Frame will disappear).

Entry Using Your MIDI Keyboard Exclusively

You do not even need to use your computer keyboard for note entry with Speedy. Instead of using the number keys to specify note duration, you can program them to specific MIDI pitches. To do this, use the MIDI Modifier Key Map. This feature is new to Finale 2002. Click the Speedy menu and choose Speedy Options. Click the Create Key Map button, and the Edit MIDI Modifies dialog box will open.

Figure 3.10
Assign MIDI notes to
Speedy Entry
commands with the
MIDI Modifier Key Map.

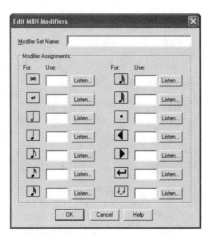

To program a MIDI pitch to one of the commands, simply click the corresponding Listen button and press a note on your MIDI keyboard (choose a note used rarely or not at all in the piece on which you are working). Do this for any duration or other command you would like to use in this box. Once you have finished programming, click OK twice to return to the score. Click a measure and use the notes you programmed just as you would keys on your computer keyboard for note entry.

Entering Articulations

Whether you plan to enter all of your articulations at once or during the note entry process, it is important to make the most of the time-saving tricks Finale has to offer. In this section, we will describe how to most efficiently enter staccato markings, accents, fermatas, and any other articulation. We will also cover how to choose from an extended variety of articulations, how to space them properly and also define them for playback. We'll get started with the fastest way to set articulations on individual notes.

To prepare for this chapter, we need a document containing notes without articulations. You can use the scratch document you used in one of the previous sections or open one of the Finale tutorial files. To open a tutorial, click the File menu and choose Open. Navigate to the Finale folder and doubleclick the Tutorials folder. Open the file "Tutorial 2.MUS." This is an arrangement of "O Susannah" that will suit our needs just fine.

Basic Articulation Entry

To get acquainted with the Articulation tool, let's start by adding articulations to individual notes. Click the Articulation tool (if it isn't selected already). Now, click a note. The Articulation Selection dialog box will appear on your screen.

Figure 3.11
Choose articulations for entry in the Articulation Selection dialog box.

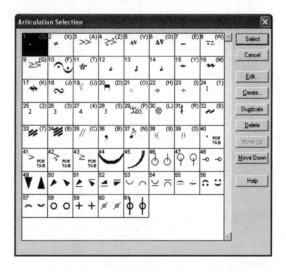

This dialog box shows the items in Finale's default articulation library. For now, click the accent marking and then click the Select button. Notice the accent appears on the note you clicked. You can add any one of the articulations in the Articulation Selection window by simply clicking a note, choosing the articulation and clicking the Select button. If you don't like the placement, click its handle and either drag it with your mouse or nudge it using the arrow keys (we'll get into more specific placement techniques later). To delete the articulation, click its handle and press the Delete key.

To edit individual articulations, right-click/Ctrl-click an expression handle to open the context menu. From here, you can easily access the Articulation Definition dialog box to edit that particular articulation. We will cover the usage of this dialog box in this section. You can also delete any articulation from the context menu.

Metatools

Metatools are time-saving shortcuts available in many areas of Finale, and are integral to using the program most effectively. Learning to use articulation metatools is a great introduction to this concept. You will see more discussion of metatools throughout this book.

While working on a score you will find yourself entering some articulations frequently and others not at all. To click a common articulation into your score without even entering the Articulation Selection dialog box, use a metatool. Click a note in your score to open the Articulation Selection dialog box. Notice the numbers or letters in parenthesis in the upper right corner on some of the articulation boxes. These are preset metatool assignments. Take note of the staccato marking in the far upper left, metatool (S). Click the Cancel button to close the Articulation Selection dialog box. Next, hold down the S key and click any note to enter a staccato marking. Hold down the A key and click another note to add an accent. Use these metatools to enter articulations quickly throughout the score. Refer to the Articulation Selection dialog box to reference all of the preset metatool assignments.

Programming a Metatool

Not all of the articulations in the Articulation Selection dialog box have a preset metatool assignment. However, there is a simple way to assign any letter or number to any articulation. For instance, let's say you want to use the 2 key to enter accent markings instead of the letter A. Hold down the Shift key and press the number 2. The Articulation Selection dialog box opens. Now, choose the accent marking and click select. The accent is now assigned to 2 key. Hold down the 2 key and click any note to add an accent. If you open the Articulation Selection dialog box again, you will notice the number 2 in the upper right corner of the accent box.

Entering an Articulation on Several Notes at Once

Finale makes it easy to add articulations to a region of notes. Simply click and drag over a region of your staff. You will notice a black square highlighting part of the staff. Encircle an area containing several notes and release the mouse button to open the Apply Articulation dialog box. Click the Select button and highlight an articulation in the Articulation Selection dialog box. Click the Select button, then OK. Finale adds the articulation you selected to all of the notes in the area you surrounded. You can also use metatools when applying articulations to a section of music. To enter an articulation to a region of notes faster, hold down a metatool key and drag over the region. To delete all articulations from any region, hold down the Delete key and drag over the region.

Adding New Articulations to the Library

If the articulation you are looking for does not exist in the Articulation Selection dialog box, you can create it. To do this, doubleclick a note in the score to open the Articulation Selection dialog box and click the Create button. This brings us to the Articulation Designer.

Figure 3.12
Specify the visual definition, placement, and playback for an articulation in the Articulation Designer dialog box.

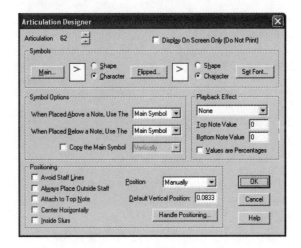

You will notice two buttons in the Symbol section: Main and Flipped. These refer to the articulation as it will appear above or below the staff, depending on your settings in the Symbol Options section. To select from a list of font characters, click the Main button. Find the character you want to use and click the Select button. If you want the same character to appear on the opposite side of the staff, click the Flipped button and do the same. If you can't find the character you are looking for, click the Set Font button to choose a different font. Once you have selected characters to add to your Articulation Selection, click OK and Select to return to the score.

Finale offers several music fonts that contain articulations that you might find useful. For a complete list of characters in all Finale fonts, click the Help menu on Mac (on Windows, click Help, then User Manual) and select the Engraver, Jazz or Maestro character map. Of course, you will be able to select a character from any font that exists on your system in the Articulation Designer dialog box.

Editing Articulations

You may need to modify the size, font or character of an existing articulation. To do this, click a note in your score to bring up the Articulation Selection dialog box. Highlight the articulation you would like to change and click the Edit button. This brings up the Articulation Designer dialog box. To modify the articulation, click the Set Font button. This launches the Font dialog box.

Figure 3.13
Choose the font, size, and style for an articulation in the Font dialog box.

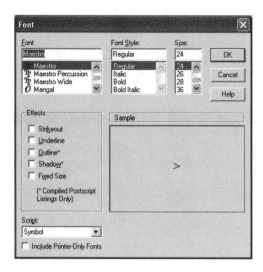

Select a new size, style or font for the articulation here. Click OK, OK, and then Select to return to your score. Any changes you make to an articulation will apply to every instance of that articulation in your score.

Using Articulations from Other Documents

If you already have created or edited articulations in another document, or have a document that contains articulations you would like to use, you can transfer these articulations between documents by saving and opening an articulation library. Open the document containing the existing articulations. Click the File menu and choose Save Library. You should see the following dialog box:

Figure 3.14
Save a library of articulations to open in any document by choosing Articulations in the Save Library dialog box.

Choose Articulations and click OK. Enter a name and save the file to your Libraries folder in your Finale directory (Finale should take you there by default). Open the document you are working on, click the File menu and choose Load Library or Open Library. You will see the Open Library dialog box:

Figure 3.15
Add articulations to a document by opening an articulation library from the Open Library dialog box.

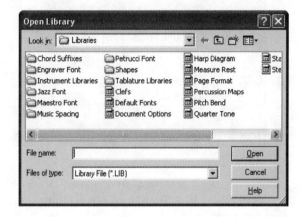

Doubleclick the library you saved to open it. Click a note to open the Articulation Selection dialog box, and all of the new articulations will be available. Finale will check for duplicate articulations, so only new ones will appear in the Articulation Selection window.

Articulation Placement

If an articulation does not appear where you want it to by default, you can change its placement settings in the Articulation Designer dialog box. This will change the placement of the articulation throughout the document. With the Articulation tool selected, click a note to bring up the Articulation Selection dialog box. Choose the articulation you would like to change and click Edit. Use the items in the Positioning section to specify the articulation's position in relation to the note.

Defining Articulations for Playback

There are three ways articulations can affect playback of a note or chord: when it starts (attack), how long it is (duration), and how loud it is (key velocity). To set an articulation to playback, doubleclick a note to enter the Articulation Selection, choose the articulation you would like to edit and click the Edit button. In the playback section, click the dropdown to choose the type of effect. An articulation can have more than one effect; for example, an accent with a dot should be played with increased attack and decreased duration. In this case, you would change both the velocity and duration setting.

Figure 3.16
Define an articulation
for playback in the
Playback Effect section
of the Articulation
Designer.

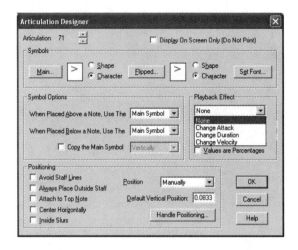

Next, specify the percentage of change in the box after Top Note Value. Most of the time, you can simply leave Bottom Note Value blank. Both the top and bottom note value fields will only apply to articulations that you want to scale from the bottom to top (or top to bottom) note of a chord. You can use both these settings with the Attack function to create a rolled chord.

Copying Articulations Within Your Score

You can copy articulations independently by using the Mass Edit Tool. To try this, enter two measures of quarter notes and add some articulations on every note in the first of these measures. Click the Mass Edit Tool and highlight the first measure. Make sure that Select Partial Measures is turned off in the Edit menu. From the Mass Edit menu, choose Copy Entry Items. Check Articulations and click OK. Now, drag the highlighted measure to the second measure. Finale will paste the original articulations on any note that lines up with the beat placement of the original articulation.

Automatically Copy Articulations to Similar Rhythmic Passages

You may have a recurring passage in your score that demands the same set of articulations at each occurrence throughout the piece. A feature new to Finale 2002, SmartFind and Paint, allows you to find and copy articulations to these passages automatically. To demonstrate this, fill a measure with a combination of eighth and quarter notes on different pitches with the Simple or Speedy Entry tool. Click the Mass Edit Tool, highlight this measure and drag-copy it to a different measure. In the Copy Measures dialog box, type 10 and click OK. Now, click the Articulation tool and add several various articulations to the original measure. Click the Mass Edit Tool again and highlight the measure containing the articulations. Click the Mass Edit menu and choose Set SmartFind Source. Next, click the Mass Edit menu again and choose Apply SmartFind and Paint. You will see the following dialog box:

Figure 3.17
Choose elements to
copy to similar
rhythmic passages in
the SmartFind and Paint
dialog box.

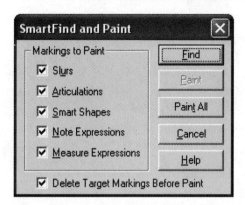

Click the Find button and the measure containing the similar passage becomes highlighted.
Click the Paint button and the articulations appear on the notes just as they did in the original
measure. This is also a great technique for copying Slurs, Smart Shapes, Note Expressions and
Measure Expressions to identical rhythmic passages throughout your score.

Entering Expressions

What exactly is an expression? Well, in Finale, expressions are most commonly used for
dynamic markings (forte, piano, etc.). However, you will be using expressions to enter many
other items, including rehearsal letters, tempo indications, style indications, etc. The main
benefit of an expression, as opposed to a text block, is spacing and metatool assignment. While
editing your score, there will usually be a good deal of spacing changes to notes and measures.
Therefore, there are two basic types of expressions: note-attached and measure- attached. In
addition, any note-attached or measure-attached expression can be in the form of text or a shape.
We refer to these as text expressions and shape expressions.

There are many situations that lend themselves to one or the other of these types, depending on
the type of marking, number of staves in your score and other factors. Generally, if you plan to
enter the text once and spacing isn't an issue, use the Text tool. If you will use the text more
than once, the Expression tool is a better choice. In this section, we'll discuss the best way to
enter expressions and also when to use each type.

To prepare for this section, either use the scratch document from the previous section or open
tutorial number 2. To do this, click the File menu and choose Open. Navigate to the Finale
folder and doubleclick the Tutorials folder. Open the file "Tutorial 2.MUS." Again, this is an
arrangement of "O Susannah" that will suit our needs just fine.

Basic Expression Entry

Since dynamic markings are usually the most common expressions, let's enter some of those
first. Click the Expression tool if it isn't selected already. Doubleclick below the first measure of
your score. This opens the Expression Selection dialog box.

CHAPTER 3

Figure 3.18
Choose an expression
for entry in the
Expression Selection
dialog box.

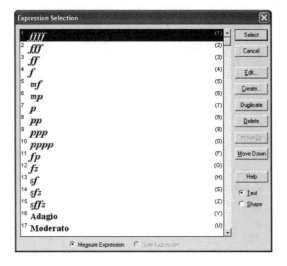

Here, you will see a list of default dynamic markings, tempo indications and rehearsal letters. Click the forte (f) expression to highlight it and then click the Select button. Click OK again and the forte marking appears where you originally clicked. You will be able to enter any expression in the Expression Selection dialog box this way. You can click above or below a measure to enter an expression. Make sure the arrow on the cursor is pointing to the correct staff before you click. If you don't like the placement of an expression, click its handle and either drag it with your mouse or nudge it using the arrow keys (we'll get into more specific placement techniques later). To delete the expression, click its handle and press the Delete key.

To edit individual expressions, right-click/Ctrl-click an expression handle to open the context menu. From here, you can easily access the Expression Assignment, Expression Definition or Font dialog boxes to edit that particular expression. We will cover the usage of these dialog boxes throughout this section. You can also delete any expression from the context menu.

Note Expressions

As mentioned earlier, note expressions are designed to adjust accordingly with the note or rest to which they are attached. They are particularly useful when working with single staff documents, because unlike measure expressions, they are designed to appear on one staff only and can affect playback of individual layers (we'll cover the benefits of measure expressions next). To enter a note-attached expression, move your cursor directly above or below a note or rest so you see a small quarter note appear to the upper right of your cursor. With the cursor in this state, doubleclick. At the bottom of the Expression Selection dialog box, you will see two radio buttons: Note Expression and Measure Expression. Make sure Note Expression is selected and click the Select button. Next, you will see the Note Expression Assignment dialog box. Here you can adjust the expression's placement and the layer at which you want it to affect playback. You will only see this dialog box while entering note expressions. Click OK and the expression appears in your score. You can distinguish between note- and measure-attached expressions in your score by the color. By default, note expressions are red and measure expressions are green.

Measure Expressions

Measure expressions are designed to adjust their positioning depending on the width and placement of the measure to which they are attached. As you adjust your barlines and move measures around, the associated measure expressions move with them. To enter a measure expression, doubleclick above or below a measure to open the Expression Selection dialog box. Click an expression and make sure the Measure Expression radio button is selected at the bottom of this dialog box. Click Select and you will see the Measure Expression Assignment dialog box. You will be able to specify spacing and where to affect playback here. The Show On section and the Allow Individual Positioning checkbox are for managing measure expressions attached to several staves. For now, just click OK to enter the expression into your score. The main benefit of measure expressions comes into play while working with multistaff scores, since they can be entered on multiple staves at the same time. This concept will be explained in detail in chapter 7 where we focus on multiple staff documents.

Metatools

Like articulations, you will also be able to enter any expression with a metatool. Again, this is a much faster way to enter them into your score than opening the Selection dialog all the time. Hold down the 4 key and click underneath the second measure. A forte (f) marking will appear. Now, doubleclick an empty space below the staff to open the Expression Selection dialog box. Notice the numbers and letters to the right of each expression. These are the preset metatool assignments. While working on your score, hold down one of these numbers or letters and click to quickly enter its associated expression into the score.

You can also specify the type of expression (note-attached/measure-attached) to enter while using expression metatools. Click the Expression menu. Choose Metatools: Note-Attached to automatically enter note expressions, or Metatools: Measure-Attached to automatically enter measure expressions as you click expressions into your score. Choose Metatools: Context Sensitive to choose the type of expression based on where you click in the score.

Click the Expression menu and choose Metatools: Context Sensitive. Move your cursor directly above or below a note so you see a small quarter note appear to the upper right of your cursor. Next, use a metatool to enter an expression and it will be attached to the note directly above or below the position you clicked. Move your cursor so the small note vanishes from the cursor, and enter another expression with a metatool into your score to specify a measure expression.

Programming an Expression Metatool

You can program your own expression metatools just like an articulation metatool. Hold down the Shift key and press a number or letter key. Choose the expression you would like to assign to that key and click Select. Hold down the key you programmed and click in the score to enter the expression you chose.

On Macintosh, you can use TGTools to quickly assign expressions to metatools. From the TGTools menu, choose Select Text Expression to do this (see chapter 15 for details). If you do not see the TGTools menu, install the TGTools demo from the companion CD-ROM.

Creating a Text Expression

You will want to create expressions for any text in your score that refers to the performance of the music. Tempo markings, style indications, volume or performance practice (andante, crescendo, arco, etc.) will all be added with the Expression tool. To create an expression, doubleclick above or below a staff to open the Expression Selection dialog box. Click the Create button. This opens the Text Expression Designer dialog box.

Figure 3.19
Create or edit text for entry as an expression in the Text Expression Designer dialog box.

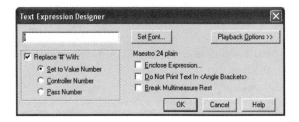

Type your text into the entry field. To change the size, font or style, click the Set Font button. The Font dialog box opens. Here, you can choose any size, style or font on your system. When you have finished, click OK, OK and Select to return to your score. The expression will appear in the size, style and font you specified. You will be able to enter the expression you just created at any time while working on this document. Doubleclick above or below a staff. Scroll to the bottom of the list and notice your custom expression at the bottom. If you plan to use this expression often, program a metatool for it.

TIP

If you want to ensure that an expression will remain the same size, regardless of staff, system or page resizing, set it to a fixed size. You will find this checkbox at the bottom of the Effects section of the Font dialog box while editing your expression.

Editing and Creating Similar Text Expressions

There may be many expressions in your score bearing similar characteristics. To avoid the redundancy of creating each one from scratch, duplicate existing expressions and edit them. To do this, doubleclick above or below a staff to enter the Expression Selection dialog box. Click the expression you just created (or any existing expression) and click the Duplicate button. This adds a duplicate of the expression at the bottom of the list, which will automatically be highlighted. Click the Edit button to edit this expression. Change the text or any other attribute, then click OK, OK and Select to return to your score. You can duplicate and/or edit any expression that exists in the Expression Selection dialog box.

TIP
While editing your expression in the Text Expression Designer, you may want to define an expression to display on your screen, but not in the printout. Type angled bracket characters on each side of the text expression and check Do not Print Text in <Angled Brackets>. Click OK and Select. The expression will appear on your screen display in angled brackets, but will not appear on the printout.

For Windows, there is an alternative way to manage and edit text expressions. If you have many expressions in your library, you may find the Expression Selection dialog box inadequate for quickly finding the expression you are looking for. In response to this problem, an Expression Browser has been included with TGTools for better management and availability of expressions. From the TGTools menu, choose Browser. Use this window to arrange, edit and select your expressions (see the TGTools documentation at www.tgtools.de for more details).

Enclosing an Expression

You may want to enclose an expression within a box, circle or rectangle. This is a common trait in rehearsal letters, but is also used for various other text in music. Doubleclick above or below a staff to enter the Expression Selection dialog box. Click one of the existing rehearsal letters in the selection and click the Edit button to enter the Text Expression Designer. Click the Enclose Expression checkbox. You will see the Enclosure Designer dialog box.

Figure 3.20
Specify an enclosure for an expression in the Enclosure Designer dialog box.

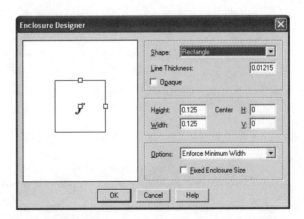

Choose the shape of the enclosure from the dropdown in the upper right corner, then use the handles in the display window to make any manual adjustments (or use the Height/Width fields to specify the size of the enclosure). Click OK, OK and then Select to return to your score and see the enclosed expression.

CHAPTER 3

Creating a Shape Expression

You may want to enter a measure or note-attached item in your score that is not in the form of text but shape. Doubleclick above or below the staff to enter the Expression Selection dialog box. Click the Shape Radio button in the lower right corner of this dialog box. You will now see a bunch of shapes in the display window. These are the items in your default Shape Expression Library. You can enter any of these just as you would a text expression. For access to more shapes, click the Create button. This opens the Shape Expression Designer dialog box. Click the Select button to see an expanded number of shapes. These are all of the shapes in your Shape library.

Figure 3.21
Choose a shape for entry
as a shape expression in
the Shape Selection
dialog box.

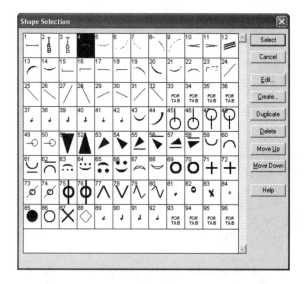

To use one of these shapes, click it, then click Select, OK and Select to return to your score. Like text expressions, these can be defined as either measure- or note-attached expressions.

You can modify any shape expression while looking at your score. Double-click the handle on the shape expression. You will see it's now surrounded with black boxes. Click and drag these boxes to modify your shape.

NOTE
If you have multiple occurrences of a shape expression in your document, modifying it in the score will change every occurrence of the shape expression. If you would like to be able to edit each shape expression independently, enter them with metatools. Each time you use a metatool to enter a shape expression, Finale creates a duplicate shape ID in the Shape Selection dialog box. Therefore, changes to one shape in the score will not apply to any other occurrence of that shape.

Creating Your Own Custom Shape

You can design and enter any shape by creating or editing a shape expression. Doubleclick above or below a staff to open the Expression Selection dialog box. Click the Shape radio button in the lower right corner. Now, click the Create button. Click the Select button to display the shapes in your Shape library. To design your own shape, click the Create button. This opens the Shape Designer dialog box.

Figure 3.22
Design your own shape
for entry as an
expression in the Shape
Designer.

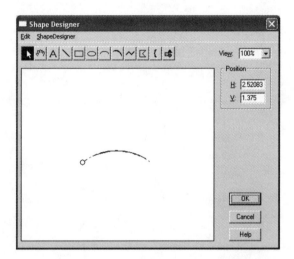

Use the tools available in this box to create your own custom shapes, brackets or even import graphics to edit and place in your score. Once you have created your shape, to return to your score, click OK, Select, OK, Select and OK. Once you have created the shape, it will exist in this document's Shape library (we'll talk about libraries at the end of this chapter).

Aligning and Positioning Expressions

If simply dragging expressions into place isn't consistent enough, you can specify the precise location of any expression related to the note or measure to which it is attached. Rightclick a note expression handle (remember note expressions are red) and choose Edit Note Expression Assignment. In the Distance from field, click the drop-down arrow to specify whether you want to position the note from the top or bottom note in a chord. Then, specify the distance from that notehead in the H: (horizontal) and V: (vertical) fields to the right. Click OK to return to your score and see the new placement. To edit the position of a measure expression, rightclick the handle on a measure expression and choose Edit Measure Expression Assignment. Now, use the H: and V: fields to specify the distance from the beginning of the measure and above or below the top staff line. The beginning of a measure in this case usually relates to the default position of the first note or rest (after the Time or Key Signature).

To select your unit of measurement (inches, centimeters, etc.), click the Options menu and choose Measurement Units. There is a description of all the measurement units in Chapter 1.

CHAPTER 3

TIP
To automatically align or move expressions in any region of your score, use the Align/Move Dynamics TGTools plug-in. For more information, see chapter 10.

Defining an Expression for Playback

Any expression can be defined to affect playback of the score. To define an expression for playback, first double-click above or below a staff to open the Expression Selection dialog box. Click the forte (f) expression, then click the Edit button. In the Text Expression Designer, click the Playback Options button and the dialog box will expand.

Figure 3.23
Click Playback Options to extend the Text Expression Designer dialog box to define an expression for playback.

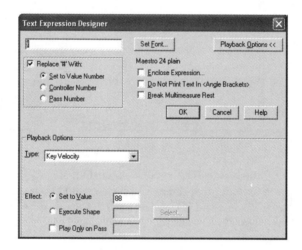

Here you will see that this expression already has a playback definition assigned. This expression, like all the dynamic expressions, has a Key velocity assigned to it. Key velocity is basically the volume of the MIDI note (it actually relates to the velocity of a key as it is struck on a MIDI keyboard). To increase the key velocity (make the note play back "louder"), enter a higher number into the Set to Value field. You can define an expression to affect playback in many ways, including tempo, pitch, panning, and channel. You will find a more complete description of any shape or text expression's playback capabilities in chapter 14.

Using Expressions from Other Documents

Like articulations, you can transfer any expression between documents by saving and opening a library. Open the document containing the existing text or shape expressions that you would like to transfer to another document. Click the File menu and choose Save Library. Choose Text Expressions or Shape Expressions and click OK. Enter a name and save the file to your Libraries folder in your Finale directory (Finale should take you there by default). Now, open the document you are working on, click the File menu and choose Open Library or Load Library. Double-click the library you saved to open it. These expressions now will be available in this document's Expression Selection dialog box.

You may see some duplicate expressions that existed in both documents to begin with. To clean this up, highlight the duplicates and click the Delete button. To avoid these duplicate expressions, you can delete them from the original document before saving the library. If you do this, make sure not to save changes when closing the file.

You can delete unused expressions with the Text Expression Sorter plug-in that's available in the TGTools plug-in set.

TIP

If you want your own custom expressions available in every new default document or document created with the Setup Wizard, customize your Maestro Font Default file. To do this, click the File menu and choose New, then Default Document. After the file opens, load any libraries containing expressions you want to add into the document. Next, click the File menu and choose Save As. On Windows, name the file "Maestro Font Default.FTM"; on Macintosh, simply name the file "Maestro Font Default." Save the file to the Components folder in your Finale folder and replace the existing file. Now, any time you start a new default document, or use the Document Setup Wizard, these expressions will be available in your Expression Selection dialog box.

Creating a Simple Arrangement

Let's apply the skills we've learned so far to create a simple score. In the following example, we'll begin a new document with the Setup Wizard, enter the notes with Simple or Speedy Entry, program metatools to enter articulations and expressions, finalize layout, and print. For this example, we'll notate an arrangement of "Greensleeves." When complete, our arrangement will look like this (Figure 3.24):

Figure 3.24
"Greensleeves"
arrangement

CHAPTER 3

1. From the File menu, choose New > Document with Setup Wizard. For Title, enter "Greensleeves," and for Composer, enter "Arr. by" followed by your name. Then click Next to move to page two.

2. Now, let's choose our instrument. We'll create a part for flute, so double-click Flute in the second column. Then, click Next to move to page three.

3. Our arrangement will be in 6/4. Notice this isn't one of the available time signatures on page three of the Setup Wizard, so we'll have to define it ourselves. Under Select a Time Signature, click the icon with two question marks. The Time Signature dialog box appears. After Number of Beats, click the right arrow twice, so 6/4 appears in the display window. Then, click OK to return to the Setup Wizard. Now, we'll select the key of the piece. Under Select a Concert Key Signature, click the drop-down/popup arrow to the right of the preview window and choose Minor Key (notice the preview window updates accordingly). This arrangement will be in A minor, so click Next to move to page four.

4. Check Specify Initial Tempo Marking. Then, in the text box to the right, enter "90." Our arrangement will also have a one beat pickup, so check Specify Pickup Measure and make sure the quarter note icon is selected to the right. Click Finish. Your new document appears as shown in Figure 3.25.

Figure 3.25
After competing the Setup Wizard, our score is ready for entry.

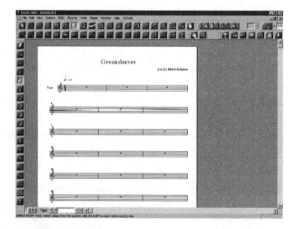

5. Now, use the Simple or Speedy entry tool (as described earlier in this chapter) to enter notes into the first four measures, as they appear in Figure 3.24.

6. Now, notice measures five and six are duplicates of measures one and two. Let's save time by copying with the Mass Edit Tool. Click the Mass Edit Tool and then drag over measures one and two so they are highlighted. Then click the highlighted area and drag to measure five (you will see a black boarder around measures five and six). Release the mouse button and click OK.

7. Now, use the Simple or Speedy Entry Tool to enter notes into measures seven through twelve.

8. Use the same procedure described in step six to copy measures nine and ten into measures thirteen and fourteen.

9. Enter notes into the final two measures with the Simple or Speedy Entry tool.

10. To delete the extra measures, click the Mass Edit Tool, then click to highlight measure seventeen (the first empty measure). Then, while holding down the Shift key, press the right arrow key to select every measure to the end of the piece. Press Delete to delete these measures (notice there is now a final barline at the end of the piece).

11. Now that we have entered notes into the score, let's enter the dynamic markings. We'll use the Expression tool to do this. Click the Expression tool, then double-click beneath the pickup measure. The Expression Selection dialog box appears. Choose the *mf* expression and click Select. Then click OK. The *mf* expression appears below the staff. Click the handle and drag the expression into place. Now, let's use predefined metatools to enter the remaining two dynamic markings. While holding down the 4 key, click beneath measure nine to add the *f* marking. Then, while holding down the 5 key, click beneath measure fifteen to enter the *mf* marking. To see all of the metatool assignments, double-click anywhere in the score to open the Expression Selection dialog box. All of the metatool assignments appear to the right of each expression. Click Cancel to return to the score.

12. Next, let's enter the articulations. Click the Articulation tool. Double-click the quarter note in the pickup measure. The Articulation Selection dialog box appears. Choose the tenuto marking (number 7–notice the E in the upper right corner indicating the metatool assignment), then click Select. The tenuto marking appears beneath the note. To enter the remaining tenuto marking, use a metatool. While holding down the E key, click the last note in measure four. Now, hold down the A key and click each note in measure nine and thirteen to enter the accent articulations. Hold down the F key and click the last note to add the fermata. Click its handle and drag up to move it above the staff.

13. If you wish, click the Play button in the playback controls to hear your piece.

14. Now, let's finalize the layout. We have some extra space at the bottom of the page, so let's evenly space the systems on the page. Click the Page Layout tool. Click the page layout menu, and choose Space Systems Evenly. Now, leave the settings alone and click OK. Notice all systems are evenly spaced on the page.

15. Your piece should now look similar to the example in Figure 3.24. To print the score, from the File menu, choose Print. In the Print dialog box, Click OK/Print to print the piece.

Congratulations! You have just created a new score from scratch using Finale's entry tools, the Mass Edit Tool, and you've also added expressions and articulations quickly with metatools. These skills can be used whenever you are working on a score, and they provide a good groundwork for more time-saving concepts you will come across in the following chapters.

CHAPTER 3

4

Advanced Note Entry, Chords, and Lyrics

If Speedy Entry still isn't quick enough for you, there are a few other methods of note entry that could prove very effective, especially if you are a pianist. Here, we'll cover the variety of methods you can use to enter music in real time with either an external MIDI device (MIDI Keyboard/MIDI Guitar) or even an acoustic wind instrument. You will also learn how to easily create, and enter, your own chord suffixes, as well as enter lyrics. By the end of this chapter, we will have covered the topics necessary to quickly produce lead sheets and most other single staff documents. Here's a summary of what you will learn in this chapter:

▶ Real-time Entry: HyperScribe.

▶ Entering Chord Symbols.

▶ Entering Lyrics.

▶ Creating a Lead Sheet.

Real-time Entry: HyperScribe

HyperScribe is Finale's tool for translating a live musical performance into sheet music. Recording into Finale with a MIDI keyboard is the most common way to do this. In this section, you will learn how to enter notes in real time while playing along with a click track or tapping the tempo with the sustain pedal. Since you are entering music without interruption, there is a little more preparation involved than with Simple or Speedy Entry. However, once you find the settings that work best for you, HyperScribe can really move. While going through this chapter, you can expect a certain amount of editing needed to make finishing touches on your HyperScribe sessions. Plan to use HyperScribe in conjunction with Simple Entry or Speedy Entry to most effectively enter notes overall. In reality, the key to efficiency is finding the most comfortable combination of note entry tools as you approach each individual project.

To prepare for this chapter, set your keyboard to the most basic piano sound (without any effects). Then, open a new default document (File > New > Default Document).

NOTE:
To use a MIDI keyboard (or any external MIDI device) for input, you will need to ensure that it is properly connected to the computer and properly setup in Finale. For complete instructions on MIDI setup, consult the Finale Installation and Tutorials manual.

Playing into the Score Along With a Metronome Click

We'll start by using the most common method of HyperScribe: playing over a click track. Click the HyperScribe tool, then click the HyperScribe menu and choose Click and Countoff (yes, it's already checked, but click it anyway). You should now see the Playback and/or Click dialog box, as shown in Figure 4.1.

Figure 4.1
Specify a beat duration, tempo and start signal for your HyperScribe session in the Playback and/or Click dialog box.

This is where you will choose the beat subdivision of your score, tempo of the click track, and start signal for recording. Since we are in common time, choose the quarter note box. In the future, you might need to select a different note value depending on the Time Signature of your piece. In cut time, you would choose a half note; in 6/8, probably a dotted quarter note, and so on. Click the drop-down arrow to the right of Start Signal for Recording. From this list, choose Any MIDI Data. This tells Finale to begin the metronome click on a MIDI note command. For now, let's leave the tempo at 96 beats per minute. Click the Click and Countoff button to open the Click and Countoff dialog box (Figure 4.2).

Figure 4.2
Choose the countoff,
and MIDI attributes for
the click in the Click
and Countoff dialog
box.

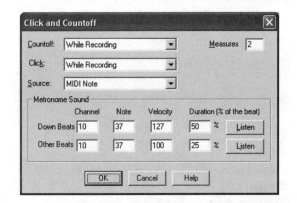

CHAPTER 4

Here, leave both Countoff and Click fields set to While Recording. The Measures field in the upper right corner controls the number of measures in the countoff. By default, it is set to click for two measures before recording. Leave this at two for now. In the future, you may want to set this to one.

In the Metronome Sound section, you will find parameters for your metronome click. The Downbeats row indicates properties for the first click in every measure, and the Other Beats row indicates properties for, well, the other beats. The default settings should work fine, as most synthesizers will use channel ten for percussion. The Key Velocity and Duration of Downbeats is higher, so the first click in each measure will be more pronounced. Click OK twice to return to the score.

When Finale records your performance, it will roundoff the notes you play to the nearest sixteenth note, eighth note, or other rhythmic subdivision depending on your quantization settings. Unlike other MIDI sequencers that use quantization to perfect playback, the quantization settings in Finale are used to accurately translate a performance into notation. You can, however, tell Finale to also play back the resulting quantized music if you want. As you record, you will find that even the most rhythmically accurate performance will vary somewhat with Finale's concrete timing. For example, if you tend to anticipate the beat slightly, a perfectly accurate transcription would result in unwanted sixty-fourth notes or one-hundred-twenty-eighth notes. You would probably also see a number of unwanted rests and ties scattered throughout your score. To specify a reasonable rhythmic value for Finale to use as a rounding marker during your HyperScribe session, use the Quantization Settings dialog box (Figure 4.3). Choose Quantization Settings from the Options menu now.

Figure 4.3
Round your notated
rhythms to the nearest
eighth note or other
rhythmic value by
configuring the
Quantization Settings
dialog box.

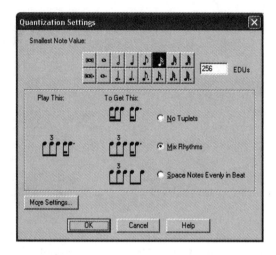

The value you choose for Smallest Note Value should generally depend on the smallest note used most frequently in the piece you are transcribing. If your piece has many small note values, you may consider choosing a slower recording tempo in the Playback and/or Click dialog box. If you intend to enter tuplets, keep in mind the duration of notes in a tuplet is smaller than the base note value. To accurately choose a tuplet duration for the Smallest Note Value, note the number of EDUs for the full duration of the tuplet and divide it by three. For instance, an eighth note tuplet is the same duration as a quarter note—1,024 EDUs. Enter 341 EDUs (one-third of 1,024) to specify an eight note tuplet as the smallest note value.

Don't attempt to HyperScribe ornaments more complex than grace notes, such as trills or tremolos, in a HyperScribe session. These should be added afterwards (with one of the TGTools Smart Playback plug-ins perhaps). For now, click the Quarter Note box for Smallest Note Value. Leave Mixed Rhythms selected and click the More Settings button. You should now see the More Quantization Settings dialog box, as shown in Figure 4.4.

Figure 4.4
Make settings for
playback, treatment of
rests, and grace notes for
a HyperScribe session in
the More Quantization
Settings dialog box.

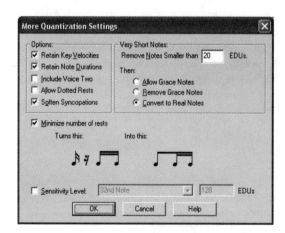

Here, you can fine-tune your quantization settings. If you plan to record a number of syncopated rhythmic passages in your score, you may want Finale to eliminate ties between beats and use larger note durations. If this is the case, leave Soften Syncopations checked. If you want notes across beats ties, uncheck Soften Syncopations (Figure 4.5).

Figure 4.5
Hyperscribe results with
and without Softened
Syncopations

Tied Syncopation   "Softened" Syncopation

Click OK twice to return to your score. You are now ready to begin. Click the first measure of your score. You will see the HyperScribe frame appear on the measure you clicked. Finale is now waiting for a MIDI pitch. Press a note on your keyboard; Finale will begin to click, giving you two measures before recording. At the completion of the second countoff measure, begin entering quarter notes into your score. After the HyperScribe frame moves on to the subsequent measure, you will see your notes appear. When you are finished, click anywhere in the score to stop recording. To enter more complicated music, click the Options menu > Quantization Settings and choose the eighth or sixteenth note for Smallest Note Value. Then, begin your HyperScribe session again. Existing notes are overwritten when you HyperScribe over them.

TIP:
You can specify the enharmonic spelling of accidentals for nondiatonic pitches entered with HyperScribe by editing the spelling tables. From the Options menu, choose Enharmonic Spelling > Edit Major and Minor Key Spellings or Edit Modal or Chromatic Key Spellings (see chapter 10 for details).

After completing a HyperScribe session, you may notice extra rests where notes should be held. You can use TGTools to easily clean up your HyperScribe results with the Modify Rests plug-in. For complete instructions, view the TGTools Quick Start Video available on the companion CD-ROM. Also, make sure you have installed TGTools (also available on the companion CD-ROM).

CHAPTER 4

Playing into the Score While Tapping the Tempo

You may want to control the tempo of HyperScribe as you record. You can do this easily by tapping the tempo with the sustain pedal (or using another MIDI signal). Click the HyperScribe menu > Beat Source > Tap. You will now see the Tap dialog box, as shown in Figure 4.6.

Figure 4.6
Tap to specify the beat for a HyperScribe session by first setting up the Tap Source dialog box.

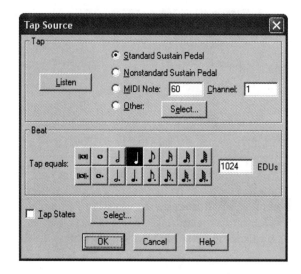

At the top, choose the type of MIDI signal you will be using to send the Tap information. The most common is a standard sustain pedal. It should be chosen by default. In the Beat section, after Tap Equals, choose the rhythmic duration of each beat. Since we are in common time, choose the quarter note. For now, click OK (we'll talk about Tap States soon). Click the first measure to see the HyperScribe frame around measure one. Finale will assume the first tap on the sustain pedal is beat 1. Begin playing while tapping the tempo on the sustain pedal. Feel free to adjust the tempo while you play. After the HyperScribe frame moves on to the subsequent measure, you will see your notes appear. When you are finished, click anywhere in the score to stop recording.

You may want to record into a score over a meter change without having to stop to change the beat unit. For example, you may want to record over a Time Signature change from 4/4 to 6/8 and have the Tap Equals setting change from a quarter note to a dotted quarter note. You can do this by setting up Tap States. From the HyperScribe menu, choose Beat Source and then Tap. In the Tap Source dialog box, click the Select button for Tap States. This will bring up the Tap States dialog box, as shown in Figure 4.7.

Figure 4.7
Switch the beat
duration per tap on the
fly by setting up the Tap
States dialog box.

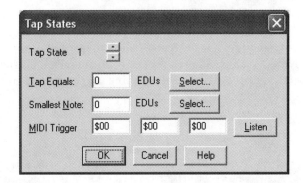

CHAPTER 4

Here, click the Select button to the right of Tap Equals to choose a new beat value. You will also
need to set up a MIDI trigger to tell Finale to switch to the new Tap State. Then, select a new
Smallest Note Value if necessary. Click the Listen button and then press a MIDI note you won't
be using (perhaps a really high or low note). This will be your trigger for Tap State 1. You can
program up to three Tap States. Click the spinner arrows at the top of this box to program any
other tap states you are using; you can program up to three. Click OK twice to return to your
score. Now, record into the score, and just before the downbeat of the new meter, stop tapping
and press the appropriate trigger. Then, resume with your performance while tapping along with
the tempo. Click anywhere in the score to finish.

CAUTION:
Once you trigger a Tap State, you will not be able to go back to your original
Beat Equals setting. If you want to return to the original meter during a Tap
session, program another Tap State with your original Beat Equals setting.

Recording into Two Staves at Once

Whether you are using a metronome click or are tapping the tempo, you may want to record
music directly into a grand staff (both treble and bass clef) in a single HyperScribe session. To do
this, click the HyperScribe menu, choose Record Mode and then Split into Two Staves. You will
now see the Fixed Split Point dialog box, as shown in Ffgure 4.8.

Figure 4.8
Tell Finale where to
split between the treble
and bass clef staves in a
grand staff with the
Fixed Split Point dialog
box.

Fixed Split Point

Split at MIDI Note: [60]   Listen

OK   Cancel   Help

The split point is the lowest pitch Finale will enter into the upper staff. Any notes entered below the split point will be entered into the lower staff. Click OK to return to your score. Now, click on the first measure to begin a new HyperScribe session. Notice there is now a box surrounding both staves. Click anywhere in the score when you are finished recording. For information on more advanced topics, such as entering into more than two staves at once and cross-staff notation, see chapter 7.

TIP

To easily open a new grand staff document, use the Setup Wizard (File menu > New). Choose Piano from the Keyboards category on page 2. To easily add a grand staff to an existing score, click the Staff Tool and choose New Staves (with Setup Wizard) from the Staff menu.

Using HyperScribe with a MIDI Guitar

In addition to using a MIDI keyboard for note entry, you can also use a number of other external MIDI devices, such as a MIDI guitar. To use a MIDI guitar for entry, follow the same instructions above. You can use a guitar (or other MIDI device) just as you would a MIDI keyboard.

MIDI guitars require an interface between the guitar and the computer to translate the acoustic pitches into MIDI information. As a result of the extra processing necessary, there might be a slight, yet consistent, delay in the time it takes from the moment the string is plucked until it reaches Finale. This is called latency, and can cause the HyperScribe transcription to lag behind the beat. To compensate for this, you can tell Finale to leave a specific amount of time between clicks/taps, and the actual recording tempo. To do this, choose MIDI Setup from the MIDI menu. Enter a MIDI Latency value anywhere from 25 to 150 milliseconds (the precise amount of time will depend on your interface and hardware configuration). Once you have established the correct amount of latency, you should be able to use HyperScribe normally.

Finale comes with many new features specifically for guitar and notation of other fretted instruments. One of these is the ability to record directly into a TAB staff with HyperScribe. When you do this, Finale will even record the actual fret numbers you play during the HyperScribe session. For more information on creating and editing TAB staves, see chapter 8.

Playback

After recording, there are several ways to adjust the way Finale plays the transcription back for you. For instance, you may want to play the music back exactly as you performed it, or exactly as it appears in the score. From the Options menu, choose Playback Options. Here, you can specify playback of individual elements of your recording. In the Options section, specify whether you want Finale to play back key velocities and note durations as you recorded them or as they appear in the score. You can also use the Playback Settings to specify other parameters such as base key velocity and swing playback. On Windows, open the Playback Settings by clicking the speaker icon on the right of the Playback Controls. On Mac, click the little expander triangle on the left side of the Playback Controls to expand the dialog. If you don't see the

Playback Controls onscreen, select them from the Window menu. For information on more advanced playback options, see chapter 14.

Other Entry Methods

There are a couple other methods of entry that are less frequently used, but worth mentioning. If you want to record an entire piece into Finale and then go back afterwards to assign the measure and beat information, you could use the Transcription tool. The Transcription tool is basically Finale's built-in miniature MIDI sequencer. To enter music in transcription mode, click the HyperScribe tool and choose Transcription Mode from the HyperScribe menu. Now, when you click a measure, you will see the Transcription dialog box. Here, record the entire piece and then assign Time and Measure tags to indicate the tempo and barlines (you can find step-by-step instructions for how to do this in the Finale User Manual). Once you have recorded the piece and assigned Time and Measure tags, click the Transcribe button to translate the music into staves in your score.

If you play a wind instrument, you may find the MicNotator useful for note entry. Use this feature to record into a microphone for transcription into a staff. To use this method of entry, choose MicNotator from the MIDI menu and check the Enable MicNotator box. Also, use the Mic Level indicator to ensure you are getting a signal from the microphone (which should be plugged into the "Mic In" port on your computer). When you see a signal in the Mic Level indicator, click OK. Then, use the HyperScribe tool just as you would with a MIDI keyboard.

When you use the MicNotator, be sure to play notes as evenly and cleanly as possible for best results. The translation from acoustic pitch to MIDI can be somewhat less accurate that a direct connection to an external MIDI device. If you are using a newer Macintosh, there may not be a Mic In port available on your computer. If this is the case, visit http://www.griffintechnology.com/products/imic/index.html for information on a USB Mic adaptor.

The Auto-Dynamic Placement Plug-in

After entering any music using HyperScribe, you can easily tell Finale to scan the music and place dynamic markings in the score based on the recorded key velocities. To do this, click the Mass Edit Tool, and press Ctrl/Command-A to Select All. From the Plug-ins menu, choose Auto-Dynamic Placement. You will now see the Auto-Dynamic Placement dialog box containing several parameters for expression placement and spacing. You may need to adjust these depending on your results. Click OK to see dynamic markings placed in your score automatically as note-attached expressions.

Working with Chord Symbols

Chord symbols are an integral part of music notation. You find them in lead sheets, jazz charts, guitar tablature and many other types of music. Chord symbols in Finale are basically entries of text placed on a baseline above entries in a staff. They consist of three elements: a symbol, suffix, and alternate bass. The symbol contains the bass pitch information of the chord (F sharp,

B flat, etc.); the suffix contains the quality of chord (major, minor, inversion, etc.). The suffix will also contain higher tertian information (7, 9, etc.) and their pitch alterations. An alternate bass pitch can also be added to any chord symbol. When entering chord symbols, you will always start with the symbol and then specify a suffix and alternate bass if necessary.

Often, when creating notation for fretted instruments, fretboard diagrams accompany the chord symbols to indicate a specific fingering. You can easily include fretboard diagrams beneath each chord suffix using Finale's default fretboards, or define your own custom fretboard diagrams. In addition to adding chord symbols, you will also learn how to enter, and even customize, fretboard diagrams.

Entering Chord Symbols

There are several ways to enter and edit chord symbols in Finale. You will be able to type them directly above a staff, define them manually for each entry or even tell Finale to analyze the music and insert the appropriate chord symbol. You will be able to customize the font, style and size of chord symbols, suffixes and fretboards, and even transfer a library of custom chord symbols between documents. In this section, you will learn how to handle chord symbols efficiently.

To prepare for the exercise, open a new default document (File > New > Default Document). Unless specified otherwise, we'll assume the Chord tool is selected.

Type into Score

Typing chords directly into the score is the most basic method of chord entry. It is also perhaps the fastest for entering basic chord symbols. To demonstrate this, first enter any single line melody into a staff with the Simple Entry tool. Then, click the Chord tool. From the Chord menu, choose Type Into Score. You will see four arrows to the left of the staff. These indicate the vertical positioning of your chords (we'll talk more about them soon). Click the first note in the staff. You will see a blinking cursor above the note you clicked. Type "CMaj" to indicate a C major chord. When you first type a chord symbol, it will appear as normal text. Press the space bar. The "CMaj" turns into a chord symbol with Maj as the suffix, and a fretboard is also displayed. To hide or show fretboards at any time, choose Show Fretboards from the Chord menu. Your cursor is now above the next note. Now, type "Abmin7/Db" and press the space bar. You will see an A flat minor seven chord over D flat (Figure 4.9).

Figure 4.9
Elements of chords

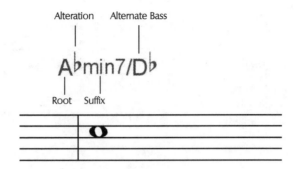

Chord symbols are case-sensitive. You can indicate the root of a minor chord by entering a lowercase letter, or the root of a major chord by using an upper case letter. The case of the root letter will affect the playback (major or minor) of the chord symbol.

While typing chords into the score, use the following method:

1. Type the letter representing the root of the chord.

2. Type the alteration of the root of the chord using "b" for flat and "#" for sharp.

3. Type the suffix abbreviation (Maj, min, 7, 9, etc.).

4. Type the alternate bass. Precede the alternate bass note with a forward slash (/) to place it to the right of the suffix, a bar symbol (|) to place it below and slightly to the right, and an underscore (_) to place the alternate bass directly below the symbol and suffix.

In addition to using "b" for flat and "#" for sharp, you can also use keystrokes for diminished and half-diminished symbols. Use the "o" key (lowercase O) for a fully diminished symbol and the "%" key (shift-5) for half diminished.

Manual Input

To enter chords with more complicated suffixes, and for more control while entering chords, you may want to use Manual Input mode. From the Chord menu, choose Manual Input. You will now see the Chord Definition dialog box (Figure 4.10).

Figure 4.10
Choose the suffix,
fretboard and playback
attributes for a chord in
the Chord Definition
dialog box.

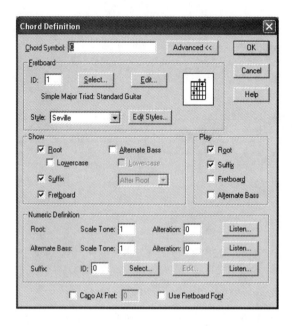

Enter the chord just as you would while typing into the score in the Chord Definition text box. Instead of typing the suffix, you can also choose from a list of available chord suffixes. Click the Advanced button and click the Select button in the Numeric Definition section (at the bottom). You will see a list of available chord suffixes. Click the one you want to use so it is highlighted, then click the Select button. You will see the suffix to the right of the root in the Chord Definition text box. Click OK to see the chord appear in the score above the note you originally clicked.

While typing into the score or using manual input, you can use keyboard shortcuts to easily select any of the available chord suffixes. After entering the root, type a colon (:) and then the number of the suffix as it appears in the Chord Suffix Selection dialog box. For example, type C:1 to enter "Cmaj." If you don't remember the number of the suffix, type :0 after the root and then press the space bar to view the Chord Suffix Selection dialog box. Choose the chord suffix and click the Select button to return to the score (or Chord Definition dialog box) with the suffix added.

TIP
By default, chords are set to playback. To silence playback for all chord symbols, uncheck Enable Chord Playback from the Chord menu.

MIDI Input

Use MIDI Input to enter chords easily with a MIDI keyboard. Choose MIDI Input from the Chord menu. Click a note in your score. You will see an ear appear above the staff. This means Finale is listening. Play a chord on your MIDI keyboard (in any inversion). Finale will analyze the chord you play and enter the corresponding chord suffix into the score. If Finale does not recognize the chord, you will be prompted with the Unknown Chord Suffix dialog box. Click "Let Finale do it" to tell Finale to automatically choose the closest chord symbol. Choose "I'll do it" to teach Finale the chord you played. Finale will take you to the Chord Definition dialog box to define a chord symbol for the chord you played.

You can edit the chord suffix associated with any chord played from the MIDI keyboard. To do this, choose Edit Learned Chords from the Chord menu. You will be prompted with the Edit Learned Chords dialog box, as shown in Figure 4.11.

Figure 4.11
Customize the chord to input for a combination of MIDI notes while using MIDI Input in the Edit Learned Chord dialog box.

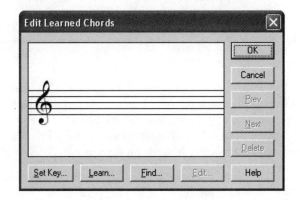

Choose a key for the learned chord and click the Learn button. Then play the chord you want to reassign. Click the Edit button to define its associated chord symbol.

One/Two Staff Analysis

If you already have a staff or staves with existing chords in the form of notation, Finale can analyze the music and enter the appropriate chord symbol automatically. Enter a chord into a staff. Then, choose One or TwoStaff Analysis from the Chord menu (depending on the number of staves you want to analyze). Click above a chord to tell Finale to place a chord symbol in the score automatically. If Finale cannot recognize the chord, you will see the Unknown Chord Suffix dialog box. Click "I'll do it" to define a chord symbol manually in the Chord Suffix Selection dialog box, or choose "Let Finale do it" to let Finale make its best guess.

Creating and Editing Chord Suffixes

If you can't find the suffix you want to use in the Chord Suffix Selection dialog box, you can create one yourself. From the Chord menu, choose Manual Input. Click a note in the score to bring up the Chord Definition dialog box. Click the Advanced button (to extend the lower portion), then click Select in the Numeric section to open the Chord Suffix Selection dialog box. Click the Create button (or, if you see a suffix similar to the one you are looking for, highlight it, click Duplicate, and then Edit). You will now see the Chord Suffix Editor dialog box, as shown in Figure 4.12.

Figure 4.12
Edit or create your own
suffix in the Chord
Suffix Editor dialog box.

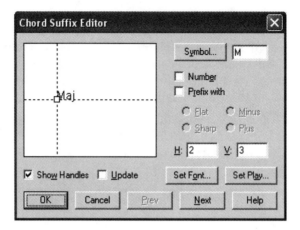

Enter a suffix symbol in the text box to the upper right (click the Set Font button to change the font). If the symbol is a number, check the Number box. To precede the symbol with a sharp, flat, plus or minus, check Prefix with and select the prefix below. If you want another character, click the Next button and repeat the process. Use either the handle in the editing window or the H: (horizontal) or V: (vertical) text boxes to position each symbol.

You may want to assign the suffix (pitches relative to the defined root) for playback. To do this, click the Set Play button. This will bring up the Suffix Keynumber Offsets dialog box, where you can enter MIDI Note numbers for playback. If you are using an external MIDI device (such as a MIDI keyboard), click the Listen button to enter the root and then the chord. Finale will record the MIDI information for you and calculate the offsets. Click OK, OK, Select and OK to return to the score and review the suffix.

TIP
When you play a chord into the Suffix Keynumber Offsets dialog box, Finale will not retain the octave information, only the pitch. To raise or lower an offset for playback for an octave, add or subtract twelve from the MIDI Note number (negatives are OK).

Changing Chord Fonts

You may want to change the default fonts of your chord symbols, suffixes, alterations, or fretboards. To do this, click the Options menu and choose Document Options. Then, click the Fonts category. Click the drop-down/popup menu for Chords and choose the element you want to change. Click the Set Font button to select a new font, size, and style. Do this for all elements of the chord you want to change. Click OK to return to the score. Changing the fonts for chord suffixes in the Document Options dialog box will only affect newly created ones, and will not affect suffixes already existing in the score or in your Suffix Selection. To change the font of existing chord suffixes, select the Chord tool and choose Change Chord Suffix Fonts from the Chord menu. In the Replace With section, click the Set Font button. Choose the Font, Size, and Style and click OK. Check the Font, Size, and Style boxes (as needed) and click OK. Existing suffix fonts will change the one you specified. If you find that the chords no longer line up on the same baseline, make sure to select "Fix Baseline Positioning" in the Change Chord Suffix Fonts dialog box.

Chord Metatools

Use chord metatools to quickly enter chords into a score. Choose Manual Input from the Chord menu. Hold down Shift and press any number or letter. You will now see the Chord Definition dialog box. Enter the chord symbol in the text box at the top (and make any other settings), then click OK. Now, hold down the letter you assigned and click on any note in the score to add the defined chord.

Chord Positioning

You can easily move any chord or fretboard diagram by clicking its handle and dragging or using the arrow keys to nudge it around. More than likely, however, you will want all of the chord symbols or fretboards to align to the same distance above the staff along a baseline. You can easily adjust the vertical placement (or baseline) of chord symbols by using the four positioning arrows on the left side of the screen. The arrow you use will depend on the region of chord baselines you want to position. Here is an explanation.

- ▶ Use the first arrow (from the left) to adjust the baseline of all chords or fretboards in the whole document.
- ▶ Use the second arrow to adjust the baseline of all chords or fretboards in that staff.
- ▶ Use the third arrow to adjust the baseline of all chords or fretboards in a particular staff in a system (in Page View).
- ▶ Use the fourth arrow to predetermine the baseline of the next chord or fretboard you enter.

To use the arrows for chord positioning, choose Position Chords from the Chord menu. To use the arrows for fretboard positioning, choose Position Fretboards from the Chord menu.

To space chords horizontally, you can drag them by the handle or reposition the notes to which they are attached. If you find your chords and/or fretboards overlap, you can tell Finale to automatically respace your music to avoid collision of chord symbols and fretboads. To do this, from the Options menu, choose Document Options and select Music Spacing. In the Avoid Collision of section, check Chords and click OK. Now, select the Mass Edit Tool, press Ctrl/Command-A to Select All, and then press the 4 key (to apply Note Spacing). Your music respaces to accommodate the chord symbols. There will be more information regarding Music Spacing in chapter 9.

Fretboard Diagrams

If you are working on a score for guitar, you may want to include fretboard diagrams that display a fingering for the chord. As mentioned earlier, you can activate or deactivate the presence of fretboard diagrams on chord symbols by choosing Show Fretboards under the Chord menu. If you decide to show fretboards, Finale will display them with a standard fingering for the specified chord. Since there are many ways to finger any given chord, you may want to edit a fretboard diagram so the chord is played on a different fret, for example. To customize a fretboard, first choose Manual Input from the Chord menu. Click a note in the score to open the Chord Definition dialog box. In the Fretboard section, click Select to see any alternate fretboards that already exist for that chord in Finale's default fretboard library. If you see the one you want, click it, then click Select and OK to return to your score. If you do not see the desired fretboard diagram, create your own. Click a note in your score to open the Chord Definition dialog box, enter the chord symbol, then click the Edit button in the Fretboard section to open the Fretboard Editor dialog box, as seen in Figure 4.13.

Figure 4.13
Edit or create your own fretboard in the Fretboard Editor dialog box.

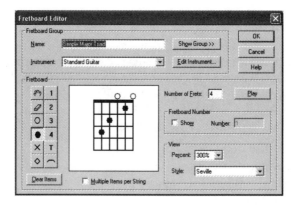

Here, make modifications to the existing fretboard using the tools on the left side of the Fretboard section. You can Edit the number of strings and string tuning of the fretboard instrument by clicking the Edit Instrument button. Once you have finished editing the fretboard diagram, click OK and Select to return to the Chord Definition dialog box. Click OK to return to the score to see the custom fretboard. If you find that the fretboards are too big or too small, choose Resize Fretboards from the Chord menu. Here, you can enter a percentage of the original size (the higher the number the bigger the fretboard gets—set it to 100% to see the original size).

TIP
To easily access the Fretboard Editor or the Chord Definition dialog box to edit a chord individually, right/control click a chord suffix handle and select Edit Chord Definition or Edit Fretboard. Also, use this context menu to show or hide chords and fretboards or to delete chord symbols independently.

Transferring Custom Chord Libraries Between Documents

If you have already created or edited chord symbols or fretboards in another document, or have a document that contains chords or fretboards you would like to use, you can transfer these between documents by saving and opening a chord and fretboard library. Open the document containing the existing chords. Click the File menu and choose Save Library. You should see the Save Library dialog box. Choose Chords and Fretboards and click OK. Enter a name and save the file to your Libraries folder in your Finale directory (Finale should take you there by default). Now, open the document you are working on, click the File menu and choose Open Library or Load Library. You will see the Open Library dialog box. Doubleclick the library you saved to open it. You will now be able to choose these chords and fretboards for entry in the new document.

Entering Lyrics

You will find entering lyrics in Finale is a breeze, as long as you use the right methods. Experimentation can get you into quite a mess if you aren't careful. We'll go over the right way to enter lyrics so as to avoid any of these unnecessary hurdles. In this chapter, you will learn how to type lyrics directly into the score, or type the lyrics first and then click them into the score.

To prepare for this section, open any document, and add a single line melody. Then, click the Lyrics tool. In this section, we'll assume you have the Lyrics tool chosen unless directed otherwise.

Type Lyrics into the Score

The easiest and most intuitive way to enter lyrics is to type them directly into the score. From the Lyrics menu, choose Type Into Score. Now, click on a note to see a blinking cursor below the staff. Type a syllable and press the space bar to advance the cursor to the next rhythmic subdivision. If you would like a hyphen between syllables, press the – (dash) key instead of the space bar. Use the left and right arrow keys to move the cursor between letters. Use the Tab key to move to the next syllable and Shift-Tab to move to the previous syllable. Click any lyric to highlight it, or doubleclick it to activate the cursor. Use the Delete/Backspace key to delete syllables like you would in a word processor.

To enter a second verse, click the first lyric so it is highlighted. Press the down arrow and you will see the cursor shift into position for the second verse. Do this to enter as many verses as you like. Press the up arrow to move to the previous verse. You can begin a new verse at any time.

TIP
You may want to change the distance between hyphens in your lyrics. To do this, click the Lyrics menu and choose Lyric Options. Here, change the value in the text box for Space Between Hyphens.

Click Assignment

Though typing into the score is adequate for simple scores, you will want to use Click Assignment in any document that contains repeating lyrics. To use this method of lyric entry, you will type all of the lyrics into a separate text window and then click the lyrics into the score accordingly. You will be able to click the same text into the score many times, saving the trouble of retyping the same lyric. Also, you will be able to edit the lyrics once to change a phrase for every occurrence in the document. We'll start by opening the Edit Lyrics dialog box (Figure 4.14) where you will be entering text. Choose Edit Lyrics from the Lyrics menu.

Figure 4.14
Enter lyrics in the Edit Lyrics dialog box for entry later with Click Assignment.

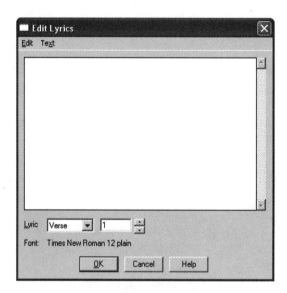

Here, enter your lyrics. You can treat this dialog box much like a basic word processor. Place a hyphen at the end of a syllable to hyphenate it to the next. Simply use a space between nonhyphenated syllables. To enter verse two, click the up arrow to the right of Verse. The editing window will appear empty. Enter the second verse just as you did the first. Do this for as many verses as you need. If you don't know all the lyrics beforehand, don't worry, you can come back to the Edit Lyrics window any time. Now that you have entered some text in the Edit Lyrics box, click OK to return to the score. From the Lyrics menu, choose Click Assignment. You will see the Click Assignment dialog box appear, as shown in Figure 4.15.

Figure 4.15
Click in the score to enter the left-most syllable shown in the Click Assignment box.

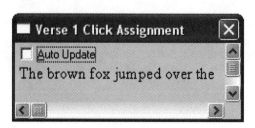

CHAPTER 4

Click a note in the staff to enter the left-most lyric. All of the lyrics in this verse will scroll to the left. The left-most lyric always indicates the next lyric ready for entry. Use the horizontal scroll bar to advance to any lyric in the verse. Move between verses by using the vertical scroll bar. Hold down Ctrl/Option and click a note to enter all lyrics to the end of the verse automatically.

You may have noticed that in addition to verses, you can also specify choruses and sections. These are no different than verses, and can be treated the same. Use them for organization if necessary. You can enter up to 512 of each. To easily specify a current lyric (verse, section or chorus) for entry in Type into Score or Click Assignment, choose Specify Current Lyric from the Lyrics menu. Choose the lyric type and the number and click OK.

TIP
You can easily copy text from a word processing program into Finale for lyric entry. Highlight the text in the word processing program with Ctrl/Command-C. Then, from the Lyrics menu, choose Edit Lyrics. Press Ctrl/Command-V to place the lyrics in the Edit Lyrics window. Then, use Click Assignment to enter them into the score.

Setting or Changing the Font for Lyrics

To set the font for your lyrics before you have entered them, choose Document Options from the Options menu. On the left, click Fonts to see the font options. Click the drop-down/popup menu for Lyrics, choose Verse, Section or Chorus, then click the Set Font button. Set the font, size or style here and click OK, and then OK again to return to the score.

If you want to change the font of existing lyrics, use the Edit Lyrics dialog box. Choose Edit Lyrics from the Lyrics menu. Move the verse section, or chorus you want to change, and highlight the text (Ctrl/Command-A to Select All). From the Text menu, choose Font. Select the font, size, or style and click OK. You will see the lyrics change in the Edit Lyrics window. Click OK to return to your score and review the font change.

You can change the font of all lyrics at once by using the Change Fonts plug-in. Click the Plug-ins menu and choose Change Fonts. Click the Change button for Lyrics to open the Font dialog box. Here, choose the font, size and style to which you would like to change your lyrics. Click OK, and then click OK again to return to the score. All existing lyrics will change to the new font, size, or style you specified.

After running the Fonts plug-in, you may find that your verses overlap, or there is too much space between verses due to a new font size or style. To fix this, you can tell Finale to reset your lyric spacing automatically. From the Options menu, choose Document Options, and select Fonts. From the Lyric drop-down/popup menu, select the type of lyric in the score, and then click the Set Font button to the right. In the Font dialog box, choose the new font and size you selected with the Change Font plug-in. Click OK twice to return to the score, and then Select. Next, with the Lyrics tool selected, go to the Lyrics menu and choose Adjust Baselines. Click Set Piece Offsets to Default Font and click OK. The vertical spacing for lyrics will be even for all verses automatically.

Positioning Lyrics

If you change the font of your lyrics, you may want to space them out vertically. You can adjust the baseline (vertical placement) of each verse, section or chorus independently. To choose the lyric you want to move, choose Specify Current Lyric from the Lyrics menu. Choose the lyric type and number, and then click OK. Notice the four arrows on the left. You can easily adjust the vertical placement (or baseline) of the chosen lyric by using the four positioning arrows on the left side of the screen, just as you would for chords. The arrow you use will depend on the region of lyrics you want to position.

- ▶ Use the first arrow (from the left) to adjust the baseline of all lyrics in the whole document.
- ▶ Use the second arrow to adjust the baseline of all lyrics in the staff.
- ▶ Use the third arrow to adjust the baseline of all lyrics in a system (in Page View).
- ▶ Use the fourth arrow to predetermine the baseline of the next chord or fretboard you enter.

Like chords, to space lyrics horizontally, you will need to reposition the notes to which they are attached. Like chord symbols, avoiding overlapping syllables is most easily done with Finale's Automatic Music Spacing capabilities. From the Options menu, choose Document Options, and select Music Spacing. Under Avoid Collision Of, make sure Lyrics is checked. Click OK to return to the score. Now, select the Mass Edit Tool, press Ctrl/Command-A to Select All, and then press the 4 key (to apply Note Spacing). Your music respaces horizontally to accommodate the lyrics. There will be more information regarding Music Spacing in chapter 9.

You can also edit the positioning of lyrics manually. From the Lyrics menu, choose Adjust Syllables. Double-click the lyric you want to move. You will see a handle appear by the lyric. Now, click and drag, or use the arrow keys to position the lyric manually. When you move lyrics vertically this way, you are actually separating them from their baselines. After using Adjust Syllables, you can move them back to their original position by using the Clear Lyric Positioning plug-in. Click the Mass Edit Tool. Highlight the region of lyrics you want to reset, then choose the Plug-ins menu > Lyrics > Remove Lyric Positioning. The Backspace/Clear key will also clear the manual positioning for a single syllable.

Editing Lyrics

While you enter lyrics, there are a number of editing techniques than can come in handy. In this section, we'll cover the common ways you can modify your lyrics while entering or after you have entered them.

Word Extensions

You can enter word extensions easily with the Word Extension plug-in. Choose the Plug-in menu > Lyrics > Word Extensions. Finale will automatically place word extensions appropriately after all syllables.

If you want the word extensions to extend farther to the right, or want to define your own customized word extensions, use TGTools. From the TGTools menu, choose Lyrics > Word Extensions. The Word Extensions dialog box appears. Here, you can set values for the length and offset for word extensions. Click Go to apply word extensions to your lyrics. If you do not see the TGTools menu in the menu bar, install the TGTools demo from the companion CD-ROM.

You can also enter or edit word extensions manually. From the Lyrics menu, choose Edit Word Extensions. Now, click any lyric to see a handle appear to the lower right of the lyric. Drag this handle to edit the word extension (or use the arrow keys to nudge for fine adjustments).

If you choose to enter word extensions manually, you will find that word extensions do not automatically extend over system breaks (from the end of one system to the beginning of the next, as shown in Figure 4.16).

Figure 4.16
Use a hard space to enter word extensions across a system break.

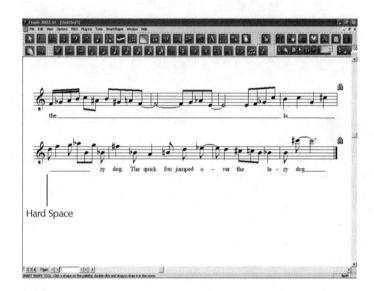

To do this, you will need to enter a hard space (empty character) at the beginning of the second system. Double-click the first note of the second system to get a cursor below the staff. On Windows, type Alt-0169 (type the numbers on the Num Pad). On Macintosh, type Option-Space Bar. Then choose Edit Lyric Extensions from the Edit menu, click the first note of the second system (you will see a handle by the hard space). Drag the handle to the right to create the word extension. If you used Finale's Word Extension plug-in, or TGTools to create your word extensions, this hard space, and following word extension, is added for you automatically.

Shifting Lyrics

You may want to shift all or some of your lyrics to the right or left after they have been entered. Click the Lyrics menu and choose Shift Lyrics. You will see the Shift Lyrics dialog box, as shown in Figure 4.17.

Figure 4.17
Shift lyrics left or right according to settings in the Shift Lyrics dialog box.

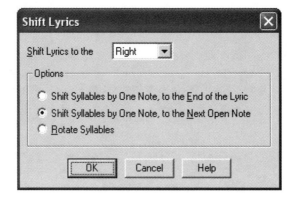

Choose Shift Syllables by One note, to the End of the Lyric, or Shift Syllables by One note, to the Next Open Note—depending on the region of lyrics you want to shift. Then, in the drop-down/popup menu, select left or right depending on the direction you want to shift the lyrics. Click OK. If you chose to shift lyrics to the left, click the note to the left of the region you want to shift to move the lyrics toward the beginning of the score. If you chose to shift lyrics to the right, click the first note of the region you want to shift to move the region toward the end of the score.

Copying and Deleting Lyrics

Click Assignment, as explained above, is the best way to enter repeated lyrics to any location in a document. However, there are some other ways to copy lyrics. If you want to copy a region of music with lyrics, use the Mass Edit Tool. Click the Mass Edit Tool, highlight the region you want to copy and drag the region to its destination. When you copy lyrics in this way, the lyrics are dynamically linked. In other words, editing lyrics in the destination region will also change lyrics in the source region respectively.

CAUTION
If you copy any music containing lyrics with the Ctrl/Command-C, Ctrl/Command-V method, or use the Insert command from the Mass Edit menu, all lyrics move down one verse in the destination region, and will appear lower in the score. To avoid this, either drag-copy with the Mass Edit Tool, or use the Clone Lyrics option under the Lyrics menu. For information on copying individual elements of any region, see chapter 9.

If you need to copy music to a region of your score not visible on the screen, select the measures you want to move. Then, navigate to the new section of the piece, hold down Ctrl-Shift (or Option/Shift on Mac), and click on the first measure in which you'd like the selected lyrics and music to appear.

You can also copy lyrics independently with the Lyrics tool. From the Lyrics menu, choose Clone Lyrics. Now, highlight a region containing lyrics and drag it to another measure containing music. Finale will copy all syllables according to the rhythmic placement of the original lyrics (so you will need the same rhythmic passage in both measures for all lyrics to copy).

To delete a region of lyrics, first click the Mass Edit Tool. Highlight the region of music containing the unwanted lyrics. From the Mass Edit menu, choose Clear Items. Choose Only Selected Items, then click the Entries checkbox. Check Lyrics and click OK. Click OK again to return to the score. Lyrics in the highlighted region will be deleted. Note that even though you've deleted the lyrics from your score, the lyrics remain in the Edit Lyrics Window.

More than One Syllable under a Note (Elisions and Melismas)

You may need to place more than one syllable on a note. To do this, simply enter a hard space between the two syllables. Enter the first syllable, either in the score or in the Edit Lyrics window. On Windows, type Alt-0169 (type the numbers on the Num Pad). On Macintosh, type Option-Space Bar. Then, enter the second syllable. You can also enter a "hard hyphen" to place a hyphen between two syllables. To do this, follow the same instructions, only use the keystroke Alt-0173 on Windows or Option- - (hyphen) on Macintosh.

Beam to Lyrics

In vocal music, it is common to coordinate the beaming pattern to the lyrics. Finale can do this automatically with the Mass Edit Tool. Click the Mass Edit Tool and select the region of music you want to rebeam (Ctrl/Command-A to Select All). Click the Mass Edit menu > Rebeam > Rebeam to Lyrics. Click OK and Finale will change the beaming of notes according to the lyrics.

TIP
You can also change the beaming of your score manually by using the Simple Entry or Speedy Entry tool. Use the B keystroke in either of these tools to beam from the previous note. You can also use the B key to remove a beam from the previous note.

Extract Lyrics Plug-in

If you want to export lyrics from Finale to another program, such as a word processor, use the Extract Lyrics plug-in. From the plug-ins menu, choose Extract Lyrics. Here, you can choose a particular verse, section, or chorus for extraction, or choose to extract all lyrics at once. Also, modify the extracted lyrics by removing hyphens or line breaks. Click Extract to save the lyrics as a text file. Then, copy the lyrics from the text file into the other program.

Rhymer

Finale 2003 contains a new feature you can use for help in the lyric creation process—a rhyming dictionary. From the Lyrics menu, choose Rhymer. Enter a word you would like to rhyme and click the Rhyme button to generate a list of rhyming words. You can even specify the type of rhyme (ending, beginning, etc.) from the Type of Rhyme drop-down/popup menu. Click the Options button to specify number of syllables, letters, or the first letter in words, to customize your results.

Creating a Lead Sheet

At this point, we have covered all the material necessary for creating a lead sheet with a melody, chord symbols, and lyrics. Let's apply the skills we have learned to create our own lead sheet, all the way from starting a new document to the final printout. For this example, we'll create a lead sheet arrangement of "Amazing Grace," as shown in Figure 4.18 (you can also find the completed Finale "Amazing Grace" on the companion CD-ROM, in the Musical Examples folder).

Figure 4.18
"Amazing Grace"
arrangement

There are a few layout issues that apply specifically to lead sheets (like the left barline on each system, for example). To save us the headache of defining these layout changes ourselves, we'll begin this process by opening the Lead Sheet template.

From the File menu, choose New > Document From Template. You should see the contents of the Finale/Template folder. Double-click the General Templates folder, then double-click Lead Sheet (Jazz Font) to open the Jazz Font Lead Sheet Template. The Jazz Font gives a lead sheet a nice handwritten look. If you prefer, choose the Lead Sheet template to use Finale's standard fonts. Now, let's begin our arrangement.

1. First, we'll add the title and composer. From the File menu, choose File info. The File Info dialog box appears. For Title, enter "Amazing Grace." Then, for composer, enter "Arr. by" followed by your name. Click OK to return to the score.

2. The meter for this piece is 3/4, so we'll need to adjust the Time Signature. Click the Time Signature tool and then double-click the first measure. The Time Signature dialog box appears. After Number of Beats, click the left arrow once, so the preview window displays 3/4 meter. Click OK to return to the score.

3. There is a one-beat pickup, so we'll need to set up a pickup measure. From the Options menu, choose Pickup Measure. The Pickup Measure dialog box appears. Choose the quarter note icon and click OK.

4. This arrangement will be in the key of F Major, so we'll need to change the key. Click the Key Signature tool and double-click the pickup measure. The Key Signature dialog box appears. To the right of the preview display, click the down arrow once so the key of F (with one flat) is displayed. Then, click OK to return to the score.

5. There are twenty-three measures in this arrangement (two more than the default twenty-one measures). Double-click the Measure tool twice to add two measures to the end of the score (you can add a measure at any time by double-clicking the Measure tool).

6. We'll finish setting up the template by adding a tempo marking. Click the Mass Edit Tool and highlight the pickup (first) measure. From the Plug-ins menu, choose Create Tempo Marking. The Create Tempo Marking dialog box appears. Check Define Expression for Playback. Then, in the text box, enter "90" (in place of 96). Also, make sure the quarter note icon is selected. Click OK. The tempo marking now appears as an expression above the staff. Your piece is now ready for note entry (Figure 4.19).

Figure 4.19
Your template should
now look like this. We
are ready to start
entering notes.

7. In this example, the theme is repeated twice. If you have an external MIDI device (MIDI keyboard, for example), I encourage you to enter the first sixteen measures using HyperScribe. Since there are not any notes under an eighth note in duration, change your quantization settings for greater accuracy. From the Options menu, choose Quantization settings. For Smallest Note Value, choose the eighth note icon and click OK. Now, begin your HyperScribe session and enter the melody for the first sixteen measures, as seen in Figure 4.18 (see information earlier in this chapter on the HyperScribe tool for more details). If you do not have an external MIDI device, use Simple or Speedy Entry to enter notes into the first sixteen measures.

8. Let's use the Simple or Speedy Entry tool to enter into measures seventeen through twenty-three. In measure seventeen, you will need to enter a triplet on the last beat of the measure. In Speedy Entry, use the Ctrl/Command-3 method to predefine the triplet. In Simple Entry, use the Simple Entry Tuplet tool to predefine the triplet (see chapter 3 for more details on entering tuplets with the Speedy and/or Simple Entry Tool). Enter notes into the remaining measures.

9. Now, let's put five measures on a system. Click the Mass Edit Tool, and then press Ctrl/Command-A to Select All. From the Mass Edit menu, choose Fit Music. Type "5" and click OK. Your piece now has five measures per system (besides the last system, which has three).

10. To enter the chord symbols, click the Chord tool. From the Chord menu, make sure Manual Input is selected. Click the first note in measure one. The Chord Definition dialog box appears. F is already selected (in the future, enter the bass chord symbol here), so click OK. Now, click the first note in measure two. Click

in the text box at the top of the Chord Definition dialog box so there is a cursor to the right of F. Type "7" and click OK. The "F7" chord symbol appears above the note. Continue entering chord symbols this way until you get to measure seventeen. Click the first note in measure seventeen. Now, click Advanced/Show Advanced to extend the lower section of the Chord Definition dialog box. Click the Select button on the bottom to open the Chord Suffix Selection dialog box. Choose "Maj7" and click Select, then OK to return to the score. For the remaining chord symbols, when necessary, add the suffix by choosing it from the Chord Suffix Selection dialog box. After you have finished entering the chord symbols, move them closer to the staff by dragging the left-most positioning arrow down closer to the staff. See section earlier in this chapter on "Entering Chord Symbols" for more chord entry and positioning techniques.

11. Now, enter the lyrics. The easiest way to enter lyrics is to type them directly into the score. Click the Lyrics tool, and then, from the Lyrics menu, choose Type Into Score. Click the first note and type the first syllable "A", then a "-" (hyphen) followed by the space bar to move to the next syllable. Continue, entering each syllable, leaving the hyphen out where it isn't necessary (don't worry about the word extensions yet).

12. After you have entered all of the lyrics, from the Plug-ins menu, choose Lyrics > Word Extensions. Finale adds all the word extensions for you.

13. Now, let's make the lyrics a little bigger. From the Plug-ins menu, choose Change Fonts. After Lyrics, click the Change button and then set the size to "16." Click OK to return to the score. Your lyrics are now a little larger and more readable (adjust the lyric baseline if you wish by clicking the Lyrics tool and using the left positioning arrow while in Type into Score mode).

14. Now, let's make the whole page a little bigger. Click the Resize tool, then click the upper left corner of the page (away from any staves or notes). In the Resize Page dialog box, enter 112 and click OK. Everything on the page is now slightly larger and more readable.

15. Now, click the Page Layout tool. Notice the bottom staff system extends only halfway across the page. Click the lower right handle of the bottom system and drag it to the left to move the margin to the middle of the page. Then, make any other desired layout changes. For example, to move all the music up on the page, drag the top left handle on the first system down a bit, then click in the middle of the system and drag it up to the top. You might also want to click the Text tool and drag the title and composer up a bit to give more space on the page for music.

You can use the above procedure as a general guide any time you create a lead sheet. After creating your own piece, you may want to add expressions, articulations, slurs, fretboard diagrams, or any number of other figures not included in the above steps. We'll be touching on most of the common notational possibilities in the remaining chapters (if you haven't seen what you're looking for already).

5

Clefs, Key Signatures, and Time Signatures

Back in chapter 2, we covered most of the basics for entering and changing clefs, Key Signatures and Time Signatures. Now, it's time to isolate each one of these items and explore a variety of common editing techniques. There are a number of similarities in the way these items are handled in Finale, and for that reason, they have been grouped together into one chapter. Here, you'll learn how to enter mid-measure clefs, standard and nonstandard key changes, large Time Signatures, and how to make a variety of changes to clef, key, and Time Signatures on an individual or global basis.

Here's a summary of what you will learn in this chapter:

> ▶ How to work with clefs.
> ▶ How to work with Key Signatures.
> ▶ How to work with Time Signatures.

As you read through this chapter, keep in mind that you can always use the Setup Wizard to start a document with predefined instruments, and also choose the opening Key or Time Signature. For more information on editing any of the settings you specify in the Document or Staff Setup wizard, refer to chapter 2. If you find the information in chapter 2 isn't in-depth enough for what you're trying to do, refer to this chapter.

Working with Clefs

For starters, if you want to add a staff to your score with a standard clef for a specific instrument, try using the Staff Setup Wizard. Click the Staff tool. Then, from the Staff menu, choose New Staves (with Setup Wizard). Choose the instrument category in the left column and the specific instrument in the second. Once the new instrument appears in the right column, click Finish and the staff will appear at the bottom of your score with a standard clef for that instrument. To change the opening clef, make adjustments to the Staff Attributes (as described in chapter 2).

In addition to changing the opening clef of a staff, there are many other cases where adding or editing clefs will be necessary. You will be using the Clef tool to make most of these changes. In this section, you'll learn how to use the Clef tool to space clefs, enter mid-measure clef changes, and even create your own custom clef. In addition, there are a variety of other document settings that relate to clefs throughout your document, such as cautionary clef changes. We'll start with the most common—entering clef changes—and then move into how to modify them.

To prepare for this section, open a new default document (File > New > Default Document), then enter a melody with the Simple or Speedy Entry tool. Click the Clef tool. For most of this section, we'll assume the Clef tool is selected unless specified otherwise.

Changing the Clef at the Beginning of a Measure

Clef changes within a staff are common, and often appear at the beginning of the measure. With the Clef tool selected, double the second measure of a staff. You will see the Change Clef dialog box, as shown in Figure 5.1.

Figure 5.1
Enter a clef change by choosing from one of the available clefs in the Change Clef dialog box.

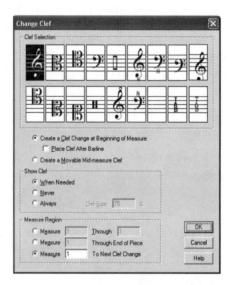

Choose the new clef from the eighteen available options. Once the clef is highlighted, click OK to return to the score and review the clef change. It will appear to the left of the measure you clicked. All of the music after the clef change will adjust according to the new clef. Now, let's say you only want the clef change to affect a single measure. Click measure three to open the Change Clef dialog box. Choose the original clef, then click OK. You should now have a clef change back to the opening clef of the staff.

NOTE
If you have an instrument with a "Set to Clef" transposition (such as bass clarinet or baritone saxophone), you will first need to uncheck Set to Clef in the Staff Transposition dialog box. Choose the Staff tool, double-click the staff to open the Staff Attributes, then click the Select button next to Transposition. Uncheck Set to Clef and click OK twice to return to the score.

In the Change Clef dialog box, you can also specify the region of a clef change when you enter a clef. Double-click a measure to open the Change Clef dialog box. Choose the new clef. In the Measure Region section, click the top radio button and specify the first and last measure number of the clef change. Click OK and Finale will enter the new clef change and then change back to the original clef at the measure you specified.

If you would like the clef to appear to the right of the barline, check the Place Clef After Barline in the Change Clef dialog box after selecting the new clef.

Entering Mid-Measure Clefs

Sometimes, clefs appear in the middle of a measure, most often at a slightly reduced size. To enter a mid-measure clef change, click where you would like to place the clef. The Change Clef dialog box appears. Choose the new clef, then check Create a Moveable Mid-Measure Clef. Click OK and you will see the new clef appear within the measure. Click and drag the handle on the mid-measure clef to move it horizontally. Notes in the measure will change staff positions accordingly as you move it. To delete any mid-measure clef, click its handle and press Delete, or right/Option-click the handle and choose Delete.

You can easily edit mid-measure clefs, or change any mid-measure clef to a regular clef change in the Mid-Measure Clef dialog box (Figure 5.2). Right/Option click the handle on the mid-measure clef and choose Edit Clef Definition to open this dialog box.

Figure 5.2
Specify the size and placement of a mid-measure clef in the Mid-Measure Clef dialog box.

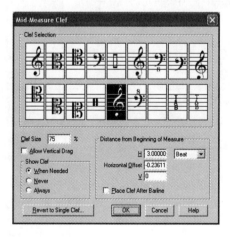

Here, choose a new clef in the clef selection, or resize the clef by entering a different percentage in the Clef Size text box. In the Show Clef section, specify when you want Finale to display the clef in the score, and pinpoint the positioning of the mid-measure clef on the right under Distance from Beginning of Measure (we'll talk more about these settings soon). If you want to be able to drag the clef vertically, check Allow Vertical Drag.

CAUTION

With Allow Vertical Drag checked, you will be able to drag or nudge clefs up or down in the staff. When you do this, notes will not reposition according to the vertical staff placement. To enter a clef that accurately repositions notes in a staff according to standard notation rules, choose one of the existing clefs from the clef selection or design your own clef with the Clef Designer.

If you like, you can also change the clef back to a regular clef change at the beginning of the measure. To do this, choose Revert to Single Clef. You will be taken back to the Change Clef dialog box. Make any desired settings and click OK to return to the score.

Clef Metatools

Like articulations and expressions, you can also enter mid-measure clef changes easily by using metatools. Hold down the Shift key and press "1" to open the Clef Selection dialog box (Figure 5.3). In the upper right corner, you will see the preset metatool assignments for each type of clef. For example, note the "6" in the vocal tenor clef box. Click OK to return to the score. Hold down the 6 key and click in the staff to enter a mid-measure vocal tenor clef. Do this for any existing clef in the Clef Selection dialog box.

Figure 5.3
The Clef Selection
dialog box.

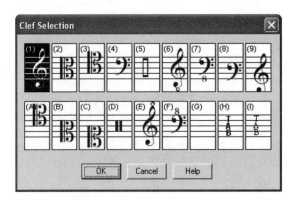

You may want to assign your own clef metatools. For instance, let's say you want to use the T key to enter a treble clef instead of the number 1. Hold down the Shift key and press the letter T. The Clef Selection dialog box opens. Now, choose the treble clef and click OK. The treble clef is now assigned to the T key. Hold down the T key and click anywhere in a staff to enter a mid-measure treble clef. If you open the Clef Selection dialog box again (by holding down Shift and pressing a number or letter), you will notice the letter T in the upper right corner of the treble clef box.

Clef Spacing and Placement

In addition to dragging or nudging mid-measure clefs, there are a number of ways to specify placement of clefs in a staff. You may want to change the default positioning of clef changes relative to the barline. To do this, click the Options menu and choose Document Options. Choose Clefs from the column on the left to display the Clef options (Figure 5.4). Specify a value for Space After Barline or Space Before Barline in these options and click OK to apply these settings to the entire document.

Figure 5.4
In the Clef portion of the Document Options dialog box, make document-wide settings for the appearance and spacing of clefs.

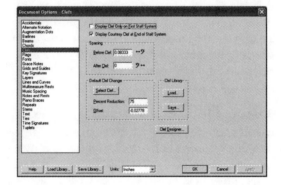

To choose the measurement unit (inches, points, EVPUs, etc.) for any parameter in the Document Options, click the drop-down/popup menu to the right of Measurement Units and make a selection. You can find a description of all the measurement units in Table 1.1 (in chapter 1).

To position a mid-measure clef, right/Option-click the mid-measure clef handle and choose Edit Clef Definition from the context menu. In the Distance from Beginning of Measure section, use the H (horizontal) text box to indicate the beat of the mid-measure clef change. If you prefer, you can also specify the rhythmic placement of the clef in EDUs (Enigma durational units) by clicking the drop-down/popup menu to the right. Use the Horizontal Offset text box to specify the space between the mid-measure clef and the next entry. Use the V (vertical) text box to indicate the vertical offset of the clef. Use a positive number to move the clef up and a negative number to move the clef down. Check Place After Barline to place the clef just to the right of the barline. Click OK to return to the score and review any changes you made.

Showing or Hiding Clefs and Courtesy Clefs

You may want to show the clef at the beginning of the first measure only. This is common practice in certain types of documents, such as lead sheets. To do this, from the Options menu, choose Document Options. Click the Clefs category on the left and check Display Clef Only on First Staff System. Click OK to apply your settings and return to the score.

CHAPTER 5

To hide all clefs in a staff, click the Staff tool and doubleclick a staff to display the Staff Attributes. Under Items to Display, uncheck Clefs. Click OK to return to the score. All clefs in the specified staff will be hidden. Check this box in the Staff Attributes to show clefs in the staff.

TIP
You can show or hide clefs in any number of staves at once by using the Global Staff Attributes plug-in. From the Plug-ins menu, choose Global Staff Attributes. Under Items to Display, check or uncheck Clefs. Specify the staves you want to affect on the left and click OK to apply changes and return to the score. Also use this method for Key Signatures and Time Signatures.

If there is a clef change at the beginning of a system, it is customary to place a "courtesy" clef at the end of the previous system to warn the performer of the upcoming change in clef. To show or hide courtesy clefs, click the Options menu and choose Document Options. Click the Clefs category on the left and check or uncheck Display Courtesy Clef at End of Staff System. Click OK to apply your settings and return to the score.

Creating a Custom Clef (The Clef Designer)

There may be a clef you want to use that doesn't exist among the eighteen available clefs in the Clef Selection dialog box. In this case, you can actually create your own clef that will contain all the properties of a legitimate clef predefined in Finale. To design a custom clef, click the Options menu and choose Document Options. Select the Clefs category on the left and click the Clef Designer button among the options on the right. This will open the Clef Designer dialog box, as seen in Figure 5.5.

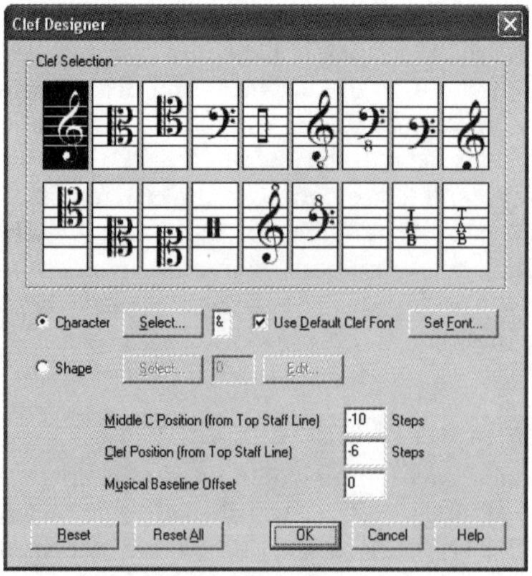

Figure 5.5
Create a custom clef
definition in the Clef
Designer dialog box.

First, choose the clef you want to edit from the selection boxes at the top. You will be redefining one of these clefs, so make sure you choose one you do not plan to use in this document. To change the appearance of the clef, click the Select button to the right of Character. This will take you into the Symbol Selection Window. Choose the character you want to use for your new clef and click Select. If you can't find the character for the clef you want to use, you could try selecting a character from a different font. To do this, click the Set Font button in the Clef Designer. This will open the Font dialog box, where you can choose the new font, size and style for your clef.

NOTE

Finale offers several music fonts that contain clef symbols that you might find useful. For a complete list of characters in all Finale fonts, click the Help menu on Mac (on Win, click Help, then User Manual) and select the Engraver, Jazz, or Maestro character map. Of course, you can also select a character from any font that exists on your system in the Font dialog box.

If you cannot find a font with an existing clef, you could also design your own. In the Clef Designer, click the Shape radio button, then click the Select button. Click Create. You will see the Shape Designer window. Use this editor to create a custom shape for your clef. You can even import existing graphics with the Graphics tool available in this window. Click OK and then Select to return to the Shape Designer. Now, it's time to configure the functional clef characteristics (how the clef will affect the notation).

For Middle C Position (from Top Staff Line), indicate the staff position of middle C in the clef you are defining. Enter 0 to place middle C on the top staff line. Subtract one for each line and space below the top staff line or add one for each line and space above the top staff line. In the Clef Position (from Top Staff Line), use the same parameters to position the clef in the staff. You may need to adjust the Musical Baseline Offset for mid-measure (reduced) clef changes after defining a custom clef, particularly if you created a custom shape for the clef. Click OK to return to your score to see your new custom clef.

Transferring Custom Clefs Between Documents

Like articulations and expressions, you can transfer custom clefs (created in the Clef Designer) between documents by saving and opening a library. Open the document containing the existing clefs. Click the File menu and choose Save Library. Choose Clefs and click OK. Enter a name and save the file to your Libraries folder in your Finale directory (Finale should take you there by default). Now, open the document you are working on, click the File menu and choose Open Library. Doubleclick the library you saved to open it. Your custom clefs will be available in this document's Clef Selection window.

Key Signatures

In chapter 2, we touched on the basics for changing the Key Signature at the beginning of a document. Here, you will learn how to make key changes at any measure or even create a customized Key Signature. Keep in mind the instructions in this section refer to changing the concert pitch of a score; therefore, the Key Signature of a transposed staff may appear in a different key. To view your score in concert pitch at any time, select Display in Concert Pitch from the Options menu (choose the same options again to display the transposed parts).

To prepare for this section, either continue using the document from the previous section, or open a new default document (File > New > Default Document). You should also use the Simple or Speedy Entry tool to enter a simple melody into the document for the purpose of demonstration. Then, click the Key Signature tool. We'll assume you have the Key Signature tool selected unless specified otherwise.

Entering/Changing the Key Signature

Unlike clefs, Key Signatures generally affect all staves in a system, so at any given measure you will only need to make one key change. Let's say you want to change to the key of A major in measure three. With the Key Signature tool chosen, double-click on measure three (or right/Control-click the measure and choose Edit Key Signature). The Key Signature dialog box opens, as shown in Figure 5.6.

Figure 5.6
Define a key change in the Key Signature dialog box.

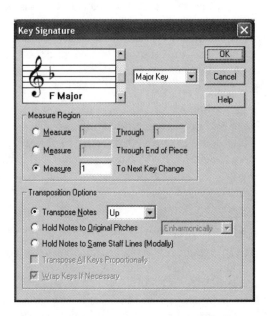

Next to the Key Signature preview window is a vertical scroll bar. Click the up arrow three times to add three sharps to the Key Signature. The display now indicates a key of A major. Since any notes in your score will transpose into the new key, you will need to choose in which direction to move them. In the Transposition Options, for Transpose Notes, click the drop-down/popup menu and choose up to transpose them up, or down to transpose them down. Click OK to return to your score and review the key change.

In the Key Signature dialog box, you can also click the down arrow next to the display window to add flats or remove sharps from a Key Signature. Click the drop-down/popup menu to the right of the preview window to specify a major, minor, or nonstandard key (we'll discuss nonstandard Key Signatures soon). By specifying a major or minor key from the drop-down/popup menu, you tell Finale how to assign accidentals accurately in a HyperScribe session and also how to assign chord definitions properly.

Specify a region for the Key Signature change in the Measure Region section. Note that every time you enter the Key Signature dialog box, the setting for Measure Region will reset to Measure _ To Next Key Change, so you will need to make adjustments to this setting when necessary.

If you want to change the key of a region of your score that already contains a key change, and want the existing key change (or any number of key changes) to adjust accordingly, check Transpose all Keys Proportionally (note that this option is not available if Measure_To Next Key Change is selected). When you do this, all affected key changes will transpose proportionally from the new key you specify (Figure 5.7).

Figure 5.7
Transposing keys
proportionally

A Key Signature that appears after transposing keys proportionally could contain unwanted double sharps or double flats. To avoid this, make sure Wrap Keys if Necessary is checked (at the bottom of the Key Signature dialog box). Click OK to return to the score.

Key Signature Metatools

If you intend to enter many key changes in a document, you may want to program Key Signature metatools. Hold down the Shift key and press the 1 key to open the Key Signature dialog box. Specify the new key here and click OK to return to the score. Hold down the 1 key and double-click a measure to enter the specified key change to a measure. Program a Key Signature metatool to any number or letter key on your QWERTY keyboard.

Managing Notes while Changing the Key

You may want to change the key of a region without transposing the music. To do this, double-click the measure of the key change to open the Key Signature dialog box. Select the Key Signature you wish to use. Under Transposition Options, select Hold Notes to Original Pitches. From the drop-down menu, choose Enharmonically to respell the notes according to the new key. Choose Chromatically to leave the spelling the same.

To leave all notes at the same staff position and change only the pitches affected by the change of key, choose Hold Notes to Same Staff Lines Modally.

TIP

If you want to transpose notes without changing the Key Signature, choose the Mass Edit Tool and select the region of notes you want to transpose. Then, from the Mass Edit menu, choose Transpose. Select an interval and click OK. There will be more information on transposition in chapter 9.

Changing the Key on a Single Staff Only

If you are working on a bitonal score (one that oversteps traditional Key Signature usage), you may need to specify a concert Key Signature change on one staff without affecting the concert key of the other staves. To do this, click the Staff tool and doubleclick the staff you want to change. In the Independent Elements section, check Key Signature and click OK. Now, use the Key Signature tool to change the key on the staff you modified with the Staff tool. Key changes to this staff will not affect the key of other staves, and key changes in other staves will not affect this staff.

Selecting the Default Font for Key Signatures

You may want to change the font of your Key Signatures to one of the other available Finale fonts, or to a different music font installed on your computer. To do this, from the Options menu, choose Document Options, and select Fonts. Click the drop-down/popup menu for Notation and select Key. Click the Set Font button for Notation to open the Font dialog box, where you can specify the font, size, and style for your Key Signatures. Click OK to return to the Document Options dialog box and click the Apply button to apply the change in font.

Since Finale expects the accidental characters to be in one of the Finale music fonts, you may need to reassign the accidental characters for your Key Signatures if you are using an external music font. To do this, from the Options menu, choose Document Options, and select Key Signatures. Click the drop-down/popup menu for Characters and choose the type of accidental you want to assign. Then, click the Select button to open the Symbol Selection dialog box. Choose the character and click Select to return to the Document Options dialog box. Choose any other character you need to assign and click the Apply button to apply your new character settings.

Spacing Key Signatures

There are a couple ways to adjust the spacing of Key Signatures in a document. You may want to increase or decrease the space between the Key Signature and the barline or the following entry. To do this on a document-wide basis, from the Options menu, choose Document Options, and select Key Signatures from the list on the left (Figure 5.8). Enter a value in the Space Before Key text box to indicate the distance between the barline and the Key Signature. Enter a value in the Space After Key text box to indicate the distance between the Key Signature and the following entry.

Figure 5.8
Make document-wide settings for Key Signature spacing, characters and appearance in Document Options-Key Signatures.

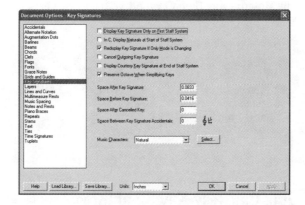

In the Document Options dialog box, you can also change the distance between the sharp or flat characters in a Key Signature. To do this, enter a new value for Space Between Key Signature Accidentals. Click OK to apply changes and return to the score.

To choose the measurement unit (inches, points, EVPUs, etc.) for any parameter in the Document Options, click the drop-down/popup menu at the bottom of the dialog box, to the right of Units, and make a selection. You can find a description of all the measurement units in Table 1.1 (in chapter 1).

Showing or Hiding a Key Signature, in Staves and Measures

You may want to show the Key Signature at the beginning of the first measure only. To do this, from the Options menu, choose Document Options. Click the Key Signature category on the left and check Display Key Signature Only on First Staff System. Click OK to apply your settings and return to the score.

To hide all Key Signatures in a staff, click the Staff tool and doubleclick a staff to display the Staff Attributes. Under Items to Display, uncheck Key Signatures. Click OK to return to the score. All Key Signatures in the specified staff will be hidden. Check this box in the Staff Attributes to show Key Signatures in the staff.

CAUTION
Hiding the Key Signature will not automatically make accidentals appear on diatonic notes. You can show these accidentals by using the A key with the Simple or Speedy Entry tool.

You can also show or hide a Key Signature at the beginning of any measure with the Measure tool. Click the Measure tool and doubleclick a measure. Click the drop-down/popup menu to the right of Key Signature and choose Always Show to show the Key Signature in that measure. Choose Always Hide to hide the Key Signature in that measure. Click OK to return to the score and review your changes.

TIP

To show or hide Key Signatures or Time Signatures for a region of measures, select the region with the Measure tool and doubleclick the highlighted area. Changes you make in the Measure Attributes will apply to all selected measures.

Showing or Hiding Courtesy Key Signatures

If there is a key change at the beginning of a system, it is customary to place a "courtesy" Key Signature at the end of the previous system to warn the performer of the upcoming change in key. To show or hide courtesy Key Signatures, click the Options menu and choose Document Options. Click the Key Signatures category on the left and check or uncheck Display Courtesy Key Signature at End of Staff System. Click OK to apply your settings and return to the score.

Outgoing Key Signatures

While changing Key Signatures in a score, it is common to indicate changes from the previous Key Signature to the left of the new key. For instance, in a key change from F major (one flat), to G major (one sharp), you may see a natural to the left of the new key "canceling" the B flat in the key of F major (Figure 5.9).

Figure 5.9
Canceling the outgoing
Key Signature.

Outgoing Key Signature Cancelation

To show or hide the canceled Key Signature by default, from the Options menu, choose Document Options and select Key Signatures from the list on the left. Check Cancel Outgoing Key Signature to show the canceled Key Signature, or uncheck this box to hide the canceled Key Signature.

You can also adjust the spacing of the canceled Key Signature indication in the Program Options by entering a value in the Space After Canceled Key text box.

Nonstandard Key Signatures

In addition to major and minor keys, you can also create your own custom Key Signatures with any combination of accidentals on any staff position. Though seldom used, this feature does warrant a few words. To define a nonstandard Key Signature, double-click a measure to open the Key Signature dialog box. To the right of the preview display, click the drop-down/popup menu and choose Nonstandard. This will open the Nonstandard Key Signature dialog box, as shown in Figure 5.10.

Figure 5.10
Define a custom Key Signature in the Nonstandard Key Signature dialog box.

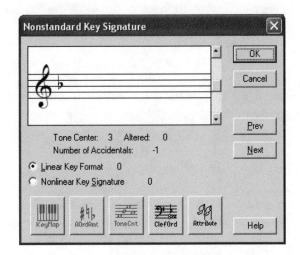

There are two types of nonstandard Key Signatures: linear and nonlinear. Choose the Linear Key Format to define a Key Signature with a recurring sequence of whole and half steps. All linear Key Signatures will cycle through a "circle of fifths" type of relationship (though your Key Signature may cycle through sixths, fourths or another interval). Major and minor Key Signatures both fall into the linear category, and are already defined as Format 0 (Major) and 1 (minor). While defining a linear Key Signature, use the scroll bar to the right of the preview display to add sharps, flats, double-sharps, double-flats, etc.

Nonlinear Key Signatures are not based on a system of related keys. Choose Nonlinear Key Signature to define a key with any number of accidentals in any order. The scroll bar in the preview display will not be available while defining a nonlinear key. You will need to use the options below.

The five buttons at the bottom of the Nonstandard Key Signature dialog box can be used to define linear or nonlinear Key Signatures (though some parameters will be limited with linear keys). Choose KeyMap to define the number of steps in an octave and the sequence of whole and half steps. Click AOrdAmt to specify where you want to place the accidentals in the staff. Click ClefOrd to assign the octave to place each accidental. Click the ToneCnt button to specify a root for your Key Signature. Click Attributes for more options, such as assigning special characters to accidentals for quarter tone Key Signatures. Whether you are creating a linear or nonlinear Key Signature, click the Next button to move to the next format or Prev to move back to the previous one.

CHAPTER 5

Time Signatures

Like clefs and Key Signatures, there are many ways to enter and edit Time Signatures beyond the options available in the Setup Wizard. Here, you will learn how to enter meter changes at any measure, create compound and composite meters, specify beaming patterns and make other settings related to Time Signatures on an individual or global basis. Since Time Signatures and Key Signatures exhibit many of the same characteristics in Finale, some of these instructions will look familiar.

To prepare for this section, use the same document you have been working with, or open a new default document (File > New > Default Document). You should also use the Simple or Speedy Entry Tool to enter a simple melody into the document for the purpose of demonstration. Then, click the Time Signature tool. We'll assume you have the Time Signature tool selected unless specified otherwise.

Entering/Changing the Time Signature

Like Key Signatures, Time Signatures usually affect all staves in a system, so at any given measure you will only need to make one meter change (we will cover independent meters later in this section). Since the document you have open is in common time, we'll start by creating a time change to 6/8. With the Time Signature tool chosen, double-click on measure three. The Time Signature dialog box opens. as shown in Figure 5.11.

Figure 5.11
Define a meter change
in the Time Signature
dialog box.

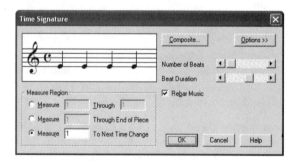

For Number of Beats, click the left arrow on the scroll bar twice. The preview display now reads 2/4. We will be counting our 6/8 meter in two (beat=dotted quarter) and beaming eighth notes in two groups of three. For Beat Duration, click the right arrow on the scroll bar once. The quarter note in the preview window will update to a dotted quarter and the Time Signature will change to 6/8. While defining Time Signatures, always think of the number of beats in the measure, and then the rhythmic value (duration) of each beat. Finale will translate the values you enter into the appropriate Time Signature automatically. Click OK to return to your score and review the change in meter.

In the Time Signature dialog box, specify a region for the Time Signature change in the Measure Region section. Note that every time you enter the Time Signature dialog box, the setting for Measure Region will reset to Measure _ To Next Time Change, so you may need to make any adjustments from this setting as needed.

Shortcuts: Context Menu/Metatools

You can enter Time Signatures quickly with a context menu. Right/Option-click a measure to see the Time Signature context menu. Choose one of the available Time Signatures to enter the time change instantly. Time Signatures entered this way will apply for all of the music up to the next time change.

If you intend to enter many Time Signature changes in a document, you may want to program Time Signature metatools. Hold down the Shift key and press the 1 key to open the Time Signature dialog box. Specify a meter here and click OK to return to the score. Hold down the 1 key and double-click a measure to enter the specified key change to a measure. Program a Time Signature metatool to any number or letter key on your QWERTY keyboard.

Abbreviated Time Signatures

You may or may not want to abbreviate 4/4 Time Signatures as **C** and 2/4 Time Signatures as **¢**. To change these settings, from the Options menu, choose Document Options and select Time Signatures. Check or uncheck Abbreviate Cut or Common Time. Click the Select button to specify a character you wish to use as an abbreviation in the default Time Signature font.

Selecting the Default Font for Time Signatures

You may want to change the font of your Time Signatures to one of the other available Finale fonts, or to a different music font installed on your computer. To do this, from the Options menu, choose Document Options and select Fonts. Click the drop-down/popup menu for Notation and select Time. Click the Set Font button for Notation to open the Font dialog box, where you can specify the font, size and style for your Time Signatures (regular and abbreviated). Click OK to return to the Document Options dialog box and click the Apply button to apply the change in font.

TIP

Try using the EngraverFontSet or Engraver Time font for an alternative style for your Time Signatures. For a complete list of characters in all Finale fonts, click the Help menu on Mac (on Win, click Help, then User Manual) and select the Engraver, Jazz or Maestro character map.

Using a Different Time Signature for Display

For a number of reasons, you may need to display a different Time Signature than the actual one defined in the Time Signature dialog box (pickup measures, measures across systems, etc.). To do this, doubleclick a measure to open the Time Signature dialog box. Set up the actual Time Signature as you would normally. Click the Options (Macintosh: More Choices) button in the upper right to expand the lower section of the dialog box (Figure 5.12).

CHAPTER 5

Figure 5.12
Click Options to
Expand Time Signature
dialog box where you
can create
a separate Time
Signature for display.

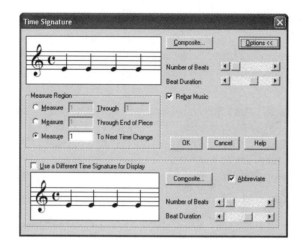

Set up the Time Signature as you want it to display in the lower section, then check Use a Different Time Signature for Display. Click OK to return to the score. The Time Signature you choose to display will only be visible if it is different than the Time Signature of the previous measure.

TIP
For information on assigning specific beaming groups for Time Signatures, see chapter 10 under "Beaming Patterns and Time Signatures."

Changing the Time Signature on a Single Staff Only

You may need to specify a meter change on one staff without affecting the meter of the other staves. To do this, click the Staff tool and doubleclick the staff you want to change. In the Independent Elements section, check Time Signature and click OK. Now, use the Time Signature tool to change the key on the staff you modified with the Staff tool. Meter changes to this staff will not affect the meter of other staves, and meter changes in other staves will not affect this staff. Finale will continue to line up all barlines regardless of the meters being used. There will be a more in-depth discussion of isorhythmic notation (in which the barlines do not line up) in chapter 12.

Spacing Time Signatures

You may want to increase or decrease the space between the Time Signature and the barline or the following entry. To do this on a document-wide basis, from the Options menu, choose Document Options and select Time Signatures from the list on the left (Figure 5.8). Enter a value in the Space Before Time Signature text box to indicate the distance between the barline and the

Time Signature. Enter a value in the Space After Time Signature text box to indicate the distance between the Time Signature and the following entry.

You can also move any Time Signature vertically. Click the Options menu and choose Document Options, then select Time Signatures. In the Vertical Adjustment section, specify a value for the bottom and top number in your Time Signature. To move a 4/4 Time Signature (in the default font and size) above the staff, enter 100 EVPUs for both Top Symbol and Bottom Symbol. Then, make any fine adjustments. If you are using an abbreviated Time Signature, you need only modify the Abbreviated Value text box.

Showing or Hiding Time Signatures in Staves or Measures

To hide all Time Signatures in a staff, click the Staff tool and doubleclick a staff to display the Staff Attributes. Under Items to Display, uncheck Time Signatures. Click OK to return to the score. All Time Signatures in the specified staff will be hidden. Recheck this box in the Staff Attributes to show Time Signatures in the staff.

You can also show or hide a Time Signature at the beginning of any measure with the Measure tool. Click the Measure tool and doubleclick a measure. Click the drop-down/popup menu to the right of Time Signature and choose Always Show to show the Time Signature in that measure. Choose Always Hide to hide the Time Signature in that measure. Click OK to return to the score and review your changes.

Showing or Hiding Courtesy Time Signatures

If there is a time change at the beginning of a system, it is customary to place a "courtesy" Time Signature at the end of the previous system to warn the performer of the upcoming change in meter. To show or hide courtesy Time Signatures, click the Options menu and choose Document Options. Click the Time Signatures category on the left and check or uncheck Display Courtesy Time Signature at End of Staff System. Click OK to apply your settings and return to the score.

Multiple Time Signatures

You may want to enter a Time Signature followed by a second Time Signature in parentheses indicating an alternate subdivision, as shown in Figure 5.13.

Figure 5.13
Multiple Time
Signatures.

To do this:

1. Doubleclick a measure to display the Time Signature dialog box.

2. Use the scroll bars to specify the "real" Time Signature (the Time Signature here is not the one that will be displayed in your score.)

3. Click Options (Mac: More Choices) to display the lower portion of the dialog box.

4. Check Use a Different Time Signature for Display.

5. Click the Composite button in the lower section.

6. Enter the first Time Signature in the first set of boxes and the second in the second set of boxes (with the top number in the Beat Groups row and the bottom number in the Beat Duration row).

7. Click OK to return to the Time Signature dialog box, then click OK again to return to the score. You should now see the multiple Time Signature separated with a + sign.

8. If you want to remove the + sign, from the Options menu, choose Document Options and select Time Signatures. Click the Plus Character button and choose the blank character (#9 on Mac and #32 on Win). Click Select and OK to return to the score.

9. Now, you may want to increase the distance between the two Time Signatures. To do this, from the Options menu, choose Document Options and select Fonts. For Notation, click the drop-down/popup menu and choose Time Signature Plus Sign and click the Set Font button. Choose a larger font size, like 96, and click OK. Click OK again to return to the score. If this is too much space, you can go back and adjust the font size of the blank character accordingly.

10. You may want to surround one of the Time Signatures with parentheses. To do this, you'll need to create an expression. Click the Expression tool. Then, doubleclick the first measure to open the Expression Selection window.

11. Click Create.

12. In the Text Expression Designer, enter "( )" (with a space).

13. Click the Set Font button. Change the size to 28, and click OK.

14. Click OK, Select and OK to return to the score.

15. Drag the parentheses into place around the Time Signature.

Large Time Signatures Placed Above the Staff

It is not uncommon to see large Time Signatures in a score placed between staves, as shown in Figure 5.14.

Figure 5.14
Large Time Signatures.

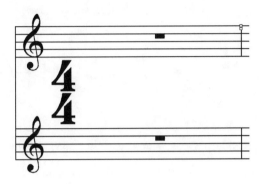

Here is a method for creating these:

1. From the Document Options menu, choose Document Options and select Fonts.
2. Click the drop-down/popup menu for Notation and choose Time.
3. Click the Set Font button for Notation.
4. In the Set Font dialog box, choose the font EngraverTime, and set the size to 48.
5. Click OK to return to the Document Options.
6. Choose the Time Signature category.
7. At the bottom of the Document Options, click the drop-down/popup menu and choose EVPUs.
8. For Top Symbol, enter 190; for Bottom Symbol, enter 135.
9. Click OK to apply these settings and return to the score.

The values in these steps assume you are using the default staff spacing, and want the Time Signature to appear above the staff. You will most likely need to adjust the font size for the Time Signature and/or the vertical offset of the top and bottom symbol. Since these Time Signatures sometimes apply to more than one staff, you may need to hide Time Signatures in some staves. Look at the instructions above for Showing or Hiding Time Signatures in Staves or Measures for details on how to do this.

TIP
Another font to build large Time Signatures with is the EngraverTime font. You can use Engraver Time to make large, narrow numbers that extend through multiple staves.

Pickup Measures Within a Score

Often, pickup measures appear somewhere within a score instead of before the first measure (Figure 5.15).

Figure 5.15
Pickup measures within a score.

Pickup Within a Score

Here are steps for creating a pickup measure at any point in a document.

1. With the Time Signature tool selected, double-click the measure you would like to change into a pickup measure.

2. Change the Time Signature to reflect the beat duration of the pickup. For example, for a quarter note pickup, use 1/4.

3. Click the Options (Mac: More Choices) button to expand the lower portion.

4. Check Use a Different Time Signature for Display.

5. Enter the Time Signature of the following measure (the measure directly after the pickup).

6. In the Measure Region section, enter the same measure number in both fields (to indicate that measure only).

7. Click OK to return to the score. Notice that you do not see a Time Signature displayed in the pickup measure. Use the Time Signature tool again to set the Time Signature in the measure following the pickup.

Now, there will be a pickup measure that will space the notes properly as you enter them. This pickup measure will also play back properly.

Isorhythmic Notation

Isorhythmic notation is the practice of using several different Time Signatures at once. When you do this, each staff will be in a completely independent meter, so barlines for each staff will not line up vertically most of the time (Figure 5.16).

Figure 5.16
Isorhythmic notation.

This is a particularly unconventional notation practice, so getting it to work in Finale is a bit of a rigamarole. Nonetheless, it can be done, and here's how:

1. You will need to set all of your staves to use Time Signatures independently. Click the Staff tool, doubleclick a staff to open the Staff Attributes. Then, in the Independent Elements section, check Time Signatures. Do this for all staves in the score. To view the attributes for a different staff, select the staff name from the drop-down menu at the top of Staff Attributes, then put a check in Independent Elements for Time Signature. Click OK when you have done so for all staves in your score.

2. Now, you will need to create a Time Signature that will encompass all of the Time Signatures you wish to use. To do this, you basically need to determine the lowest common denominator for the multiple meters. For example, if you want to use 3/4 in one staff and 2/4 in another, use 6/4 - (3×2)/4=6/4. This is the shortest measure that will encompass both a 3/4 and 2/4 meter.

3. Click the Time Signature tool and doubleclick the first measure in the top staff to open the Time Signature dialog box.

4. Enter the Time Signature that represents the lowest common denominator (as calculated above), then click the Options (Mac: More Choices) button to expand the lower portion of this dialog box.

5. Check Use a Different Time Signature for Display.

6. In the lower portion, set the Time Signature you want to display for the staff.

7. Click OK. Then repeat steps three through six for all staves in the score. Remember, if you will be doing this frequently, set up appropriate metatools for each Time Signature needed to save yourself the trouble of going to the dialog box every time.

8. Now, you will need to add additional barlines manually. To do this, click the Smart Shape tool, and choose the Line tool from the Smart Shape palette. Doubleclick and drag to enter the remaining barlines. To constrain dragging (for perfectly vertical lines), hold down the Shift key while entering the Smart Shape barlines. You will probably want to do this as you add the notation for accurate placement.

6

Slurs, Hairpins, Other Smart Shapes, and Repeats

In chapter 3, we covered the basics for adding articulation markings and text expressions to a score. There are many other common markings in notation that require curves, brackets, wavy lines, and other shapes. For these, use the Smart Shape tool. You can use the Smart Shape tool to enter slurs, hairpins, trill extensions, brackets, bend shapes, glissandi, and other markings. Like Expressions, Smart Shapes are designed to adjust intelligently while you work. As you edit and adjust the layout of your score, each Smart Shape moves with the measure or note it is attached to, and can even adjust automatically to avoid collision with notes, accidentals, and other items. In this chapter, you'll learn when to use Smart Shapes and how to enter, edit and copy them. You'll also learn how to make global changes and create your own custom Smart Shapes.

The end of this chapter will be devoted to repeats. Repeats are represented by both text and barline figures. You will learn how to easily enter repeats barlines and text repeats, as well as how to edit their appearance and get them to play back.

Here's a summary of what you will learn in this chapter:

▶ How to work with Smart Shapes, Slurs, and Hairpins.

▶ How to enter glissandi, guitar bends, lines, and other Smart Shapes.

▶ How to define repeats

Intro to Smart Shapes

When you click the Smart Shape tool, you will see the Smart Shape Palette appear (Figure 6.1).

Figure 6.1
Choose a shape from
Smart Shape Palette for
entry into the score.

Use the Smart Shape Palette to choose the shape you'd like to enter. To enter a Slur, for example, click the Smart Shape tool, then choose the Slur tool from the Smart Shape Palette. Doubleclick and drag to enter the slur in the score (we'll talk more about entering slurs and other shapes soon). By default, any Smart Shape you enter will appear red in the score (to distinguish them from text

CHAPTER 6

blocks, measure expressions and other items). In addition to the Smart Shape Palette, you will also see the Smart Shape menu appear at the top of your screen (Figure 6.2).

Figure 6.2
Customize the appearance, placement, and other attributes of Smart Shapes by choosing an item from the Smart Shape menu.

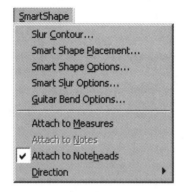

Each Smart Shape has its own properties relating to how it can be edited and to what it can be attached (notes, noteheads, or measures). In addition, there are a number of placement and graphical changes you can make from this menu at a documentwide level. Throughout this chapter, we will be referring to this menu to apply some of these changes.

A preassigned metatool has been assigned to each Smart Shape. Whenever the Smart Shape tool is selected, hold down one of these metatool keys and double-click and drag to enter its corresponding Smart Shape. Table 6.1 displays a list of Smart Shape metatools. Use these at any time as a substitute for choosing one of the tools in the Smart Shape Palette.

Table 6.1
Smart Shape Metatools

Tool	Metatool	Tool	Metatool
Slur	S	Bracket Tool	K
Dashed Curve	V	Dashed Bracket	R
Decrescendo	>	Line	L
Crescendo	<	Dashed Line	D
Trill	T	Glissando Tool	G
Trill Extension	E	Guitar Bend	B
8va/8vb	8	Bend Hat	N
15ma/15mb	1	Tab Slide	A
Double-Ended Bracket Tool	0	Dashed Double-Ended Bracket Tool	H
Custom Line	C		

General Smart Shape Editing

Before we begin to explore the various Smart Shape types, there are some techniques for editing that are common to many Smart Shapes. Whenever the Smart Shape tool is selected, you will see a handle appear on every Smart Shape in the score. I will refer to this handle as the primary handle. Click and drag this handle to move Smart Shape around. Use the arrow keys to nudge it for fine-positioning adjustments. Click and drag over several primary Smart Shape handles to move several of them at once. Press the Delete key to delete all selected Smart Shapes.

Measure, Note, and Notehead-Attached Smart Shapes

Like Expressions, many Smart Shapes can be set to attach to either a measure or a note. Before entering a Smart Shape, from the Smart Shape menu, you can choose Attach to Measures, Attach to Notes or Attach to Noteheads, depending on the role of the Smart Shape you are about to enter (note: Some of these options are limited to certain Smart Shapes). Measure-attached Smart Shapes can be entered anywhere in the score and will attach to the measure closest to the point of entry. They will adjust to their corresponding measure like a measure-attached expression. Note-attached Smart Shapes will adjust according to their corresponding notes much like a note-attached expression. Their position is determined by settings in the Smart Shape Placement dialog box (Smart Shape menu > Smart Shape Placement). The Attach to Notehead option is used for the tab slide and glissando Smart Shape. The default setting for Measure/Note/Notehead-Attached is usually adequate for the common usage of each Smart Shape, so you may never need to change this setting. However, making the distinction between these three Smart Shape types is fundamental to the way Smart Shapes are organized in Finale.

Other Techniques

There are some other tricks that apply to all Smart Shapes.

▶ Drag-enclose to select several Smart Shapes. You may also select several Smart Shapes by holding down the Shift key and clicking in each handle. Then, use the mouse to drag all selected Smart Shapes uniformly, or the arrow keys to nudge them.

▶ Hold down the Shift key while creating or editing a Smart Shape to "constrain" dragging to either vertical or horizontal movement.

▶ Hold down the Delete key and drag over as many Smart Shapes as you like to delete them.

▶ When a Smart Shape's primary handle is selected, press the Tab key to cycle selection through the editing handles of any Smart Shape. Pressing Esc will select the primary handle again and hide the diamond-shaped editing handles. When there are no editing handles showing, the Tab key will cycle through the primary handles of the various Shapes in the document.

The Smart Shape Context Menu

Any Smart Shape can be edited in the score with a context menu. Right/Control-click any Smart Shape handle to invoke the Smart Shape context menu, as seen in Figure 6.3.

Figure 6.3
Quickly edit Smart
Shapes in the score with
the Smart Shape context
menu.

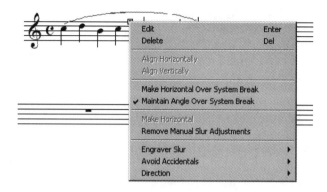

This menu can be used to quickly make a number of adjustments to individual Smart Shapes, including direction and alignment. The available options in this context menu will depend on the type of Smart Shape (certain options will be grayed out with some smart shapes). Choose Edit from the context menu to show the editing handles on a Smart Shape, or choose Delete from the context menu to delete one. There are also some other options in this context menu that apply to many or all Smart Shapes. Learn to use the context menu frequently while editing Smart Shapes to save time.

Context Menu - Aligning Smart Shapes

You can easily align any number of measure-attached Smart Shapes, such as hairpin crescendo or decrescendos, vertically or horizontally. Click and drag to select several measure-attached Smart Shape handles. Right/Control-click one of the highlighted handles to open the context menu. Choose Align Horizontally to horizontally align all selected Smart Shapes. Click Align Vertically to vertically align all selected Smart Shapes. Then, press the up or down arrow keys, or click one of the highlighted handles, to position all of the aligned Smart Shapes at once.

Context Menu - Smart Shapes over System Breaks

Many Smart Shapes can be extended over a system break. When this is done, Finale basically generates a new Smart Shape at the beginning of the second system (and any subsequent system as necessary). If you would like to "flatten" the Smart Shape as it is moved over a system break, from the context menu, choose Make Horizontal Over System Break. This option can also apply to existing Smart Shapes. To allow Smart Shapes to retain their angle across system breaks, choose Maintain Angle Over System Break from the context menu.

Slurs

Slurs can be used to indicate a legato, uninterrupted performance style, or to indicate a musical phrase. To enter a slur, click the Slur tool in the Smart Shape Palette. Double-click the first note of the slur and drag it to the destination note. When you release the mouse button, the slur will adjust automatically to avoid collision of notes and accidentals. As you drag the cursor over subsequent notes, refer to the highlighted note to specify the endpoint of the slur (Figure 6.4).

Figure 6.4
Specify the slur
endpoint by referring to
the highlighted note.

After you have entered the slur, you will notice a surrounding pentagon with small diamonds at
each corner. You can use these diamond editing handles to manually edit the shape of the slur.
Click and drag them, or click a handle and use the arrow keys to make fine adjustments. Use
these reshaping handles to edit the arc and endpoints.

If you want to remove all manual changes you have made to a slur, press the Backspace/Clear
key with the handle selected. Or, right/Control-click the slur handle and choose Remove Manual
Slur Adjustments.

Flipping Slurs Over or Under a Staff

After you have entered a slur, you might want to move it to the other side of the staff. To do this,
right/Control-click the slur handle to open the context menu. From the Direction submenu, choose
Flip. The slur will flip to the other side of the staff. You can also flip a slur easily by pressing
Ctrl/Control-F with a slur handle selected. Flipping is only available for note-attached slurs.

Editing the Slur Contour Globally

If you are not satisfied with Finale's default slur contour settings, you can adjust them for an
entire document. To do this, from the Smart Shape menu, choose Slur Contour. This will open
the Slur Contour dialog box, as seen in Figure 6.5.

Figure 6.5
Edit the default contour
of slurs in the Slur
Contour dialog box.

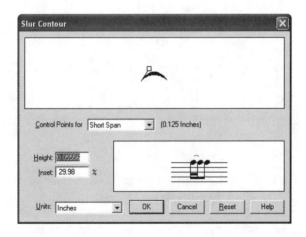

CHAPTER 6

First, click the drop-down/popup menu and choose from the four available slur lengths. Since
no one contour will work for every slur length, Finale divides the contour settings into four
different lengths. Choose the length that most closely compares to the slurs you want to change.
Then, use the handle in the editable preview window to adjust the default slur contour. Notice

the preview window at the bottom will update to display any changes you make. Hold down the Shift key to constrain dragging to vertical or horizontal movement only. If you prefer, enter values in the Height and Inset text boxes for more precise control over slur contour. Click Reset to revert to the default settings for the chosen length. Click OK to apply any changes and return to the score. Contour settings will affect existing slurs in the score.

Editing the Slur Width

You can edit the thickness of slurs in the Smart Shape Options dialog box. With the Smart Shape tool selected, from the Smart Shape menu, choose Smart Slur Options. On the right side of the Smart Slur Options dialog box, use the Thickness Left, Thickness Right, and Tip Width parameters to adjust the thickness of slurs and slur tips.

Editing Default Slur Placement

Finale offers a great deal more flexibility for editing slurs globally. You can change the default placement for any slur based on the surrounding notation. From the Smart Shape menu, choose Smart Shape Placement. You will see the Smart Shape Placement dialog box, as shown in Figure 6.6.

Figure 6.6
Edit the default placement of slurs, tab slides, glissandi, and guitar bends in the Smart Shape Placement dialog box.

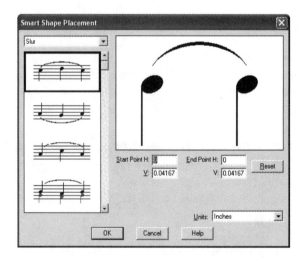

First, choose the general type of slur from the list on the left. Use the scroll bar to view all the options. Notice the placement of the slur related to the stem settings to determine which type of slur to adjust. In the large, editable preview window, make adjustments to the slur manually. Click the left and right endpoints to adjust the slant and length of the slur. Click the middle of the slur and drag to adjust the vertical placement. You can also enter specific values for the start and end points in the H: (Horizontal) and V: (Vertical) text boxes. Click Reset to revert back to the original default settings. Click OK to return to the score and review your changes.

Changes made in the Smart Shape Placement dialog box will affect any new slurs you create, as well as existing slurs in the score, provided they have not been adjusted manually.

S-Slurs

Sometimes, slurs need to extend from one staff to another, requiring an "S" shape instead of a simple curve, as shown in Figure 6.7. This type of slur is quite simple to create in Finale. Enter the slur as you normally would, between notes in two adjacent staves (a grand staff, for example). Then, drag the endpoints of the slur to the desired location. Drag the editing handles to create the S shape, as seen below.

Figure 6.7
Creating an s-curve.

Dashed Curves or Slurs

Dashed curves behave just like slurs. Click the Dashed Curve tool in the Smart Shape Palette, then double-click in the score to create a dashed curve/slur. Most settings made in the Smart Slur Options dialog box will apply to dashed slurs as well as regular slurs.

The width of dashed slurs/curves is customizable. Dashed slurs/curves are not tapered, unlike regular slurs, and are basically just curved lines. To change the width of a dashed slur, the dash length, or the space between dashes, use the Smart Shape Options dialog box. From the Smart Shape menu, choose Smart Shape Options. In the right side of this dialog box, specify a value for Line Thickness, Dash Length and/or Dash Space. Then, click OK to return to the score. Note that these changes will also apply to Line and Bracket Smart Shapes as well.

Avoiding Collisions with Articulations (TGTools)

If you find that some of your slurs collide with articulation markings, you can use TGTools to tell Finale to automatically reposition the endpoints of slurs to avoid this collision. Here's how:

1. Click the Mass Edit Tool.
2. Select a region of your score containing slurs that collide with articulations, or Ctrl/Command-A to Select All.
3. From the TGTools menu, choose Modify > Slurs.
4. Click the Resolve Collisions tab.
5. Here, you can specify the offset for slurs that collide with articulations. The default values usually work fine.
6. Click Go. Slurs in the selected region adjust to avoid collision with articulations.

Depending on the musical passage, you may want to adjust slurs colliding only with certain articulations. Select the Articulation Types tab in the TGTools Slurs dialog box to choose specific articulations to avoid.

TIP
You can define an articulation to be placed inside a slur by default in the Articulation Designer dialog box. This is especially handy for staccato and tenuto articulations that typically are placed inside slurs.

Engraver Slurs

Finale 2002 introduced a variety of slur improvements, one of which is the ability to automatically avoid collision of slurs with notes, accidentals, and beams. These slurs will even update as you edit notes in the score. Slurs that include this functionality are called engraver slurs, and are used by default in Finale 2002 documents and later. (Finale will not automatically adjust the appearance of slurs in documents converted from Finale versions 2001 or earlier). As a result of these improvements, there are a number of new parameters available that help control the behavior of engraver slurs. From the Smart Shape menu, choose Smart Slur Options. On the left side of this box, make adjustments to the way Finale configures engraver slurs.

Any time you edit a slur manually, it will change into a normal slur, meaning its shape will no longer automatically adjust with the changes you make to your document. Essentially, the slur will be frozen into position and will no longer automatically adjust its shape to avoid collisions. To convert it back to an engraver slur, highlight its handle and press Backspace/Clear.

To set all slurs in a converted document (or selected region) to engraver slurs:

1. Click the Mass Edit Tool.
2. Select a region of your score, or Ctrl/Command-A to Select All.
3. From the Mass Edit menu, choose Utilities > Remove Manual Slur Adjustments.
4. Click the Smart Shape tool.
5. From the Smart Shape menu, choose Smart Slur Options.
6. Check Engraver Slurs.
7. Click OK. Slurs in the selected region are now set to adjust to avoid collision with notes, accidentals, and beams.

Hairpins (Crescendos and Decrescendos)

Hairpins in music notation are used to indicate a gradual dynamic contrast. They are also referred to as crescendos and decrescendos, an increase or decrease in dynamics, respectively. In Finale, hairpins generally appear as measure-attached Smart Shapes, and can be entered with either the Crescendo or Decrescendo tool in the Smart Shape Palette.

With the Crescendo tool selected (or while holding down the < key), doubleclick below a staff and drag to the right. Release the mouse button to create the crescendo. You will notice three diamond editing handles on the crescendo in addition to the main handle (if not, double-click the main handle to display the diamond handles). Click and drag the right-most diamond handle to adjust the placement of the end of the hairpin. Click the left-most handle to adjust the placement of the beginning of the hairpin. Move your cursor over the diamond handle on the right side of the hairpin (on the line) to adjust the width of the opening (Figure 6.8).

Figure 6.8
Use handles to edit the length and opening width of hairpins.

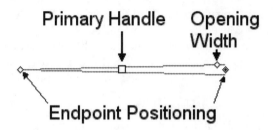

Decrescendos can be entered and edited the same way as crescendos (use the > key stroke for a decrescendo). Press Backspace/Clear to revert a hairpin back to the way it looked when originally entered.

With either hairpin tool selected, you can create both shapes. For example, Click the Crescendo tool, double-click and drag to the left. Instead of a crescendo, you get a decrescendo.

To specify the line thickness and opening width for all hairpins you create, from the Smart Shape menu, choose Smart Shape Options. In the Crescendo/Decrescendo section, specify a value for Line Thickness and Opening Width, and click OK. All hairpins that have not been edited manually will change to the values you specified. Also, new hairpins will use these values.

TIP

If you want to indicate a crescendo simply as text (i.e. Cresc.), create a text expression (as described in chapter 3). To create the text "cresc." followed by an adjustable dashed horizontal line, create a custom Smart Shape. You can find information on how to create custom shapes later in this chapter.

Creating Horizontal Hairpins

Hold down the Shift key while entering any hairpin to make it perfectly horizontal. If you would like to tell Finale to automatically constrain dragging horizontally for all hairpins, from the Smart Shape menu, choose Smart Shape Options. In the Crescendo/Decrescendo section, check Make Horizontal and click OK. Now, all new hairpin Smart Shapes you create will be horizontal.

If you already have entered hairpins, and want to make them horizontal, right/Control-click to open the context menu and choose Make Horizontal. This will affect all selected hairpins.

Aligning Hairpins

Aligning hairpins horizontally is easy. Drag to select the hairpins you want to align (or Shift-click to select the desired hairpins). Then, right/Control-click one of the selected handles and choose Align Horizontally. They all become aligned with the one you right/Control-clicked.

You may want to align all hairpins horizontally at a certain position above or below the staff. You can do this with the Align/Move Dynamics plug-in. Choose the Mass Edit Tool. Highlight the region of your score containing hairpins (Ctrt/Command-A to Select All). From the Plug-ins menu, choose TGTools > Align Move Dynamics. You will see the Align/Move Dynamics dialog box. On the right, make sure Hairpins is checked (and uncheck any other items if you do not want them to align). Choose the appropriate option on the left. If you choose Set To Value, enter an offset from the bottom staff line in the Move Vertically text box. Click Apply to align your hairpins.

Defining Hairpins for Playback

You can automatically define hairpins for playback with the Smart Playback plug-in. Choose the Mass Edit Tool. Highlight the region of your score containing hairpins (Ctrt/Command-A to Select All). From the Plug-ins menu, choose TGTools > Smart Playback. This will open the Smart Playback dialog box. Check Hairpins. Click Apply to define the hairpins for playback using the default settings. Play the document back to hear the volume changes. They are defined as MIDI controller 7 (volume) data. To change the intensity of the volume change, increase or decrease the value for Volume changes per quarter note in the Smart Playback dialog box.

TIP
You can find more information on defining and editing a document for playback in chapter 14.

Hairpins Over System Breaks

You may need to create a crescendo or decrescendo over a system break (from the end of one system to the beginning of the next). To do this, simply doubleclick where you want the hairpin to begin, and drag it down to the next system. When you release the mouse button, there will be a break in the hairpin lines at the beginning of the second system, as shown in Figure 6.9.

Figure 6.9
Drag the right editing handle of a hairpin down to extend it across a system break.

You can drag a hairpin over as many systems as there are on a page. The width of the opening on each one can be adjusted independently.

Generating Hairpins Between Expressions Automatically (TGTools)

If you have already entered dynamic expressions into your score, you can use TGTools to easily extend crescendos or decrescendos between them automatically, as long as they are both note-attached or both measure-attached. Here's how:

1. Click the Mass Edit Tool.

2. Select a region of your score containing dynamic expressions you want to extend hairpins between.

3. From the TGTools menu, choose Music > Create Hairpins. The Create Hairpins dialog box appears.

4. Click Go. A hairpin extends between dynamic markings in the selected region. If you do not like the results, press Ctrl-Z to undo. Then, try again to specify values for offset, and opening width in the Create Hairpins dialog box. You can also choose to add hairpins between specific dynamic expressions in the dialog box.

Other Smart Shapes

There are a number of other Smart Shapes you can use for a variety of other purposes. These include trills, ottavas (8va/8vb), glissandos, bend hats and curves, brackets, lines, and custom shapes. These will all have the note- or measure- attached properties as described earlier in this chapter, as well as many of the same editing capabilities.

Trills and Trill Extensions

These can be entered with the Smart Shape tool, as well as with the Articulation tool, although with the Smart Shape tool, you will be able to create an adjustable extension. Click the Trill tool in the Smart Shape Palette. Then, doubleclick and drag to the right to create a trill indication with an extension. Use the primary handle to move the entire figure around. Use the left and right handles to adjust the endpoints individually.

TIP

Trills, hairpins, and glissandi entered with the Smart Shape tool can be defined for playback with the Smart Playback plug-in. Click the Mass Edit Tool, highlight a region of the score with a trill, then choose the Plug-ins menu > TGTools > Smart Playback. For more information, see chapter 14.

The Trill Extension tool in the Smart Shape Palette can be used to indicate guitar tremolos as well as trill extensions. They can be edited just like regular trill Smart Shapes. To add an accidental at the beginning of a trill figure to indicate the pitch variation, use a custom Smart Shape. There is more information on creating custom Smart Shapes later in this section.

Ottavas (8va/8vb) and 15va/15vb

To tell the performer to transpose a section of music up or down an octave, an 8va or 8vb symbol is often used (Figure 6.10). Both of these can be created with the 8va Smart Shape tool. Simply double-click above a staff to enter an 8va, or below the staff to enter an 8vb. Take note of your mouse cursor, as the arrow points to the staff to which the shape will be attached. Finale will use the appropriate figure and adjust the playback of the region accordingly. You can extend the dash line over system breaks, and Finale will place the 8va or 8vb symbol in parentheses automatically at the beginning of each subsequent system. 8va and 8vb figures will always be measure-attached.

Figure 6.10
Click above the staff to enter an 8va; click below the staff to enter an 8vb.

Use the 15va tool the same way as the 8va tool. This figure is used to indicate a two-octave transposition from the written pitches.

If you are not satisfied with the text attached to default ottava or 15va/vb figures, you can choose your own. To change the attached text, from the Smart Shape menu, choose Smart Shape Options. This opens the Smart Shape Options dialog box, as seen in Figure 6.11.

Figure 6.11
Choose the font, character, style, and other Smart Shape attributes in the Smart Shape Options dialog box.

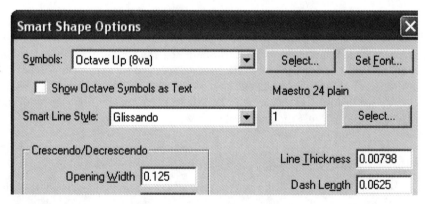

In the Symbols drop-down/popup menu, choose the marking you want to edit. Then, click the Set Font button to choose the font of your new character. Once you have chosen the font, size, and style, click OK. Click the Select button to open the Symbol Selection dialog box. Choose the character you would like to use, and click Select. Click OK to return to the score. Create the figure you edited to review your changes.

Glissandi and Tab Slides

Glissandi are used to indicate a rapid slide through ascending or descending pitches. They appear as wavy lines between adjacent notes (Figure 6.12). Creating these in Finale is easy. Click the Glissando tool in the Smart Shape Palette and double-click a note. Finale will automatically extend a glissando to the next note. Tab slides are generally used in tablature notation to indicate a pitch change by sliding up or down the fretboard of a fretted instrument (Figure 6.12). Enter these the same as you would a glissando.

Figure 6.12
Double-click to extend a glissando or tab slide to the next note.

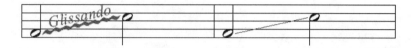

Both of these Smart Shapes are notehead-attached by default. However, you can create a glissando anywhere in your score (not attached to any notehead). To do this, choose Measure-Attached from the Smart Shape menu, then double-click and drag anywhere in the score.

When a glissando reaches a certain length, you will see the text "Gliss" or "Glissando" attached to the Smart Shape (depending on its length). To enter a glissando without this text, Ctrl/Option-click the Glissando tool in the Smart Shape Palette to open the Smart Line Style Selection dialog box. Choose the regular wavy line (without text) and click Select. Now, any glissando you enter will not include the attached text.

The endpoints of glissandos and tab slides can be adjusted relative to the noteheads to which they are attached. To specify placement of these items throughout your document, select the Smart Shape menu and choose Smart Shape Placement (Figure 6.6). From the drop-down/popup menu, choose either Tab Slide or Glissando. For tab slides, specify the type of tab slide from the list box on the left (depending on whether the notes are on staff lines or spaces, ascending or descending). Click the left and right endpoints to adjust the slant and length of glissandi and tab slides. Click the middle of the glissando or tab slide and drag to adjust the vertical placement. You can also enter specific values for the start and end point in the H: (Horizontal) and V: (Vertical) text boxes. Click Reset to revert back to the original default settings. Click OK to return to the score.

NOTE
For tab slides, the V: value indicates the offset from the staff line or space of the notehead, depending on the selection in the list box to the left of this dialog box.

Changes made to tab slides and glissandi in the Smart Shape Placement dialog box apply to new Smart Shapes and existing Smart Shapes in the score that have not been edited (Finale will not make changes to tab slides or glissandi you have already adjusted manually). You can find more information on tab slide Smart Shapes in chapter 8.

Bend Hats and Guitar Bends

Bend hats and curves are used to indicate a bend in pitch. To enter a bend hat, click the Bend Hat Smart Shape, and double-click a note. Finale will extend the bend hat to the next note automatically (Figure 6.13). You will see three diamond editing handles attached to the bend hat in addition to the primary handle. Drag the diamond handles on the ends of the bend hat to adjust the placement of the endpoints, and the handle at the joint to adjust the angle. To create a bend hat that isn't bound to two notes, click the Smart Shape menu and choose Attach to Measures. Then, doubleclick and drag anywhere in the score.

Figure 6.13
Use bend hats to
indicate a pitch bend.

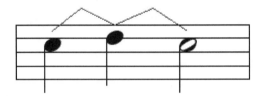

The guitar bend Smart Shape was introduced in Finale 2003 and is used primarily for bend and release figures in guitar tablature notation. This is perhaps the smartest Smart Shape, due to its ability to analyze the notation and create the appropriate pitch change text for the existing notes, as well as hide unnecessary notes. To enter a guitar bend in a TAB staff, simply choose Guitar Bend Smart Shape and double-click a fret number to create the guitar bend. Finale will hide the following fret number and indicate the appropriate pitch change in text (Figure 6.14).

Figure 6.14
Use the Guitar Bend
tool to create bend
curves with text
automatically generated
to indicate the pitch
variation.

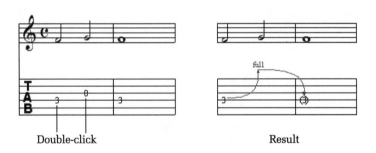

Double-click   Result

After creating a guitar bend, press Ctrl/Command-D to redraw the screen. You can customize Finale's handling of Smart Shapes (generated text, font, etc.) with the Guitar Bend Options. From the Smart Shape menu, choose Guitar Bend Options. There is a more complete discussion of how to use, enter, and edit guitar bends and how to create guitar tablature in chapter 8.

Brackets and Lines

There are six remaining Smart Shape tools for creating brackets and lines. The four bracket Smart Shapes (bracket, dashed bracket, double-ended bracket, and dashed double-ended bracket) pretty much behave the same. With one of them selected, double click and drag to create a horizontal bracket. Use the diamond editing handles to adjust the length and the primary handle to move it around. To create a line, click the Line or Dashed Line tool, then double-click and drag anywhere in the score. Unlike brackets, lines can be drawn at any slope. Bracket and line Smart Shapes are always measure-attached.

There are a several ways to customize brackets and lines throughout your document. Change the width, dash length, dash space, and length of bracket hooks in the Smart Shape Options dialog box. From the Smart Shape menu, choose Smart Shape Options. The Smart Shape Options dialog box appears (Figure 6.11). In the four text boxes on the right, you can specify line thickness, dash length and dash space. These parameters affect both bracket and line Smart Shapes, as well as dashed curves. To change the length of the bracket hooks (the vertical lines on the ends of brackets), enter a new value in the Hook Length text box (of course, the Hook Length setting only applies to brackets). Click OK to review changes in your score.

Custom Smart Shapes

There are a number of other available Smart Shapes that do not exist in the Smart Shape Palette. To see a list of other Smart Shapes, Ctrl/Option-click the Custom Line tool. You will see the Smart Line Style Selection dialog box, as seen in Figure 6.15.

Figure 6.15
Edit or create a smart line in the Smart Line Style Selection dialog box.

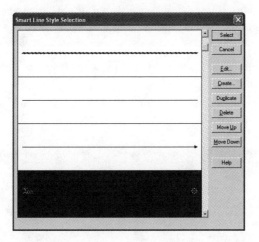

Here, there are a number of other Smart Shape line styles available for you to choose from. They are basically specialized lines for figures not available in the Smart Shape Palette. To use any of the following, click to highlight it, then click the Select button. Doubleclick and drag in the score to create the figure you chose.

▶ Glissando: Choose a glissando with or without text. These are the same as regular glissandi.

▶ 𝒫𝑒𝑑. and ✳ (sustain): These figures are generally used to indicate the beginning and end of a sustained section of piano music (requiring the sustain pedal).

Many custom Smart Lines, such as this one, do not contain a line at all. This Smart Shape only displays a figure at the beginning and end of an "invisible" line. Also, notice the graphical pedal markings available here.

▶ Lines with arrowheads: These are just like regular lines, only with an arrowhead attached.

▶ Ritardando: Often, ritardandos are indicated with "rit." followed by a dashed horizontal line.

▶ Trills: Choose from a number of trill markings, set to indicate possible pitch variations with accidentals.

▶ Figures for Guitar Notation: Choose from a variety of figures for guitar notation, including harmonics (A.H., N.H.), mute indications (P.M.) and picking symbols, hammer-ons, and pull-offs. There will be more information on guitar notation in chapter 8.

Like regular lines, custom lines are measure-attached. As the name of the tool suggests, you can edit any of the available lines, or create your own from scratch.

Creating Custom Smart Shapes

Create a custom Smart Shape for any type of line you need. Perhaps the most common Smart Shape is the crescendo marking followed by a horizontal line. Here are steps for creating a crescendo marking followed by a dashed line. Before you begin, from the Options menu, choose Measurement Units, and then Inches.

1. Hold down the Ctrl/Option key and click the Custom Line tool. The Smart Line Style Selection dialog box appears.

2. Click the Create button. You should see the Smart Line Style dialog box, as shown in Figure 6.16.

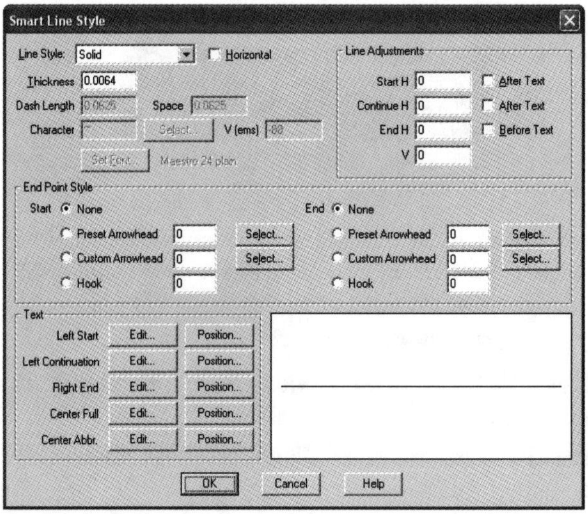

Figure 6.16
Define the appearance and add text to a smart line in the Smart Line Style dialog box.

3. Click the Style drop-down/popup menu and choose Dashed. Notice the updated preview in the lower right. We'll leave the line thickness and dash settings alone for now.

4. Now, let's increase the frequency of the dashes. Some find the default dashes a bit too long. For Dash Length, enter .04. For Space, enter .04 (inches). Notice the preview in the lower right updates after leaving each text box.

5. Check Horizontal if it isn't already. We'll want to constrain to horizontal dragging while entering the crescendo markings in the score.

6. Now, let's add the text. In the text section, at the bottom of this dialog box, click the Edit button for Left Start (since we'll want the text at the beginning of the line). The Edit Text box opens.

7. Type "Crescendo.".

8. Most often, this type of marking is italicized. Hold down Ctrl/Command and press A to Select All.

9. From the Text menu, choose Style, then Italic. The text becomes italicized.

10. Click OK. You will return to the Smart Line Style dialog box.

11. We'll want the dashed line to begin after the text. In the upper right, for Start H, check After Text.

12. Click OK to return to the score.

13. Double-click and drag to create the marking anywhere in the score.

You can edit custom lines in the score just as you would a regular line (though we confined this line to horizontal dragging only). If you want to change the text, line thickness, dash length, etc., Ctrl/Option-click the Smart Line tool. Your custom Smart Shape will now always appear in the Smart Line Style Selection dialog box. Click it and choose Edit to make any edits to the line.

If there is a custom line similar to the one you would like to create, you can save time by duplicating and then editing the smart line. In the Smart Line Style Selection dialog box, click the Smart Line similar to the one you want to create and click the Duplicate button. A duplicate of the Smart Line will appear at the bottom of the list. Click the duplicate Smart Line, then click the Edit button to make the adjustments.

One additional benefit to custom Smart Shapes is the ability to rotate text. If you need text to appear vertically, for example, create a custom Smart Shape line, then create the shape vertically.

Copying Smart Shapes

When you copy music with the Mass Edit Tool, Finale will copy all Smart Shapes along with the notation. You can, however, copy Smart Shapes independently from one area of your score to another. Before following these steps, click the Edit Menu and uncheck Select Partial Measures (if it is checked).

1. Click the Mass Edit Tool.

2. From the Mass Edit menu, choose Copy Measure Items if you want to copy measure-attached Smart Shapes. Choose Copy Entry Items if you want to copy note-attached Smart Shapes. The Measure or Entry Items dialog box appears. If

you copy note-attached Smart Shapes (Entry Items), notes in the destination measure will need to have the same rhythmic configuration for the Smart Shapes to copy properly.

3.   Put a check in Smart Shapes (Attached to Notes or Attached to Measures).

4.   Click OK.

5.   Select the region of your score containing the Smart Shapes you want to copy, and drag to the new measures (or Ctrl/Option-Shift-click the first measure in the destination region).

6.   The Smart Shapes copy to the new location. If they do not, make sure the Smart Shapes in the region you selected are measure-attached if you chose Copy Measure Items, or note-attached if you chose Copy Entry Items from the Mass Edit menu.

Automatically Copy Smart Shapes to Rhythmically Identical Passages

You may have a recurring motif or ostinato in your score that demands the same set of Smart Shapes at each occurrence throughout the piece. The SmartFind and Paint feature introduced in chapter 3 also allows you to find and copy Smart Shapes to rhythmically identical passages. To demonstrate this, fill a measure with a combination of eighth and quarter notes on different pitches with the Simple or Speedy Entry tool. Click the Mass Edit Tool, highlight this measure, and drag-copy it to a different measure. In the Copy Measures dialog box, type 10 and click OK. Now, click the Smart Shape tool and add several Smart Shapes to the original measure. Click the Mass Edit Tool and highlight the measure containing the Smart Shapes. Click the Mass Edit menu and choose Set SmartFind Source. Next, click the Mass Edit menu and choose Apply SmartFind and Paint. Click the Find button, and the measure containing a passage with an identical rhythm becomes highlighted. Click the Paint button and the Smart Shapes appear on the notes just as they did in the original measure. This is also a great technique for copying articulations, note expressions and measure expressions to similar phrases throughout your score.

Defining Repeats

Repeats are a common way to tell the performer to go back and play a section of music once, twice, or several more times. Often, a new ending is specified for each run through the same section of music. In notation, repeat barlines and text are used to indicate these repeated sections. In Finale, these markings can be entered with the Repeat tool and by using Repeat plug-ins. They can even be defined for playback.

Basic Repeat Creation and Editing

Defining basic repeats in Finale is easy. To indicate a single repeated section, or a repeat with a first and second ending, use the Repeat plug-ins. To create a single repeat with two repeat barlines, one at the beginning, and one at the end:

1. Click the Mass Edit Tool.

2. Highlight the region of your score that will be included in the repeated section (click the first measure, then Shift-click the last measure of the desired region).

3. From the Plug-ins menu, choose Repeats > Easy Repeats.

The selected region now begins and ends with a repeat barline and will play back correctly. Creating a repeat with a first and second ending is almost as easy:

1. Click the Mass Edit Tool.

2. Highlight the region of your score that will be included in the repeated section, including the first ending (click the first measure, then Shift-click the last measure of what will be the first ending).

3. From the Plug-ins menu, choose Repeats > First Ending Repeats. The First Ending Repeats dialog box appears, as shown in Figure 6.17.

Figure 6.17
Choose the number of total passes and the number of measures under the first ending in the First Ending Repeats dialog box.

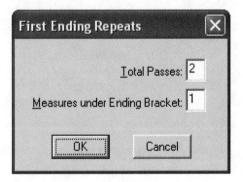

4. For Measures Under Ending Bracket, type the number of measures in your first ending. (Leave Total Passes at 2).

NOTE

The term "passes" sometimes causes confusion among Finale users. Passes are the number of times playback will "pass" through a section. For example, if you tell Finale to repeat something once, there are two passes through that portion of the music.

5. Click OK. The highlighted region is now between two repeat barlines with a bracket over the fist ending.

6. Click the Repeat tool.

7. Click the measure following the end repeat bar. The Repeat Selection dialog box opens, as shown in Figure 6.18.

CHAPTER 6

Figure 6.18
The Repeat Selection
dialog box

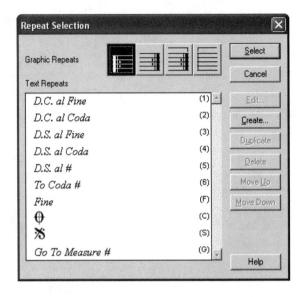

8. After Graphic Repeats, click the fourth icon (the bracket with a hook on the left).

9. Click Select. The Ending Repeat Bar Assignment dialog box opens, as shown in Figure 6.19.

Figure 6.19
The Ending Repeat Bar
Assignment dialog box

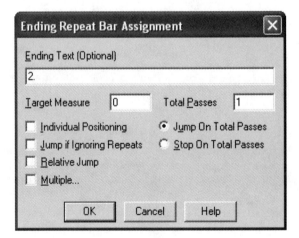

10. Type "2" to indicate a second ending.

11. Click OK. A second ending will appear in your score after the end repeat.

After creating repeat endings, you may want to edit the repeat brackets. To do this, click the Repeat tool. Click a measure containing an ending bracket to display repeat handles. Drag or nudge these handles to edit the length of the bracket, or bracket hooks (Figure 6.20).

Figure 6.20
Use the handles to edit
repeat bars and brackets.

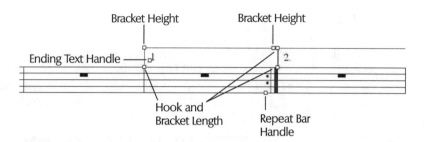

NOTE

As you edit repeat brackets, you may notice two brackets overlapping. Since ending brackets contain a hook only at one end, two brackets are required for double-ended brackets (for first endings, for example). If you adjust the height of any such bracket, simply move both brackets so they overlap. Use the Zoom tool to zoom in for greater accuracy while dragging. Instead of dragging handles, you can also type in global values for the repeat ending brackets to maintain uniformity for all ending brackets in a document. To do this, from the Options menu, choose Document Options > Repeats and click Repeat Endings.

Deleting Repeats

To delete repeat indications from any region of your score:

1. Click the Mass Edit Tool.
2. Highlight the region containing the repeat barlines and/or text.
3. From the Mass Edit menu, choose Clear Items. The Clear Items dialog box appears.
4. Choose Only Selected Items.
5. Check Measures. The Measure Items dialog box appears.
6. Check Repeats.
7. Click OK to return to the Clear Items dialog box.
8. Click OK to return to the score.

Repeat definitions in the highlighted area of your score are removed.

Hiding Repeat Brackets and Text in a Staff

It is common to display the repeat brackets and text on the top staff, and not on subsequent staves (in a piano grand staff, for example). To remove these repeat items from a staff, click the Staff tool. Then, doubleclick the staff containing the unwanted repeat markings to open the Staff Attributes. Under Items to Display, uncheck Endings and Text Repeats. Click OK to return to the score with repeat endings and text removed from the staff you selected.

D.S. al Coda/Fine

It is common for repeat markings to indicate a return to a sign (D.S. and Segno), then jump to a Coda. The following instructions can be a continuation of the previous instructions for creating first and second ending repeats. After you have created a repeat definition, use the following steps to enter the D.S., Segno and Coda. After following these steps, you will be able to create a score containing all of the repeat symbols in the following musical example (Figure 6.21).

Figure 6.21
First and second ending repeat example with D.S. al Coda

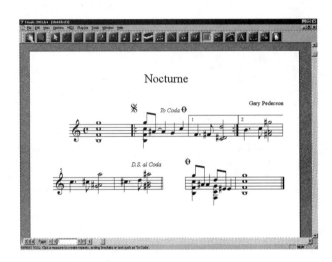

1. Choose the Repeat tool.

2. Doubleclick the measure you want to place the Segno (sign). The Repeat Selection dialog box appears (Figure 6.18).

3. Doubleclick the Segno in the Text Repeats list. The Repeat Assignment dialog box appears, as shown in Figure 6.22.

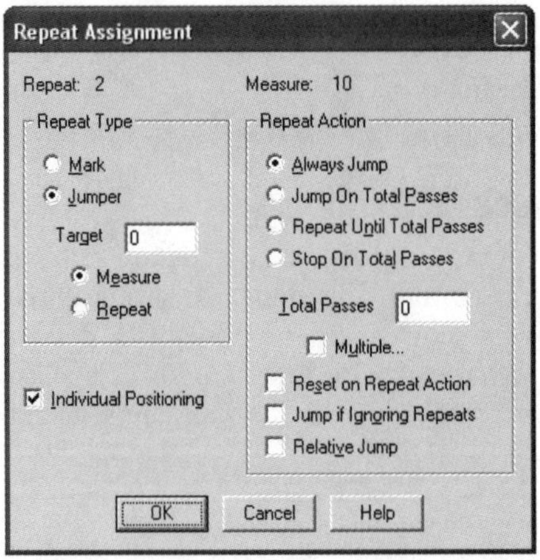

Figure 6.22
Choose the Repeat Assignment dialog box.

4. For Repeat Type, choose Mark. Take note of the repeat number assigned to the Segno in the upper left corner of the dialog.

5. Click OK.

6. Click and drag the handle of the Segno to reposition it (you may have to click the measure to show the Segno's handle). The Segno sign should be placed at the beginning of the measure to which it is attached. Now, we'll enter its corresponding D.S. al Coda indication.

7. Double-click on the measure you want the D.S. al Coda to appear. The Repeat Selection dialog box appears (Figure 6.18).

8. Doubleclick the D.S. al Coda in the Text Repeats list. The Repeat Assignment dialog box opens.

9. The music does jump from this point back to the Segno, so for Repeat Type, choose Jumper. For Target, choose Repeat and then type the number of the repeat that was assigned to the Segno (as you noted in step 4).

10. For Repeat Action, choose Always Jump. Click OK.

11. Click and drag the handle of the D.S. al Coda to reposition it. Again, you may have to click on the measure to show the D.S. al Coda's handle. Now, we'll enter the Coda sign.

12. Doubleclick the first measure of your Coda section.. The Repeat Selection dialog box opens.

13. In the Repeat Selection, doubleclick the Coda sign. The Repeat Assignment dialog box appears.

14. The Coda sign itself is just a marker, so select Mark and take note of the repeat number assigned in the upper left corner.

15. Click OK. Click and drag the handle of the Coda sign to reposition it. Now, we'll enter its corresponding To Coda indication.

16. Double-click the measure that will contain the To Coda indication. The Repeat Selection dialog box appears (Figure 6.18).

17. Singleclick the To Coda # in the Text Repeats list, and click Edit. Put a check in "Replace '#' with Repeat Mark in Target." Click OK; you are now back to the Repeat Selection box. The To Coda # should be highlighted. Click Select. The Repeat Assignment dialog box opens (Figure 6.22).

18. The music does jump from this point to the Coda, so for Repeat Type, choose Jumper. For Target, select Repeat and type the repeat number that was assigned to the Coda sign as you noted in step 14.

19. For Repeat Action, choose Jump on Total Passes, and for the number of Total Passes, type 2.

20. Click OK. Notice the Coda symbol appearing after the To Coda indication.

21. Click and drag the handle of the To Coda to reposition it. Notice that the # has been replaced with the measure number of the Coda, the target measure.

Text Repeats

In addition to using the available text repeats, you can create your own or edit those already available. Click the Repeat tool, then doubleclick a measure. Click Create to open the Repeat Designer dialog box. Enter the text of your repeat marking here (highlight the text and click Set Font to change the font, size, or style). You can use the # character to indicate a customizable measure number or symbol for the text repeat, depending on settings you will make in the Repeat Assignment dialog box. Click OK to return to the Repeat Selection dialog box. From now on, the repeat text you created will appear in this dialog box. Like articulations, expressions, and other items, you can transfer text repeats between documents by saving and opening a library.

Playback

You may find that a score containing repeats hangs as you initiate playback (the Message/Status bar will seem to process measures indefinitely). If this is the case, it is likely there are repeats in your score that are defined to loop infinitely. To fix this problem, double-check the playback definitions of your repeats. To view or redefine the playback definitions of your repeats, right/Control click the handle of the repeat and click Edit Repeat Assignment. In the Repeat Assignment dialog box, you can edit the Target Repeat or Measure number, as well as the Repeat Action and number of Total Passes.

After defining the repeats as described above, they will play back correctly. However, you may want to specify a performance indication for playback the second time only (for example). You can tell Finale to play back at a specific volume, tempo, or even patch number (sound) for the first, second, or third pass only. To do this:

1. Click the Expression tool.
2. Doubleclick at the beginning of a repeated section. The Expression Selection dialog box opens.
3. Click Create.
4. In the text box, enter a description in <angled brackets> of the playback definition you are entering (<Play 1st time only> for example).
5. Since you won't want this expression to print, check Do Not Print Text in <Angled Brackets>.
6. Click Playback Options/More Choices.
7. For Type, click the drop-down/popup menu and choose the type of MIDI data you want to modify. In this example, select Key Velocity.
8. For Effect, enter the value of change. For this example, enter 0.
9. For Play Only on Pass, enter the number of the pass you want this expression to affect playback. In this example, enter 2. The second time these measures are played, the notes will be silent.
10. Click OK, click Select.

11. Click OK to return to the score.

12. You will notice that on the second time through the repeated area, the notes do not sound on this staff. The playback definitions of expressions affect channels. To make sure this expression affects only the staff you intend, make sure all of you staves are set to their own channel in the Instrument List. You'll also notice that this staff will continue to be silent after that point. This is because you need to add another expression that contains a key velocity greater than 0.

13. Double-click a measure after the repeated area, or in your second ending. When the Expression Selection appears, click Create. Type your text in <angled brackets> and click Do Not Print Text in <Angled Brackets>.

14. For type, choose Key Velocity and enter a value greater than 0 but less than 127, such as 64. Note: the dynamic markings in your document are already assigned a key velocity, so you may use a dynamic instead.

Click the Play button in the playback controls to hear your results. There will be a more complete discussion of the playback capabilities of the Expression tool in chapter 14.

7

Creating and Working With Multiple Staff Scores

So far, our topics have emphasized documents with a single staff, or perhaps a piano score with two staves. The aim of this chapter is to get acquainted with procedures applicable to working with scores of two, three, or many staves. To cover material fundamental to working with multiple stave scores, we will explore properties of the Staff, Measure, Page Layout and Expression tools. You will learn how to position, view, and reorder staves, manage barlines, group staves in brackets, remove empty staves from systems, add expressions to any number of selected staves, and perform a variety of other tricks that apply specifically to multiple-stave documents.

Here's a summary of what you will learn in this chapter:

> ▶ How to work with multiple staves.
> ▶ How to work with staff groups.
> ▶ How to enter expressions in documents with multiple staves.
> ▶ How to create and work with optimized scores.
> ▶ Other tricks for multiple stave scores.

Working with Multiple Staves

A Finale document can contain any number of staves, limited only by the available memory on your machine. Much of the work of beginning a new score can be done automatically by starting with the Setup Wizard or a Template. Refer back to chapter 2 for information on starting a new document. This section focuses on adding and removing staves in any existing document, as well as viewing and editing them most efficiently.

To prepare for this section, open a new default document (File > New > Default Document). Then, from the View menu, choose Scroll View. Scroll View is best for demonstrating staff creation and management. You will see a single staff extend across the page. Click the Staff tool. Unless specified otherwise, we'll assume the Staff tool is selected for this section.

Adding, Removing, and Positioning Staves

There are a couple ways to add staves to an existing document, with or without the Setup Wizard. To add new, empty staves, with no staff name, or other attributes, from the Staff menu, choose New Staves. The New Staves dialog box opens, as shown in Figure 7.1.

Figure 7.1
Choose the number of staves, and their spacing, in the New Staves dialog box.

Type the number of staves you want to add. For now, leave it at 1. Click OK. You return to the score with the new staves at the bottom. Also, in Scroll View, double-click on your document to create a new staff. Then, use the staff handle to drag it into position (we'll talk more about staff positioning later in this section). After you have added staves this way, you will need to specify the staff name, clef, transposition, and any other necessary staff attributes (as described in chapter 2). To do this automatically while you add staves, use the Staff Setup Wizard.

With the Setup Wizard, you will be able to choose the instruments and order of several new staves at once. With Staff tool selected, from the Staff menu, choose New Staves (with Setup Wizard). You will see the Choose Parts page of the Setup Wizard (Figure 2.2). Choose the new instruments and order just as you would in the Document Setup Wizard. For this example, let's add a brass quartet. Choose the Brass category on the left, then double-click Trumpet in Bb, Horn in F, Trombone, and Tuba. The four instruments appear in the right column. For Score Order, click the drop-down/popup menu and choose Concert Band to put them in a more standard order. Click Finish to return to the score. The four staves have been added to the score beneath the two undefined staves. Notice the blue bracket to the left. This is called a group bracket, which is used to indicate staves of a similar instrumental group (we will be talking more about groups soon). Right/Option-Command-click and drag the score so the left edge of the system is in view (from this point on, to move around the score horizontally in Scroll View, always use the scroll bar at the bottom on the screen).

Removing Staves

Now, let's delete the top two staves. Click the handle on the upper left corner of the top staff, then from the Staff menu, choose Delete Staves and Reposition. This clears the top staff and shifts the subsequent staves up to take its place (you can also choose Delete Staves and reposition from the Staff context menu—right/Control-click the staff handle). Now, click the handle on the top staff (the remaining undefined staff). Hold down Shift and press the Delete key. This is the shortcut for deleting a staff and repositioning. To delete a staff without changing the positioning of any of the other staves, simply click the staff handle and press the Delete key. To delete many staves, hold down the Shift key and click all of the staff handles on staves you want to delete. Then, follow one of the previous methods for deleting the selected staves.

Inserting a Staff Between Existing Staves

Let's say we want to insert a second trumpet part above the horn staff in the document on which we are working. Click the handle on the horn staff. Then, from the Staff menu, choose New Staves (with Setup Wizard). Choose Brass on the left, then doubleclick Trumpet in Bb. Click Finish. The new trumpet staff appears above the horn staff, and all subsequent staves are shifted down.

Positioning Staves

You can move staves manually with the staff handles. Simply click a staff handle (or number of staff handles) and drag to reposition the staves. In the document we have been working on, let's say we want to drag the trombone staff above the horn staff, but leave the spacing the same. Click the handle on the trombone staff and drag it up between the trumpet and horn staves (it will look cramped initially). Then, from the Staff menu, make sure Auto Sort Staves is checked, and then, choose Respace Staves. You will see the Respace Staves dialog box, as shown in Figure 7.2.

Figure 7.2
Set the distance between staves in the Respace Staves dialog box.

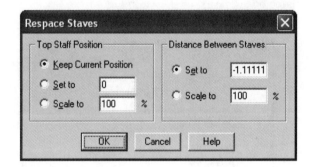

For now, just click OK. You return to the score with the original spacing. The trombone staff is now above the horn staff.

You may want to increase or decrease the space between your staves to make more room for music on ledger lines, or to fit additional staves. Let's say we want to bring the staves of our quintet a bit closer together. From the Staff menu, choose Respace Staves to invoke the Respace Staves dialog box (Figure 7.2). Click Scale To and type 90 in the text box to tell Finale to respace the staves at ninety percent of their original spacing. Click OK to return to the score. Notice the staves respace proportionally, bringing them closer together.

To increase the space, use the same instructions, only in the Respace Staves dialog box, enter a value over 100 in the Scale To text box. If you know a precise value, choose Set To, and enter the space between each staff in the corresponding text box (the default is 1.111 inches). To change the unit of measurement, from the Options menu, choose Measurement Units.

NOTE

When you choose to scale the spacing percentage in the Resize Staves dialog box, Finale will retain the original proportions of the space between staves. To space the staves evenly, choose Set To, then enter a value in the Respace Staves dialog box. You may want to then go back and respace to a percentage, with even staff spacing.

Resizing Staff Systems

If you add many staves to your score, they may end up running beyond the lower page margin. If this is the case, first try respacing the staves so the system takes up less vertical space. If you do this, and find that after all staves fit on the page, there is not enough space between the staves to fit music and/or expressions and other markings, you will need to resize the systems (reduce them). To do this, first respace the staves so there is an adequate amount of space between them. Click the Resize tool, then click an area between two staves in the system. The Resize Staff System dialog box appears, as shown in Figure 7.3.

Figure 7.3
Resize systems and/or staff heights in the Resize Staff System dialog box.

Resize Staff System
┌─ Staff Sizing ─────────────────────────┐
Staff Height: `0.28472` Inches ▼
And Resize System: `100` %
Resulting System Scaling: 85 %
☑ Hold Margins   ☑ Resize Vertical Space
┌─ Staff System Range ───────────────────┐
○ System `1` Through `1`
● System `1` Through End of Piece
☑ Update Page Format
[OK] [Cancel] [Help]

After And Resize System, enter a new percentage. For example, type "80" in this box to reduce the system to eighty percent of its original size. You will probably want to resize all systems in your score at once. In the Staff System Range section, select System 1 Through End of Piece. Click OK to return to the score and review the system reduction. You may need to experiment with several different system reductions to find the one that fits best on the page.

Working with Barlines

When you edit the appearance of barlines, the changes you make automatically apply to all staves in the system. They can also have implications on parts extracted from the score, such as breaking multimeasure rests. To create double, dashed, solid, or other barline styles, first click the Measure tool. Doubleclick a measure to open the Measure Attributes dialog box, as seen in Figure 7.4.

Figure 7.4
Choose a barline style in the Measure Attributes dialog box.

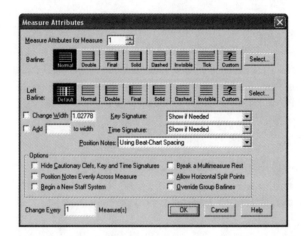

In the top row of barline icons, choose the one you want to use and click OK to return to the score. The new barline appears on all staves at the end of the measure you clicked.

To quickly change barlines, use the Measure tool context menu. Right/Control-click a barline handle to open the context menu (barline handles are located on the top staff). Choose the barline style here to edit the barline instantly.

Creating and Editing Barlines

If you can't find the barline style you want to use, create your own. With the Measure tool selected, double-click a measure to open the Measure Attributes dialog box. In the top row of barline icons, click the right-most option (the Custom Barline icon), then click the Select button beside it. The Shape Selection dialog box appears. Click the Create button. The Shape Designer dialog box appears. Use the tools in this window to design your own custom barline (you can find more information on the Shape Designer in chapter 10). Once you have finished, click OK, Select, and OK to return to the score. Your custom barlines now appear on every staff.

To manage barlines throughout your document, use the Barlines portion of the Document Options. From the Options menu, choose Document Options and select Barlines. The Barline options appear, as seen in Figure 7.5.

Figure 7.5
Make document-wide
settings for barlines in
the Barlines category of
the Document Options.

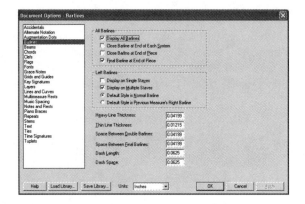

Following are some common ways to edit barlines using the Document Options. These settings apply to barlines throughout the document:

▶ Uncheck Display All Barlines to hide all barlines in the score.

▶ By default, there is usually a final barline at the end of the document. To remove this, uncheck Final Barline at End of Piece.

▶ Check Display on Single Staves to place a barline on the left edge of each system. This is particularly useful for lead sheets.

▶ Use the text boxes to control the thickness of barlines, distance between double barlines and the length and frequency of dashes on dashed barlines.

Adjusting Measure Width

You can use the Measure tool to increase or decrease the width of measures. With the Measure tool selected, click and drag or use the arrow keys to nudge a barline handle horizontally. Notice that music in the measure respaces proportionally in all staves as the width of the measure changes. Also note that note-attached items will also respace along with the notes. You can use this method to give a measure more space for chord symbols, lyrics, expressions, and other note-attached items.

NOTE
You may notice two handles on some barlines. The lower one can be used to assign spacing for beats in the measure with a "Beat Chart." You can find more information on Beat Chart spacing, and other music spacing methods, in chapter 9.

You can also set the width of measures to a specific value. With the Measure tool selected, highlight a measure or number of measures. Then, double-click the highlighted region to open the Measure Attributes dialog box (Figure 7.4). For Change Width, enter the amount of space you would like between barlines in the selected measures. You can also add space between barlines by entering a value for Add_to Width. Click OK to return to the score and review changes. If you don't see a change, your measures may be locked so that they will not reflow across systems (for example, if there are three measures in a system, and you set the measure width for each to .5 inches, Finale needs to be able to reconfigure the number of measures per system to compensate for the extra space. Finale will not adjust the system margins to fit the measure widths you set.). To unlock a system, choose the Mass Edit Tool and highlight the system and adjacent systems. From the Mass Edit menu, choose Unlock Systems. Then, go back and change the measure width with the Measure tool.

TIP
Use the Page Layout tool to adjust system margins.

Adding Double Barlines at Key Changes Automatically

In conventional notation, you will sometimes find a double barline at every key change. In Finale, instead of using the Measure Attributes to add these double barlines for each key change, you can do it for your whole score automatically with the Automatic Barlines plug-in. To apply these changes to a region of your score, choose the Mass Edit Tool, and select a region of your score (for the whole document, no selection is necessary). From the Plug-ins menu, choose Automatic Barlines. Double barlines appear at key changes in the region you selected, or throughout the document.

Customize Staff Viewing: Staff Sets

With large scores, you may not be able to see all staves at the same time while entering or editing your music. Or, to see all your staves, the view percentage needs to be small to effectively work with them. With Staff Sets, you can specify certain staves for viewing and eliminate staves you don't need to see.

To demonstrate this, let's add some more staves to our score. First, select the top trumpet staff so that staves will be inserted above this staff. Click the Staff Menu and choose New Staves (with Setup Wizard). In the Setup Wizard, choose the Woodwinds category. Add a Flute, Oboe, Bassoon, Clarinet in Bb and a Bass Clarinet. For Score Order, click the drop-down/popup menu and choose Concert Band. Click Finish to return to the score. The woodwind parts appear above the brass staves. Now, let's say you are beginning the piece with a flute and tuba duet. Depending on your screen resolution, monitor size, and view percentage, both of these staves may not appear on your screen at the same time (if they do, let's pretend they are spaced too far apart). To isolate the flute and tuba staves for viewing:

1. Move to Scroll View (if you are in Page View). From the View menu, choose Scroll View.

2. With the Staff tool selected, hold down the Shift key and click the handles of the

staves you want to isolate, in this case, the flute and tuba staves. If you can't see the tuba staff, use the scroll bar on the right to move the score vertically.

3. While holding down the Ctrl/Option key, click the View menu.

4. Continue holding down the Ctrl/Option key and choose Program Staff Set > Staff Set 1.

The display now shows the flute and tuba staves only. You can use this view to enter and edit music as you would normally. To see the full score again, from the View menu, choose Select Staff Set > All Staves. You can program up to eight staff sets, each with any number of staves. Select any staff set you program by choosing View > Select Staff Sets.

TIP

For even greater control over staff viewing (including the ability to define a view percentage for your staff sets), try the Patterson Staff Sets plug-in. This plug-in is part of the Patterson Plug-in Collection available for download from Robert Patterson's website at www.robertgpatterson.com and also included on the companion CD-ROM. You can find more information regarding the Staff Sets plug-in in Chapter 15.

Staff Groups

Staves in large scores are often divided into groups of instrumental families (Figure 7.6). All staves in a group are enclosed by brackets to the left of the score. In addition, barlines usually extend through all staves of a group throughout the score.

Figure 7.6
Group brackets

Often, within each group there are also secondary groups, such as the secondary clarinet group in Figure 7.4. Whenever you use the Setup Wizard to begin a new score, Finale will enter these group indications for you automatically. This is also the case while adding several staves to a score with the Setup Wizard (Staff menu > New Staves (with Setup Wizard)). In this section, you will learn how to create your own group definitions and edit the ones Finale creates for you.

We'll start by defining groups for a score from scratch. To prepare for this section, open a new default document (File > New > Default Document). Move to Page View (View menu > Page View). Then, click the Staff tool and from the Staff menu, choose New Staves. Type 3 and click OK. Change your view percentage so all staves are visible (try 50%—View menu > Scale View To > 50%). Also, from the Options menu, choose Measurement Units and make sure Inches is selected.

Adding Groups

To add a group, from the Staff menu, choose Add Group and Bracket. The Group Attributes dialog box appears, as shown in Figure 7.7.

Figure 7.7
Define the enclosed staves, group name, and bracket style for a group in the Group Attributes dialog box.

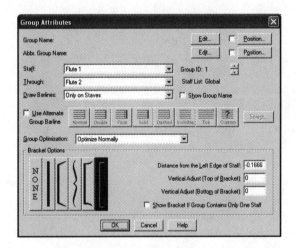

From this dialog box, you will be able to create and manage all group definitions. Let's say we need to create a "Strings" group containing the top four staves.

1. In the Group Attributes, click the Edit button for Group Name. The Edit Text dialog box appears. Type the name of the group here. Type "Strings". In the future, you may want to highlight the text and use the Text menu to edit the font size and style of the group name.

2. Click OK to return to the Group Attributes.

3. Click the Edit button for Abbr. Group Name. Type "Str.".

4. Click OK to return to the Group Attributes.

5. For Staff:, leave the setting [Staff 1] since the top staff in the score is the top staff of our group.

6. For Through:, leave the setting [Staff 4] since it is the bottom staff in our group.

7. For Draw Barlines, leave the setting at Through Staves (this is most common). Use this setting in the future to specify barlines only on staves (for choral music) or Mensurstriche (only between staves) barlines.

8. In the Bracket Options section, choose the style of your bracket. For now, let's choose the bracket second from the right (the straight bracket with curved hooks).

9. Place a checkmark on Show Group Name.

10. Click OK to return to the score.

You will see a bracket (blue by default) to the left of the four staves, and barlines through them. You should also see the text "Strings" to the left of the group bracket on the first system and "Str." to the left of the second system. The abbreviated group name you define in Group Attributes will appear on the second and all subsequent systems.

Now, let's say you want to add a secondary bracket to the top two staves as if they were both violins.

1. From the Staff menu, choose Add Group and Bracket. The Group Attributes dialog box appears. Notice the number for Group ID: is 2. Whenever you choose Add Group and Bracket from the Staff menu, Finale will begin a new group definition. You can use the arrows here at any time to move between group definitions. Text is often unnecessary for secondary group brackets, so we'll leave the Name and Abbr. Name alone.

2. For Staff: leave the setting [Staff 1], since, again, this is the top staff of our group.

3. For Through:, click the drop-down/popup menu and choose [Staff 2], since this is the bottom staff in our group.

4. In the Bracket Options section, choose the right-most bracket (the thin one with perpendicular hooks). This is the most common secondary bracket figure.

5. Finale will always leave the same amount of space between the left edge of the system and the group bracket by default. Since you want this bracket to the left of the existing one, enter a greater value in the Distance from Left Edge of Staff text box. In this case, enter "–0.1666" (inches). You can also adjust the bracket length in this section if necessary, though the defaults should be fine.

6. Click OK to return to the score.

The secondary group bracket appears to the left of the main group bracket. You can use the above methods to enter any number of group and secondary group definitions into a score, specifying the appropriate text, top and bottom staff, bracket style and positioning for each group.

In the score, drag or nudge text and bracket handles to position them manually. To further edit any group bracket, right/Control click its handle and choose Edit Group attributes. The Group Attributes dialog box will open where you can modify its definition.

To delete a group, as well as the barline settings of the group, click its handle in the score and press the Delete key. You can also Right/Control-click a group bracket handle and choose Delete. Hold down the Delete key and drag over any number of group brackets to delete them.

Removing Barlines Between Staves

You can remove barlines between any two staves, regardless of the group definition. To do this, doubleclick the lower of the two staves connected by barlines. The Staff Attributes dialog box appears. Check Break Barlines Between Staves, and click OK to return to the score. Barlines will no longer connect the two staves. Recheck this box to allow barlines between this and the above staff.

Entering Expressions in Multiple Stave Documents

In chapter 3, we described the basics for entering expressions in documents with a single staff. In large scores, you may want to enter an expression so that it appears on many or all staves at once. While entering a measure expression, you can also assign it to all staves, or any number of staves in your score using staff lists. You can even store staff list information to use for any future expression, to save you the trouble of entering it on each staff individually.

To prepare for this section, let's use the same multiple-staff document we have been working with. You could also begin a new document and add three staves. Click the Expression tool. For this section, we'll assume the Expression tool is selected unless specified otherwise.

Assigning Measure Expressions

Let's start by assigning an expression to a measure so that it appears on every staff. With the Expression tool selected, double-click above the first measure of the top staff. The Expression Selection dialog box appears. Double-click an expression and you will see the Measure Expression Assignment dialog box. In the Show On section, choose All Staves and click OK. You return to the score with the expression above each staff. Click and drag a handle to position the expressions uniformly.

Any measure expression you enter with a metatool will appear on all staves automatically. To tell Finale to use measure expressions while entering with metatools, from the Expression menu, choose Metatools: Measure-Attached.

Assigning Measure Expressions to Specific Staves Using Staff Lists

Now, let's say you want to enter an expression in the top two staves only. Double-click the top staff to open the Expression Selection dialog box. Select the Forte expression (make sure Measure Expression is selected at the bottom of this dialog box), then click Select. The Measure Expression Assignment dialog box appears. In the Show On section, select Staff List. Then, click on the dropdown menu and choose New Staff List. You will then see the Staff List dialog box, as seen in Figure 7.8.

CHAPTER 7

Figure 7.8
Assign an expression to
the score and/or parts in
the Staff List dialog box.

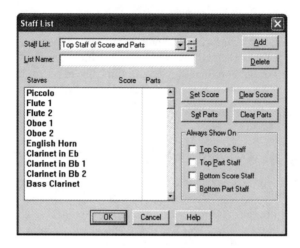

Here, we'll define the list of staves on which we want the expression to appear. For List Name, type "Violin 1 and 2", then click the Add button. These expressions can appear in both the score and parts, so click to place an X under both the Score and Parts column for Staves 1 and 2. Click OK to return to the Measure Expression Assignment dialog box and OK again to return to the score. The expression appears on the top two staves. Click a handle and drag to move them into place.

NOTE

The Parts column in the Staff List dialog box refers to expressions in parts extracted from a score. We'll dive into part extraction in chapter 11.

Now, any time you want to place an expression on staves one and two, you can use the same Staff List. Double-click on the top staff to open the Expression Selection dialog box. Choose the Piano expression and click Select. Now, in the Measure Expression Assignment dialog box, choose Staff List. The staff list you just defined is already selected, so click OK to return to the score. The expression now appears on the top two staves.

You can also easily edit the assignment of existing expressions in your score. Simply right/Control-click an expression handle and choose Edit Measure Expression Assignment. Then, choose All Staves, This Staff Only or Staff List to modify the assignment of the expression. Click OK to return to the score.

TIP

To show expressions that you have specifically assigned to appear in the extracted parts in the staff list, from the Expression menu, choose Display Expressions for Extracted Parts.

CHAPTER 7

Measure Expression Positioning

You have probably noticed that moving any measure expression also moves the corresponding expressions on other staves. To move any measure expression independently, right/Control-click the expression's handle and choose Edit Measure Expression Assignment. Check Allow Individual Positioning and click OK (or check this box while assigning the expression initially). Now, drag or nudge to position each occurrence of the expression individually. If you want to move a number of expressions uniformly, drag-enclose them (or Shift-click each handle), then drag to position all selected expressions.

You can also use the H: and V: parameters in the Measure Expression Assignment dialog box to position expressions to a specific distance from the beginning of the measure or top staff line (as described in chapter 3). Note that if you do this, corresponding expressions in other staves will adjust respectively. In other words, they will remain the same distance apart even if you have checked Allow Individual Positioning.

Copying Measure Expressions

You may want to copy measure-attached expressions to another area of your score, but not the notation. To do this, click the Mass Edit Tool. From the Mass Edit menu, choose Copy Measure Items, then check Measure Expressions and click OK. Next, select the measures (in any staff) containing the measure-attached expressions and drag to the new location (or Ctrl/Option-Shift-click). The expressions will appear in the new measures, and any staff list information is retained (so they appear on the original staves). Edit the staff lists on the copied expressions to edit their staff assignment.

CAUTION

Any time you copy measure expressions between documents, the staff list information will be lost and the expressions will appear on every staff. Either reassign the copied expressions in the staff list of the destination document or enter new ones. Transfer all expressions available in the Expression Selection dialog box between documents by saving and opening an expression library (as described in chapter 3). You can also use the TGTools Modify Expressions plug-in to convert measure-attached expressions to note-attached before copying between documents. Note-attached expressions will copy between documents. You can find the TGTools demo on the companion CD-ROM.

Optimization

In large scores, it is often unnecessary to show all staves on every system. The empty staves in systems are usually removed to "optimize" the amount of music that fits on a page (Figure 7.9). In Finale, you can remove these unnecessary staves by optimizing with the Page Layout tool. In addition to removing empty staves, optimization allows staves in a system to be positioned independently, without affecting the staff positioning in other systems. Also, changes to group definitions in an optimized system will not affect group definitions on any other system. For these, and other reasons (which will be explained in this section), you will want to wait until after you have finished editing the notation of a score before optimizing. Nonetheless, optimization is an important topic to understand in all stages of score preparation.

Figure 7.9
A score before and after optimization—notice the empty staves are removed and groups adjust accordingly.

To prepare for this section, click the Page Layout tool. Note that any time you click the Page Layout tool, you will automatically be moved to Page View. Optimization, and any page layout changes, affect Page View only, and will not have any effect on the representation of the score in Scroll View. We can continue using the same document we have been working on, or you can begin a new default document and add several staves.

Removing Empty Staves in a System

First, make sure there are no entries in the document. If there are, click the Mass Edit Tool, press Ctrl/Command-A, then press Backspace/Clear. Next, click the Simple Entry tool and enter some notes into the top two staves of the first system. Also, enter some notes in the fourth staff of the first system. Let's say we want to remove the third staff in the top system from the score. With the Page Layout tool selected, right/Control-click anywhere within the top system margins and choose Optimize Staff Systems. The Staff System Optimization dialog box appears, as shown in Figure 7.10.

Figure 7.10
Choose systems to optimize, or remove optimization, with the Staff System Optimization dialog box

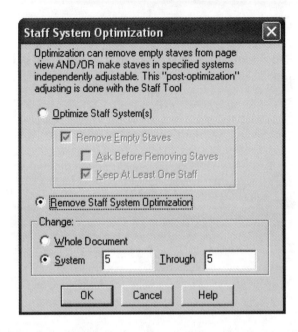

Make sure Optimize Staff Systems is checked. For now, we'll leave the rest of the settings alone. Click OK. You return to the score with the third, and all other empty staves, removed from the top system. You can optimize any number of systems or even the whole document by specifying a system range in the Optimize Staves dialog box.

From the View menu, choose Scroll View. Notice all of the staves remain visible.

CAUTION
If you enter music in Scroll View on a staff that has been removed in Page View as a result of optimization, the staff and notation will remain hidden in the score when you return to Page View. Make sure you have entered all notation into a system before you optimize it, to avoid missing music. If you notice notes in Scroll View that do not appear in Page View, reapply optimization to the appropriate system to add the staff back to the system.

Individual Staff Spacing

Normally, when you use staff handles to position staves vertically, the staff will adjust in every system. You can adjust the vertical staff placement within optimized systems independently. To do this, click the Staff tool. Notice there are two handles on each staff, as shown in Figure 7.11.

Figure 7.11
Spacing staves in
systems independently

Click and drag or use the arrow keys to nudge the lower handle to reposition the staff vertically within that particular system. This will not have any effect on the staff placement in other systems. Use the upper handles to reposition staves in all systems as you would normally.

Groups in Optimized Systems

If you have the document open that we started at the beginning of this chapter, there are still two groups defined. Group brackets will always adjust to include the remaining staves in a group after optimizing a system. Any changes you make to these, or any groups in an optimized system, will not have any effect on other systems. For example, with the Staff tool selected, click and drag the group bracket handles on the top system. Notice there are no changes to the group brackets on the second system. Press the Delete key to delete the group bracket. Again, brackets in other systems are not affected. To reset a system to include the original bracket definitions and staff spacing, optimize the system again or remove optimization on the system.

If there is a piano, harp, or other part in your document that requires more than one staff, you can set the group attributes so that all staves for that instrument will always be optimized together (so that Finale will leave both staves visible if there are any notes in either staff in the system). In the Group Attributes for the part, click the drop-down/popup for Group Optimization, and choose Only Remove if All Staves are Empty.

Removing Optimization

When you remove optimization, all staves return to the system. In addition, staff spacing and group brackets return to their original appearance (i.e. before optimization). Let's remove optimization from the system we have optimized. Right/Control-click the system and choose Optimize Staff Systems. The Staff System dialog box appears. Choose Remove Staff System Optimization and click OK. The system returns to its original appearance before optimization.

Other Tricks for Multiple Stave Scores

Here are some other tricks you can use while working with large scores:

Selecting Specific Playback Staves

In addition to setting a staff to a General MIDI instrument (as described in chapter 2), in large scores, you may want to mute or select certain staves for playback. To do this, from the Window menu, choose Instrument List. The Instrument List dialog box appears. To the right of the list of staves, there are two columns: P (Play) and S (Solo). By default, there will be a box for each staff under the P column, assigning each staff to playback. Click the square box under the P column for any staff to mute it on playback. Click the S column to choose a specific staff for playback and mute others (a circle will appear in the S column). You can select as many "Solo" staves as you want (In a score of twenty staves, just click the S column for the two staves you want to play back, for example, instead of removing eighteen boxes in the P column).

View Several Regions of your Score on the Screen

If you are copying music between remote areas of your score, or referencing a different area during entry, you can avoid having to scroll back and forth between sections by using multiple windows. From the Window menu, choose New Window. A new window appears on your screen with the same score visible. Any changes you make to the score in one of these windows will apply to the other as well (these are just two views of the same score). You can scroll to any region of the score independently, or even set one view to Scroll View and the other to Page View. In Figure 7.12, a staff set has been programmed to the top two staves in the left window, and the full score appears in the right.

Figure 7.12
Use multiple windows to see any combination of views for the same score, or to view more than one document at the same time.

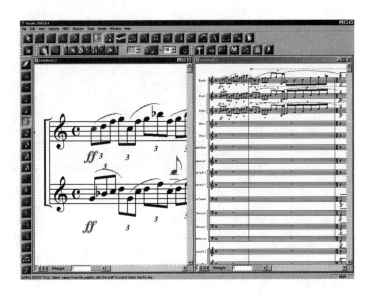

CHAPTER 7

Also, notice the windows in Figure 7.12 fit nicely within the active region of the screen. You can set this automatically by choosing Tile Vertically or Tile Horizontally from the View menu. All open windows will resize and arrange themselves horizontally or vertically on your screen. You can use as many windows as you like to view your score on screen.

Faster Redraw

The more staves and notes you have in a score, the longer it takes Finale to redraw the screen. This can be a nuisance, especially while working in Simple Entry. For faster redraw, try moving to Scroll View, and program staff sets (as described earlier) to eliminate staves from the view that you are not currently working with. The fewer staves, the faster Finale redraws. To cut down the number of times Finale redraws the screen, you could also turn off Automatic Music Spacing from the Edit Menu. Note that if you do this, your music will not respace proportionally as it usually does as you enter music. Finale will recalculate the spacing of all entered music once you turn Automatic Music Spacing back on.

You also have control over the specific items on the screen Finale recalculates during each redraw. To eliminate certain items from redraw, from the View menu, choose Redraw Options. The Redraw Options dialog box appears, as shown in Figure 7.13.

Figure 7.13
Specify items to redraw and make other redraw settings in the Redraw Options dialog box.

In the Draw section, uncheck items you are not concerned about viewing as you work on the document. If you are using multiple windows to view your score, check Redraw Only the Active Window to eliminate background windows from redraw. Sometimes, you will not need the screen to redraw completely; for example, if you are scrolling through your music, you may only need to see the first couple measures. In the Redraw Options, check Allow Redraw Interrupt to stop redraw before Finale has finished redrawing the screen. With this option checked, any click or keystroke will immediately halt redraw.

Add Cue Notes Automatically

While working on a score with many staves, you may want to add cue notes of existing music in another staff. Add cue notes to any number of staves in your score automatically with the Create Cue Notes plug-in. Select the Mass Edit Tool, and highlight the region of your score containing the original notes. From the plug-ins menu, choose Add Cue Notes. The Add Cue Notes dialog box appears, as shown in Figure 7.14.

Figure 7.14
Assign cue notes to staves and edit their appearance in the Add Cue Notes dialog box.

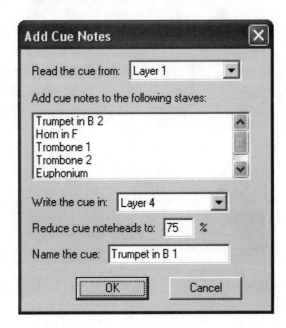

From the drop-down/popup menu, choose the layer of the original music. Then, hold down the Ctrl/Option key and click each staff to which you want to add cue notes. Type the name of the cue notes (the part/staff name of the original notes). Choose the layer you wish Finale to place the cue notes into and click OK. They will also be reduced to 75% of their original size. If you want, you can also change the size of the resulting cue notes in the Add Cue Notes dialog box.

TIP
The Add Cue Notes plug-in will not be able to write cue notes over existing notes in the same layer. In the Add Cue Notes window, be sure to choose to Write the cue notes into a layer that is not being used.

Global Staff Attributes Plug-in

We already have touched on the Global Staff Attributes concerning specific tasks. Note that this plugin is particularly useful while working with large scores. From the Plug-ins menu, choose Global Staff Attributes to display the Global Staff Attributes plug-in, as seen in figure 7.15.

Figure 7.15
Assign staff attributes to several staves at once by using the Global Staff Attributes plug-in.

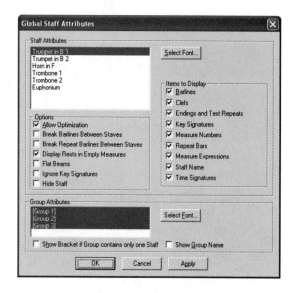

Here, you see many of the options available in the Staff Attributes dialog box. Apply these attributes to many or all staves of your document at once. In the list of staves, select all staves you want to affect (Ctrl/Command-click to choose noncontiguous staves). Then, mark the appropriate checkbox in the Options and Items to Display sections to modify all selected staves.

In the Group Attributes portion of this dialog box, you can apply settings for groups on a global basis as well. Select the group(s) you want to change, and use the check the boxes to show/hide brackets on single staves and show/hide group names for the selected groups. Click the Set Font button to select the font, size, and style for staff names or group names. Click Apply to update your score without leaving the Global Staff Attributes, or click OK to apply settings and return to the score.

Generate a Piano Reduction Automatically

Finale can generate a reduction of any number of staves automatically, and place the results in a grand staff. To create a piano reduction from any score, from the Plug-ins menu, choose Piano Reduction. You will see the Piano Reduction plug-in, as shown in Figure 7.16.

Figure 7.16
Create a piano reduction
for any number of staves
with the Piano
Reduction plug-in.

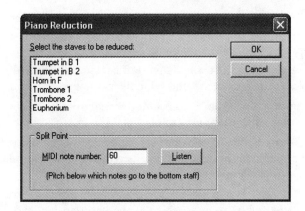

Hold down the Ctrl/Command key and click the staves you want to reduce. You can also click and drag to select contiguous staves. In the Split Point section, enter the MIDI note number of the lowest note in the treble clef staff. Notes in the original staves lower than this number will go into the bass clef staff. Click OK. A grand staff appears below your score with a reduction of the staves you selected. Note that there will probably be some cleanup necessary.

TIP

Finale will quantize to the smallest note duration while generating a piano reduction. If you want to create independent lines of music in the reduction, try using the Move Layers feature to distinguish voices in your staves before running the Piano Reduction plug-in. With the Mass Edit Tool selected, highlight some music, then choose the Mass Edit menu > Move layers. After creating the piano reduction, you may want to move the music back to its original layer on the staves above.

Customizing the Document Setup Wizard

In chapter 2, you learned how to begin a new score with any number of predefined staves by using the Document Setup Wizard. If there are instruments you use regularly that do not exist in the Setup Wizard, you can define your own, then use them at any time while beginning a new document. The information used by the Setup Wizard is stored in the "Instrumen.txt file" located in your Finale/Component Files folder. To customize any of the available staves in the Setup Wizard or to create your own (Note: You can leave any parameter out if you do not care to specify a preference):

1. On your computer, navigate to the Finale folder and open the Component Files folder. Doubleclick on the file named "Instrument.txt". The file will open in a text editor (Figure 7.17).

2. If you are creating a new instrument, begin the entry with [INS:<InstrumentName>] followed by a carriage return. Otherwise, you can edit any existing instrument's existing settings.

3. For Name, (to the right of the = sign), enter the staff name as you would like it to appear in the score. For accidental symbols, use ^flat() for a flat, ^sharp() for a sharp and ^natural() for a natural.

4. For Abbr., enter the abbreviated staff name as you would like it to appear in the score. You can use the same symbols mentioned above for accidentals

5. For useKeySigs, type "1" to use Key Signatures. Type "0" to leave them out (for percussion staves, for example).

6. For Transposition, specify a transposing instrument by typing the number of half-steps up or down from the concert pitch. For example, B flat trumpet sounds down a whole step, so you would enter "–2".

7. For Transclef, type a clef for a transposing instrument. Your options are: treble, bass, alto, treble8vb, percussion, tenor, baritone, bass8vb, frenchviolin, cbaritone, mezzosoprano, soprano, altpercussion, treble8va, bass8va, tabl, or blank.

8. For StaffType, enter the type of staff. Your options are: standard, percussion, single, grand, tab, or organ.

9. For Clef, enter the clef. Your options here are the same as for TransClef.

10. For Patch, type the General MIDI patch number minus 1 (0-127). This controls the playback instrument of the staff. You can find a list of MIDI patches, and their corresponding numbers, in table # (chapter 14).

11. For PercMap, enter the name of a percussion map (either one you have defined, or an existing one). You can also enter a single General MIDI note number. Enclose a percussion map name in quotes if it contains a number.

12. Now, scroll down until you see [GRP:WW] heading.

13. If you created your own staff, enter the instrument name (not the staff name) in one of the groups. These groupings represent the category you will find them in while in the Setup Wizard, as well as how they will be grouped together in the score. If you want, you can even create a new group, or edit the existing ones in this section. The "x" tells Finale to include the instrument in the Setup Wizard list.

14. Now, scroll down to the [ORD:] section.

15. If you created your own staff, enter it in the order you want it to appear in the score. Notice that there are several different score orders. These correspond to the list for Score Order on page 2 of the Setup Wizard.

16. Save the file (File menu > Save).

17. Launch Finale and run the Setup Wizard. The instruments you created or edited will appear among the staff lists on page 2.

8

Alternate Notation, Staff Styles, and Guitar Tablature

In addition to setting up a staff name, clef and transposition for a part, there are also a number of other ways to configure a staff for specific notation styles. You can set up a staff for slash notation, rhythmic notation, or tablature, or change the number of lines on a staff for percussion notation. All of these notation styles can be applied to an entire staff, or they can be applied to any portion of a staff using Staff Styles.

Here's a summary of what you will learn in this chapter:

▶ How to set up a staff for slash, rhythmic and other alternate notations.

▶ How to apply alternate notation to part of a staff only: Staff Styles.

▶ How to create tablature, percussion, and other notation styles.

▶ More on guitar notation and tablature.

▶ How to create a guitar part with TAB.

Staff Setup for Slash, Rhythmic, and other Notation Styles

Any time you want to create notation with slashes, enter one or two bar repeats, or hide the existing music in a staff, you can apply alternate notation to the staff. To prepare for this section, open a new default document (File > New > Default Document). Click the Staff tool. In this section, we'll assume you have the Staff tool selected unless specified otherwise.

Slash and Rhythmic Notation

Slash and rhythmic notation are often used in conjunction with chord symbols to indicate comping, or the background harmonic progression of a piece. This type of notation is particularly common in guitar and piano parts, where rhythm and style take precedence over exact pitches.

In slash notation, there is one slash for each beat of the measure, and usually chord symbols above the staff (Figure 8.1). The precise rhythm is left up to the performer.

Figure 8.1
Apply alternate
notation in the Staff
Attributes to create
slash notation.

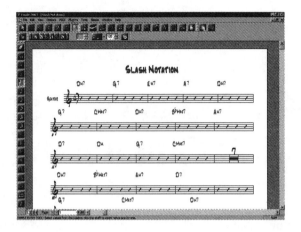

To set up a staff for slash notation with chord symbols:

1. First, use the Simple or Speedy Entry tool to enter rests into the staff on each beat. Finale needs an entry in the staff for the chord symbols you will be entering. If you do not intend to enter chord symbols, skip ahead to step 4. Since we are in common time, enter four quarter rests into the first measure (consult chapter 3 for information on entering rests in Simple or Speedy entry).

2. Click the Mass Edit Tool. Select the first measure and drag it to the second. In the Copy Measure dialog box, enter "20" and click OK. Now, all twenty-one measures of the default document are filled with rests. Of course, in the future you will need to choose the rhythmic value and number of measures specific to the piece on which you are working.

3. Click the Chord tool and enter the chord symbols on any rest you have entered to indicate a harmonic change (see chapter 4 for more information on entering chord symbols).

4. Click the Staff tool and double-click the staff. The Staff Attributes dialog box appears.

5. Click the Select button under Alternate Notation. The Alternate Notation dialog box appears, as shown in Figure 8.2.

Figure 8.2
Choose a type of
alternate notation in the
Alternate Notation
dialog box.

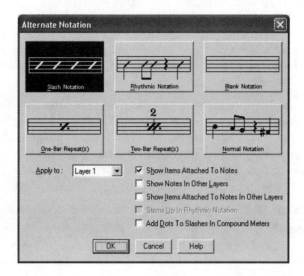

6. Select Slash Notation. In the future, if your piece is in a compound meter, such as 6/8, and you want to add dots to your slashes, check Add Dots to Slashes in Compound Meters. For now, leave this box unchecked.

7. Click OK to return to the Staff Attributes. Notice there is now a check in the Alternate Notation checkbox.

8. Click OK to return to the score. You should now see slashes throughout your staff. To enter or edit existing chord symbols, you can click on the slashes (since there is a rest hidden under each one).

Rhythmic notation is similar to slash notation, but more closely resembles regular notes and indicates the specific rhythmic pattern (Figure 8.3). The slashed notes in rhythmic notation are often used to notate strumming patterns for guitar.

Figure 8.3
Apply alternate notation
in the Staff Attributes to
create rhythmic
notation.

CHAPTER 8

Before we continue, let's remove the slash notation we applied. Double-click the staff, and in the Staff Attributes, uncheck Alternate Notation. Click OK to return to the score with the alternate notation removed. Use the Mass Edit Tool to highlight the measures and the Backspace/Clear key to remove the rest entries and chord symbols. Now, to set up a staff for rhythmic notation with chord symbols:

1. Use the Simple or Speedy Entry tool to enter notes and rests into the staff in the rhythmic pattern you want. With rhythmic notation, the pitch of any notes you enter will convert to standard slashes. Rests will remain rests (consult chapter 3 for information on entering notes and rests in Simple or Speedy Entry).

2. Click the Chord tool and enter any chord symbols (see chapter 4 for more information on entering chord symbols).

3. Click the Staff tool and doubleclick the staff to open the Staff Attributes dialog box.

4. Click the Select button under Alternate Notation to open the Alternate Notation dialog box.

5. Select Rhythmic Notation.

6. By default, Finale will place stems down on rhythmic notation. If you want to change the stem direction, check Stems Up In Rhythmic Notation.

7. Click OK to return to the Staff Attributes and OK again to return to the score. You should now see slashes with stems for each note you entered in the staff and rests wherever you entered a rest.

Since there are underlying notes in the slash and rhythmic notation we applied, you can enter note-attached Smart Shapes or expressions to your slashes as needed. If you want to apply slash or rhythmic notation to only a portion of your staff, apply a Staff Style (we'll talk about Staff Styles soon).

Managing Playback for Staves with Slash or Rhythmic Notation

You will notice that Finale will play back any underlying notes that exist beneath the alternate notation. You may want to eliminate playback of these notes from rhythmic or slash notation. To do this. from the Window menu, choose Instrument List. Click the drop-down/popup menu to the left of the staff with alternate notation. Under the P (Play) column, click the black box to remove playback from any layer. Do the same for chords, or expressions to remove them from playback. Note that this staff is silenced for the entire piece.

Managing Layers in Rhythmic and Slash Notation

If there is more than one layer in the staff that you want to apply alternate notation to, you may want to show the notes in other layers, or items attached to them. For example, you may have a staff that has slash notation throughout, but in a couple of measures, you want standard notation in a different layer to appear as well. To do this, doubleclick a staff and click Select under Alternate Notation. In the Alternate Notation dialog box, choose the layer you want the alternate notation to occupy from the Apply to: drop-down/popup menu (any notes in this layer will be overwritten with the alternate notation). Then, from the checkboxes on the right, choose Show Notes in Other Layers, or Show Items Attached to Notes in Other Layers to display them. Click OK twice to return to the score.

Blank Notation

Blank notation can be used any time you want to hide a layer of notation. This type of alternate notation is often used to hide notes in a layer that you want to use exclusively for playback. For example, you may have notated a trill in layer one and entered the notes as you want the trill to play back in layer four. Use Blank Notation to hide the notes in layer four.

1. With the Staff tool selected, double-click the staff to open the Staff Attributes.

2. Click the Select button under Alternate Notation to open the Alternate Notation dialog box.

3. Choose Blank Notation.

4. From the Apply to: drop-down/popup menu, choose the layer you want to hide; in this case, layer four.

5. Click OK to return to the Staff Attributes and OK to return to the score.

Notes in the layer you specified are hidden in the staff, and will play back. To hide notes and eliminate them from playback, use the H key command in Speedy or Simple Entry (see chapter 3 for details). You can also eliminate playback for any layer of a staff (even one hidden by blank alternate notation) with the instrument list (see the earlier entry "Managing Playback for Staves with Slash or Rhythmic Notation" for steps to remove a layer from playback).

Hide notes with blank notation in any region of a staff, or apply any set of staff attributes to a specific staff region using Staff Styles.

Apply Staff Attributes to Part of a Staff Only: Staff Styles

The alternate notation types described above, as well as any staff attribute, can be applied to part of a staff using Staff Styles. A Staff Style is a collection of staff attributes you can apply to any region of your score. Hide portions of a staff, change the staff transposition, or define any set of attributes for any region using Staff Styles. You can apply one of Finale's preset Staff Styles or create your own.

Let's continue to use the file we've been working with. Double-click the staff to open the Staff Attributes, uncheck Alternate Notation and click OK to return to the score.

Applying a Staff Style

First, let's apply rhythmic notation to a portion of a staff using Staff Styles. This happens to be one of the styles that already exists in Finale's default Staff Style library. With the Staff tool selected, highlight a couple measures of a staff or a partial measure. From the Staff menu, choose Apply Staff Style. The Apply Staff Style dialog box appears, as shown in Figure 8.4.

Figure 8.4
Choose a collection of staff attributes (Staff Style) to apply to a portion of a staff in the Apply Staff Style dialog box.

Select Rhythmic Notation and click OK. The highlighted region of your staff converts to rhythmic notation. You will also see a blue line above the staff. A (nonprinting) blue line will appear above every region of a staff containing a Staff Style whenever the Staff tool is selected.

To easily assign a Staff Style, right/Control-click a highlighted region of your staff and choose the Staff Style you want to apply from the list. You can also apply any Staff Style with a metatool. With a region of a staff highlighted, from the Staff menu, choose Apply Staff Styles. In the Apply Staff Styles dialog box, notice the letter in parentheses to the right of each option. While working with the Staff tool, you can use any one of these letters to apply the corresponding Staff Style to the selected region of the staff.

Apply as many Staff Styles as you like to the same region of a staff. You will see a new blue line appear above the staff for each new Staff Style you apply. If you find yourself applying several Staff Styles to the same region, define your own Staff Style that includes all of the desired attributes. We'll talk about defining your own Staff Style soon.

TIP
To easily define an instrument transposition for a region of your staff, simply highlight the region with the Staff tool, right/Control-click the highlighted region, and choose the transposition. If you don't see the transposition you are looking for, define your own Staff Style (see "Defining a New Staff Style" below).

One- and Two-bar Repeats

One- and two-bar repeats tell the performer to repeat the previous one- or two-bar segment of music (Figure 8.5). In Finale, one- and two-bar repeats are handled with Staff Styles.

Figure 8.5
Use Staff Styles to create one- and two-bar repeats.

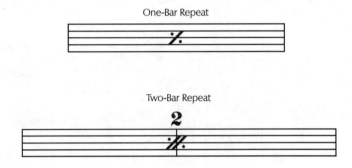

To enter a one- or two-bar repeat, or a number of consecutive one- or two-bar repeats, highlight a region of the staff. Right/Control-click the highlighted region and choose One-Bar Repeat or Two-Bar Repeat. The staff automatically updates to reflect the selection you made. You can also use the metatool "O" to apply a one-bar repeat, or the metatool "T" to apply a two-bar repeat Staff Style to the selected region of a staff.

The Staff Style Library

There are twenty Staff Styles in Finale's default file library. You can use these any time you begin a document with the Setup Wizard, the default file, or one of Finale's templates. If the file you are working on does not contain these preset Staff Styles (such as an older Finale file), you can import them by saving and opening a library. To import the default Staff Style library, from the File menu, choose Open Library or Load Library. Navigate to your Finale folder and open the Libraries folder. Double-click the file "Staff Styles.lib." Now, the default Staff Styles will appear in the context menu and in the Apply Staff Styles dialog box.

Like articulations and expressions, all Staff Styles in a document can be transferred to another by saving and opening a library.

Removing Staff Styles

To remove the Staff Style, highlight any region of a staff containing a Staff Style (refer to the blue lines above the staff) and press Backspace/Clear. You may also right/Control click the highlighted region to open the Staff Style context menu and choose Clear Staff Styles. All staff styles are removed from the highlighted region.

CHAPTER 8

Defining a New Staff Style

If the staff attributes you want to apply to a staff do not exist in the default Staff Style library, create your own. To create your own Staff Style:

1. With the Staff tool selected, from the Staff menu, choose Define Staff Styles. The Staff Styles dialog box appears, as shown in Figure 8.6. This dialog box is almost identical to the Staff Attributes.

Figure 8.6
Define a custom Staff Style in the Staff Styles dialog box.

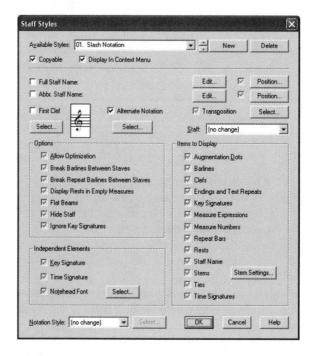

2. Click the New button in the upper right corner.
3. Click in the text box to the right of Available Styles and type a name for your Staff Style.
4. Make sure Display in Context Menu is checked if you want this definition to appear in the Staff Styles context menu.
5. Make any setting you would like to apply to a region of a staff. Change the number of staff lines, the transposition, the clef, or adjust any other parameter. Gray checks in the checkboxes tell Finale to leave the setting alone in the applied region of the staff.
6. Make sure Copyable is checked if you want this Staff Style to be copied via the Mass Edit Tool.

7. Click OK to return to the score.

8. Highlight a region of your staff, then right/Control click the highlighted area to open the Staff Styles context menu. The Staff Style you just defined will appear at the bottom. Choose it to apply your Staff Style to the highlighted region of the staff.

You can also define a new Staff Style by choosing Define Staff Style from the Staff Style context menu, or by clicking the Define button in the Apply Staff Styles dialog box.

To assign a metatool to any Staff Style, hold down the Shift key and press any number or letter on the QWERTY keyboard. The Apply Staff Styles dialog box appears. Choose the Staff Style you want to assign to the number or letter you pressed and click OK. Now, press the metatool number or letter to apply the Staff Style to any selected region of a staff.

Viewing Staff Styles

You have already seen that any Staff Style applied to a region of your staff is indicated with a blue line. However, there is no indication of which Staff Style is applied. To tell Finale to include the name of each Staff Style within this blue line, from the Staff menu, choose Show Staff Style Names. Now, each blue Staff Style indicator line includes the name of the applied Staff Style. Zoom in using the Zoom tool (or the View menu) to see these Staff Style names more clearly. To remove Staff Style names from the blue indicator line, uncheck Show Staff Style Names again from the Staff menu.

While working with the Staff tool, if you want to remove the blue indicator lines, from the Staff menu, choose Show Staff Styles. Check Show Staff Styles again from the Staff menu to display them.

Tablature, Percussion, and Other Notation Styles

In addition to alternate notation, there are a number of other notation styles you may want to use throughout a staff or in a Staff Style. Double-click a staff to open the Staff Attributes. Click the drop-down/popup menu to the right of Notation Style. There are four options here: Standard, Percussion, Note Shapes and Tablature (Figure 8.7).

Figure 8.7
Choose a notation style for a staff from the Notation Styles drop-down/popup Menu of the Staff Attributes.

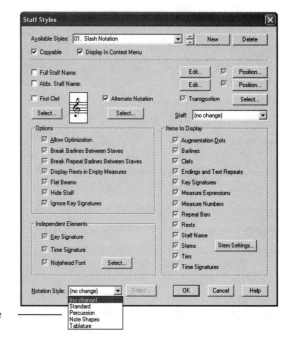

Notation Style ——————
Submenu

Most staves in Finale are in the standard notation style, so this option is usually selected by default. If you intend to create percussion, note shape or tablature notation, choose the corresponding style from this list.

NOTE

When you choose staves for a document with the Setup Wizard, or begin with one of Finale's templates, the notation style for percussion, and tablature staves will be set up for you already.

Percussion

If you are notating for a nonpitched percussion instrument, all of the special parameters, including music font, number of staff lines, and the percussion clef can be set in the Staff Attributes dialog box. If you begin by choosing a percussion staff with the Setup Wizard, many or all of the parameters you want might already exist. If you begin with a new default document, or want to change existing parameters in a percussion staff, use the instructions in this section.

In your score, double-click a staff to open the Staff Attributes dialog box. In most percussion parts, the Key Signature is absent, and a percussion clef appears at the beginning of each staff line. Under Items to Display, uncheck Key Signatures. Note also that accidentals do not appear in percussion staves. If you intend to use a pitched percussion instrument for a portion of the staff later on, you can always apply a Staff Style then include the Key Signature and accidentals. Next, for First Clef, click the Select button. Choose one of the two available percussion clefs and click OK. The clef you chose should appear in the preview window. Again, if you intend to use a pitched instrument for a portion of the staff, you can apply a Staff Style including a nonpercussion clef for any region. Make sure there is no check in the Transposition checkbox.

Changing the Number of Staff Lines

You may want to change the number of staff lines. Many percussion parts contain staves with only one line. To change the number of lines in the staff, click the drop-down/popup menu for Staff: and choose 1-line with Short Barline. This setting will remove all but the middle staff line from the score. Of course, choose any of the other options depending on the part you are defining.

If you want, you can set up a staff to include any number of staff lines. To do this, from the Staff: drop-down/popup menu, choose Other. The Staff Setup dialog box appears, as shown in Figure 8.8.

Figure 8.8
Customize the number and placement of staff lines in the Staff Setup dialog box.

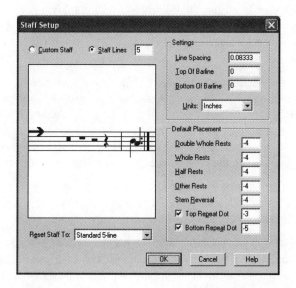

Click the Custom Staff radio button. Then, click the handles to the left of the staff in the preview window to add or remove staves from the custom staff (as seen in the preview window). Adjust the length of the barlines for the staff in the Settings section. For Top Barline, enter the length you want your barlines to extend above the top staff line. For Bottom barline, enter the length you want your barlines to extend below the bottom staff line. Click OK to return to the Staff Attributes.

Specifying a Notehead Font

You can set an independent percussion font for your percussion staff. To do this, in the Independent Elements section of the Staff Attributes, click the Select button for Notehead Font. The Font dialog box appears. To use Finale's standard percussion font, choose Maestro Percussion. You may also want to choose the tamburo font, which is also a percussion font included with Finale (tamburo is an older percussion font.) Of course, you can choose any font on your computer from this dialog box. Click OK to return to the Staff Attributes dialog box.

Percussion Maps

In your percussion staff, you also might want to assign certain noteheads to staff positions and configure your staff for playback using the appropriate percussion sounds. Playback of percussion is unique because each staff line or space will play back a unique percussive sound. You can assign noteheads and configure playback for percussion staves by creating a percussion map.

Before moving on, it is important to understand the purpose of percussion maps. When using a MIDI keyboard for entry, a percussion map allows you to assign a staff position for any key (or MIDI note) struck on the keyboard. In a tonal patch, such as Grand Piano (or any tonal instrument sound), each key on a MIDI keyboard represents a unique pitch. When you strike a key, Finale is wired to automatically place a notehead on the correct staff position (according to the clef, transposition, etc.). In a percussion MIDI patch (or when using channel 10 in General MIDI), each key represents a unique percussive instrument. Without a percussion map assigned to a staff, a key struck very low on a MIDI keyboard will display a notehead well below the staff in Finale. With a percussion map applied to the staff, you can assign a specific line or space in the staff for any key, so a very low key struck on a MIDI keyboard will translate to a notehead on the middle staff line, for example.

When entering into Finale without a MIDI keyboard, percussion maps are important if you want the score to play back properly. Without a percussion map assigned, any note entered on the third space, for example, will sound like a whistle (if you are using General MIDI) because the third space is assigned to MIDI note 72 in Finale. In General MIDI percussion, note number 72 is set to the whistle sound. With a percussion map, you can assign a staff position for any MIDI note, so your score will play back using the desired percussive instrument for each staff line or space.

If you are still in the Staff Attributes, click OK to return to the score. Let's say you want to enter a snare drum part on the middle staff line. To avoid confusion later on, always set up a percussion map before entering notes onto the staff.

1.   First, assign the staff to play back on channel 10 (the standard MIDI percussion channel). From the Window menu, choose Instrument List. Under the Instrument Column, click the drop-down/popup menu for your percussion staff and choose Percussion. The channel for the staff should change to 10.

2.   Close out of the instrument list.

NOTE

If you are using a MIDI keyboard, setting up a percussion map will be easier. Before moving on, from the MIDI menu, choose MIDI thru, then Smart, and click OK. Then, click the Speedy Entry tool and click on the percussion staff. Play a few notes on the keyboard. You should hear percussion sounds. If you do not, make sure you have properly set up your MIDI keyboard with the computer. Also, in the MIDI Setup dialog box (under the MIDI menu), make sure a General MIDI output device is selected. Most sound cards will use General MIDI by default.

3. Click the Staff tool, and double-click the staff to open the Staff Attributes dialog box.

4. For Notation Style, make sure Percussion is selected and click the Select button. The Percussion Map Selection dialog box appears.

5. Choose General MIDI Entry and Playback and click the Duplicate button. Then, click the Edit button. The Percussion Map Designer dialog box appears, as shown in Figure 8.9.

Figure 8.9
Assign a staff position, notehead, and playback note in the Percussion Map Designer dialog box.

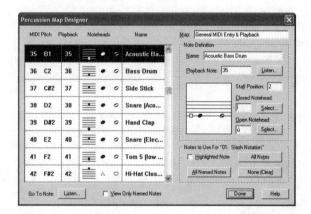

6. In the Map: text box, type the name of your custom percussion map. For now, type "Test Percussion Map."

7. Now, find the percussion instrument you want to define. If you are using a MIDI keyboard, click the Listen button in the lower left corner. The Listen dialog box appears. Press the pitch on your keyboard that sounds like a snare drum (D2).

   If you are not using a MIDI keyboard, use the vertical scroll bar to find, then highlight, Snare (Acoustic). It's MIDI playback note 38.

8. Next, choose the staff position in the fiveline staff preview window. In this case, drag the handle on the note up to the middle staff line. The staff position number represents the number of lines and spaces above the first ledger line below the staff (0). The space below the staff is 1, first line, 2, etc.

9. Under Open Notehead, click the Select button to choose a symbol for noteheads. Do the same for Closed Noteheads. You can do this to select "X"s or any other character from the font you are using (an open notehead will be used for durations of a half note and larger; closed noteheads will be used for durations of a quarter note and smaller).

10. In the Notes to Use section, check Highlighted Note. If this is not checked, Finale will disregard settings you have just made.

11. Click Done, click Select and then OK to return to the score.

12. Now, in Simple Entry, enter a note on the middle staff line and it will play back

CHAPTER 8

as a snare drum. To enter a note on the middle staff line from Speedy Entry, hold down the note on your keyboard that sounds like a snare drum (D2) before typing the rhythmic duration. Finale will place the note on the middle staff line.

13. To add more instrument parts to the percussion staff (setup noteheads and playback for a different staff position), doubleclick the staff to open the Staff Attributes. Click the Select button for Notation Style, and select "Test Percussion Map" (or the name you assigned the map) and click Edit.

Any percussion map you define can be applied to any portion of the staff using Staff Styles. To define a percussion map Staff Style, from the Staff menu, choose Define Staff Style. In the Staff Styles dialog box, click the new button and name the new Staff Style (after Available Styles). Change the Notation Style to Percussion and click the Select button to the right. In the Percussion Map Selection dialog box, choose the desired percussion map and click Select. Click OK to return to the score. Now, apply the Staff Style to use the percussion map for any portion of a staff.

Transfer percussion maps between documents by saving and opening a percussion map library. From the File menu, choose Save Library. In the Save Library dialog box, choose Percussion Maps, click OK, and save the library file. Open the destination document, and from the File menu, choose Open Library. Then, navigate to the library file you saved and double-click it. The new percussion maps will appear in the Percussion Map Selection dialog box.

To save time, you may want to use a percussion map that already exists in your document, or edit one that is similar to what you need in your score. Double-click a staff to open the Staff Attributes—for Notation Style choose Percussion—then click the Select button to the right to open the Percussion Map Selection dialog box. Notice the available percussion maps. To use one of these, click it so it is highlighted, then click the Edit button to the right. Highlight the instrument you want to use, then make sure to check Highlight Note. Do this for all pitches you want to use. If you want to use all the defined instruments/MIDI notes, click All Named Notes. Make any further desired edits to the percussion map, then click Done, Select and OK to return to the score. The percussion map now applies to the staff.

Note Shapes

Some notation, like chant, sometimes uses note shapes for scale degrees. To select note shapes for noteheads in a staff, and to assign them to scale degrees:

1. With the Staff tool selected, double-click a staff to open the Staff Attributes dialog box.

2. Click the drop-down/popup menu for Notation Style, and choose Note Shapes. The Note Shapes dialog box appears, as shown in Figure 8.10.

Figure 8.10
Assign a notehead
character for rhythmic
values and/or scale
degrees in the Note
Shapes dialog box.

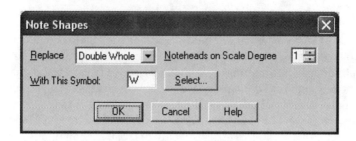

3. Click the drop-down menu for Replace, and choose the notehead type you would like to replace with a shape.

4. Choose the scale degree with the up and down arrows for Noteheads on Scale Degree. Or, click and enter a scale degree in this text box manually. Finale will use the Key Signature of the piece to discern the appropriate note for each scale degree.

5. Click the Select button to choose a shape from the list of characters in your default music font.

TIP
To set the default music font, from the Options menu, choose Set Default Music Font.

6. Repeat steps 2 through 5 for each notehead type and scale degree you want to assign to a shape character.

7. When you have finished assigning note shapes, click OK to return to the Staff Attributes and OK again to return to the score.

8. If you plan to use this notation often, save this file as a template. See chapter 13 for details.

Now, any notes you add in the staff will use the note shapes you assigned. If you want to use note shapes for all staves in your document, from the Options menu, choose Document Options and select Notes and Rests. Check Use Note Shapes and use the same procedure to assign shape characters to notehead types and scale degrees.

The steps above set up shape note notation on a staff by staff basis. If you want to do this globally, go to Options > Document Options and select Note Shapes. Here, you can define shape note notation throughout your document, and even save your note shape settings in a Library.

CHAPTER 8

Guitar Notation and Tablature

This brings us to whole new topic. The tablature notation style is one of many features revised in Finale 2003 as part of a program-wide improvement for notation of fretted instruments. In fact, the Automatic Tablature plug-in, which was previously central to tab notation, has been entirely removed from the software in favor of improvements to the Staff, Simple Entry and Mass Edit Tools. In this section, you will learn how to begin a new score for guitar with tablature, and create one from scratch. Also, we'll cover how to enter fret numbers, bends, hammer-ons, pull-offs, and other items specific to tablature notation.

Setting up a Tablature Staff

If you are beginning a new document, and plan to include any fretted instrument (guitar, lute, dulcimer, etc.), use the Document Setup Wizard. From the File menu, choose New, and then Document With Setup Wizard. Page one of the Setup Wizard appears. Type the composer, title and copyright (as necessary), and click Next to move to page 2. Now, in the left column, choose Fretted Instruments. A list of fretted instruments and TAB appears there, as shown in Figure 8.11.

Figure 8.11
Choose a fretted
instrument and
corresponding TAB staff
on page 2 of the Setup
Wizard.

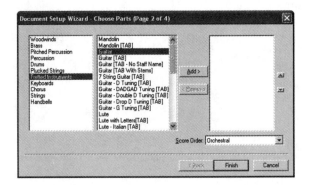

Double-click the fretted instrument you would like to use so it appears in the third column. For now, double-click Guitar. Then, double-click its corresponding TAB staff; in this case, Guitar [TAB]. Each type of TAB staff is designed to accommodate for string tuning, number of strings and number of frets for its accompanying fretted instrument. You should now see Guitar and Guitar [TAB] in the third column. Click Next to set up the time and Key Signature for you piece. Click Next again to choose the tempo, pickup measure and music font, then click Finish to generate the score. The notation and TAB staves appear in your new custom document. Now, let's enter some tablature notation.

Entering Tablature

There are a number of ways to enter tablature into a TAB staff. You can copy music from a notation standard staff, enter directly into a TAB staff with Simple or Speedy Entry, or use a MIDI guitar for entry into a TAB staff. Let's start by demonstrating the easiest: copying notation directly into a tablature staff from a standard notation staff.

Copying Music to a TAB Staff

We'll assume you have a score with both standard and tablature notation open. If not, go back to the previous section and create a new score with the Setup Wizard containing a notation and tablature staff. For the remainder of this section, we'll refer to the regular five-line staff as the "notation staff" and the tablature staff as the "TAB staff."

1. Select the Simple Entry tool.

2. Enter the melody seen in Figure 8.12 into the first three measures of the notation staff (you can find information of Simple Entry in chapter 3).

Figure 8.12
Use the Mass Edit Tool to copy notation to a TAB staff, and vice versa.

3. Click the Mass Edit Tool.

4. Click the first measure of the notation staff so it is highlighted. Then, hold down the Shift key and click the third measure. Measures one through three of the notation staff should be highlighted.

5. Click within the highlighted area and drag down over the first three measures of the TAB staff. When you see black boarder around the first three measures of the TAB staff, release the mouse button. The Change Lowest Fret dialog box appears.

6. Click OK. The TAB staff now contains fret numbers that correspond to the above notation.

You can also copy existing tablature into a notation staff. To demonstrate, highlight measure one in the TAB staff. Then, drag the highlighted area to measure four of the notation staff. Click OK and you will see the notes appear in the notation staff.

Now, while copying to a TAB staff, you may want to indicate that the notes should be played higher on the fretboard. For this reason, the Change Lowest Fret dialog box appears (Figure 8.13) any time you copy from a notation staff into a TAB staff (as you saw in the previous steps).

Figure 8.13
Specify the lowest fret
for music copied to a
TAB staff in the Change
Lowest Fret dialog box.

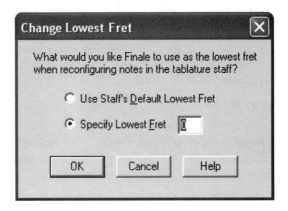

In this dialog box, you can specify the lowest fret, and Finale will distribute the fret numbers to the appropriate strings. Let's use the same document we have been working with to demonstrate this.

1. Select the Mass Edit Tool.
2. Click to the left of the notation staff to highlight the entire staff.
3. Click within the highlighted area and drag down over the TAB staff (yes, right over the existing music). The Change Lowest Fret dialog box appears.
4. For Lowest Fret, enter "5".
5. Click OK. The tablature now recalculates with fret numbers on new strings, all on fret five or above.

As we saw in this example, you can copy over existing tablature, or an empty TAB staff. Finale will recalculate the tablature each time you do this to account for any changes in the notation staff and the value you set in the Change Lowest Fret dialog box.

You can also change the lowest fret of any region of a TAB staff independently. To do this, click the Mass Edit Tool and highlight a region of the TAB staff. Then, from the Mass Edit menu, choose Utilities > Lowest Fret. The Change Lowest Fret dialog box opens. Enter the new lowest fret and click OK to modify the highlighted region of the TAB staff.

Entering TAB with Simple Entry

You can also enter fret numbers directly into a TAB staff with the Simple Entry tool. Click the Simple Entry tool. Under the Simple menu, make sure Select Fret Numbers on Entry is checked. Select a note duration from the Simple Entry Palette and click in a TAB staff. By default, you will see a "0" appear in the score, and it will be selected. Simply type the fret number using the number keys on your keyboard. Press the up and down arrows to move the fret number up or down a string and the number will adjust accordingly (to represent the same pitch). Use the left and right arrows to move the selection horizontally between fret numbers. Ctrl/Option-click any fret number to select it.

TIP

While entering fret numbers into a TAB staff, Finale will warn you if a fret number is beyond the range of a string by turning it orange. If it is below the range of the string, you will also see a – (minus sign) preceding the fret number. If a fret number is orange, try moving it to a different string, changing the string tuning, changing the default lowest fret of the staff, or changing the number of frets in the staff. You can find information on how to do all of this later in this chapter.

Entering TAB with Speedy Entry

If you decide to enter fret numbers into a TAB staff with Speedy Entry, there are a couple things to know. First of all, you will not be able to see the TAB staff in the Speedy Frame, only a standard fiveline staff (in treble clef, an octave up, by default). As you enter notes, only the notation appears (and no fret numbers) until the frame leaves the measure. For this reason, it is recommended to use only Speedy Entry to enter TAB if you are using a MIDI keyboard. As long as you are using a MIDI keyboard, you can enter into a TAB staff just as you would normally (see chapter 3 for more information about Speedy Entry).

While entering into a TAB staff with Speedy Entry, you may want to adjust the clef of the staff visible in the Speedy Frame, so the notes you are entering are visible. To do this, click the Staff tool, then doubleclick the TAB staff. In the Staff Attributes, click the Select button next to the Notation Style: drop-down/popup menu to open the Tablature Staff Attributes. Then, click the Edit Instrument button. Click the Speedy Clef button to open the Clef Selection dialog box, where you can choose the clef for your Speedy Frame. Choose the clef you would like to use, then click OK all the way back to the score. Now, click the Speedy Entry tool and enter some notes into the TAB staff. The notes you play on your MIDI keyboard will translate to the staff lines corresponding to the clef you chose. When the frame advances to the next measure, the fret numbers appear.

Entering TAB with a MIDI Guitar

In chapter 4, we covered the basics for entering music into Finale with a MIDI guitar. You can enter into a TAB staff just as you would a standard notation staff by using the HyperScribe tool. When you do this, Finale can even record the correct string you play and place fret numbers on the appropriate TAB line. Finale can distinguish between strings because each string is set to a different MIDI channel. Your guitar to MIDI interface will send the MIDI data to Finale on specified channels. You can coordinate the MIDI string channels assigned on your guitar to MIDI interface with Finale by editing the MIDI Channels for Tablature dialog box (Figure 8.14).

Figure 8.14
Coordinate MIDI notes to strings in the MIDI Channels for Tablature dialog box.

First, check the guitar to MIDI interface device to see which channel is assigned to each string. Consult the MIDI interface's instruction manual for information on how to assign and view the string channels. Then, assign the corresponding channel for each string in the Tablature MIDI Channels dialog box (located under the MIDI menu). Now, Finale will be able to translate your performance properly into a TAB staff.

Adding Tablature Markings

Beyond fret numbers, there are several other figures standard in tablature notation. These include bends, releases, tremolos, hammer-ons, hammer-offs, and tab slides.

Entering Bends and Releases

In tablature, bends are usually indicated with a curved line pointing up and text indicating the pitch variation from the original note. A bend can be followed by a release, telling the performer to "bend back down" to the original pitch. You can see an example of a bend and release in Figure 8.15.

Figure 8.15
Easily create a bend and release with the Guitar Bend tool.

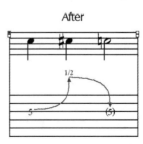

Creating these in Finale is easy with the Guitar Bend Smart Shape:

1. First, enter three fret numbers on a string, "5," "6," then "5" again (as in the "Before" example in Figure 8.15). Then, click the Smart Shape tool.

2. In the Smart Shape Palette, choose the Guitar Bend tool.

3. Double-click the first "5" you entered (then press Ctrl/Command-D to redraw). Notice Finale creates the bend, adds the "_" text and hides the second fret number. Any time you create a new guitar bend, Finale will add text corresponding to the pitch variation of the fret numbers (whole step=1, minor third= 1 _, etc.).

4. Now, doubleclick on the hidden fret number and redraw the screen (it should be on the same TAB line directly under the _ text). Finale creates a release for you automatically, and parenthesizes the destination fret number.

To create a quarter bend, Ctrl/Option-double-click on any fret number.

You can also generate bends and releases automatically by copying any music from a standard notation staff into a TAB staff that contains a bend hat Smart Shape. Finale automatically takes into account the pitch variation.

Use the primary handle to reposition the entire guitar bend, or use the small diamond arrows to reposition the end points. You can set the default placement for your bends in the Smart Shape Placement dialog box. From the Smart Shape menu, choose Smart Shape Placement. From the drop-down/popup menu on the upper left, choose Guitar Bend. You will see a list of three options for default placement of guitar bends (Figure 8.16).

Figure 8.16
Edit the default placement of guitar bend Smart Shapes in the Smart Shape Placement dialog box.

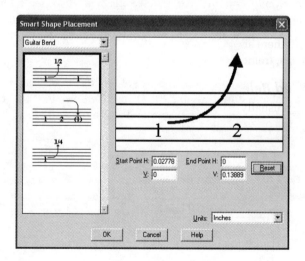

CHAPTER 8

Drag the figure in the preview window to reposition the default appearance of bends, releases and quarter bends. Changes here will apply to all new guitar bends you enter, as well as all existing guitar bends that have not been manually repositioned.

In addition to placement, you can manipulate other default characteristics of the guitar bend Smart Shapes with the Guitar Bends Options. From the Smart Shape menu, choose Guitar Bend Options. The Guitar Bend Options dialog box appears, as shown in Figure 8.17.

Figure 8.17
Make settings for
default text,
parentheses, and other
attributes of
guitar bends in the
Guitar Bend Options
dialog box.

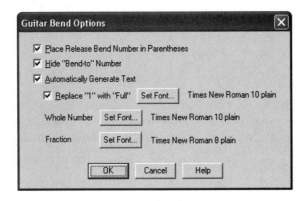

Here, choose Finale's default behavior while entering guitar bends. You can tell Finale to place release bend numbers in parentheses, hide the "Bend-to" number, and automatically generate text. You saw Finale do all of these things in the above example. They are all turned on by default. Changes here apply to all guitar bends in the score, as well as newly created ones. Sometimes, the text "Full" is used to indicate a bend of a whole step instead of the number "1". Check Replace "1" with "Full" to use "Full" for any guitar bend of a whole step. Then, click the Set Font button if you want to modify its font, size, or style. Also, set the font, size, and style for whole numbers and fractions by clicking the corresponding Set Font button at the bottom of this dialog box. Click OK to return to the score and review any settings you made.

Tremolos and Tab Slides

Like guitar bends, tremolos and tab slides can be entered as Smart Shapes. Tab slides tell the performer to slide to a note without leaving the string. Tremolos are used to tell the performer to add vibrato to the pitch. You can see an example of a tremolo and tab slide in Figure 8.18.

Figure 8.18
Create tab slides with
the Tab Slide tool and
tremolos with the Trill
Extension tool.

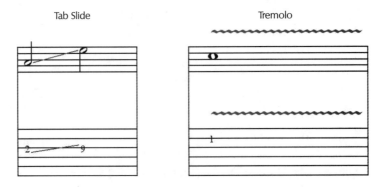

Simply double-click a note or fret number with the Tab Slide tool selected to extend a tab slide to the next note or fret number. When you copy regular notation that contains tab slides into a tablature staff, the tab slides copy with it. In the tablature staff, tab slides will always begin near the bottom of the first fret number and slant upwards to end near the top of the second fret number (since tab slides will always appear between fret numbers on the same TAB line).

To enter a tremolo above a staff, use the glissando Smart Shape. Click the Glissando tool in the Smart Shape Palette. From the Smart Shape menu, choose Attach to Measures. Now, Ctrl/Option-click the Glissando tool. The Smart Line Style Selection dialog box appears. Choose the wavy line without text and click Select. Now, hold down the Shift key (to constrain dragging), click and drag above the staff to create the tremolo.

Entering Hammer-ons and Pull-offs

Hammer-ons tell the performer of a fretted instrument to temporarily "capo" a string with one finger, and use another for the next fret number. A pull-off tells the performer to release the top fret position to sound the lower of the two pitches. You can see an example of a hammer-on and pull-off in Figure 8.19.

Figure 8.19
Add hammer-ons and
pull-offs with the
Custom Line tool.

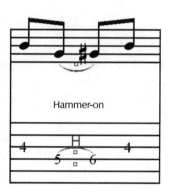

CHAPTER 8

To enter a basic hammer-on, or pull-off requires a regular Smart Shape slur. Click the Slur tool in the Smart Shape Palette. From the Smart Shape menu, select Attach to Notes. Then, double-click a fret number to extend the slur to the next fret number. You now have a basic hammer-on or pull-off figure. To add accompanying text for hammer-ons ("H") or pull-offs ("P"), as shown in Figure 8.19, use one of Finale's preset custom shapes. To do this:

1. Ctrl/Option-click the Custom Line tool to open the Smart Line Style Selection dialog box.
2. Scroll down and click to highlight the "H" or "P" custom line. These are basically hidden Smart Shape Lines with attached text.
3. Click Select to return to the score.
4. Double-click on the first of two fret numbers and drag to the right until the "H" or "P" appears in the desired location.

Entering Picking Figures

It is common to see picking indicators in tablature that tell the performer which direction to pluck the string or strings (Figure 8.20).

Figure 8.20
Use articulation to specify picking.

For these, use articulations. Click the Articulation tool, then double-click a fret number. The Articulation Selection dialog box appears. Choose either the up pick marking (#19) or the down pick marking (#20) and click Select. You return to the score with the marking above the staff directly above the fret number you clicked. For more information regarding adding articulations, see chapter 3.

Editing TAB staves

There are a number of ways to modify existing tablature staves in a document. You can add stems and beams to fret numbers in a staff, change the default lowest fret for a specific fretted instrument, change the string tuning, or even customize the pitch variation between frets for diatonic fretted instruments such as dulcimer.

To make general settings for any TAB staff, click the Staff tool, and doubleclick the TAB staff to open the Staff Attributes dialog box. Click the Select button next to Notation Style to open the Tablature Staff Attributes, as seen in Figure 8.21.

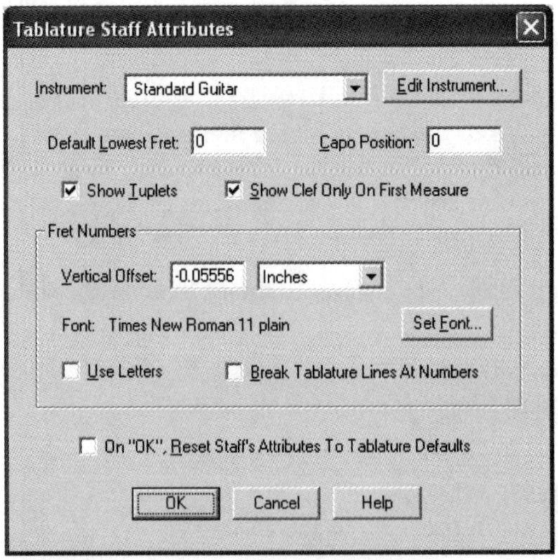

Figure 8.21
Set up a TAB staff for use with any fretted instrument in the Tablature Staff Attributes dialog box.

Tablature Staff Attributes

Instrument: Standard Guitar ▼   Edit Instrument...

Default Lowest Fret: 0   Capo Position: 0

☑ Show Tuplets   ☑ Show Clef Only On First Measure

Fret Numbers

Vertical Offset: -0.05556 Inches ▼

Font: Times New Roman 11 plain   Set Font...

☐ Use Letters   ☐ Break Tablature Lines At Numbers

☐ On "OK", Reset Staff's Attributes To Tablature Defaults

OK   Cancel   Help

Here, click the Instrument: drop-down/popup menu to choose from a number of predefined fretted instruments. Each one contains a different string tuning. Choose the instrument you are writing for here so fret numbers will display properly. You can also create your own custom instrument (we'll explain how to do that soon).

The Default Lowest Fret and Capo settings dictate the lowest fret number you want to allow in the TAB staff with which you are working. In the Fret Numbers section, you can change the font and vertical placement of your fret numbers. If you want to use Finale's default TAB settings in its Staff Attributes, make sure On "OK", Reset Staff Attributes To Tablature Defaults is checked before clicking OK. If this box is checked, when you click OK, all of the settings in the Staff Attributes (number of staff lines, staff line spacing, items to display, etc.) will reset so your TAB staff will appear as it would after creating it with the Setup Wizard. If you have changed settings in the Staff Attributes, and do not want these settings to be reset, leave this box unchecked and click OK. If you have changed any settings in your Tablature Staff Attributes, which affects the number of strings in your TAB staff, then you must check "On 'OK' Reset Staff's Attributes To Tablature Defaults" in order to see the changes in your document (as the number of lines on the staff is directly linked to Staff Attributes.) This includes selecting a different instrument that contains a different number of strings in the Tablature Staff Attributes, or editing the number of strings of the current instrument by clicking Edit Instrument.

Add Stems and Beams

To tell Finale to add stems and beams to fret numbers in a tablature staff, do the following:

1. Click the Staff tool.
2. Double-click the TAB staff to open the Staff Attributes.
3. In the Items to Display section, click the Stem Settings button to the right of Stems. The Staff Stem Settings dialog box appears, as shown in Figure 8.22.

Figure 8.22
Customize stems for a specific staff in the Staff Stem Settings dialog box.

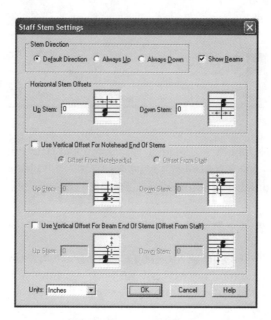

4. Here, specify how you want your stems to appear in the score. Choose the stem direction, placement, and whether or not to show beams. If you want to use Finale's default TAB stem settings, you can leave these parameters as they are.

5. Click OK to return to the Staff Attributes.

6. Click OK to return to the score. Stems and beams appear in the TAB staff reflecting the settings in the Staff Stem Settings dialog box.

Create a Custom Fretted Instrument Definition for your TAB Staff

If you are using an instrument in your score that requires a special number of strings or string tuning, you can define your own fretted instrument. To do this:

1. Click the Staff tool.

2. Double-click the TAB staff to open the Staff Attributes.

3. Click the Select button next to Notation Style to open the Tablature Staff Attributes.

4. Click the Edit Instrument button in the upper right to open the Fretboard Instrument Definition dialog box, as seen in Figure 8.23.

Figure 8.23
Specify tuning, number of strings and number of frets for a fretted instrument in the Fretboard Instrument Definition dialog box.

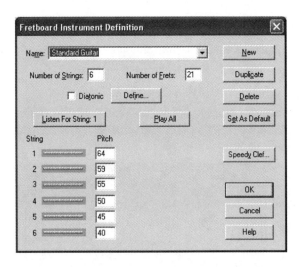

5. Click the New button to begin a new Instrument Definition. Then, click in the Instrument text box to enter a name for your custom instrument.

6. Enter the number of strings on your fretted instrument in the Number of Strings text box.

7. Enter the number of frets on your fretted instrument in the Number of Frets text box.

8. Now, specify the pitches for each open string as MIDI notes. If you are using a MIDI keyboard (or other external MIDI device), simply click in the text box for a string, click the Listen button, and then play the open string pitch. Repeat for

each string on your instrument. If you do not have a MIDI keyboard, click in each text box and enter the MIDI note number that corresponds to each open string (60 = middle C). Click the Play All button to hear the pitches you've assigned.

9. If you are creating an instrument with a nonchromatic fretboard (dulcimer, for example), click the Define button to open the Diatonic Instrument Definition dialog box, as seen in Figure 8.24. If you are not creating an instrument with a diatonic fretboard, skip to step 12.

Figure 8.24
Specify fret tuning in the Diatonic Instrument Definition dialog box.

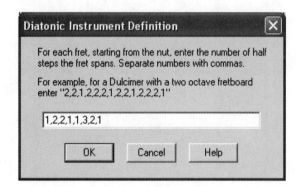

10. Enter the pitch variation between each fret here. Enter "1" for a half-step, "2" for a whole step, "3" for a minor third, etc. For example, if you want a note played on the first fret to sound a whole step higher than the open string, enter "2" as the first number. Separate each entry with a comma.

11. Click OK to return to the Fretboard Instrument Definition dialog box.

12. Click OK. In the Tablature Staff Attributes box, be sure to check On 'OK', reset Staff's Attributes to Tablature Defaults. Click OK twice to return to your score. Your TAB staff now contains the number of strings you specified. Any music you copy to the TAB staff will accurately reflect the string tuning, fret tuning, and number of frets for the instrument you defined.

Creating a Guitar Part with TAB

Let's use the skills we have learned in this chapter (and previous chapters) to create a guitar part with TAB, chord symbols, and custom fretboard diagrams.

Finale 2003 comes with some nice guitar templates. We'll use one of these to begin. From the File menu, choose New > Document from Template. In the Finale/Templates folder, double-click the Tablature Templates folder to open it. Then, double-click the file "House Style 3." A new document appears containing a standard, and TAB staff. In the future, if you are creating a score for another fretted instrument, use the Document Setup Wizard to choose from a variety of fretted instruments with other string tunings.

Now, use the following steps to create a short guitar score with TAB. After following these steps, your document should look like this (Figure 8.25):

Figure 8.25
Guitar notation example with TAB (you can also find this example as a Finale file in the Music Examples folder on your companion CD-ROM).

Before going through the following steps, I recommend opening and printing the file "Guitar Example" located on the companion CD-ROM. Then, refer to this printout as you go over these steps.

1. First, we'll add the title and composer. From the File menu, choose File info. The File Info dialog box appears. For Title, enter "Guitar Example". Then, for composer, enter "Arr. by" followed by your name. Click OK to return to the score.

2. This piece is in the key of A major, so we'll need to change the key. Click the Key Signature tool and double-click the first measure. The Key Signature dialog box appears. To the right of the preview display, click the up arrow three times so the key of A (with three sharps) is displayed. Then, click OK to return to the score.

3. Now, enter the notation into the standard (top) staff using any of the available entry methods. Use the Smart Shape tool to enter the slurs and TAB slides. If you own a MIDI guitar, you could also use HyperScribe to enter the music into the standard or TAB staff (see "Entering TAB with a MIDI Guitar" above). When you get to measure nine, use the TAB slide Smart Shape to add the TAB slides on beat four.

4. After you have entered the notation, click the Mass Edit Tool. Click to the left of the standard (top) staff so the entire staff is highlighted. Now, dragclick in the highlighted area and drag down into the TAB staff. Release the mouse button. The Lowest Fret dialog box appears. Click OK. Fret numbers for each note now appear in the TAB staff.

5. In this template, you may want to move the fret numbers down a bit so they are more centered on the line. To do this, click the Staff tool, then double-click the TAB staff. In the Staff Attributes, click the Select button at the bottom (to the right of Tablature). The Tablature Staff Attributes dialog box appears. In the Fret Numbers section, for Vertical Offset, enter "-0.05" inches. Then click OK twice to return to the score.

6. Click the Mass Edit Tool and press Ctrl/Command-A to Select All. Then, from the Mass Edit menu, choose Fit Music. Type 4 and click OK. Now, there are four measures per system. To delete the extra measures, click measure 17 so it is highlighted, hold down the Shift key and press the right arrow button, then press the Delete key.

7. Click the Simple Entry tool. Notice the third beat of measure three contains fret numbers on the B and E strings. Ctrl/Command-click and drag these down a string. Notice the numbers update accordingly. Also, do this to modify the fret numbers in measure seven, ten, thirteen, and fifteen so they appear as shown in Figure 8.25 (and/or in your example printout).

8. Click the Smart Shape tool. To enter the "Let Ring" indications, Ctrl/Option-click the Custom Line tool in the Smart Shape Palette. The Smart Line Style Selection dialog box appears. Scroll down and click to highlight the "Let Ring" smart line. Click Select. Now, double-click and drag in the score to enter the Let Ring indications.

9. Now, we'll enter the hammer-ons and pull-offs. Click the Smart Shape tool, then click the Slur tool in the Smart Shape Palette. In measure four, beats three and four, notice the slurs didn't carry over from the standard staff. Double-click the lower "2" on the third beat. The slur actually is now overlapping the slur above. Click the handle on the slur attached to the top "2" on the third beat. Then, press and hold the down arrow key to nudge it over the lower fret numbers. Do the same for the fret numbers on the fourth beat. To place the letter "H" above the slur, click the Ctrl/Option-click the Custom Line tool to open the Smart Line Style Selection dialog box. Scroll down and click the H smart line to highlight it, then click Select. Click the first note of the hammer-on and drag the second. Notice the H appears above and between the two fret numbers. Now, we need to enter pull-offs in measures eight and twelve. Click the Slur tool again and double-click the fret number on the "and of two" in measures eight and twelve. Now, to add the P, ctrl/Option-click the Custom Line tool again, but this time, choose the P smart line and click Select. Double-click the fret number on the "and of two" in measure eight and drag to the next fret number. Do the same in measure twelve.

10. Now, enter the chord symbols (as described in chapter 4). Then, to show fretboard diagrams, from the Chord menu, choose Show Fretboards. When you get to measure three, notice the fretboard diagrams shown in Figure 8.25 are slightly

different. To add the thumb indication on the low E string, create a custom fretboard diagram. With the Chord tool selected, right/Control-click the chord symbol handle and choose Edit Chord Definition. In the Fretboard section, click Select, then click Create. The Fretboard Editor appears. Click the T tool and then click the second fret E string to place the T on the fretboard diagram. Then, click OK, Select and OK to return to the score. Now, the second fretboard diagram in measure three is quite different than the default fretboard. Right/Control-click the second chord symbol handle in measure three and choose Edit Chord Definition. In the Fretboard section, click Select, then click Create. Now, use the available tools to create the new freatboad (as shown in Figure 8.26). This chord will need to be fingered higher on the fretboard, so in the Fretboard Number section, check Show, and then for Number, enter "4". The Fretboard Editor dialog box should now look like Figure 8.26. Click OK, Select and OK to return to the score. Your custom fretboard now appears above the staff. Use the same method to create custom fretboards as necessary for the remaining measures (you won't have to create the same fretboard twice for the same chord; just choose the one already created in the Fretboard Selection dialog box by clicking Select in the Fretboard section of the Chord Definition dialog box).

Figure 8.26
Use the Fretboard Editor to quickly edit fretboard diagrams in your score.

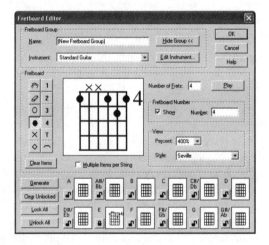

11. Now, you may notice the chord symbols overlap, particularly in measure fifteen. To resolve this, from the Options menu, choose Document Options, then select Music Spacing. Under Avoid Collision of, check Chords and click OK. Your music adjusts to avoid collision of chord symbols.

12. Now, click the Page Layout tool. From the Page Layout menu, choose Space Systems Evenly and click OK. Make any other changes to the layout as necessary.

If you like, play back the piece for review. If you want to disable chord playback, click the Chord tool, and then, from the Chord menu, uncheck Enable Chord Playback. You can use the general method above at any time while creating a guitar part with TAB. If a guitar part you are writing requires slash or rhythmic notation, look at the beginning of this chapter under "Staff Setup for Slash, Rhythmic, and Other Notation Styles" for more information.

9

Editing Your Music

One of the great advantages of creating music notation with a computer is the ability to make large-scale changes to an existing score. If, after finishing a score, you find that one of your articulations or note-expressions is the wrong character, font, size or style, you can change every one in seconds in a score of any size (using the Mass Edit Tool). Or, perhaps you need to change all G sharps in a certain motif of a score to A flats. Again, it can be done in seconds (with the Note Mover tool). The number of possible changes you might need to make to specific regions, or the whole score, are endless. In this chapter, you will learn the most common ways to change existing notation in any sized score.

Here's a summary of what you will learn in this chapter:

▶ How to copy and clear music
▶ How to change music en mass (transpose, edit entry items, move pitches, etc.)
▶ How to space your music
▶ How to change and manage fonts

Copying and Clearing Music

As we briefly covered in chapter 2, you can copy music from a selected region of your score to any other region with the Mass Edit Tool. As basic as this concept seems, there are a variety of ways to copy music depending on what you want to move (everything, just notes, just expressions, etc.), and where you want to move it (across staves, across documents, across programs). You may also need to perform more advanced operations, like search and replace for specific pitches, or find similar rhythmic passages to apply articulations and expressions consistently. In this section, we'll cover a variety of ways to move and change music with the Mass Edit and Note Mover tools.

The first step to copying will always include selecting a region. For information on selecting measures and partial measures, see chapter 2 under "Selecting Regions."

Methods of Copying

We already discussed the basics for cutting, copying, replacing, and inserting music in chapter 2. This might be a good time to go back and review these basics before moving on, as the topics in this chapter expound on those concepts. Here, we'll use the same methods previously described to select measures/partial measures, and copy music (drag-copy, Ctrl/Option-Shift-click copy, etc.). You'll learn how these methods also apply to copying specific items from any selected region and copying across documents.

To prepare for the following instructions, open a new default document (File menu > New > Default Document).

Copying Single Layers

You can isolate any layer for copying by showing the active layer only. First, choose the layer you want to copy from the Layer selection buttons/popup menu in the lower left corner of the screen. Then, from the View menu, choose Show Active Layer Only. Now, copy the music as you would normally. Only the layer that displays will be copied. Also, music in other layers in the destination measures will not be affected.

TIP

Move music from one layer to another with the Mass Edit Tool. Choose the Mass Edit Tool, highlight a region of music, then, from the Mass Edit menu, choose Move Layers. Note that this method will not combine music into one layer. If there is music in the destination layer, it will be replaced.

Selecting Specific Items to Copy

By default, when you copy music within a document, Finale copies everything (notes, expressions, articulations, Smart Shapes, etc.). You can isolate any entry item or measure-attached item for copying. To copy measure-attached items:

1. Click the Mass Edit Tool.

2. From the Mass Edit menu, choose Copy Measure Items. The Measure Items dialog box appears as shown in Figure 9.1.

Figure 9.1
Specify measure-attached items to copy in the Measure Items dialog box.

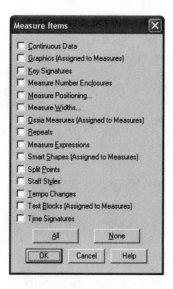

3. Check each item you want to copy from the selected region. Click All if you want to copy all measure items.

4. Click OK.

5. Highlight a region of your score containing the measure items you want to copy. Make sure to highlight the measures to which the items are attached for all measure items you wish to copy.

6. Ctrl/Option-Shift-Click the first measure of the destination region (or drag-copy to the destination region). All of the measure-attached items appear in the new location.

Now, click the Mass Edit menu. Notice that Copy Measure Items is still checked. You can continue to copy the measure items you selected (in the Measure Items dialog box) for other areas of your score. When you want to go back to copying everything, choose Copy Everything from the Mass Edit menu.

In addition to copying measure-attached items, you can also isolate entry and note-attached items for copying (notes, note-attached expressions, lyrics, chords, etc.). To do this:

1. Click the Mass Edit Tool.

2. From the Mass Edit menu, choose Copy Entry Items. The Entry Items dialog box appears, as shown in Figure 9.2.

Figure 9.2
Specify note/entry-
attached items to copy
in the Entry Items
dialog box.

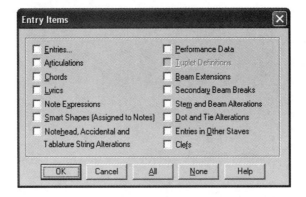

3. Check each item you want to copy from the selected region. Click All if you want to copy all Entry items.

4. Click OK.

5. Highlight a region of your score containing the entry items you want to copy. Make sure to highlight the notes to which the entries are attached for all note-attached items you wish to copy.

6. Ctrl/Option-Shift-Click the first measure of the destination region (or drag-copy to the destination region). All of the note-attached items, with a note on the corresponding beat, appear in the new location.

When copying note-attached items, keep in mind that each will require a note on the same beat in the destination measure. If a there is no corresponding note, the note-attached item will be left out of the destination region. Like copying measure items, you will need to choose Copy Everything from the Mass Edit menu to copy all items in a region.

Copying Between Documents

You can copy notation between documents just as you would within the same document. First, open the source and destination document. Then, from the Window menu, choose Tile Horizontally (or Tile Vertically), so you can see both documents simultaneously on your screen. Now, drag-copy to move music between documents.

Aside from drag-copying music between documents, you can use the commands under the Edit menu. After selecting a region with the Mass Edit Tool and choosing Copy from the Edit menu (or Ctrl/Cmd-C), there are two ways Finale can transfer this information to the destination document: by replacing the existing entries, or inserting a new measure containing the copied material.

▶ Replacing existing entries only transfers note entries and note-attached items. This option is called Replace Entries under the Edit menu, or is otherwise invoked by the traditional Ctr/Cmd-V (for paste) command. While using Replace Entries to copy music between documents, Finale will leave measure items (such as measure expressions and Key Signatures) out of the destination region. Note that new measures are not added, but the destination measures are overwritten with the copied material.

▶ Inserting the copied material into a new measure (or measures) transfers everything Replace Entries does, as well as measure expressions, Key and Time Signatures. After highlighting a region of music and selecting Copy from the Edit menu (or Ctrl/Cmd-C), highlight a measure in the destination document and from the Edit menu, choose Insert. Inserting to another document transfers the most amount of material from the destination region. The disadvantage of this method is that staff lists for measure expressions are not transferred.

If you want to copy measure expressions across documents, and retain staff list information, you can use the TGTools Transfer plug-in. First, make sure you have installed the TGTools demo from the companion CD-ROM.

To transfer measure-attached expressions (and other items) between documents:

1. In your source document, highlight the desired region with the Mass Edit Tool (note that this plug-in may not work properly if the first measure is included in the source region).

2. From the TGTools menu, choose Modify > Transfer. The Transfer dialog box appears.

3. Check the items you want to copy. Make sure Read Now is checked (at the top).

4. Click Go.

5. View the destination document.

6. With the Mass Edit Tool, highlight a region of measures.

7. From the TGTools menu, choose Modify > Transfer. The Transfer dialog box appears.

8. Make sure Write Now is checked, and click Go. The measure expressions appear in the destination region. You can "paste" by pressing Write Now as many times as you like in the destination document, as long as Write Now is checked in the Transfer dialog box.

TIP
If you want to view documents on the entire screen while copying, switch between documents by choosing the file name at the bottom of the Window menu.

Copying Music to a Clip File

There may be a region of music you want to save and archive for use later, in a different or future document, perhaps. To do this, save a clip file. With the Mass Edit Tool selected, highlight a region of your score. Then, hold down the Ctrl/Option key, click the Edit menu and choose Copy or Cut to Clip file. The Save Clipboard File dialog box appears. Name the clip file, choose a location, and click Save. Then, when you want to use the clip file, open the destination document and highlight the desired region with the Mass Edit Tool. Hold down the Ctrl/Option key, click the Edit menu and choose Replace or Insert from Clip File. The Paste (Mac: Open) dialog box appears where you can choose a clip file you have saved. Select the desired clip file and choose Open to place the music from the clip file into the selected region.

Clearing Items

You can clear any type of musical item from a selected region of your score. With the Mass Edit Tool selected, highlight a region of your score. Then, from the Mass Edit menu, choose Clear Items. The Clear Items dialog box appears, as shown in Figure 9.3.

Figure 9.3
Specify measure or entry items to clear in the Clear Items dialog box.

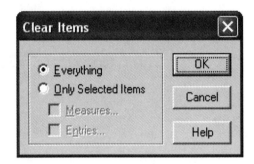

In this dialog box, choose Only Selected Items. Then, click the checkbox for Measures to open the Measure Items dialog box (Figure 9.1), or the checkbox for Entries to open the Entry Items dialog box (Figure 9.2). Choose the type of items you want to clear from the Measure or Entry Items dialog box, then click OK to return to the Clear Items dialog box. At this point, either click the other checkbox (Measures or Entries) to specify more items to clear, or click OK to return to the score. The items you specified are cleared from the highlighted region.

Changing Music

Anything you enter in Finale can be changed, moved or deleted. In this section, we will focus on the many ways to edit existing notes, expressions, chords, tuplets and other items for any region of your score or the whole document. Unlike editing items individually, which usually requires the tool used to create the item, the following techniques require the use of either the Note Mover or Mass Edit Tool only.

Changing Notes: Search and Replace

There may be a recurring passage of music in a score, or even a short motif, that you want to edit for every occurrence. You can change the pitch or enharmonic spelling of individual notes in a recurring musical passage with the Note Mover tool's search and replace function. To do this:

1. Choose the Note Mover tool (on Windows, first click the Window menu and choose Advanced Tools, then choose the Note Mover tool from the Advanced Tools Palette).

2. Click a measure containing an arrangement of notes that you want to change for another or all other occurrences in the score. You will see a handle on every note, as shown in Figure 9.4.

Figure 9.4
Selecting a region for search and replace

3. Drag over a region of handles to choose the notes in your source region. If you want to select nonconsecutive notes, hold down the Shift key and click the handle on each note you want to include.

4. From the Note Mover menu, choose Search and Replace. The Search and Replace dialog box appears, as shown in Figure 9.5.

Figure 9.5
Customize your search in the Search and Replace dialog box.

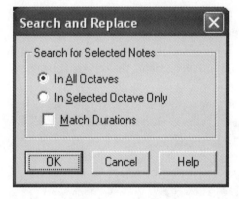

5. Here, choose In All Octaves if you want Finale to search for the selected notes in every octave of your score. Choose In Selected Octave Only to isolate the search to the octave of the selected notes. Check Match Durations if you want Finale to search only for the selected arrangement of notes in their rhythm alone.

6. Click OK. The Alteration for Slot dialog box appears.

7. Each "Slot" is a selected note. The first selected note is Slot 1, the second, Slot 2, etc. Move to the slot of a selected note you want to change by clicking Next. If you want to change the enharmonic of the slot, select Enharmonic. If you want to change the pitch, select Transposition. If you select transposition, the Transposition dialog box appears. Choose an interval to transpose the note in the

specified slot. If you wish to apply the same transposition to each selected note, set your transposition first, then click Set All. Click OK.

8. Once you have finished specifying the changes, click OK to return to the score. You will now see a new menu at the top of the screen, the Search menu.

9. From the Search menu, choose Find. Finale will look for a matching arrangement of notes and will highlight their handles.

10. From the Search menu, choose Replace Then Find to apply the changes you specified to the region, and automatically select the next occurrence. To find and replace all occurrences at once, from the Search menu, choose Replace All.

Changing Entry Items En Mass

In addition to changing notes with the Note Mover tool, Finale can also modify the appearance of several other items in any region of the score with the Mass Edit Tool.

Swapping Articulations and Expressions

You can swap a note-attached expression or articulation for another in any selected region of your score with the Mass Edit menu's Change Articulations Assignments and Change Note Expression Assignments features. If you would like to swap an expression or articulation, first make sure the new figure exists in the Expression Selection or Articulation dialog box (you can find information in creating and editing expressions and articulations in chapter 3). Use the following steps to change articulations in a selected region of your score:

1. Click the Mass Edit Tool, and select a region of your score containing articulations you want to change.

2. From the Mass Edit menu, choose Change > Articulation Assignments. The Change Articulation Assignments dialog box appears, as shown in Figure 9.6.

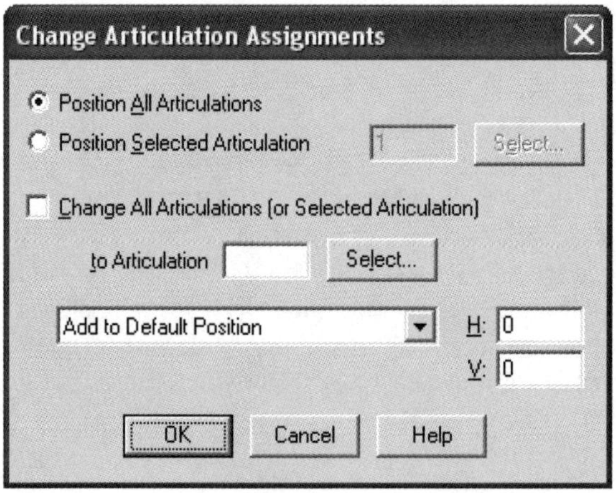

Figure 9.6
Swap articulations with the Change Articulation Assignments dialog box.

3. Select Position Selected Articulation. If you want to change all articulations in the selected region to the same one, leave Position All Articulations chosen and move to step 6.

4. Click the Select button to the right of Position Selected Articulation. The Articulation Selection dialog box appears.

5. Choose the existing articulation that you would like to change from the list and click Select. You return to the Change Articulation Assignment dialog box and the number of the articulation you selected appears in the top text box.

6. Check Change All Articulations (or Selected Articulation).

7. Click the Select button next to "to articulation". The Articulation Selection dialog box appears.

8. Choose the new articulation from the list and click Select. You return to the Change Articulation Assignment dialog box and the number of the articulation you selected appears in the middle text box

9. For H: and V:, enter a value if you wish to adjust the default positioning of the new articulations. Or, click the drop-down/popup menu and choose Add to Current Position to make adjustments from where they are currently positioned.

10. Click OK to return to the score and review your changes. The articulations you specified (or all articulations) change and reposition accordingly.

To change a specific note-attached expression assignment, or all note expressions in a region, follow the same steps, only choose Change Note-Attached Expressions from the Mass Edit menu.

Chords

Like articulations and note expressions, every chord symbol in a selected region can be changed at once. You can edit their transposition, playback, and visual definition. To do this:

1. Click the Mass Edit Tool, and select a region of your score containing chord symbols you want to change.

2. From the Mass Edit menu, choose Change > Chord Assignments. The Change Chord Assignments dialog box appears, as shown in Figure 9.7.

Figure 9.7
Change the visual definition, playback, or transposition of an existing chord symbol in the Change Chord Assignments dialog box

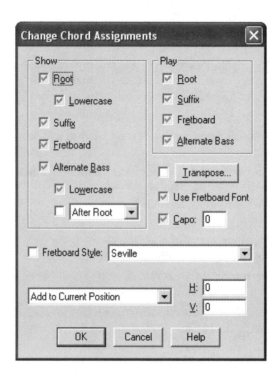

3. Here, choose how you want to change the selected chord symbols (any checkboxes in gray means the settings will be unaltered). In the Show section, choose chord components to show or hide. In the Play section, assign components of the chords for playback. Click the Transpose button to open the Transpose dialog box, where you can choose a new transposition for the selected chord symbols. Transposition will apply to fretboard diagrams as well as to chord symbols.

NOTE
When you change the key of a piece using the Key Signature tool, all chord symbols will also transpose accordingly. Use the Change Chord Assignments dialog box only to transpose chord symbols independently from the Key Signature.

4. When you have finished specifying changes, click OK to return to the score. All chords and fretboads in the selected region change according to the settings you made.

To make global changes to the appearance of accidental characters on chord symbols, from the Options menu, choose Document Options, then select Chords. In the Chords portion of the Document Options, you can set the baseline (vertical placement) and change font characters for accidentals in chord symbols. Note that any changes you make in Document Options only apply to the document on which you are working.

Ties and Tuplets

The placement and visual definition of ties and tuplets can be altered in a selected region like expressions, articulations, and chords. With a region of the score selected, choose Mass Edit (menu) > Change > Ties to change ties, or MassEdit > Change > Tuplets to change tuplets. However, you will most likely want these items to remain consistent throughout an entire document. To edit the placement, visual definition, and other attributes of ties and tuplets throughout a document, from the Options menu, choose Document Options. In the Document Options dialog box, choose the Ties or Tuplets category to make global changes to ties and tuplets.

TIP

To alter tie and tuplet definitions and placement for a region of music, try the Patterson Tuplet Mover and Tie Mover plug-ins available on the companion CD-ROM.

Change Note Durations and Appearance

With the Mass Edit Tool, you can easily change the note duration, notehead character, and note size for any selected region of music. Like the previous features, these can be found in the Mass Edit > Change submenu.

Changing Note Durations

You have a great deal of control over the duration of notes in a selected region. You may need to change note durations if you decide to change the Time Signature (doubling note durations while changing from common time to cut time, for example). To modify the duration of notes in any region, use the following steps:

1. Click the Mass Edit Tool, and select a region of your score containing notes you want to change. If you want to change note durations in a specific layer, choose the layer, then from the View menu, choose Show Active Layer Only.

2. From the Mass Edit menu, choose Change > Note Durations. The Change Note Durations dialog box appears, as shown in Figure 9.8.

Figure 9.8
Edit the duration of a region of notes according to settings in the Change Note Durations dialog box.

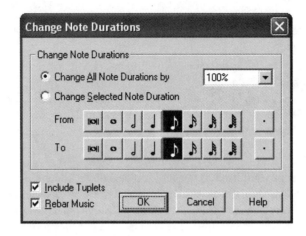

3. To change all note durations, ensure Change All Note Durations By is selected. Then, click the drop-down/popup menu and choose the new percentage (200% doubles the note values, 50% reduces durations by half, etc.). If there is a specific note duration within the selected region you want to change, choose Change Selected Note Duration. In the From row, click the duration of the note you want to change (use the dot on the right to indicate a dotted note). In the To row, click the new duration you want to assign.

4. Check Rebar Measures if you want the resulting notes to flow into different measures as dictated by the Time Signature. If this box is not checked, Finale will leave the resulting notes in their original measures (likely creating overfilled or incomplete measures).

5. Click OK to return to the score and review changes to note durations.

When you use these steps, all notes and rests in the selected region change except default whole rests. If you would like to include default whole rests while changing note durations with this method, use the Change To Real Whole Rests plug-in. With the Mass Edit Tool, highlight the region of your score you want to change. Then, from the plug-ins menu, choose Note, Beam and Rest Editing > Change to Real Whole Rests. Now, rests in the selected region are "real" and will be affected by note duration changes with the Mass Edit Tool.

Changing Notehead Characters

You can change the notehead character in any selected region of your score. However, for the most flexibility, there are a few preliminary steps to ensure you can set noteheads to characters in any font, which is not supported by the Change Noteheads feature directly.

NOTE
If you are creating percussion notation, use the Percussion Map Designer to assign notehead characters to staff lines (see chapter 8).

If the character of the notehead you want to use is in your existing Notehead font, use the Change Noteheads plug-in in the Notes, Beams and Rests submenu of the Plug-in menu. The following steps point out the true power of Finale.

To change noteheads in any region to characters in any font:

1. First, find the font containing the character you want to use. From the Help menu, choose a font character set (Windows: Help > User Manual > Character Map) to see each character in the Finale Music Fonts. Note the keystroke required for the character you want to use ("Q", "Alt-0130", etc.). If you are using a third-party music font, locate the keystroke for the desired character in that font. After you have found it, move back to Finale. If the character exists in the document's default music font (Maestro by default), skip ahead to step 8. You can see your current default music font by choosing Set Default Music Font from the Options menu.

2. Click the Staff tool.

3. From the Staff menu, choose Define Staff Styles. The Staff Styles dialog box appears.

4. Click New, and after Available Styles, type "Notehead Font", then the name of the font containing the character you want to use (for future reference).

5. In the Independent Elements section, click the Select button and choose the font containing the character you want to use. Click OK to return to the Staff Styles dialog box. Then, click OK to return to the score.

6. Highlight the region containing the noteheads you want to change.

7. Right/Control-click the highlighted region and choose the "Notehead Font _(font name)" Staff Style you just created. The Staff Style (with the independent notehead font setting) is applied and marked with blue bars.

8. Click the Mass Edit Tool and highlight the measures containing the noteheads you want to change (if they are not highlighted already). If you want to change noteheads in a specific layer, choose the layer, then from the View menu, choose Show Active Layer Only.

9. From the Mass Edit menu, choose Change > Noteheads. The Change Noteheads dialog box appears, as shown in Figure 9.9.

Figure 9.9
Change noteheads for a region of your score according to settings in the Change Noteheads dialog box.

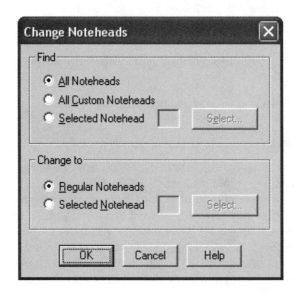

10. In the Find section, choose All Noteheads if you want to change all noteheads in the region. If you want to change noteheads you have already changed, choose All Custom Noteheads. Choose Selected Notehead if there is a specific notehead character in the highlighted region that you want to change.

11. In the Change to section, click Selected Notehead, then click in the text box to see a blinking cursor. Type the keystroke of the character (as seen in its Font Character Set/Map). You can also click the Select button to open the Symbol Selection dialog box containing a list of fonts in the current default music font. If your character is not in the default music font, your choices in this box do not reflect how the character will appear in the score (since we applied an independent notehead font to the region).

12. Click OK to get back to the score to review the new notehead characters.

TIP
To apply a Staff Style to a region containing partial measure, from the Edit menu, choose Select Partial Measures.

Changing the Note Size

You may want to change the size of notes in a region (to create cue notes, for example). To change the size of notes, and their corresponding stems and beams:

1. Click the Mass Edit Tool, and select a region of your score containing notes you want to resize. If you want to change note size in a specific layer, choose the layer, and then from the View menu, choose Show Active Layer Only.

2. From the Mass Edit menu, choose Change > Note Size. The Change Note Size dialog box appears, as shown in Figure 9.10

Figure 9.10
Change the size for a region of notes according to settings in the Change Note Size dialog box.

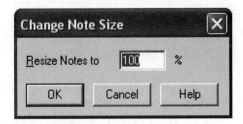

3. Enter a new percentage for notes in the selected region (200% doubles the note size, 50% reduces the size by half, etc.).

4. Click OK to return to the score. All visible notes in the selected region are resized.

TIP
You can also change the size of notes individually by clicking them with the Resize tool. Notice that when you click on the stem, you get the Resize Note dialog, and when you click directly on the notehead, you get the Resize Notehead dialog box.

Transposing

We already have seen how to transpose music by changing the Key Signature (in chapters 2 and 5). You may, however, need to transpose music without changing the key. To transpose notes diatonically or chromatically in any region of your score within the key, do the following:

1. Click the Mass Edit Tool, and select a region of your score containing music you want to transpose.

2. From the Mass Edit menu, choose Transpose. The Transposition dialog box appears, as shown in Figure 9.11

CHAPTER 9

Figure 9.11
Specify an interval
to transpose a
selected region in
the Transposition
dialog box.

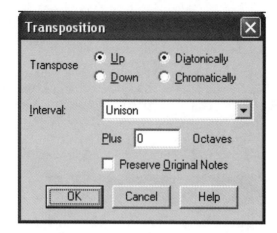

3. For Transpose, choose the direction you want to transpose the music (Up or Down). Then, choose Chromatically to transpose any number of half-steps, or Diatonically to transpose within the key.

4. Click the drop-down/popup for Interval and choose an interval to transpose the notes. The options you have here depend on the Diatonic/Chromatic setting above.

5. In the text box for Plus_Octaves, enter the octave displacement. "1" = up one octave, "-1" = down one octave, etc.

6. Choose Preserve Original Notes if you want to leave the existing notes in the score and make copies of them at the specified transposition. For example, this works well for quickly creating octave doubling in a staff or doubling at the third, etc.

7. Click OK to return to the score. Music in the selected region is now transposed to the interval you specified.

To quickly transpose your music, assign transposition metatools. With the Mass Edit Tool selected, hold down the Shift key and press the 6, 7, 8, or 9 key on the QWERTY keyboard. The Transposition dialog box appears. Define a transposition and click OK. Now, highlight a region of music and press the number key you assigned to transpose it.

TIP

Try assigning metatools for four transposition settings; up a whole step, up a half step, down a whole step, and down a half step. Then, you can use the number keys you assign to increment to the desired transposition (for example, press the 6 key four times to transpose up a fourth).

If you want to transpose the music for an instrument doubling, remember to use a Staff Style, which will display the new Key Signature, play back correctly, and affect only the region to which the style is applied. If you want to transpose music by semitones, try the Canonic Utilities plug-in under the Plug-ins menu.

Music Spacing

By default, Finale is configured to do most music spacing for you. You may have noticed notes shifting after you enter them. This is Finale's attempt to space music proportionally during entry. If you are not satisfied with the default spacing, or want to make manual adjustments, Finale offers you plenty of power to do so. Manipulating the automatic music spacing settings, stretching measures by moving barlines, or moving notes around individually are just a few ways to adjust the spacing of your music in Finale. In this section, you'll learn how to use several of Finale's most effective music spacing methods.

Music spacing is largely affected by the width of systems, so for the following instruction, it is best to be working in Page View (remember, there are no systems in Scroll View). From the View menu, choose Page View.

Automatic Music Spacing and Music Spacing Libraries

Automatic Music Spacing is turned on by default, so it is likely you have put it to use without even knowing it. It affects the spacing of your music after entering notes with any of the available entry methods. It can automatically adjust the space between notes and the width of measures. It can also make fine adjustments to your music to avoid collisions. Automatic Music Spacing can be turned on or off from the Edit menu.

TIP
Highlight a region of measures with the Mass Edit Tool and press the 4 key to easily apply note spacing to the region.

You can modify the parameters Finale uses for spacing in the Music Spacing category of the Document Options dialog box (Figure 9.12). From the Options menu, choose Document Options, then select Music Spacing from the list on the left.

Figure 9.12
Make changes to
document-wide settings
to music spacing in the
Music Spacing portion
of the Document
Options dialog box.

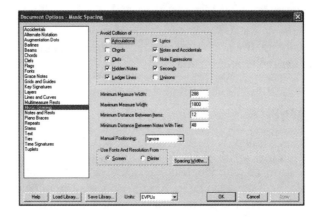

In this dialog box, you can make adjustments to Finale's default music spacing settings. Here, tell Finale to avoid collision of certain items, choose a minimum and maximum measure width, and specify the minimum and maximum space between notes. You can also tell Finale to ignore, clear, or incorporate spacing of notes you have positioned manually by choosing one of these items from the Manual Positioning drop-down/popup menu. For example, if you have manually positioned some notes or barlines, and later decide you want to space your music using Finale's defaults, select Clear for Manual Positioning, then apply Note Spacing to your document.

You can have further control over Finale's automatic spacing by modifying the spacing widths. Click the Spacing Widths button to specify a number of EDUs allotted to each rhythmic duration. The process of adjusting spacing widths manually and reviewing the score can be quite time-consuming and tedious. Instead, choose from a number of preset spacing width configurations by loading one of Finale's available music spacing libraries.

Click the Load Library button in the Document Options dialog box (or, from the File menu, choose Open Library or Load Library). The Open Library dialog box appears. Double-click the Music Spacing folder. Now, double-click one of the available music spacing libraries to open it (then click OK to return to the score if necessary). Now, Finale will use the spacing widths defined by the library you opened. One of the five music spacing libraries should meet your needs. If not, configure custom music spacing settings in the Spacing Widths dialog box, and save your own music spacing library to use with any document. After customizing the spacing widths, click the Save Library button in the Document Options to save a Music Spacing library.

Updating the Layout

By default, Finale updates the page format and number of measures per system during entry, while adding measures, or making other changes that have an effect on the page layout (in Page View only). You may have seen measures jumping between systems while entering music. This is a result of Automatic Update Layout, Finale's attempt to create evenly spaced measures within systems. Updating the layout also brings together other elements of the page format, such as the number of systems per page while resizing systems, staves or pages. If you want to update the layout manually, you can turn off Automatic Update Layout by selecting it from the Edit menu. Then, press Ctrl-U on Windows or Cmd-\ on Mac (or choose Update Layout from the Edit menu) to update the layout at any time.

Locking Measures Per System

To tell Finale how to handle the number of measures per systems while updating the layout, use the Update Layout Options. From the Options menu, choose Update Layout Options. The Update Layout Options dialog box appears, as shown in Figure 9.13.

Figure 9.13
Tell Finale how to reconfigure systems and pages while updating the layout in the Update Layout Options dialog box.

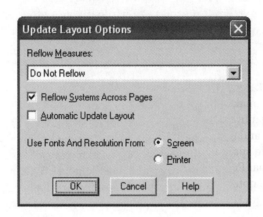

Click the drop-down/popup menu for Reflow Measures and choose Only Within Systems. Then, click OK to return to the score. Now, Finale will not change the number of measures per systems while updating the layout.

You may want to lock certain systems with a specific number of measures, but leave other systems unlocked. If you want to continue to use Automatic Update Layout to reflow unlocked measures across remaining systems, from the Options menu, choose Update Layout Options, and from the drop-down/popup menu choose Across Systems (Maintain System Locks). This is Finale's default setting and perhaps the most flexible setting. Click OK to return to the score. From the View menu, make sure Show Page Layout Icons is checked so that any system locks will be visible. To lock a system or systems, click the Mass Edit Tool, then highlight measures in the systems you want to lock. From the Mass Edit menu, choose Lock Systems. You will notice a padlock icon to the right of the selected systems. This icon indicates that the number of measures in the system are locked and will not be changed while updating the layout. To remove system locks, highlight a region and choose Unlock Systems from the Mass Edit menu.

You may have noticed that any change you make in the measure layout results in the appearance of lock icons. While moving measures between systems manually, or using the Fit Music command to fit a number of measures to systems (described in chapter 2 under "Moving Measures Across Systems"), Finale locks changed systems automatically. To demonstrate this, clear system locks from a page with the Mass Edit Tool (as described above). Then, click the last measure of a system, and press the down arrow to move it to the next system. Notice that a lock appears to the right of both changed systems. Systems also become locked any time you change the number of measures with the Fit Music command (under the Mass Edit or Page Layout menus).

Systems Per Page

While updating the layout, you will usually want Finale to move systems across pages automatically (to update for resizing other page format changes). However, you can tell Finale to leave the same number of systems on a page in the Update Layout Options dialog box. From the Options menu, choose Update Layout Options. The Update Layout Options dialog box appears (Figure 9.13). Here, uncheck Reflow Systems Across Pages and click OK. Now, Finale will leave the same systems on each page while updating the layout. Move them manually with the Page Layout tool (as described in chapter 2). There will be more information on page layout in chapter 11.

Spacing with the Mass Edit Tool

You may want to apply spacing changes to a certain region of the score without affecting any other region. You can apply music spacing to any desired region with the Mass Edit Tool. First, turn off Automatic Music Spacing under the Edit menu. Then, click the Mass Edit Tool and highlight a region of measures containing music you want to respace. From the Mass Edit Menu, choose Music Spacing, then Apply Note, Beat, or Time Signature Spacing. Instead of choosing the menu item, simply press the 3 key to apply beat spacing to a region, or press the 4 key to apply note spacing to a region.

Beat spacing will space each beat according to the table of widths, and space notes between beats linearly (quarter note gets twice the space of an eighth note, and so on). Note spacing provides more precision by using the spacing widths table for each note (note spacing is also used for automatic music spacing). Time Signature Spacing will use linear spacing throughout the measure. For example, a half note would get twice as much space as a quarter note. This is how your music looks directly after entering it into the score with Automatic Music Spacing off.

Spacing Notes Individually

You can use the Speedy Entry tool or the Special Tools to space notes individually. Click the Speedy Entry tool and click a measure containing notes to open the Speedy Frame. Now, simply click and drag notes in the active layer to move them horizontally. To use the Special Tools for spacing, first click the Special Tools tool (on Windows, from the Window menu choose Advanced Tools Palette, then click the Special Tools tool). You will see the Special Tools Palette appear on the screen. From this palette, choose the Note Position tool. Then, click in a measure to see positioning handles appear above the measure. Click and drag these handles to move the corresponding notes left or right in the measure.

To incorporate your manual note spacing into all future music spacing applied to the region, from the Options menu, choose Document Options, then select Music Spacing. Click the drop-down menu for Manual Positioning and choose Incorporate. Or, choose Ignore to tell Finale to reapply your manual positioning after spacing the music. You can also choose clear to remove manual spacing adjustments while spacing.

The Beat Chart and Spacing With the Measure Tool

In Chapter 7, we covered how to increase or decrease the width of measures by dragging barlines with the Measure tool. When dragging the barlines, the entries in the measures will respace proportionally. There are some other music spacing techniques possible with the Measure tool.

Occasionally, you may want to respace all notes on a certain beat for all staves in a measure. You can manually adjust the placement of each beat using the Measure tool's beat chart. To space your music using a beat chart, do the following:

1. Click the Measure tool and highlight a region of measures containing notes.

2. Doubleclick the highlighted area to open the Measure Attributes dialog box.

3. Click the drop-down/popup menu for Position Notes, and choose Using Beat-Chart Spacing. This step is not necessary if Note Spacing already has been applied to the region.

4. Click OK to return to the score. You will now see two handles on each barline in the selected region.

5. Click the bottom barline handle. The beat chart appears above the top staff in the system, as shown in Figure 9.14

Figure 9.14
Specify the placement of beats for a measure in all staves of a system with the beat chart.

Beat Chart

6. Drag the bottom handle to position all notes on the beat in all staves of the system.

7. For more information about the placement of each beat, double-click the top handle to open the Beat Chart dialog box, as shown in Figure 9.15. The Elapsed Duration indicates the number of EDUs from the beginning of the measure. The remaining values use the measurement unit selected under the Options menu (Options menu > Measurement Units). You can use these values to space measure-attached items in your score relative to the placement of the note.

Figure 9.15
Specify the precise
placement of beats
using the Beat Chart
dialog box.

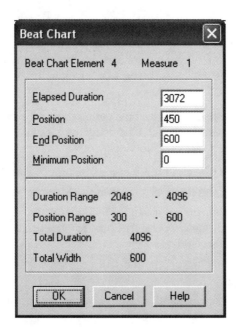

8.   Click OK to return to the score. Click anywhere in the score to hide the beat chart.

TIP

Use one of several TGTools plug-ins to edit music spacing via the beat chart. For example, you can remove white space at the beginning of a measure, or change the measure width. From the TGTools menu, choose Spacing to see the available options. The TGTools demo is available on the companion CD-ROM.

Positioning Notes Evenly in a Measure

With the Measure tool, you can also tell Finale to position notes evenly in a measure regardless of the Time Signature, measure width or number of notes in the measure. This is sometimes used for chant notation, where a measure takes up an entire staff system or a long cadenza in a solo. Also, use this method when you want to space a measure containing too many beats relative to the Time Signature, for example, in a cadenza passage.

Click the Measure tool and double-click a measure to open the Measure Attributes dialog box. In the Options section, check Position Notes Evenly Across Measure. Click OK to return to the score. Notes in the measure are now positioned evenly. Any notes you add to this measure will also be positioned evenly.

Set a Measure to Begin a Staff System

If you know you want a specific measure to always begin a new staff system, you can mark the measure with the Measure tool. With the Measure tool selected, double-click a measure to open the Measure Attributes dialog box. In the Options section, check Begin a New Staff System. Click OK to return to the score. Now, the measure will always mark the beginning of a new system. Notice that the resulting arrow icon in the left margin is a reminder to you.

Changing and Managing Fonts

Just about everything you enter into a score—music, text expressions, articulations, and other items—are font characters. Just like you can change the font, size, or style of your letters in a word processing program, you can do the same for most items in a score. All font settings are document-specific, so are saved along with each document. You can see the fonts currently selected in an open document by looking in the Document Options. From the Options menu, choose Document Options and select Fonts from the list on the left. The Font options appear, as shown in Figure 9.16.

Figure 9.16
Set the default font for any item in the Fonts portion of the Document Options dialog box.

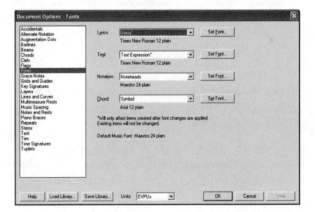

Here, you can choose any font on your system for each option under the four drop-down/popup menus. The fonts on your system include the Finale music fonts that were added when you installed Finale (you can find a list of the Finale fonts and their characters under the Help menu, on Windows, Help > User Manual). Let's say you want to set the font of your Lyric Verses to Arial. First, click the drop-down/popup menu for Lyrics and choose Verses. Then, click the Set Font button to the right. The Font dialog box opens, as shown in Figure 9.17.

Figure 9.17
Specify the font, size, and style for an item in the Font dialog box.

Use the scroll bar on the left to move up the list, and click Arial to select it. Note that you can change the point size and style of a font just as you would in a word processing program. When you have set up your font, click OK to return to the Document Options dialog box.

Notice there is an asterisk (*) next to many of the items listed under the four drop-down/popup menus. The asterisk tells you that any change to the font in the Document Options will apply only to new items added to the score, and will not apply to existing items. If you want to change the font of one of the asterisked fonts, try using the Change Fonts plug-in under the Plug-ins menu (we'll talk more about how to do this soon).

Changing Your Music Font

Finale makes changing the default music font easy. From the Options menu, choose Set Default Music Font to open the Font dialog box, where you can choose a new music font. The Finale music fonts include Maestro, Maestro Percussion, Maestro Wide, Jazz, Jazz Perc, and Engraver fonts.

TIP

If you want to use Finale's Jazz font for a new document, use the Setup Wizard (File > New > Document With Setup Wizard). On page 4, for Default Music Font, choose Jazz. You will see the music in the preview window change to the Jazz font.

Remember, you can see a list of all of Finale's fonts and their characters under the Help menu (Windows: User Manual submenu of the Help menu). Remember that Finale also gives you the ability to change different elements of music, mentioned above. The Default Music font changes all of these elements at once.

Swapping/Checking Fonts

You can change everything that exists in a certain font to another by using Finale's Font Swapping utility. From the Options menu, choose Data Check, then Swap One Font for Another. The Swap One Font for Another dialog box appears, as shown in Figure 9.18.

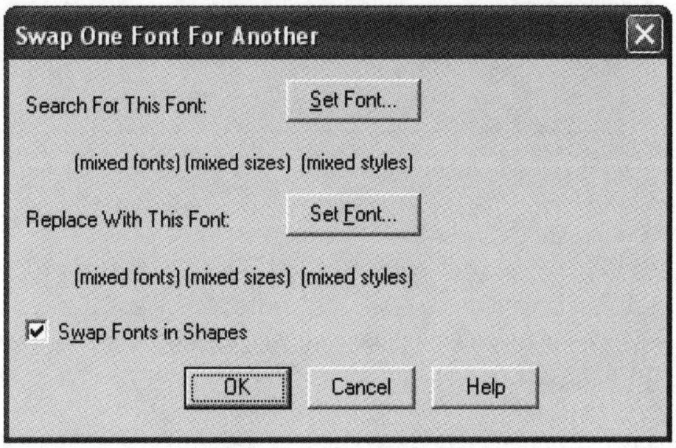

Figure 9.18
The Swap One Font for Another dialog box

> **Swap One Font For Another**   ☒
>
> Search For This Font: [S̲et Font...]
>
>   (mixed fonts) (mixed sizes) (mixed styles)
>
> Replace With This Font: [Set F̲ont...]
>
>   (mixed fonts) (mixed sizes) (mixed styles)
>
> ☑ S̲wap Fonts in Shapes
>
> [OK]   [Cancel]   [Help]

Here, click the Set Font button next to Search for This Font to open the Font dialog box. Select the font you want to change and click OK. Now, click the Set Font button to Replace with This Font. The Font dialog box appears again. Select the new font, size and style for your font and click OK. Click OK to return to your score and review the appearance of items in the new font. Keep in mind that changing the font this way will apply to all items in the selected font. Consult the Fonts category of the Document Options (as described above) to see all items that use any given font.

CHAPTER 9

The Change Fonts Plug-in

You can change the font for some existing items in the score with the Change Fonts plug-in. From the Plug-ins menu, choose Change Fonts. The Change Fonts dialog box appears, as shown in Figure 9.19.

Figure 9.19
Change the font for existing staff names, group names, text blocks, and lyrics in the Change Fonts dialog box.

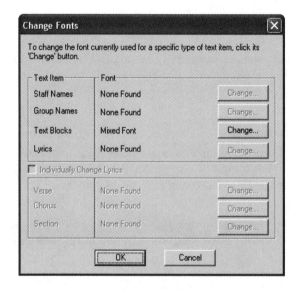

Click the Change button for any of the available items to open the Fonts dialog box, where you can set a new font for the item. If Finale does not detect any existing entries for one of these categories, the selection will not be available. Change the font for any of the desired items in this dialog box and click OK to return to the score.

Checking Document Fonts Against System Fonts

Finale remembers the fonts you use in any document after saving. When you open a file, Finale finds each font used in the document on your computer and displays it. If Finale cannot find a font on your computer that it needs to properly display one or more elements, you may end up seeing incorrect-looking music or markings in your score. This can happen when you use a third-party music font, or any uncommon font, and open the file on a computer that does not have the font installed. To check a document to ensure all fonts used in the document exist on the computer, and substitute missing fonts, use the Check Document Fonts Against System Fonts utility. From the Options menu, choose Data Check and choose Check Document Fonts Against System Fonts. If Finale finds any fonts in your document that do not exist on your computer, the Font dialog box appears, as shown in Figure 9.20.

Figure 9.20
Checking Document
Fonts Against System
Fonts

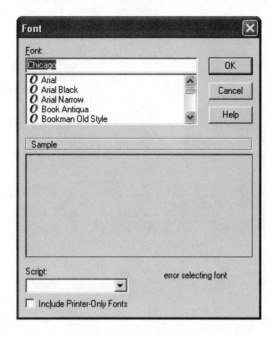

Here, choose a substitute for any missing fonts Finale finds. For example, if you are using Windows, you may see the Times font appear in this dialog box. This is a font standard on Macintosh, but not on Windows. Choose a new font (like Times New Roman—similar to Times) just as you would normally, and click OK to tell Finale to display the next missing font, or return to the score (if there are no more missing fonts).

Everything Looks Funny: Reinstalling Your Finale Music Fonts

If all music in a document looks completely messed up, you probably need to reinstall your Finale music fonts. You may have uninstalled a previous version of Finale, thus removing your music fonts. The easiest way to do this is to simply reinstall from the original Finale installation CD using a Typical (Macintosh: Easy) install when prompted to do so. You can also download the fonts from Coda's website, www.codamusic.com. Search the site for the Finale (or SmartMusic) Viewer Font pack download. Follow instructions on the site for installing these fonts.

10
Fine Tuning: The Details

In chapter 9, you learned large-scale editing procedures that are often applied during score creation. In this chapter, we'll cover additional editing techniques that allow you to have greater control over the appearance of individual items. The following instructions apply primarily to fine-tuning the appearance of markings and notation rather than creating, editing, and moving pitches and rhythms. Here, we'll focus on details that can make any score look neat, clean, and professional. Many prefer to use techniques described below after all markings and notation have been entered into a score, though the method you adopt for using any editing technique will depend on the project you are working on and your own work style. In this chapter, we'll describe how to align and position a variety of items on the page, as well as how to make global and individual changes to beams, stems, accidentals, dots, and ties.

Here's a summary of what you will learn in this chapter:

▶   Techniques for alignment and positioning.
▶   How to edit beams.
▶   How to edit stems.
▶   How to edit notes and noteheads.
▶   How to edit accidentals.
▶   How to edit dots and ties.

Alignment and Positioning Techniques

After a page of music has been created, you may want to specify precise placement for expressions, text, chords, graphics, or other markings in your score relative to the page edge and/or each other. Here, we'll talk about how to easily position items, using a ruler, grid, or guide as a reference.

Since we are only concerned with adjusting the placement of items as they will appear after printing, move to Page View (View > Page View). Remember, only in Page View can you see the score as it will appear in the printout.

NOTE

Use the following alignment and positioning techniques in Page View to place various markings before finalizing your page layout. See chapter 11 for more information on laying out your staff, system and page margins for printing.

The Selection Tool

Introduced in Finale 2001 and improved in Finale 2002, the Selection tool has made general positioning a breeze for most items. With this tool, you can select almost anything on the page and drag it into position without having to switch tools. Simply click the Selection tool, click an item and drag it around. See Figure 10.1 for a description of items you can move and delete with the Selection tool. The Finale file used for this example, "Selection Tool Guide," is also included on the companion CD-ROM.

Figure 10.1
Position items easily with the Selection tool.

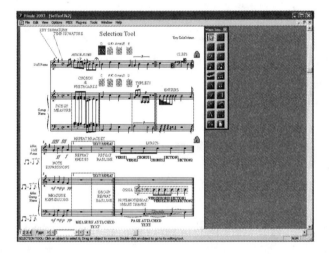

After you click an item, it will be surrounded with a rectangle. Then, you can either click and drag or use the arrow keys to nudge the item into place. Double-click any item with the Selection tool to select the item's corresponding tool for further editing. Press the Delete key to delete the item. Use the Selection tool in conjunction with the following positioning techniques to specify precise placement of items in your score.

In addition to dragging and deleting items, you can also invoke context menus for many items with the Selection tool, and make edits without leaving the Selection tool. For example, with the Selection tool chosen, right/Control-click a measure expression. The measure expression context menu appears. Choose Edit Measure Text Expression Definition to open the Text Expression Designer. Enter some new text for the expression, and click OK. You return to the score with the Selection tool still selected. While editing existing scores, make a habit of using the Selection tool as much as possible to avoid the hassle of switching tools frequently.

Rulers and Margins

By default, in Page View, only page edges and staves exist as a reference to use while positioning expressions, text, and other items. For greater control over the exact placement of an item as it will appear on the printed page, use rulers. From the View menu, choose Show Rulers. You will now see two rulers appear, one across the top of the screen and one on the left side (Figure 10.2).

Figure 10.2
Use rulers and margins for precision placement.

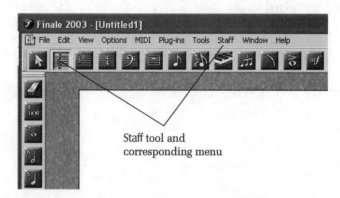

Staff tool and corresponding menu

As you click and drag any item, you will notice dashed lines extending vertically and horizontally. Use these lines to position items in your score relative to the distance from the top and left page edges. To specify inches, centimeters, EVPUs or another measurement unit to display on the rulers, from the Options menu, choose Measurement Units, then select the desired unit of measurement.

TIP

For more precision, try zooming in. From the View menu, choose Scale View To, and choose a greater percentage (or use Ctrl/Command 0,1,2,4,5,7 to quickly change view percentages). You can also use the Zoom tool to scale the view. Right/Command-Option-click and drag to move the viewable region of the page. As you change the view percentage and viewable area of the page, the rulers will adjust accordingly.

If you would like to position items relative to the system or page margins, from the View menu, choose Show Margins. Now, the system and page margins appear in a light gray line (Figure 10.2). With Show Margins selected, you can also see two vertical lines: One marks the midpoint of the page, and the other marks the midpoint of the page margins. There are two horizontal lines marking the page and page margin midpoint as well. You can hide rulers and margins by unchecking Show Rulers or Show Margins under the Edit menu.

Grids and Guides

Like rulers and margins, grids and guides can also be used as a reference to position a variety of items in your score. Grids and guides are both basically horizontal and vertical reference lines that extend through the page at specified points along the vertical or horizontal axis. A key advantage to both grids and guides is the ability to snap items to them.

Positioning With Grids

Instead of manually dragging or nudging expressions, text, Smart Shapes and other items into place, Finale contains a powerful utility for snapping items to a grid automatically. To do this, click the View menu and choose Show Grid. There is now a grid covering your page (with ? inch between each line by default). Each intersection of the grid displays as a + on your page. To tell Finale to snap specific items to the closest intersection, click the View menu and choose Grid/Guide Options. Document Options-Grids and Guides displays, as shown in Figure 10.3.

Figure 10.3
Make document-wide settings for grids and guides in the Grids and Guides category of the Document Options.

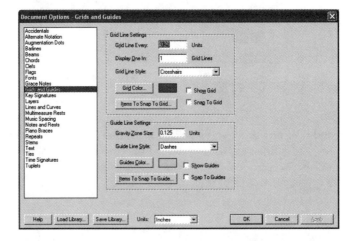

In the Grid Line Settings section, click the Items to Snap To Grid button. The Items to Snap To Grid dialog box appears. Here, check any items you want to position in the score using the grid, and click OK. Then, check Snap to Grid and click OK to return to the score. Now, any time you drag one of the items checked in the Items to Snap To Grid dialog box, it will snap to the nearest intersection. See Figure 10.4 for an example of a score with the grid visible:

CHAPTER 10

Figure 10.4
An example of a score
with the grid visible

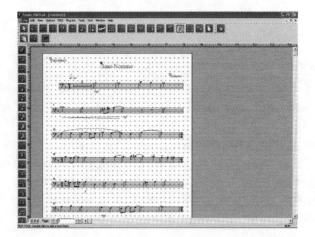

To increase or decrease the distance between each grid intersection, click the View menu, choose Grid/Guide Options and specify a value in the Grid Line Every field. In this section, you can also choose to display fewer grid lines, and, using the Grid Line Style drop-down/popup menu, change the grid line style from crosshairs to dots, dashes, or a solid line.

Positioning With Guides

A guide is basically a vertical or horizontal line that you can add as a reference point. To create a guide, right/Control-click a ruler to open the context menu and choose New Guide (or you can also double-click in the ruler to create a guide.). The New Horizontal Guide dialog box appears, as shown in Figure 10.5

Figure 10.5
Specify the guide
location in the New
Horizontal Guide dialog
box.

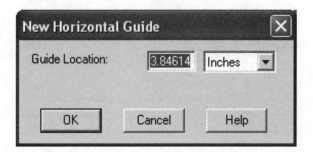

Here, specify the distance you want to position the guide from the top or left edge of the page and click OK. Notice that a triangle appears on the ruler with a dashed line extending through the score. Click and drag the triangle to reposition the guide if needed.

Like the grid, you can also snap items to this guide. From the View menu, choose Grid/Guide Options. In the Grid Line Settings section, click Items To Snap To Guide to open the Items To Snap To Guide dialog box. Make sure the items you want to position using the guide are checked, and click OK to return to the Grid/Guide Options. Check Snap To Guides. For Gravity

Zone Size, enter the region to either side of the guide you want the Snap To setting to affect. For example, enter 1 inch if you want any item moved within an inch of the guide to snap to it. Click OK to return to the score. Now, use guides to align markings vertically or horizontally. You can use grids and guides simultaneously or independently.

To see the "gravity zone" of your guides (the region in which an object will snap to the guide), Right/Ctrl-click on an existing guide in the ruler and choose Show Gravity Zone.

TGTools: The Align/Move Dynamics Plug-in

This plug-in was added in Finale 2002, and greatly enhances Finale's ability to easily position dynamic markings relative to the staff and to each other. To demonstrate how to quickly align dynamic expressions and hairpins horizontally, try this:

1. Add a number of dynamic text expressions (*mf*, *p*, etc.) at varying distances above the staff.

2. Click the Mass Edit Tool and highlight the region of the staff containing the expressions.

3. From the Plug-ins menu, choose TGTools > Align/Move Dynamics. The Align/Move Dynamics dialog box appears, as shown in Figure 10.6.

Figure 10.6
Align dynamic expressions and hairpins with the Align/Move Dynamics dialog box.

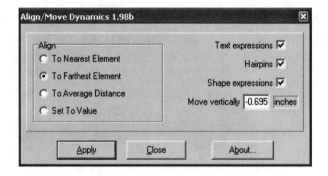

4. In the Align section, choose To Average Distance. By choosing this setting, you are telling Finale to find the average distance for the expressions and set them all to that distance from the staff.

5. Click Apply to see the expressions align (move the dialog box out of the way if necessary). They now all appear at the same distance from the staff.

6. Without leaving the dialog box, click in the score.

7. Hold down the Ctrl/Command key and press Z to undo your changes. Now, we'll align all expressions to the one closest to the staff.

8. In the Align/Move Dynamics dialog box, select To Nearest Element.

9. Click Apply. Now, the expressions all align to the expression closest to the staff. You can also choose To Farthest Element in the Align/Move Dynamics dialog box to align the expressions to the one farthest from the staff.

10. Click Close to close the Align/Move Dynamics dialog box.

You can also use the Align/Move Dynamics plug-in to align hairpins and shape expressions by checking the desired items on the right side of the Align/Move Dynamics dialog box. You can tell Finale to move these markings up or down by entering a value in the Move Vertically text box.

NOTE

As the name implies, the Align/Move Dynamics plug-in aligns only *dynamic* expressions (*mf*, *p*, etc.), and will not align expressions in your score that are not dynamic markings.

Positioning Rests

By default, Finale places rests according to standard notation conventions. In measures with a single layer, rest placement generally lies in the middle of the staff (the precise placement depends on the rest's duration). As long as you are using one of Finale's music fonts, placement of rests should look fine. However, if you are using a third-party music font, the rest characters may be offset. Or, you may be creating notation that calls for rests in a document to be repositioned vertically. You can change the default placement of rests in the Document Options dialog box. From the Options menu, choose Document Options and select Notes and Rests. The Notes and Rests options appear, as shown in Figure 10.7.

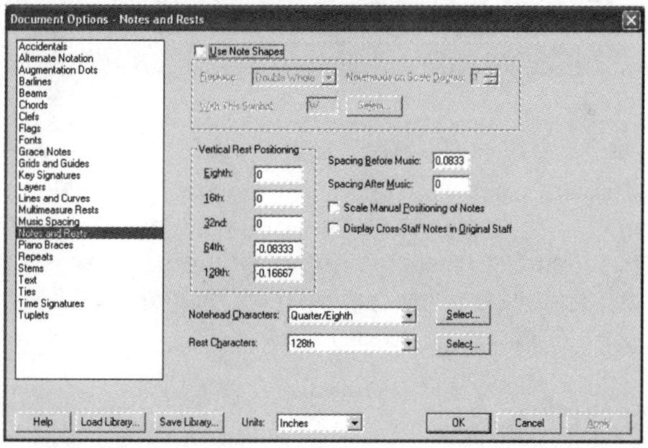

Figure 10.7
Make document-wide settings for rests in the Notes and Rests category of the Document Options.

In the Vertical Rest Positioning section, set the offset for any rest duration of an eighth or less from the middle staff line. Click OK to apply changes and return to the score.

In measures with more than one layer, Finale automatically offsets rests higher or lower in the staff to distinguish between multiple voices. These are called "floating rests." For example, enter a quarter rest in layer one, and then in the same measure, enter a quarter rest in layer two. Notice that as you enter the rest in layer two, the rest in layer one jumps up, and the rest in layer two appears lower in the staff. You can tell Finale how to treat the placement of rests while working in multiple layers in the Layer options. From the Options menu, choose Document Options and select Layers. The Layer options appear, as shown in Figure 10.8.

Figure 10.8
Make document-wide settings for layers in the Layers category of the Document Options.

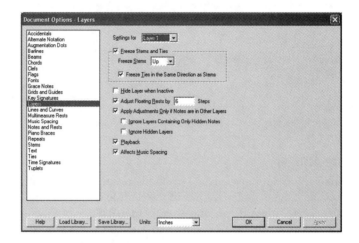

From the drop-down/popup menu at the top, choose the layer of the rests you want to change. Then, enter the offset, in steps for Adjust Floating Rests by_ (a step is a line or space in the staff). The default value is 6 for layer 1 and –6 for layer 2, so floating rests appear centered on the first ledger line above the staff for layer 1 and below the staff for layer 2. Uncheck this option to tell Finale to use the positioning for rests as specified in Document Options-Rests for all rests in the selected layer.

If you want to use the vertical rest positioning specified in the Layer options even when there are no notes in other layers, uncheck Apply Adjustments Only if Notes are in Other Layers. With this box unchecked, all rests in the layer will position themselves according to the floating rest setting. Click OK to return to the score and review your settings. Changes made will apply to all existing music and all new music added to the document.

Editing Beams

By default, Finale beams together all notes in a beat (with the exception of eighth notes in common time, which can be beamed in groups of four). You can find general beaming settings for a document in the Document Options dialog box. From the Options menu, choose Document Options, and select Beams. The Beam options appear, as shown in Figure 10.9.

Figure 10.9
Make document-wide
settings for beams in the
Beams category of the
Document Options.

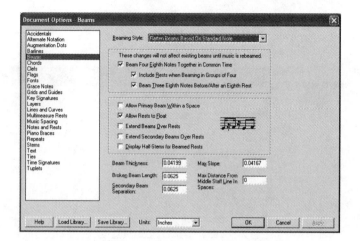

CHAPTER 10

Use these options to adjust the default appearance of beams throughout your document. Here, you can tell Finale to use flat beams (under the Beaming Style drop-down/popup menu), beam over rests, modify the maximum slope of beams, and make other document-wide adjustments. Settings here dictate largely how your beaming will look immediately after entering the notation. Following are some common ways to edit beams throughout your document in the Document Option's Beam settings:

▶ By default, Finale beams groups of four eighth notes together in common time. In other words, it breaks eighth note beams only on beat three. To break eighth note beams on every beat in common time (to always beam eighth notes in groups of two), uncheck Beam Four Eighth Notes Together in Common Time.

▶ Note the section containing five checkboxes and a preview example. This short musical example updates to display the appearance of beams based on the combination of checkboxes selected. For example, check Allow Rests to Float and Extend Beams over rests. Notice that the figure updates as you check or uncheck these options. Use this preview as a guide to customize the default appearance of beams for your document.

▶ In the lower portion, enter values to specify beam thickness, broken beam length, secondary beam separation, and max slope for beams. To change the measurement unit to use for these settings (inches, centimeters etc), click the drop-down-popup menu for Units at the bottom of this dialog box.

Besides settings for treatment of eighth note beams in common time, the beam settings in the Document Options do not apply to the default beam grouping. To specify default beam groups to use as you enter music into the score, use the Time Signature tool.

Beaming Patterns and Time Signatures

Beaming patterns are stored in Time Signatures. When you specify a Time Signature, Finale will apply a beaming pattern for the music based on the duration of the main beat. For example, in

6/8 time, with a dotted quarter note as the main beat, Finale will automatically beam six eighth notes in two groups of three, as seen in Figure 10.10.

Figure 10.10
Beaming for a 6/8 Time
Signature.

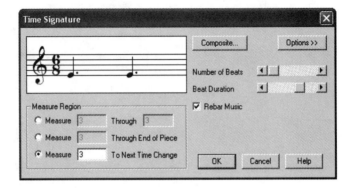

You can specify a custom beaming pattern for any Time Signature manually, and even apply a new beaming pattern without changing the Time Signature. To demonstrate this, here are steps for creating a custom beaming pattern for a 7/8 measure. In this example, we will create a beaming pattern with eighth notes in groups of two and three. Let's start fresh with a new default document (File > New > Default Document).

1. With the Time Signature tool selected, doubleclick a measure to display the Time Signature dialog box.

2. For Number of Beats, click the right arrow until 7 appears as the top number in the preview display.

3. For beat duration, click the left arrow until 8 appears as the bottom number in the preview display, indicating a Key Signature of 7/8.

4. Click the Composite button at the top to open the Composite Key Signature dialog box. This is where we will specify the beats/beaming pattern.

5. After Beat Duration, enter the rhythmic value that represents the smallest subdivision of notes you will be beaming. In this case, enter 8. This value will usually be the same as the bottom number in your Key Signature.

6. Now, after Beat Groups, in the FIRST box, specify the number of notes in each group. In this case, we will enter 3+2+2 (Figure 10.11). Notice the preview display indicates the beamed groups.

Figure 10.11
In the Composite Time
Signature dialog box,
you can specify the beat
duration and beaming
for any Time Signature.

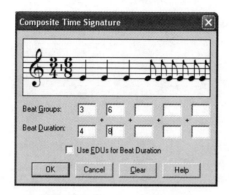

CHAPTER 10

7. Click OK. You will now see the composite Time Signature in the preview
    display, though you will probably just want to display 7/8 in the score.

8. Click the Options (Mac: More Choices) button to expand the lower section.

9. Adjust the Number of Beats and Beat Duration in the lower section as you did
    above to indicate a Time Signature of 7/8.

10. Check Use a Different Time Signature for Display. By checking this box, you tell
    Finale to use the Time Signature in the lower section for display.

11. Click OK to return to the score.

12. Enter eighth notes into the staff with the Simple or Speedy Entry tool. You will
    see the notes beamed to the pattern specified in the Composite Time Signature
    dialog box.

Rebeaming a Selected Region

At any time, you can reset the beaming for a region of music back to the settings specified in the
Time Signature and Document Options. To do this, click the Mass Edit Tool and highlight a
region of your score. Then, from the Mass Edit menu, choose Rebeam > Rebeam Music. Beaming
in the selected region reverts back to the region's Time Signature settings and updates the region
to your settings in Document Options-Beams (Figure 10.9). You would most often use this
feature after manually editing beams with Simple or Speedy Entry. For more control over the
beaming of a selected region, you can rebeam to a Time Signature with the Mass Edit Tool as
well.

Rebeaming To Time Signature

Above, you learned how to adjust beaming patterns for a Time Signature. You can also apply
beaming settings for any region of your score without changing the Time Signature, or even
going into the Time Signature tool. To do this, click the Mass Edit Tool and select a region of
music. From the Mass Edit menu, choose Rebeam > Rebeam to Time Signature. The Rebeam to
Time Signature dialog box appears, as shown in Figure 10.12.

Figure 10.12
Edit beamed groups in
the Rebeam to Time
Signature dialog box.

Here, edit the beat groups for the region as you would by changing the Time Signature. Click the Composite button to open the Composite Time Signature dialog box (Figure 10.11) where you can specify beaming groups for each beat (as described in the steps above under "Beaming Patterns and Time Signatures").

Rebeaming To Lyrics

In some vocal music, beams appear only over melismas (when more than one note is sung for a syllable). In Finale, you can rebeam music to lyrics automatically to fit this paradigm. Click the Mass Edit Tool and select a region of a score with lyrics and notes of an eighth note (or shorter) duration. From the Mass Edit menu, choose Rebeam > Rebeam to Lyrics. The Rebeam to Lyrics dialog box appears, as shown in Figure 10.13.

Figure 10.13
Specify a lyric to
rebeam to in the
Rebeam to Lyrics dialog
box.

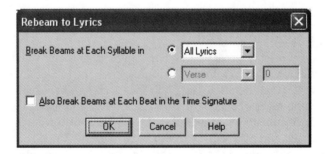

Here, after Break Beams at Each Syllable in, click the drop-down/popup menu and specify the type of lyric you want Finale to take into account while beaming to syllables. If you only have one line of lyrics, choose All Lyrics here. From the lower drop-down menu, choose a specific verse, section or chorus to which to beam. If you want Finale to break beams over melismas that carry over a beat, check Also Break Beams at Each Beat in the Time Signature. Click OK to apply lyric beaming to the selected region. See Figure 10.14 for an example of music before and after running Rebeam to Lyrics.

Figure 10.14
Beaming before and
after applying Rebeam
to Lyrics.

Editing Beams Individually

Finale lets you edit the appearance of individual beams in several ways. You can add or remove beams between notes with the Simple or Speedy Entry tool, or modify the appearance of beams using several tools in the Special Tools Palette.

Use the Simple Entry tool or Speedy Entry tool to add or remove a beam between any two notes. To add or remove beams in Simple Entry, click the Simple Entry tool, and then Ctrl/Option-click the second of two eighth notes (or any two notes of lesser value than a quarter note). Press the B key to break or join a beam from the previous note. To add or remove beaming in Speedy Entry, click the Speedy Entry tool, then move the cursor over the second of two notes and press the B key to break or join a beam from the previous note.

While in Simple Entry or Speedy Entry, you can flatten an angled beam by pressing the M key, or return to default beaming by pressing Shift-B.

TIP

To flatten all beams in a region, use the Flat Beams plug-in. Select a region of measures with the Mass Edit Tool, then from the Plug-ins menu, choose Note, Beam and Rest Editing > Flat Beams. Choose Flat Beams (Remove) to remove flat beams in a region.

Changing the Beam Angle

You can edit the angle of any beam individually with the Beam Angle tool. Click the Special Tools tool to display the Special Tools Palette (on Windows, click the Window menu and choose Advanced Tools Palette, then select the Special Tools tool from the Advanced Tools Palette). Click the Beam Angle tool in the Special Tools Palette. Click a measure to display a handle on the end of each beam in the measure. Click the right handle to adjust the angle of the beam, and the left handle to adjust the vertical placement of the beam (Figure 10.15).

Figure 10.15
Adjusting beams with
the Beam Angle tool.

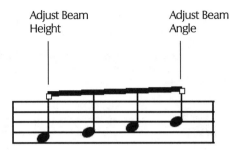

Feathered Beaming

Editing beams with the Beam Angle tool will adjust all beams in the group (eighth, sixteenth, etc.) evenly. You can also adjust the height and angle of secondary beams individually, to create feathered beaming, for example (Figure 10.16). To create feathered beaming:

1. Enter a string of consecutive 32nd notes (or notes of any duration that are connected with multiple beams).

2. Click the Special Tools tool to display the Special Tools Palette (on Windows, click the Window menu and choose Advanced Tools Palette, then select the Special Tools tool from the Advanced Tools Palette).

3. Click the Secondary Beam Angle tool in the Special Tools Palette.

4. Click the measure containing the 32nd notes so there is a handle on each end of all secondary beams.

5. Drag the left handle to position the placement of the start point for each secondary beam, and the right handle to adjust the angle and endpoint for each secondary beam as you would with the Beam Angle tool. Using these positioning handles, you can create feathered beaming in both directions, as shown in Figure 10.16. Use the up and down arrow keys to nudge handles for fine adjustments.

Figure 10.16
Feathered beaming.

6. Now, if you want to adjust the angle of all beams, click the Beam Angle tool and adjust the left handle to change the height, and the right handle to adjust the angle of all beams in the group evenly. This way, you can slant the primary beam as well, as shown in Figure 10.17.

Figure 10.17
Feathered beaming
adjusted with the Beam
Angle tool.

Extending Beams

In addition to adjusting the beam angle, you can change the length of any beam. Click the Beam Extension tool in the Special Tools Palette. Click a measure containing beamed notes. You will see a handle appear on each end of the primary beams. Click and drag, or use the arrow keys to nudge the start or endpoint of the beam.

If you want to extend a secondary beam, double-click one of the handles to open the Beam Extension Selection dialog box, as shown in Figure 10.18.

Figure 10.18
Select the beams you
want to extend in the
Beam Extension
Selection dialog box.

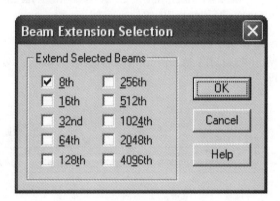

Here, check the beam type you want to extend (8th = primary beam, 16th = first secondary beam, 32nd = second secondary beam, etc.). Then, click OK. Drag a handle to adjust the beams you selected in the Beam Extension Selection dialog box. You might use this technique to beam over rests individually. If you find yourself making many changes to your score with the Beam Extension tool, try adjusting the default beaming settings in the Document Options (from the Options menu, choose Document Options and select Beams—see Figure 10.9).

CHAPTER 10

Flipping Broken Beams Across Stems

Broken beams can appear when a beamed group contains different rhythmic durations. Any broken beam can be flipped to the other side of the stem with the Broken Beam tool. To see this, enter a dotted eighth note followed by a sixteenth note, and then another eighth note in a measure. Beam the second eighth note to the previous sixteenth with the Simple Entry tool. Your measure should look like the top example in Figure 10.19.

Figure 10.19
Flipping broken beams across stems.

Click the Broken Beam tool in the Special Tools Palette. Then, click the measure. You will see a handle appear above and below the broken beam. Click the bottom handle to flip the broken beam across the stem, as shown in Figure 10.19.

Breaking Through Secondary Beams

Sometimes, secondary beams are broken within beamed groups, as shown in Figure 10.20.

Figure 10.20
Breaking through secondary beams.

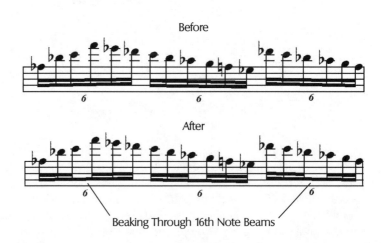

Beaking Through 16th Note Beams

To break secondary beams, click the Secondary Beam Break tool in the Special Tools Palette. Click a measure containing secondary beams. You will see a handle appear above each note. Double-click the handle on the second of two notes (you will be editing the beams to the left of the note you double-click). The Secondary Beam Break Selection dialog box appears, as shown in figure 10.21.

Figure 10.21
Specify the beams you want to break in the Secondary Beam Break Selection dialog box.

Here, check the beams you want to break. To break all beams up to the primary beam (as shown in Figure 10.19), choose Break Though, and check all boxes in the Beam Durations section. Click OK to return to the score. All secondary beams to the left of the note disappear.

You can also specify individual beams to break. Follow the same instructions as described above, only in the Secondary Beam Break Selection dialog box, choose Break Only. Then, in the Beam Durations section, check all beams you want to break.

Beaming over Barlines

Sometimes, beams extend across barlines into the next measure, as shown in Figure 10.22. Finale does not directly support beaming over barlines, so this process is basically a workaround.

Figure 10.22
Beaming across barlines.

To extend a beam across a barline:

1.   Click the Speedy Entry tool.

2.   From the Speedy menu, uncheck Jump to Next Measure and Check for Extra Notes.

3.   Click the measure to the left of the barline you would like to beam across, and enter all notes including all notes you want to include in the beamed group across the barline (there will be extra notes in this measure). Use the B key to beam the appropriate notes.

4.   Now, click the following measure to open the Speedy Frame. Enter rests that equal the duration of the extra notes from the previous measure. For example, if you want a single eighth note to appear beamed across the barline (as shown in Figure 10.22), you would enter an eighth rest. These will be placeholder rests to accommodate spacing.

5. With the Speedy Frame still open, use the H key to hide the placeholder rests.

6. After hiding placeholder rest, enter notes to complete the measure.

7. Click back on the first measure to open the Speedy Frame.

8. Use the right arrow key to move the cursor to the end of the measure (so the extra notes are visible).

9. Click and drag the extra notes to the right, over the right edge of the staff lines.

10. Click outside the Speedy Frame to see your results. Since you cannot see the barline in the Speedy Frame, you may need to go back and make further adjustments to the note placement in the Speedy Frame. Remember, you can also adjust the position of notes with the Special Tools Note Position tool.

If you would like to beam over a barline at the end of the system, you can use the Beam Extension and Beam Angle special tools to edit the beams accordingly.

TIP

To easily extend beams over barlines, try the Beam Over Barlines plug-in included with the Patterson Plug-in collection. You can download this plug-in set from Robert Patterson's website at www.robertgpatterson.com or copy the plug-ins from the companion CD-ROM. See chapter 15 for more information regarding the Beam Over Barlines plug-in.

Patterson Beams Plug-in

This plug-in can make adjustments to beam angles, widths, and stems automatically to produce a publisher-specific look to beaming for a region of measures, or for the entire score. To use this plug-in, first, from the Options menu, choose Document Options and select Beams. Check Allow Primary Beam Within a Space, uncheck Extend Beams Over Rests, and set the Max Slope to 6 EVPUs. Click OK to return to the score. Now, highlight a region of the score with the Mass Edit Tool (or, if you want to apply the plug-in to the entire score, no selection in necessary). Then, from the Plug-ins menu, choose Patterson Beams. The Patterson Beams dialog box appears, as shown in figure 10.23.

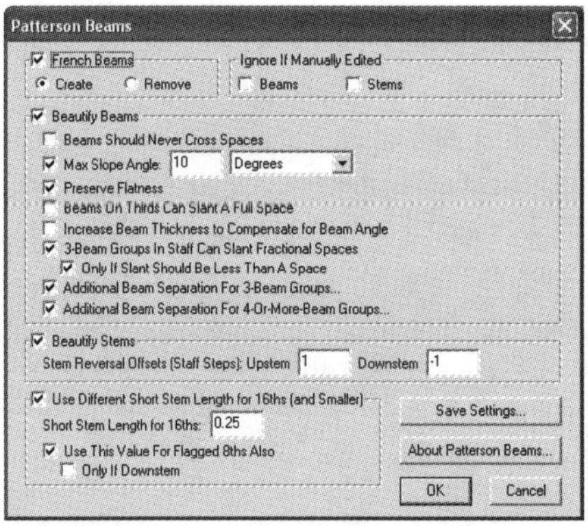

Figure 10.23
Use the Patterson Beams plug-in to specify the appearance of beams for a region or your entire document.

Here, you can choose from a variety of options for beam and stem adjustment. Robert Patterson, the third-party plug-in developer responsible for the Patterson Beams plug-in, explains each parameter in the Patterson Beams dialog box at his website <www.robertgpatterson.com>. Also, refer to this website for specific settings you can use that meet professional publishing standards. Click the About Patterson Beams button for a link to this website. After making your settings, click OK to return to the score and review your results. Note that the Patterson Beams plug-in makes static adjustments based on note position, measure width, and page layout. It is recommended that you make these adjustments near the end of your process.

Editing Stems

As you enter notes, Finale determines stem direction and length based on a number of factors. The default settings are based on standard notation practice. Stems on notes below the middle staff line go up; stems on notes on or above the middle staff line go down. Stems on notes above and below the staff always extend to the middle staff line. You can adjust several default stem settings in the Document Options dialog box. From the Options menu, choose Document Options and select Stems. The Stem options appear, as shown in Figure 10.24.

Figure 10.24
Make document-wide settings for stems in the Stems category of the Document Options.

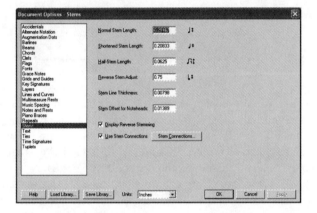

Use these options to adjust the default appearance of stems throughout your document. Change the default stem length, flipped stem length, or even modify the placement of stems relative to notes by selecting Stem Connections (we'll talk more about stem connections later). In addition to the Stem options, you can also modify the default direction of stems in measures with multiple layers in the Layer options.

Without leaving the Document Options, click the Layers category on the left. The Layer options appear (Figure 10.8). In the Layer options, you can set the default stem direction for each layer. From the drop-down/popup menu at the top, choose the layer you want to change. Check Freeze Stems and Ties, then choose the default direction from the Freeze Stems drop-down/popup menu. This setting also affects the default direction of ties. Click OK to apply all settings you have made in the Document Options dialog box and return to the score.

Stem Connections

You can modify Finale's default placement of stems relative to any notehead character for any document. Setting up stem connections may be necessary if you are using custom noteheads, or noteheads in a third-party music font. To edit stem connections for a notehead character, use the Stem Connection Editor. From the Options menu, choose Document Options and select Stems. Then, click the Stem Connections button. The Stem Connections dialog box appears, as shown in Figure 10.25.

Figure 10.25
All custom stem connections are visible in the Stem Connections dialog box.

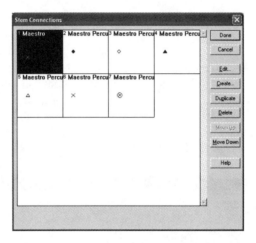

Here, you see a list of custom noteheads that require specialized stem connections. In the upper left of each selection, you will see the name of the font for each notehead character. You will not see the default noteheads here, because they use default stem connection settings (and need no adjustments, though they can be edited). To edit any of the existing stem connections, click one of the notehead characters and then click the Edit button. To create a stem connection for a character not available in the Stem Connections dialog box, click Create. After choosing either Edit or Create, the Stem Connection Editor dialog box appears, as shown in Figure 10.26.

Figure 10.26
Edit the placement of a stem for a specific notehead character in the Stem Connection Editor dialog box.

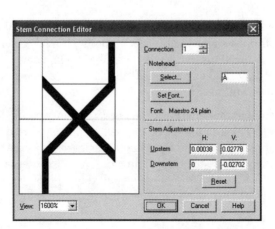

Here, make adjustments to the placement of the stem relative to the notehead. If you clicked Create, use the Set Font button to open the Font dialog box, where you can choose the font for a notehead. Click the Select button to open the Symbol Selection dialog box, where you can choose a specific character. Use the following tricks to adjust the stem connection to the selected character in the Stem Connection Editor dialog box.

▶ Click and drag the stems to move them around manually. Hold down the Shift key to constrain dragging vertically or horizontally. Notice the values change in the Stem Adjustments section as you move the stem. You can also enter specific values for the stem connections placement offset from the default placement in the Stem Adjustments section.

▶ Use the View drop-down/popup menu to adjust the view percentage to zoom in for fine adjustments, or zoom out to see the complete figure.

▶ Right/Option-Command-click and drag in the preview window to move the visible area.

▶ To change the character of the notehead, click the Select button in the Notehead section. The Symbol Selection dialog box appears, where you can choose a new character.

▶ To change the font of the existing character, click the Set Font button in the Notehead section. The Font dialog box appears, where you can choose a new font, size, and style for the notehead.

▶ Click Reset in the Stem Adjustments section to remove stem adjustments and return stems to the default placement.

▶ Use the up and down arrows for Connection (at the top) to move between notehead characters as they appear in the Stem Connections dialog box.

Once you have finished editing your stem connection, click OK to return to the Stem Connections dialog box. Click OK to return to the Document Options, and OK again to return to the score. Stems on notehead characters you edited will appear according to your settings in the Stem Connection Editor.

Editing Stems for a Selected Region

There are a number of ways to edit stem direction, placement, and visual definition for a selected region of your score. You can easily freeze stems up or down with the Mass Edit Tool. To do this, click the Mass Edit Tool and highlight a region of measures. From the Mass Edit menu, choose Utilities > Freeze Stems Up or Freeze Stems down.

TIP

To apply the Freeze Stem utility or any Mass Edit function to a specific layer, choose Show Active Layer Only from the View menu. Then, select the layer you want to edit. Now, changes with the Mass Edit Tool will apply only to the visible layer.

Define Stem Settings for Individual Staves

Starting with Finale 2003, you can edit stem placement, direction, and the visual definition for any staff in the Staff Attributes. Click the Staff tool and double-click a staff to open the Staff Attributes dialog box. In the Items to Display section, click the Stem Settings button to open the Staff Stem Settings dialog box (Figure 8.22). Here are some ways to edit stems for a staff in the Staff Stem Settings dialog box:

▶ In the Stem Direction section, define a default stem direction for notes in the staff. Note that if there is more than one layer in a measure, the stem direction settings will revert to those specified in Document Options-Layers.

▶ Uncheck Show Beams to remove all beams from a staff.

▶ Click the Units drop-down/popup menu to change measurement units (inches, EVPUs, centimeters, etc.) for values in this dialog box.

▶ To place stems directly above the staff or below the staff (as commonly used in TAB notation), check Use Vertical Offset for Notehead End of Stems. Then, choose Offset from Staff and enter 25 EVPUs for Up Stem and –25 EVPUs for Down Stem. Check Use Vertical Offset for Beam End of Stems (Offset from Staff), and then in the section beneath, set Up Stem to 115 EVPUs and Down Stem to –115 EVPUs. You can also make these settings automatically by choosing On "OK", Reset Staff's Attributes to Tablature Defaults in the Tablature Staff Attributes, and then checking Stems in the Staff Attributes dialog box. See chapter 8 for more details on TAB notation.

Once you have finished making stem settings, click OK to return to the Staff Attributes and OK again to return to the score. Stems throughout the staff change to reflect settings you configured in the Staff Stem Settings dialog box.

Since the Staff Stem Settings are a staff attribute, you can create a new Staff Style and apply stem settings to any region of your score. From the Staff menu, choose Define Staff Styles. Click New at the top and enter a name in the Available Styles text box. Click the Stem Settings button and make your custom settings. Click OK twice to return to the score. Now, highlight a region of your score, Right/Control click the highlighted area and choose the Staff Style you created. See chapter 8 for more information on Staff Styles.

Midline Stem Direction Plug-in

Usually, the stem direction for notes on the middle staff line is down. However, for a cleaner look, it is common to flip this stem if the previous note's stem is up. With this plug-in, you can tell Finale to flip the stem on notes on the middle staff line based on the stem direction of the previous and following notes (Figure 10.27). Click the Mass Edit Tool and highlight a region of music. From the Plug-ins menu, choose Note, Beam and Rest Editing > Midline Stem Direction.

Figure 10.27
Use the Midline Stem Direction plug-in to edit the midline stem direction based on surrounding notes.

Changing the Default Midline Stem Direction

You can set the stem reversal (point in the staff where stems flip automatically) in the Staff Setup dialog box. With the Staff tool selected, double-click a staff to open the Staff Attributes. Click the drop-down/popup menu for Staff, and choose Other. The Staff Setup dialog box appears (Figure 8.8). In the Stem Reversal text box, enter the position, in steps, from the top staff line you want Finale to flip stems down (the default setting is –4, so notes on the middle line and above flip down by default). Enter –3 if you want all stems on the middle line to flip up automatically, and all notes on the third space and above to flip down. Click OK twice to return to the score with the new stem reversal applied. Apply these settings to all desired staves, or create a staff style to apply them to any selected region.

Editing Stems Individually

Finale lets you edit stems individually in many ways. You can flip stem direction for any note with the Simple or Speedy Entry tool, or modify the length and appearance of stems using several tools in the Special Tools Palette.

Use the Simple Entry tool or Speedy Entry tool to flip stems. Click the Simple Entry tool, then Ctrl/Option-click a note. Press the L key to flip the stem (you may have to press it twice). To flip the stem back, simply press the L key again. To edit the stem direction in Speedy Entry, click the Speedy Entry tool and click a measure to open the Speedy Frame. Move the cursor over an entry and press the L key to flip the stem direction.

While in Simple Entry or Speedy Entry, hold down the Shift key and press L to tell Finale to use the default stem direction for the specified note.

You can also change the stem direction for a number of individual notes quickly with the Stem Direction tool. Click the Special Tools tool to display the Special Tools Palette (on Windows, click the Window menu and choose Advanced Tools Palette, then select the Special Tools tool from the Advanced Tools Palette). Click the Stem Direction tool in the Special Tools Palette. Now, click a measure to see a handle above and below each note in the active layer. Click the top handle to flip a stem up, or the bottom handle to flip a stem down.

Changing the Stem Length and Horizontal Positioning

You can change the length and horizontal positioning of any stem with the Stem Length tool. Click the Stem Length tool in the Special Tools Palette, then click a measure containing notes. You will see a handle above and below all the notes in the active layer. Now, click and drag the handle to increase or decrease the length of the stem. You can also move the stem left or right relative to the note. Use the arrow keys to nudge a selected handle to make fine adjustments. Hold down the Shift key to constrain horizontal or vertical dragging.

Changing the Appearance and Hiding a Stem

You can change the appearance or hide a stem with the Custom Stem tool. Click the Custom Stem tool in the Special Tools Palette, then click a measure to display a handle on each stem. Double-click a stem to open the Shape Selection dialog box, where you can choose from a library of shapes to use for the stem. To create your own shape, or replace the stem with a blank entry to hide it, click the Create button to open the Shape Designer. Here, use the various tools to design your own stem shape. If you want to hide the stem, leave this window blank. Click OK and Select to return to the score with your new settings applied.

Editing Notes and Noteheads

There are many ways to edit notes and noteheads individually without using the basic editing functionality of the Simple or Speedy Entry tool. Following are some special ways to edit a variety of properties of individual notes using the Edit Frame dialog box and the Special Tools.

The Edit Frame dialog box

This is a seldom-used dialog box that allows you to view and change the raw data stored with every note. Here, you can tell Finale to remove an individual note from playback, or ignore a note during music spacing, and make other changes. You will probably never need to use this dialog box, but it's good to know it exists. To get there, click the Speedy Entry tool. Then, click outside a staff to ensure that Speedy Frame is not active. Then, Ctrl/Option-click a measure containing at least one note.

Figure 10.28
Use the Edit Frame
dialog box to make fine
changes to notes
individually, or to
change their properties.

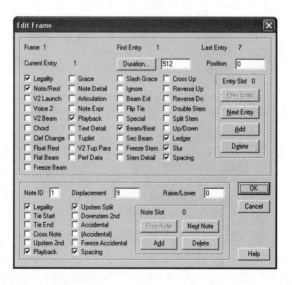

The frame number (in the upper left) tells you the number of the frame you are editing. The frame number is ordered not by measure number, but by the order in which the frame/measure was added. The First Entry and Last Entry numbers indicate the range of notes that exist in the measure. Like frames, entries are numbered sequentially (in the order they were added). The

Current Entry number is the entry you are currently editing. Use the options in the upper section to edit the entry. If the entry contains more than one note (a chord), you can specify settings for individual notes in the chord by editing the lower section.

NOTE
The Edit Frame dialog box will display notes in the current active layer.

Here are some ways to edit notes using the Edit Frame dialog box:

▶ Uncheck Playback to remove a note or entry from playback. Do this when you are using notes in another layer (hidden with a Staff Style, for example) for playback of trills, tremolos, or other figures.

▶ If you want to hide a note, but still want it to play it back, check both Ignore and Playback (pressing the O or H key in Simple or Speedy Entry both hides and mutes the entry).

▶ If you want an entry to be ignored while Finale reconfigures the music spacing, uncheck Spacing.

▶ If you have entered a tuplet in voice two overlapped by a tuplet in voice one, you will notice unwanted spacing in voice one. To correct spacing in this specific situation, check V2 Tup Para.

Editing Noteheads and Note Positioning With the Special Tools

There are three Special Tools devoted to editing notes individually. You can use the Note Position tool to reposition a note horizontally, the Notehead Position tool to position a notehead, or the Note Shape tool to change the character of a notehead individually.

To Reposition Notes Horizontally

1. Click the Special Tools tool.

2. From the Special Tools Palette, choose the Note Position tool.

3. Specify the layer containing the notes you want to reposition (choose the layer as you would normally).

4. Click the measure containing the notes. Handles appear above the staff for each note in the measure.

5. Click and drag (or user the arrow keys to nudge) a handle to reposition its corresponding note horizontally.

NOTE
You can also reposition individual notes horizontally by dragging them in the Speedy Frame.

To Reposition Noteheads Horizontally

1. Click the Special Tools tool.
2. From the Special Tools Palette, choose the Notehead Position tool.
3. Specify the layer containing the notes you want to reposition (choose the layer as you would normally).
4. Click the measure containing the notes. Handles appear by each notehead in the measure (in the active layer).
5. Click and drag (or user the arrow keys to nudge) a handle to reposition the noteheads horizontally.

To Change Notehead Characters Individually, or Remove a Notehead

1. Click the Special Tools tool.
2. From the Special Tools Palette, choose the Note Shape tool.
3. Specify the layer containing the notes you want to reposition (choose the layer as you would normally).
4. Click the measure containing the notes. Handles appear by each notehead in the measure (in the active layer).
5. Double-click a handle to open the Symbol Selection window, where you can choose from the characters available in the current music font.
6. Double-click a character to use it for the selected note. If you want to remove the notehead, choose the blank character (# 32 in the Maestro font).

After choosing the new notehead, you may need to move it so it appears correctly next to the stem. To define a stem connection for any notehead character, use the Stem Connections dialog box (from the Options menu, choose Document Options and select Stems, then click Stem Connections—see "Stem Connections" above for details).

Editing Accidentals

We already have described how to enter accidentals with the Simple and Speedy Entry tool. You can make a variety of changes to the positioning and appearance of accidentals for your entire document, or for individual entries. You can change the default character or positioning for accidentals throughout your document in the Document Options dialog box. From the Options menu, choose Document Options and select Accidentals. The Accidentals options appear, as shown in Figure 10.29.

Figure 10.29
Make document-wide
settings for accidentals
in the Accidentals
category of the
Document Options.

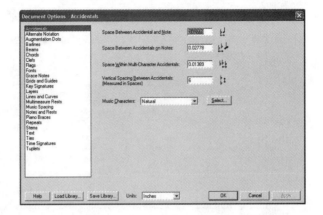

Use these options to adjust the positioning and character of accidentals throughout your
document.

▶ Enter new values in the four available text boxes for positioning of accidentals
relative to notes and each other. Click the drop-down/popup menu for Units to
change the unit of measurement.

▶ Here, you can change the character of any accidental. Click the Music Characters
drop-down/popup menu and select the character you want to change. Then,
click the Select button to the right to open the Symbol Selection dialog box,
where you can choose a new character for the accidental. Click Select to return
to the Document Options.

If you would like to select a different font for your accidentals, click the Fonts category in the
Document Options dialog box to display the font options. Click the drop-down/popup menu for
Notation and choose Accidentals. Then, click the Set Font button to the right to open the Font
dialog box, where you can choose a new font, size, and style for your accidentals.

Changing the Default Enharmonic Spelling

You can adjust the default spelling for pitches in the score that lie outside the key by using
settings under the Options menu. These settings generally apply to music entered with a MIDI
keyboard. If you want Finale to tend to use sharps while representing pitches in your score,
from the Options menu, choose Favor Sharps. Choose Favor Flats if you want Finale to tend to
use flats to represent pitches. Choose Use Spelling Tables to tell Finale to use a custom
definition for enharmonic spelling as specified in the spelling tables.

Editing the Major and Minor Key Spelling Table

Use this table to define the automatic spelling of nondiatonic pitches in major and minor keys.
From the Options menu, choose Enharmonic Spelling > Edit Major and Minor Key Spellings.
The Edit Major and Minor Key Spellings dialog box appears, as shown in Figure 10.30.

Figure 10.30
Edit the spelling of
nondiatonic pitches in
the Edit Major and
Minor Key Spellings
dialog box.

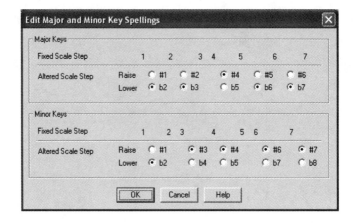

In this dialog box, choose whether to use a raised or lowered note to represent pitches between whole steps in a major or minor diatonic scale. In the key of C, for example, step 1=C, step 2=D, step 3=E, etc. To display the note between C and D as D flat (in the key of C), choose b2 under the 1 column. Finale will use the settings you specify in the Major or Minor spelling table depending on the mode (major or minor) of the key specified in the Key Signature dialog box.

If you are using a nonstandard key that is modal or chromatic, you may want to assign a spelling for each pitch in the chromatic scale. To do this, from the Options menu, choose Enharmonic Spelling > Edit Modal or Chromatic Key Spellings. The Edit Modal or Chromatic Spellings dialog box appears, as shown in Figure 10.31.

Figure 10.31
Edit the spelling of
nondiatonic pitches for
modal or chromatic Key
Signatures in the Edit
Modal or Chromatic
Spellings dialog box.

Here, choose the enharmonic spelling for each pitch of the chromatic scale. Click OK to return to the score. Notes entered with a MIDI keyboard will reflect the settings you specified in the spelling tables (be sure Use Spelling Tables is checked in the Enharmonic Spelling submenu of the Options menu if you want to use them).

Checking Accidentals

Occasionally, there may be an accidental visible at the conclusion of a tie that should be hidden. To check for and remove extraneous accidentals, run the Check Accidentals utility. Click the Mass Edit Tool and select a region of the score (Ctrl/Command-A to Select All). From the Mass Edit menu, choose Utilities > Check Accidentals. Extra accidentals in the selected region are removed.

Positioning Accidentals Individually

You can manipulate the positioning of each accidental in your score individually with the Special Tools. Click the Special Tools tool to display the Special Tools Palette (on Windows, click the Window menu and choose Advanced Tools Palette, then select the Special Tools tool from the Advanced Tools Palette). Click the Accidental Mover tool in the Special Tools Palette. Now, click a measure containing notes with accidentals. You will see a handle on each accidental. Click and drag, or use the arrow keys, to nudge accidentals horizontally.

If you are creating early music notation that requires Musica Ficta markings, click the Accidental Positioning tool, right/Control-click an accidental handle and choose Edit. Set the size of the accidental (usually 75%) and place a checkmark on "Allow Vertical Positioning." Click OK and return to the score. Click this accidental's handle and drag it up above the notehead.

TIP

Use the Canonic Utilities plug-in (under the Plug-ins menu) to show accidentals on all notes. This is a handy tool for atonal music.

Editing Augmentation Dots and Ties

Like beams and stems, augmentation dots and ties can be positioned for an entire document, or individually. To edit the default positioning and visual definition of augmentation dots, from the Options menu, choose Document Options, and select Augmentation Dots. The Augmentation Dot options appear, as shown in Figure 10.32.

Figure 10.32
Make document-wide settings for augmentation dots in the Augmentation Dots category of the Document Options.

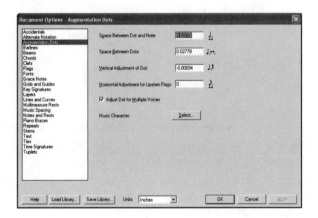

Use these options to adjust the positioning and character of augmentation dots throughout your document.

▶ Enter new values in the four available text boxes for positioning of augmentation dots relative to notes and each other. Click the drop-down/popup menu for Units to change the unit of measurement.

▶ To change the character of augmentation dots, click the Select button to open the Symbol Selection dialog box, where you can choose a new character for your augmentation dots.

If you would like to select an augmentation dot character in a different font, click the Fonts category in the Document Options dialog box to display the font options. Click the drop-down/popup menu for Notation and choose Augmentation Dot. Then, click the Set Font button to the right to open the Font dialog box, where you can choose a new font, size, and style for your augmentation dots.

To edit the default positioning and visual definition of ties, from the Options menu, choose Document Options and select Ties. The Tie options appear, as shown in Figure 10.33.

Figure 10.33
Make document-wide settings for ties in the Ties category of the Document Options. Use these options to define the default visual definition of ties.

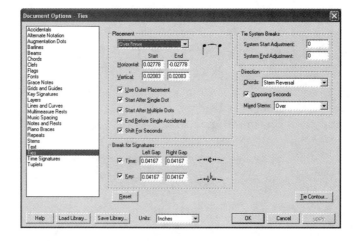

▶ In the Placement section, click the drop-down/popup menu and choose the type of tie you want to edit (depending on note placement). Look to the preview display on the right to see the selected tie style.

▶ Use the Horizontal and Vertical text boxes to enter a start and stop point for ties of the selected style. Click the drop-down/popup menu for Units to change the unit of measurement.

▶ In the Break for Signatures section, specify the treatment of ties over meter and key changes. Use the text boxes to indicate the amount of space before and after the tie break.

▶ Click the Reset button to revert all settings in this box back to the defaults.

▶ Click the Tie Contour button to open the Tie Contour dialog box, where you can specify the precise shape of ties throughout your document.

Editing Dots

You can edit augmentation dots individually with the Dot tool. Click the Special Tools tool to display the Special Tools Palette (on Windows, click the Window menu and choose Advanced Tools Palette, then select the Special Tools tool from the Advanced Tools Palette). Click the Dot tool in the Special Tools Palette. Then, click a measure containing notes with dots. A handle appears next to each dot in the measure. Click a handle and drag, or use the arrow keys to nudge augmentation dots. Hold down the Shift key to constrain dragging vertically or horizontally. Use the Zoom tool to zoom in on the measure for precision editing.

Adding and Editing Ties

Use the Simple Entry tool or Speedy Entry tool to add or remove a tie between any two notes of the same pitch. To add or remove ties in Simple Entry, click the Simple Entry tool, then Ctrl/Option-click a note to select it. Press the T key to extend a tie to the next note or remove an existing tie. Hold down the Shift key and press T to extend or remove a tie to the previous note. Finale will automatically remove extra accidentals. To add or remove a tie in Speedy Entry, click the Speedy Entry tool, and click a measure to invoke the Speedy Frame. Then, move the cursor over a note, and press the T key to extend a tie to the next note or remove an existing tie. Hold down the Shift key and press T to extend or remove a tie to the previous note.

You can edit the shape of ties individually with the Tie tool. Click the Tie tool in the Special Tools Palette. Then, click a measure containing notes with ties. Three handles appear on each tie in the measure. Click a handle and drag, or use the arrow keys to nudge these handles to adjust the start point, end point, and contour (Figure 10.34). Hold down the Shift key to constrain dragging vertically or horizontally.

Figure 10.34
Use the handles to edit ties with the Tie tool.

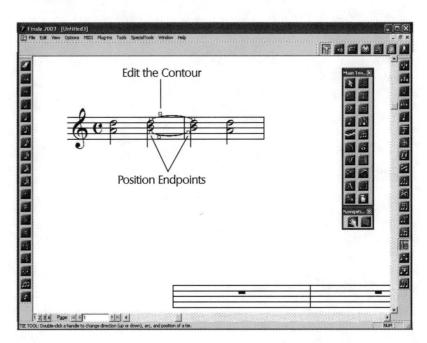

To ensure that all ties in your document will play back correctly, and appear over system breaks, run the Check Ties Utility. Choose the Mass Edit Tool and press Ctrl/Command-A to Select All. From the Mass Edit menu, choose Utilities > Check Ties.

TIP

Use the Patterson Move Ties plug-in to regionally edit the shape of ties. This is a powerful tool to mix tie appearance between Use Outer Placement and Avoid Staff Lines. Many publishers allow context to dictate the appearance of ties, and this plug-in makes the task quick and easy.

11

Measure Numbers, Graphics, Part Extraction, and Printing

In chapter 10, we covered a variety of ways to position and fine tune elements of a score in the later stages of a project. Now, we will focus on techniques for finalizing the score for printing. You will learn how to edit measure numbers and define measure number regions, add graphics, finalize system/page layout, extract parts from a multiple staff score, and print the score and parts. You will find that a number of techniques discussed in chapter 10, such as alignment and positioning, come into play throughout the final stages of score development. Some of the following topics expand on concepts introduced in earlier chapters, such as page layout and printing.

Here's a summary of what you will learn in this chapter:

▶ How to edit measure numbers.

▶ How to work with graphics.

▶ How to extract parts.

▶ Techniques for printing.

Measure Numbers

Measure numbers are an important element to any score. They can be added and manipulated with the Measure tool. By default, Finale places a measure number at the beginning of each system, though you can edit their frequency, positioning, and appearance individually, or for any region of your score. You can begin numbering at any measure, or even create several measure number regions to number multiple movements within the same file independently.

To prepare for this section, open a new default document. From the File menu, choose New > Default Document. You will see a measure number at the beginning of each system.

TIP
To add rehearsal letters, use expressions. See chapter 3 for information on creating expressions.

Editing Measure Numbers in the Score

You can make a number of adjustments to measure numbers individually in the score. Click the Measure tool to display handles on all measure numbers. Then, from the Measure menu, check Dragging Selects Number Handles. Use the following techniques to make basic changes to measure numbers.

▶ Click and drag to adjust the positioning of a measure number manually. Hold down the Shift key to constrain horizontal and vertical dragging.

▶ Select a measure number handle and press Backspace/Clear to return a measure number to its original placement.

▶ Select a measure number handle and press Delete to remove a measure number.

▶ Right/Command-click a measure number handle to open the Measure Number Context menu, where you can restore the default position, delete the measure number, or edit its enclosure.

▶ Double-click a measure number handle to edit its enclosure or add an enclosure.

When you double-click a measure number, the Enclosure Designer dialog box appears, as shown in Figure 11.1.

Figure 11.1
Create or edit a measure number enclosure in the Enclosure Designer dialog box.

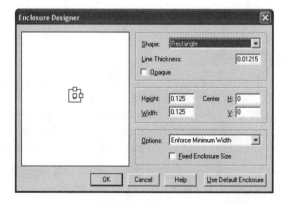

In the Enclosure Designer dialog box, click the Shape drop-down/popup menu to choose an enclosure shape. Check Opaque to tell Finale to hide any item behind the enclosure in the score. Click and drag the handles in the preview window to resize or move the enclosure. Click OK to return to the score. The enclosure now surrounds the measure number you selected.

You can also use the Measure menu to edit and manage measure numbers in the score.

▶ From the Measure menu, choose Dragging Selects Number Handles to select measure number handles while dragging, instead of barline handles.

▶ Select one or more measure number handles, and choose the Measure menu > Measure Numbers > Add Enclosures to open the Enclosure Designer, where you can define an enclosure for all selected measure numbers.

▶ To show measure numbers for every measure in a selected region of your score, highlight the region of measures and choose the Measure menu > Measure Numbers > Show Numbers. Measure numbers appear above all selected measures.

▶ Select one or more measure number handles, and choose the Measure menu > Measure Numbers > Hide Numbers to clear the selected measure numbers.

▶ Select one or more measure number handles, and choose the Measure menu > Measure Numbers > Restore Defaults to revert back to default settings for measure numbers, as specified in the Measure Number dialog box (explained below).

Creating and Editing Measure Number Regions

The default settings for measure numbers are stored in the Measure Number dialog box. From the Measure menu, choose Measure Numbers > Edit Regions. The Measure Number dialog box appears, as shown in Figure 11.2.

CHAPTER 11

Figure 11.2
Edit the frequency, font, size, style, and positioning—and create measure number regions—in the Measure Number dialog box.

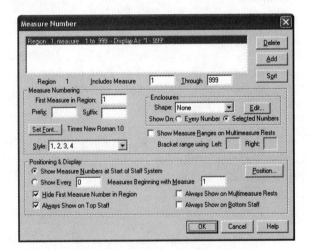

In this dialog box, make global changes to the appearance and positioning of measure numbers. All measure numbers in your score are organized by measure region. Notice the existing default entry at the top of this box: "Region 1, measure 1 to 999 --Display As: '1-999'." This entry tells Finale to number measures 1-999 as 1-999.

The predefined measure number region includes 999 measures beginning with the first measure of your document. This means each measure in the score is numbered consecutively for up to 999 measures. If each measure of your score consists of a valid musical measure, without interruption, the default measure number region will serve your purposes fine (for the first 999 measures). However, the actual measures in your score may not always serve the purpose of a "real" measure. Your numbering may need to skip a hidden measure used as a placeholder, or begin from measure one within the document for a second movement, for example. Resolve any such measure numbering problem by creating a new measure number region.

For the following example, let's say measure 11 is hidden with the "hide staff" Staff Style and should not be included in the measure numbering. "Real" measures are those as they exist in the Finale document, and "defined" measures are those you assign deliberately.

1. Click the Measure tool.

2. From the Measure menu, choose Measure Numbers > Edit Regions. The Measure Number dialog box appears (Figure 11.2).

3. Define the measures for the existing (first) region, in this case 1-10. Just below the region display window, for Includes Measures, enter the first and last "real" measure, "1" in the first box, and "10" in the second.

4. In the Measure numbering section, for First Number in Region, enter "1", since the first region begins at the first measure of the document.

5. For this demonstration, in the Positioning and Display section, choose (and enter) Show Every "1" Measures Beginning with Measure "1".

6. Click the Add button. A new region appears in the region display window. It is selected by default.

7. Now, define the measures for the new region, in this case 12-999 (the second region will extend to the end of the score). Just below the region display window, for Includes Measures, enter the first and last "real" measure of the second region. We want to skip measure 11, so enter "12" in the first box and "999" in the second.

8. In the Measure numbering section, for First Number in Region, enter "11".

9. Click OK. Notice that all measures are numbered consecutively, with an extra measure between numbers 10 and 11.

Use the above method to define as many measure number regions as you like. You can also easily assign measure number regions in your score with the Easy Measure Numbers plug-in (described below).

TIP

To tell Finale to display actual measure numbers (beginning from the first "real" measure), from the Options menu, choose Program Options and select View. Choose Display Actual Measure Numbers, and click OK. Now, from the View menu, choose Scroll View. The measure indicator at the bottom left of the screen now displays the "real" measure number.

Edit each measure region independently in the Measure Number dialog box. Simply click the desired region in the region display window, and then apply settings for the region using the available options. You can edit each region without leaving the Measure Number dialog box. Following are some common ways to edit measure numbers for a region:

▶ To set the font, size, and style for measure numbers in a region, click the Set Font button in the Measure Numbering section. The Font dialog box appears, where you can choose the font, size, and style.

▶ If you would like to use a numbering convention other than standard measure numbers, such as letters, click the Style drop-down/popup menu to choose a different format for your measure numbering.

▶ To show measure numbers only at the beginning of each system, in the Positioning and Display section, choose Show Measure Numbers at Start of Staff System.

▶ Check Always Show on Top Staff, or check Always Show on Bottom Staff to show measure numbers on the top or bottom staff regardless of measure number setting in the Staff Attributes. These settings can be particularly useful if you plan to optimize the score.

▶ To display measure number ranges for multimeasure rests, check Show Measure Ranges for Multimeasure Rests. In the Left and Right text boxes, enter the character to use (brackets, parentheses, etc.) to enclose the number ranges (Figure 11.3). Assigning measure regions for multimeasure rests will apply to multimeasure rests both in the existing score and in any extracted parts.

Figure 11.3
Measure regions on
multimeasure rests.

▶ To position measure numbers for a measure region, click the Positioning button in the Positioning and Display section. The Position Measure Number dialog box appears, as shown in Figure 11.4. Click and drag the measure number in the preview window to specify the measure positioning, or enter specific values in the H: and V: text boxes.

Figure 11.4
Use the Position Measure Number dialog box to position measure numbers for a measure number region.

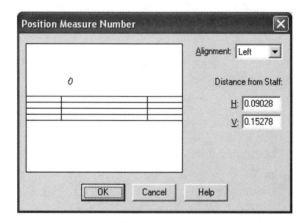

Easy Measure Numbers Plug-in

In addition to assigning measure regions in the Measure Number dialog box, you can also use the Easy Measure Numbers plug-in. Use this plug-in to apply regions to selected measures in the score. To prepare for the following instructions, delete existing measure number regions in your scratch document. With the Measure tool selected, click the Measure menu and choose Measure Numbers > Edit Regions to open the Measure Number dialog box. Now, click the Delete button several times until all regions have been removed. Click OK to return to the score. We'll then use the Easy Measure Numbers plug-in to create two measure number regions in your score.

1. Click the Mass Edit Tool.
2. Highlight measures one through ten.
3. From the Plug-ins menu, choose Measure Numbers > Easy Measure Numbers. The Easy Measure Numbers dialog box appears, as shown in Figure 11.5.

Figure 11.5
Use the Easy Measure Numbers dialog box to easily assign measure number regions.

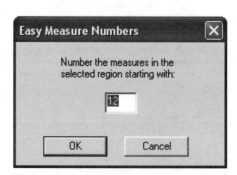

4. Type the first measure number in the selected region, in this case, "1."

5. Click OK. Measures one through ten are now defined as a measure number region. Now, let's say we want to skip a measure before you resume numbering.

6. Click the twelfth measure so it is highlighted.

7. Hold down the Shift key and press the right arrow key to select all remaining measures.

8. From the Plug-ins menu, choose Measure Numbers > Easy Measure Numbers. The Easy Measure Numbers dialog box appears.

9. Type "11" and click OK. Now, the remaining measures are numbered in a second measure number region.

To view or edit measure number regions created with the Easy Measure Numbers plug-in, open the Measure Number dialog box. Click the Measure tool, choose the Measure menu > Measure Numbers > Edit Regions. Notice the regions you defined using the plug-in appear in the measure region display window.

Show or Hide Measure Numbers on a Staff

You can show or hide measure numbers for a specific staff in the Staff Attributes. Click the Staff tool and double-click a staff to open the Staff Attributes dialog box. In the Items to Display section, uncheck Measure Numbers. Click OK to return to the score.

NOTE

Settings in the Measure Number dialog box can override the Display Measure Number setting you assign in the Staff Attributes. If editing the Staff Attributes does not change the appearance of measure numbers on the staff, edit the corresponding measure region in the Measure Number dialog box. From the Measure menu, choose Measure Numbers > Edit Regions. Uncheck the "Always Show" checkboxes under Positioning and Display.

Clear Measure Number Positioning

You can clear manual measure number positioning for any selected region of your score with the Clear Measure Number Positioning plug-in. Click the Mass Edit Tool and highlight a region of your score. From the Plug-ins menu, choose Measure Numbers > Clear Measure # Positioning. Measure numbers in the selected region return to their default placement.

Number Repeated Measures

If you have several consecutive measures that are identical, you may want to number them (independently from the measure numbering) to aid the performer. To do this, click the Mass Edit Tool and highlight a region of identical measures. From the Plug-ins menu, choose Number Repeated Measures. The repeated measures are now numbered consecutively. They are entered as measure expressions, so you can edit or delete them with the Expression tool.

Working with Graphics

Graphics are commonly used in Finale documents for figures in your score outside of music notation, such as a logo. You want to use a separate graphic program to prepare an image to place into a Finale document. You also may need to save a page or excerpt of music from a Finale document as a graphic to import into a file in another program. On Windows, Finale can open or save graphics in TIFF or EPS format. On Macintosh, Finale can open or save graphics in TIFF, EPS, PICT, or Illustrator format. Use the Graphics tool to import or export a graphic.

To prepare for this section, open a new default document (File > New > Default Document). Then, click the Graphics tool. On Windows, first choose Advanced Tools Palette from the Window menu, then click the Graphics tool in the Advanced Tools Palette.

Exporting a Graphic

You can export a portion of a page or an entire page from Finale as a graphic file. To export a graphic, you will always need to be in Page View (View > Page View). To export a rectangular section of a page, with the Graphics tool selected, doubleclick and drag to enclose the desired region. When you release the mouse button, a dashed rectangle should remain. Then, from the Graphics menu, choose Export Selection. To export an entire page, or several pages, first move to Page View (View menu > Page View). Then, click the Graphics menu and choose Export Pages. After choosing Export Selection or Export Pages from the Graphics menu, the Export Pages/Export Selection dialog box appears, as shown in Figure 11.6.

Figure 11.6
Choose properties for an exported graphic in the Export Pages/Export Selection dialog box.

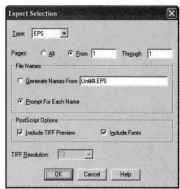

From the Type drop-down/popup menu, choose the format of the graphic you want to export. Following is a brief description of each of the available graphic formats:

▶ The TIFF (Tagged-Image File Format) is very versatile. TIFF files can be exchanged between just about any program that supports graphics. They can also be transferred from Macintosh to Windows, and vise versa. Placed TIFF files will appear in a Finale document, and print as they display on screen.

▶ Graphics in EPS (Encapsulated PostScript) format will generally produce cleaner results than graphics in TIFF. If you need professional looking graphics in the printout, EPS is the way to go. However, you will need a PostScript printer to print or create any EPS graphic. EPS files placed into a Finale document will not display on screen, only in the printout (though you may see a crude TIFF preview of the graphic on screen).

▶ The PICT file (available only on Mac) format is generally used to transfer between Macintosh applications. Like TIFF files, graphics in PICT format print as they appear on screen.

▶ The Illustrator file format (available only on Mac) can be used to save a graphic compatible with the Adobe Illustrator application. With Illustrator selected, click OK. The Illustrator Options dialog box appears, as shown in Figure 11.7. In this dialog box, from the drop-down menu, choose the version of Illustrator you will be using to open the graphic, and make other settings related to Illustrator graphics.

Figure 11.7
Choose settings for version, text, and display of an exported Illustrator graphic in the Illustrator Options dialog box

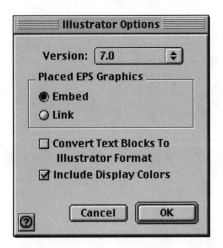

CHAPTER 11

After you have chosen the file type, specify the pages you want to export. If you are exporting the entire document, each page will be saved as a separate graphic file. Choose Generate Names From to tell Finale to name each graphic with the file name of the Finale document followed by a number (increasing by one for each successive page). If you are exporting a single page, choose Prompt for Each Name if you wish to name the file yourself.

If you are exporting an EPS graphic, choose Include TIFF Preview if you want a preview of the graphic to display on screen before printing. Choose Embed Fonts if you plan to move the file to a computer that does not have fonts used in the graphic. If you are exporting a TIFF or PICT file, click the drop-down/popup for resolution to choose a resolution for the graphic. Screen resolution is 72 dpi. Choose a higher resolution to export a sharper graphic file. Most inkjet printers print at 600 dpi or higher.

Click OK. Finale generates the graphics, or, if Prompt for Each Name is selected, the Open window appears. Choose a name and location for the file and click OK to save the graphic.

CAUTION
Due to some bugs in the Windows OS, EPS does not work properly in
Windows NT/2000/XP.

Importing a Graphic

On Windows, you can place TIFF, WMF (Windows Metafiles), and EPS graphics into a Finale
document. On Macintosh, you can place TIFF, PICT, or EPS graphics into a Finale document. To
import a graphic, with the Graphics tool selected, double-click in the score. The Place
Graphic/Open File window appears. On Windows, click the drop-down for Files of Type and
choose the format of the file you want to import. Navigate to the file and double-click to open it.
You return to the score with the graphic placed in the document.

Editing Placed Graphics

You can edit the graphic in the score in many ways. Double-click a graphic's handle to activate
six black editing handles around the graphic. Click and drag the graphic (not on the handles) to
reposition it manually on the page. To stretch the graphic, click and drag one of the editing
handles. Double-click the graphic again to open the Graphic Attributes dialog box (Figure 11.8),
where you can make specific settings for positioning and appearance.

Figure 11.8
Position and scale
graphics in the
Graphic Attributes
dialog box.

Graphic Attributes	⊠
Type: TIFF File	Height: 0.71528 Width: 3.65625
Path: C:\Documents and	

Attach to
- ⦿ Page   Single Page ▾   1   Through
- ○ Measure 1   Piccolo ▾

Alignment and Positioning
Horizontal   Left ▾   H: 3.42708
Vertical   Top (Header) ▾   V: -1.6354
Position from Page Edge ▾

Scale
H: 100 %
V: 100 %
☑ Fixed Percent

Right Page Alignment and Positioning
☐ Use Right Page Positioning   H: 3.42708
Horizontal   Left ▾   V: -1.6354

OK
Cancel
Help

Here are some common ways to edit graphics in the Graphic Attributes dialog box:

▶ In the Attach To section, choose Page to place the graphic at a set location on the page. Changes to system and page margins will have no effect on the placement of the graphic. It will remain static relative to the page edge, or page margin (depending on the setting in the Alignment and Positioning section). With this option selected, all items in the Alignment and Positioning section become active. Specify specific horizontal and vertical placement for your graphic in this section.

▶ In the Attach To section, choose Measure to attach the graphic to a specific measure. Do this if you want the graphic to always reposition with a measure respectively. Specify the measure and staff in the text boxes to the right of this option.

▶ Scale the graphic by changing the percentage in the Scale Section. When scaling, 100% always equals the original size of the graphic. Check Fixed Percent if you want the graphic to remain the same size regardless of page resizing with the Resize tool.

After you have finished editing the graphic, click OK to return to the score to review your changes.

Graphics are not embedded in Finale documents. Instead, Finale references graphics by using the path you specify when you initially place the graphic, or the folder of the Finale file. This means that if you move the Finale file or graphic to a different folder, the association will be lost and the graphic will not appear in the document (just the file name of the missing graphic). Use the Check Graphics menu item in the Graphics menu to see where Finale is expecting to find the graphics. You can copy this list to a clipboard, which could be printed and used as a reference sheet.

TIP

To avoid missing graphics, store each graphic file in the same folder as its host Finale file. Then, if you ever move the Finale document, be sure to also move the associated graphic with the Finale file. Finale will always find a graphic if it exists in the same folder as the Finale document.

Entering a Graphic as an Expression

In addition to placing graphics directly into the score, you can store and enter graphics as expressions. You might want to do this if you would like to enter the same graphic at various locations in the score. To do this:

1. Click the Expression tool.
2. Double-click the score to open the Expression Selection dialog box.
3. Choose the Shape radio button in the lower right corner of the Expression Selection dialog box.
4. Click the Create button. Then, click Select and Create to open the Shape Designer.

5. In the Shape Designer, click the Graphics tool (it looks just like the Graphics tool in the Main/Advanced Tool Palette).

6. Double-click in the Shape Designer window. The Place Graphic/Open File window appears.

7. Navigate to the file you want to import and double-click it. The graphic appears in the Shape Designer window.

8. Use the other editing tools in the Shape Designer to make any further graphical edits to the image (if needed). For example, use the Selection tool to move or scale the graphic.

9. Click OK, Select, OK to return to the Expression Selection dialog box. Notice the graphic now exists among the available options.

10. Click Select to open the Note/Measure Expression Assignment dialog box.

11. Edit the expression assignment as you would with any expression (see chapter 3 for details).

12. Click OK to return to the score. The graphic now appears where you originally clicked, and is attached to the designated measure/note as an expression.

Now, any time you want to use the graphic in the document, double-click a measure with the Expression tool, choose Shape, and select the expression you created. If you would like to be able to edit the graphic independently in the score, click Duplicate in the Expression Selection dialog box to create a duplicate of the graphic expression (or simply use a metatool to enter the shape expression, which creates a duplicate automatically). You can treat this expression just as you would any other shape expression.

Page Layout

In chapter 2, we covered the basics for editing the page layout. You learned how to edit system margins, distance between systems, and page margins. These basic layout concepts are important throughout the score production process, and can be quite adequate for smaller projects. However, there are several other options that can save you time while preparing the layout of a score. By devoting a little extra time for page layout after completing the entry process, you can produce a consistent, professional looking score.

TIP

If you are worried about mangling the layout of your score beyond repair, save a backup copy of the Finale document. In fact, you may want to save a separate version of your score specifically for the purpose of experimentation, especially if you are less familiar with this aspect of the program.

Editing the Overall Page Format for your Score or Extracted Parts

To decrease the amount of manual editing necessary in a score, you may want to define the overall page format, then go back to make additional page layout changes. You may also want to redefine the format of a document before entering any music, if you know how the overall page format should look outright. To define the overall format for a score (system margins, page margins, and spacing), use the Page Format for Score dialog box. From the Options menu, choose Page Format > Score to open the Page Format for Score dialog box.

Identical options are available for predefining the layout of extracted parts. From the Options menu, choose Page Format > Parts to open the Page Format for Parts dialog box, where you can edit the format of extracted parts before extraction (we'll cover part extraction soon). The Page Format for Score and Page Format for Parts dialog boxes appear, as shown in Figure 11.9 (these two dialog boxes are identical in structure).

Figure 11.9
Use the Page Format for
Score and Page Format
for Parts dialog boxes to
reformat the layout for
your score or future
extracted parts.

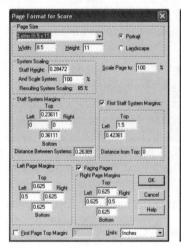
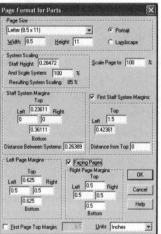

To establish consistent spacing, system margins, and page margins, redefine the layout for the score or parts in the Page Format for Score and Page Format for Parts dialog boxes.

TIP
If you intend to redefine the format for your score, note that all optimization and other adjustments made with the Page Layout tool will be lost. Apply optimization after updating the page format, then make any final manual adjustments with the Page Layout tool to completely rework the layout.

282   Measure Numbers, Graphics, Part Extraction, and Printing – Chapter 11

- Select the measurement unit you would like to use from the drop-down/popup menu in the lower right corner of this dialog box. See Table 1.1 for equivalent values for each measurement unit.

- At the top, in the Page Size section, choose the page size of the Finale document (any new page that is generated gets its dimensions here). Click the drop-down/popup menu for a list of available choices. After setting up the page size, you will need to select the actual size of the printed page in the Page Setup dialog box (File menu > Page Setup). If you want to print one "Finale" page on one "physical" page, enter the same page size in both the Page Format for Score (or Page Size) and Page Setup dialog boxes. The value for page size in the Page Format for Score dialog box is dynamically linked to the same parameter in the Page Size dialog box available from the Page Layout menu.

- For System Scaling, you can reduce or enlarge all systems in the document and their contents. Note that the values for Staff Height and Scale System are cumulative, so adjustments to either of these parameters will affect the overall system scaling. Finale calculates this value for you and displays it to the right of Resulting System Scaling.

- Enter a page reduction for all items on the page in the Scale Page to text box. The page reduction can also be adjusted with the Resize tool.

- In the Staff System Margins section, enter a specific value to control the system margins for the entire document. Here, you can also set the space between each system. Usually, the first system is indented to allow more space for the full staff name. You can define the top and left margin for the first staff system in the section to the right. First, check First Staff System Margins, then enter the top and left margin for the first staff system in the section below this checkbox.

- Under Left Page Margins, enter the space between page margins and the edge of the page. If you want to define separate page margins for odd-numbered pages, check Facing Pages, then enter the margin values in the Right Page Margins section.

Once you have finished making changes to the Page Format for the Score/Parts dialog box, click OK to return to the score. If you made settings for the layout of your current score, you will need to redefine the pages for these settings to take effect. To apply these changes, click the Page Layout tool and then, from the Page Layout menu, choose Redefine Pages > All Pages. Next, click OK. Any settings you made in the Page Format for Parts dialog box will apply to parts after they have been extracted.

Optimizing Large Scores

Whether or not you have redefined your pages as described above, you will probably want to optimize your entire score before the final printout. As you recall, optimizing is the process of removing empty staves from each system, often referred to as a French Score style. You will want to do this before making further adjustments to system margins and spacing. By removing empty staves within systems, optimization will usually change the size of systems, so it's best to do this task before tweaking your final system layout. Make sure you have completed entering all of the music before optimizing the entire score. To optimize, first click the Page Layout tool.

From the Page Layout menu, choose Optimize Staff Systems. The Staff System Optimization dialog box appears (Figure 7.10 in Chapter 7). In the Change section, choose Whole Document, then click OK. You return to the score with all systems optimized. Now, you are ready to continue editing the layout.

You can also optimize systems in your score independently. Right/Control-click a system and choose Optimize Staff Systems to open the Staff System Optimization dialog box, where you can apply optimization to the system you clicked (or to a range of systems).

Cutaway Scores

Sometimes, empty measures within systems are hidden from the score, as shown in Figure 11.10. This method of score formatting is known as a cutaway score.

Figure 11.10
Use the Hide Staff Staff Style to create cutaway scores.

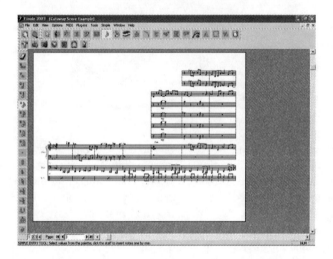

First, optimize the score to remove empty staves from systems. Then, use the Hide Staff Staff Style to hide any number of remaining measures from a score as needed. To do this:

1. Click the Staff tool.
2. Highlight the measure or measures you want to hide.
3. Right/Control-click the highlighted area and choose Hide Staff from the Staff Style context menu (or press H). The measure(s) disappear(s) and the Staff Style is marked with a horizontal blue line.
4. Repeat these steps for all occasions where a measure needs to be hidden within a staff system.

Customizing Systems and Pages

In chapter 2, you learned how to manually adjust system margins individually. You can also adjust margins for several systems at once. The following methods are particularly useful while editing the layout for extracted parts, or scores with more than one system on a page.

To quickly edit many or all system margins at once, and view results immediately, select a region of systems (to select more than one region, drag Enclose System handles or hold down the Shift key and click a handle on each desired system). Then, from the Page Layout menu, choose Edit System Margins. The Edit System Margins dialog box appears, as shown in Figure 11.11.

Figure 11.11
Use the Edit System Margins dialog box to edit margins of a selected region of systems.

In the Edit System Margins dialog box, check the box that corresponds to the margin or margins you want to edit (left, right, top, bottom). Then, specify the new system margin value in the appropriate text box. Check Distance Between Systems, and enter a value to specify the distance between systems. In the Change section, specify a system range. Click Apply to see results without leaving the dialog box. Also, pressing the Enter or Return key is the same as clicking Apply. Enter new values in this box, and click Apply as many times as you like before clicking Close to remove the dialog box.

TIP
To select several staff systems at any time, from the Page Layout menu, choose Systems > Select Staff System Range. Also, remember that you can always select the system range in the Edit System Margins dialog box.

You can also edit page margins for a selected region of pages. From the Page Layout menu, choose Page Margins > Edit Page Margins. The Edit Page Margins dialog box appears, as shown in Figure 11.12.

Figure 11.12
Edit page margins for a
region of pages in the
Edit Page Margins
dialog box.

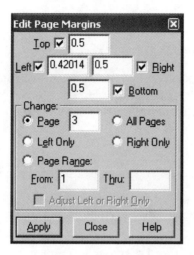

Check the box that corresponds to the margin or margins you want to edit (left, right, top,
bottom), then enter a value to specify the space between the page edge and page margin. Specify
the margins to edit in the Change section. Click Apply to update the page. Enter new values in
this box, and click Apply as many times as you like before clicking Close to remove the dialog
box. If desired, this dialog box can be open at the same time as the Edit Page Margins dialog box.

Systems Per Page

As of Finale 2003, you can specify a certain number of systems to place on each page. To do this:

1.   Click the Page Layout tool.

2.   From the Page Layout menu, choose Space Systems Evenly. The Space Systems
     Evenly dialog box appears, as shown in Figure 11.13.

Figure 11.13
Specify the number of
systems per page in the
Space Systems Evenly
dialog box.

3. In the Space Systems Evenly On section, choose the page or pages you want to change.

4. In the Distribute Systems section, choose Place _ Systems on Each Page.

5. Click OK. Finale will place the number of systems you specified on the chosen pages, provided there is room on the page. The systems will be spaced evenly as well. If there is not room on the page, or if your music looks scrunched, try reducing the system scaling with the Resize tool.

Page Turns

You can set a system to always appear at the beginning of a page by assigning a page break. To assign a page break:

1. Click the Page Layout tool. All system and page margins appear in the score.

2. From the View menu, make sure Show Page Layout Icons is checked.

3. Right/Control-click the upper left system margin handle on the system you want to assign to the beginning of the page to display the Page Layout context menu.

4. Choose Insert Page Break. The context menu disappears and a yellow box appears to the left of the measure. Now, this system will always appear at the top of a page. Note that this system is still subject to moving between pages based on other page layout changes.

Splitting Measures Across Systems

It is not uncommon to see a measure split across a system break. In other words, the first portion of a measure appears at the end of one system and the second portion at the beginning of the next, as shown in Figure 11.14.

Figure 11.14
Notice that measure six extends across the system break.

You could create two shorter measures by defining "invisible" meter changes with the Time Signature tool, but this will throw off your measure numbering. To split a measure across a system break without disturbing the measure numbering, use the Measure tool.

1. Make sure all notes have been entered in the measure you want to split. Also, for these steps, use the Mass Edit Tool to move the measure to the end of a system. We'll be moving the second half of this measure to the next system.

2. Click the Measure tool, then double-click the measure you want to split. The Measure Attributes dialog box appears.

3. In the Options section, check Allow Horizontal Split Points.

4. Click OK to return to the score.

5. Notice there are now three handles at the right edge of the measure/system. Click the lowest handle to display a rectangle above the measure.

6. Doubleclick within this rectangle to specify the split point (Figure 11.15). You will see a handle appear in the rectangle. Drag the handle to adjust the position of the split point.

Figure 11.15
Double-click within the split point rectangle to establish a split point in the measure.

7. Click the Mass Edit Tool.

8. Click the measure so it is highlighted.

9. Press the down arrow to move the right portion of the measure to the next system.

Extracting Parts

After you have finalized the notation and layout, you are ready to generate parts. Finale's ability to generate parts from a score is perhaps the biggest time saver over creating sheet music by hand. When you extract parts, you basically tell Finale to separate out each staff, or group of staves, and place them into new Finale documents. Finale will automatically include the title, composer, and staff name in each generated part, and also consolidate empty measures into multimeasure rests. You can customize the page format, and music spacing for your parts, before extraction to minimize the amount of editing necessary for each part.

Before part extraction, you will want to review your score to ensure each staff contains all the markings you want to include in your extracted parts:

▶ Click the Expression tool, and then from the Expression menu, choose Display Expressions for Extracted Parts. Review the score for any missing expressions, or expressions defined to staff lists incorrectly. Check the tempo marking and rehearsal letters to ensure they appear on all staves (for more information on setting expressions to display on the score or parts, see chapter 7).

▶ If you have excluded the appearance of repeat brackets or measure numbers for certain staves, you will want to turn those back on for part extraction. From the Plug-ins menu, choose Global Staff Attributes. Check Endings and Text Repeats (so there is a solid check in the checkbox), then click OK to place the repeat brackets and text back into all staves.

▶ Finale will save extracted parts to the Music folder designated in the Program Options dialog box. On Windows, Finale saves the extracted parts to the same location as the score file. On Mac, Finale saves the extracted parts to the Music folder designated in the Program Options dialog box. From the Options menu, choose Program Options and select the Folders category. After Music, see the path Finale will use while saving extracted parts. Click the Browse button to change the Music folder to specify a new folder for your extracted parts.

After you have made final preparations, use the following steps to extract parts from a score. If you do not have a particular score, to demonstrate part extraction, open any multiple staff score, or create a new document with the Setup Wizard (File > New > Document with Setup Wizard) and add several staves.

1. From the File menu, choose Extract Parts. The Extract Parts dialog box appears, as shown in Figure 11.16. In the Extract Parts dialog box, you can define the default appearance for all extracted parts. You could extract parts using all of the default settings, and edit each part individually as needed, or customize these parameters for more consistency (and less editing) in each extracted part.

Figure 11.16
Configure the page format, music spacing, and multimeasure rest settings for extracted parts in the Extract Parts dialog box.

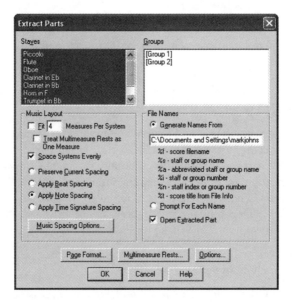

2. Under the Staves field, select the staves you want to extract. All staves are selected by default, so if you want to extract all staves, you can leave this field as is. Ctrl/Command-click staves to deselect or select them individually. Hold down the Shift key and click to select several consecutive staves.

3. Under the Groups field, you can specify any group in your score for extraction. Select them just as you would staves. For more information on groups, see chapter 7.

4. In the Music Layout section, define the measure layout and music spacing. If you like, set the number of measures per system, and type of music spacing here. Click the Music Spacing button to open the Music Spacing options, where you can make specific adjustments to spacing in the resulting parts. See chapter 9 for information on music spacing.

5. Click the Page Format button to open the Page Format dialog box, where you can set the page size, system scaling, and margins (Figure 11.9). Edit the page format for all extracted parts here (as described earlier in this chapter). To test your page format settings, try extracting a single part from the score. Go back and revise your page format settings, then extract again and overwrite the previously extracted file. Do this until the part looks good, then use the settings you have established when you generate all the parts.

6. Click the Multimeasure Rest button to open the rests portion of the Document Options dialog box, where you can make settings for rests in the extracted parts. Here, choose the number of measures to allow before creating a multimeasure rest, width between barlines of multimeasure rest, and other options. Click OK to return to the Extract Parts dialog box.

7. Click the Options button to open the Page Options dialog box, as shown in Figure 11.17.

Figure 11.17
Remove text from extracted parts, and position the instrument name in the Page Options dialog box.

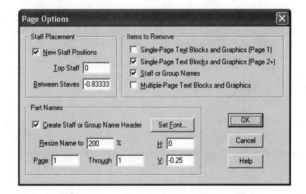

Here, select items to remove from the extracted parts, including certain text blocks, staff names, and group names. Also, select the font, size, and positioning for the part name. Finale will place the staff/instrument name in the upper left corner of the page as it would appear on a standard part. Click OK to return to the Extract Parts dialog box.

8. In the File Names section of the Extract Parts dialog box, choose Generate Names From if you want to use one of the available naming conventions for your extracted parts. They are listed below the text box (for example, type "%f%s.MUS" to tell Finale to name each new file with the score file name followed by the staff or group name). Choose Prompt for Each Name to name each extracted part yourself during the extraction process.

CAUTION

If you get the warning message: "This file already exists. Replace Existing File?" and have chosen Prompt for Each Name in the Extract Parts dialog box, be absolutely sure that you name each part with an original file name to avoid overwriting your score.

9. Check Open Extracted Part to tell Finale to open each part immediately after extraction.

10. Click OK to begin part extraction. Finale will generate new files for each chosen staff and/or group. This may take a while with larger scores.

If you get the error message: "Cannot Rename Part," there is a staff name using an illegal character (such as a slash (/), back slash (\), or comma (,). Try changing the naming convention in the Extract Parts dialog box to avoid using staff names in the file name (try "%i," the staff or group number, instead of "%s",). Then, extract again.

If you get the error message: "The generated part name is too long," go back and shorten the file name, or use a naming convention that will produce shorter file names.

If Open Extracted Part was chosen in the Extract Parts dialog box, every part will open in a new window. You can easily move to any extracted part by choosing its file name from the bottom of the Window menu. If you find yourself making many of the same layout changes to each part, it may be worth your while to go back to the score, make more adjustments to the Page Format for Parts, and extract parts again.

Editing Extracted Parts

You will usually have to manually edit some aspect of the layout of each extracted part. Use the basic page layout instructions from chapter 2 to make manual system and page adjustments. Use layout techniques described earlier in this chapter to define the number of systems per page, page turns, and measures split across system breaks. Use the Selection tool to move various elements (text blocks, expressions, etc.) into place.

Be sure to retain consistency between the score and extracted parts. If you make any adjustments to the music in the extracted part, return to the score and make the same changes. View the score and part at the same time while making these adjustments. With just the score and one part open, from the Window menu, choose Tile Vertically or Tile Horizontally to place the score and part side-by-side, or one above the other.

TIP

Plug-ins can greatly reduce the amount of time you spend editing extracted parts. If your score contains multipart staves, you can explode them into two or more parts with the TGTools Smart Explosion of Multi Part Staves plug-in. This plug-in will even look for text such as "Div." and "a2" to determine the resulting parts. See chapter 15, or the TGTools User Manual PDF, for details. Also, Use the TGTools Align/Move Dynamics to move all expressions up or down in the part staff. If you used the Patterson Beams plug-in on the score, you probably will want to run it again on each part to ensure beam angles are consistent with your style. You can find the TGTools and the Patterson plug-ins on the companion CD-ROM.

Special Part Extraction

While working on the score, you can use Special Part Extraction to display a single staff for printing. To select a single part for display while working in the score:

1. In the score, move to Scroll View (View menu > Scroll View).
2. Click the Staff tool.
3. Click the staff handle of the staff you want to display. Or, hold down the Shift key and click all staves you want to display.
4. From the Edit menu, choose Special Part Extraction. The Multimeasure Rest dialog box appears.
5. Make any desired settings for the appearance of multimeasure rests, then click OK.
6. Move to Page View (View menu > Page View). The selected staff or staves become isolated on the page.

To view your full score, from the Edit menu, uncheck Special Part Extraction.

Printing Techniques

The final step to almost any project is generating the physical sheet music from your Finale document. In chapter 2, you learned the basics for printing a document by configuring the Page Size and Page Setup dialog boxes. Here are a couple methods you can use to customize the page format, placing two-up on a single page, or printing half of a score on two pages if a printer doesn't support a page size large enough.

Printing Two-up

You can easily place two pages of your Finale document in portrait orientation on a letter page in landscape orientation (Figure 11.18).

Figure 11.18
Two-up printing

To do this:

1. From the File menu, choose Page Setup. The Page Setup dialog box appears.

2. Set the size to letter (or any preferred page size) and the orientation to landscape. On Macintosh, be sure to keep the Scale percentage at 100%.

3. Click OK.

4. From the File menu, choose Print. On Mac, click the General popup menu and choose Finale 2003 (or your version of Finale). The Finale print options appear.

5. Check 2-up, then choose the page range.

6. Check Ignore Printer Margins for N-up printing if you want to extend the music as close as possible to the page edges.

7. Click Print to print the document. Two documents appear side by side on the page.

TIP

To view more than one page in Finale, from the View menu, choose Show Multiple Pages.

Fit a Score on Two Pages: Tile Pages

If your score is too large to fit on a paper size supported by your printer, you can, for example, print two 8.5 × 11 inch pages tiled so the full score appears on the two pages stacked horizontally. This way, the score appears as if it were printed on tabloid size paper (11 × 17 inch). To print a score on tiled pages:

1. First, set the page size to Tabloid. Click the Page Layout tool and from the Page Layout menu, choose Page Size. From the Page Size drop-down/popup menu, choose Tabloid (11 × 17). Then, click OK.

2. Use the Page Layout tool to customize the layout of systems to properly fit on this page size. You may want to use the Resize tool to resize the page, or the Staff tool to change the distance between staves.

3. From the File menu, choose Page Setup. The Page Setup dialog box appears.

4. Set the orientation to landscape, the page size to 8.5 × 11, and click OK.

5. From the File menu, choose Print. On Mac, click the General popup menu and choose Finale 2003 (or your version of Finale). The Finale print options appear.

6. Check Tiled Pages.

7. If you want the pages to overlap slightly, enter the margin of overlap in the Tile Overlap text box. Specify the overlap in the unit of measurement you have selected in the Measurement Units submenu of the Options Menu. About ¼ inch usually works well.

8. Choose the page range and print the document. Half of each system will appear on each 8.5 × 11 inch page. Stack the pages horizontally to view a full page of the score.

TIP

Use TGTools and the JW plug-ins for more printing functionality. On Windows, to print multiple files at once, from the TGTools menu, choose Print Multiple Files. See the TGTools User Manual for more information. On Windows or Macintosh, if you are printing in booklet format, try the JW Booklet plug-in. The TGTools demo and corresponding User Manual PDF are located on the companion CD-ROM, as well as on the JW Booklet plug-in.

CHAPTER 11

12

Tricks for Specific Projects and Composing With Finale

In the last eleven chapters, you have learned the fundamentals for efficiently producing a score, from starting a new document to the final printout. You have seen numerous features that save you time and give you ultimate control over the details of your notation. Even still, we have only scratched the surface of Finale's capabilities. In this chapter, you will learn a variety of techniques for notation of specific instruments, such as crossstaff notation for a piano score, figured bass, and other common notation types.

Some of Finale's most impressive features are particularly useful to arrangers and composers. If you plan to arrange with Finale, you will learn how to use valuable orchestration utilities. Explode a single staff of music into many, or easily compress any sized score into a grand staff for a piano reduction. If you plan to compose with Finale, you can use the Composer Assistant, Auto Harmonizer, and other plug-ins to aid in the creative process.

Here's a summary of what you will learn in this chapter:

▶ Tricks for specific projects.
▶ How to use Finale's Orchestration tools.
▶ How to use Finale's Creative tools.

Tricks for Specific Projects

It would be impossible to cover the endless number of notational styles possible in Finale. We already have discussed percussion notation (chapter 7) and tablature (chapter 8), though there are a number of other common types of music notation made easy with Finale. These include cross-staff notation for piano, figured bass, chant, as well as notation for handbells and harp.

Cross-Staff Notation and Tricks for Piano Scores

Cross-staff notation is a common occurrence in piano music. It is a way of beaming notes placed across the right- and lefthand staff in a piano score, often with stems up and down on the same beam (Figure 12.1).

Figure 12.1
Cross-staff notation

To create cross-staff notation:

1. In a grand staff, enter all notes into one staff. For this example, the notes are entered in the top staff (Figure 12.2).

2. Click the NoteMover tool (on Windows, from the Window menu, choose Advanced Tools and click the NoteMover tool in the Advanced Tools Palette).

3. From the NoteMover menu, choose Cross Staff.

Figure 12.2
Enter notes into the same staff, and then from the NoteMover menu choose Cross Staff.

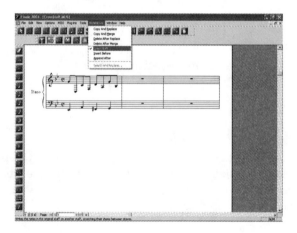

4. Click the measure. Handles appear on the notes.

5. Select the notes you want to move to the other staff. Click and drag-enclose the desired handles, as shown in Figure 12.3, or hold down the Shift key and click to select them.

Figure 12.3
Select the handles of the
notes you want to move
to the other staff.

6. Now, click and drag one of the note handles to the middle of the other staff.
    Notice all the handles move as you drag (Figure 12.4). Don't worry about
    positioning them over the correct staff position; they will snap to the correct
    pitch automatically.

Figure 12.4
Drag the note handles to
the middle of the other
staff.

7. Choose the Special Tools tool.

8. From the Special Tools Palette, select the Reverse Stem tool. For the notes you
    want above the beam, click the upper handle. For the notes you want below the
    beam, click the lower handle (Figure 12.5).

Figure 12.5
Use the Reverse Stem
tool to adjust the stem
placement.

9. From the Special Tools Palette, choose the Beam Angle tool.

CHAPTER 12

10. Click and drag the left handle of each beam and drag it to the desired position (Figure 12.6).

Figure 12.6
Use the Beam Angle
tool to position each
beam.

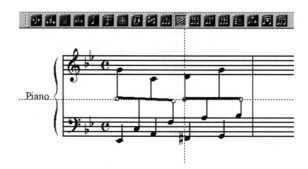

Also, with the Beam Angle tool selected, click and drag the right handle on a beam to adjust its angle.

Here are some other tips that will come in handy while working with piano scores.

▶ To begin a new piano document, use the Setup Wizard (File > New > Document With Setup Wizard). Then, on page 2, choose the Keyboards category and select Piano (or another keyboard instrument). You can also easily add a grand staff to your document with the Setup Wizard. Choose the Staff tool, and then, from the Staff menu, choose New Staves (with Setup Wizard).

▶ To add a pedal marking to your score (as shown in Figure 12.7), use the Custom Line tool. Click the Smart Shape tool, then Ctrl/Option-click the Custom Line tool in the Smart Shape Palette (the Smart Line Style Selection dialog box appears). Choose the Pedal Custom Line and click Select. Now, simply double-click and drag to add the pedal marking.

Figure 12.7
Use the Custom Line
tool to create pedal
markings.

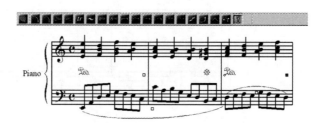

▶ Add an 8va or 8vb marking with the Smart Shape tool as well. With the Smart Shape tool selected, choose the 8va/8vb tool in the Smart Shape Palette. Double-click and drag above the staff to enter an 8va. Double-click and drag below the staff to create an 8vb (notice your cursor points to the staff to which the Smart Shape will be attached). These indications will also apply to playback.

▶ Use the Articulation tool to enter fingerings. With the Articulation tool selected, hold down the fingering number and click an entry to add it to the score (in Finale 2003, the number keys one through five are preset fingering metatools).

Figured Bass

Figured bass (or basso continuo) originated in the baroque period as a method for notating accompaniment. It is basically a system of shorthand written beneath the bass part that indicates the chord to be played above it (Figure 12.8).

Figure 12.8
Use the Chord tool to enter figured bass.

In Finale, figured bass can be entered with the Chord tool by using Finale's Figured Bass chord library.

1. From the File menu, choose Open Library. The Open Library/Open File window appears.
2. Navigate to the Finale/Libraries folder (if you aren't there already), and double-click the Chord Suffixes folder.
3. Double-click the library file "Figured Bass". You return to the score.
4. Click the Chord tool.
5. From the Chord menu, choose Manual Input.
6. Click a note in the score on which you want to add a figured bass symbol. The Chord Suffix Selection dialog box appears.
7. Click Show Advanced to display the lower portion of this dialog box (if it's not visible already).
8. Click the Select button in the Numeric Definition section. The Chord Suffix Selection dialog box appears.
9. Scroll down to the bottom to find the figured bass symbol you want to use and click to select it. You return to the Chord Definition dialog box.
10. In the Show section, uncheck Root.
11. Click OK to enter the symbol into the score.
12. Use the positioning arrows to the left to position the figured bass symbols just as you would chord symbols.

Using the Chord tool is just one way to enter figured bass in Finale. You can also use the Lyrics tool. If you do this, use different verses to stack symbols on top of each other. Use the Edit Lyrics dialog box to choose the font to use for the figured bass characters.

CHAPTER 12

> **TIP**
> There are several Figured Bass fonts available, most notably FinalFiguredBass, by Angsar Krause. You can find it at www.angsarkrause.de. Use this font as a single verse of lyrics for your figures.

Chant

There are a number of common techniques for producing chant in Finale. Generally, you will want to make some global adjustments first, like removing the Time Signature and barlines. To prepare a document for chant notation:

1. From the File menu, choose New > Default Document. A new default document opens.
2. Choose the Mass Edit Tool, then press Ctrl/Command-A to select all.
3. From the Mass Edit menu, choose Fit Music. The Fit Music dialog box appears.
4. For Lock Layout With _ Measure(s) per System, enter "1".
5. Click OK. There is now a single measure in every system. It is impossible to "eliminate" measures in Finale, so we have placed a single measure on each system to give the appearance of a measureless document.
6. Choose the Measure tool, then press Ctrl/Command-A to select all.
7. From the Measure menu, choose Edit Measure Attributes. The Measure Attributes dialog box appears.
8. In the Measure Attributes, if you want to eliminate the barline at the end of each system, choose Invisible from the row of icons next to Barline. For Time Signature, choose Always Hide. In the Options section, check Position Notes Evenly Across Measure.
9. Click OK. You return to the score. Now, tell Finale to accommodate many notes in each measure/system with the Time Signature tool.
10. Choose the Time Signature tool and double-click the first system. The Time Signature dialog box appears.
11. After Number Of Beats, click the right arrow to select the number of beats you want to place in the first measure/system. For example, if you want 24 quarter notes in the first system, create a Time Signature of 24/4.
12. Click OK. You return to the score.

Now, you have created what appears to be music without measures. If you intend to create chant notation in the future, save this document as a template to use later (and avoid having to repeat the previous steps). To do this, from the File menu, choose Save As (then on Windows, for Save As Type, choose Coda Template File). Save the file to your templates folder for use later.

Notes entered in the score will be spaced evenly across the system. You will probably want to turn off Fill with Rests under the Simple menu and in the Speedy menu > Speedy Options.

Here are some other helpful tips to use as you enter chant notation:

▶ To remove stems from all notes in a staff, click the Staff tool and double-click the chant staff. In the Items to Display section, uncheck Stems. Click OK. You return to the score with all stems removed from the selected staff.

▶ To position notes manually, choose the Measure tool, and click a system containing notes. Now, click the lower handle on the right side of a staff to display the beat chart above the measure. Use the lower handle to position any note horizontally.

▶ As you enter lyrics into chant notation, you may want to enter more than one syllable under a note. To do this, use a "hard space." Type the first syllable, then type a hard space (Win: Alt-0160 on the num pad, Mac: Option-Space Bar). Then, type the second syllable, and so on.

▶ If you want to use tick barlines for chant, without setting one measure per system, choose the Measure tool and highlight a region of your score (or press Ctrl/Command-A to Select All). Then, double-click the highlighted area to open the Measure Attributes dialog box. In the Barline row, choose Tick and click OK.

▶ Use the Note Shapes notation style to select shapes for pitches and/or note durations. With the Staff tool selected, double-click a staff to open the Staff Attributes. Click the drop-down/popup menu for Notation Style and choose Note Shapes. The Note Shapes dialog box appears. Choose the shapes you want to use and click OK back to the score. For more information on the Note Shapes notation style, see chapter 8.

NOTE

If you are interested in creating medieval notation, such as Franconian or Gregorian notation, try Klemm Music Technology's Medieval plug-in. You can find a free demo on their website at www.klemm-music.de/medieval.

Mensurstriche Notation

Due to the absence of pulse in chant and other early notation, some reproductions of this music include barlines between staves rather than through them to offer a general sense of meter. This practice is known as mensurstriche notation. In Finale, mensurstriche barlines can be specified with the Staff tool.

To create mensurstriche notation with barlines between staves:

1. Begin with any document containing more than one staff.

2. Choose the Staff tool.

3. Select any number of desired staves.

4. From the Staff menu, choose Add Group and Bracket. The Group Attributes dialog box appears.

5. Click the drop-down/popup menu for Draw barlines and select Between Staves (mensurstriche).

6. Make any other settings you would like to apply to the group and click OK. You return to the score with barlines extending between staves, and not through them.

Handbells

If you are creating a score for handbells, use Finale's handbells template. From the File menu, choose New > Document From Template. Double-click the Church Templates folder, then double-click the file "Handbells" to open it. The score opens with two bells-used charts in the first system (Figure 12.9).

Figure 12.9
Use the Handbells template to begin a new score for handbells.

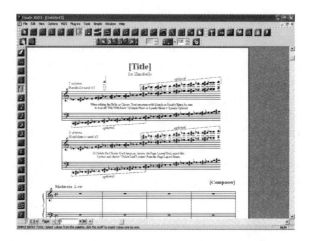

You can choose from two available bells-used charts, one with regular noteheads, and one with diamonds. To delete the extra bells-used chart, click the Page Layout tool, then right/Control-click the system you want to remove and choose Delete System. The selected system disappears. Note that this particular template will look different if you are using a version older than Finale 2003.

Now, you may need to remove some of the bells in the bells-used chart. To edit the bells-used chart:

1. Click the Simple Entry tool.

2. From the Simple menu, uncheck Fill With Rests.

3. Ctrl/Option-click a note you want to remove to select it, then press the Delete key to delete it. Leave any extra parentheses in for now.

4. Use the right and left arrow keys to select any other notes you want to remove, and use the Delete key to delete them as well.

5. Once all extra notes have been removed, click the Articulation tool.

6. Hold down the Delete key and drag over the extra parentheses. Or, click a note to display its articulation handle, select the handle and press the Delete key.

7. Click the Text tool and double-click the handle on the "Octaves and Bells Used" text block to edit it. Or, select the handle and press the Delete key to delete it. Also, delete the informational text block between the staves of the bells-used chart.

8. To edit or delete the "Optional" bracket, click the Smart Shape tool. Click the primary handle to activate the smaller editing handles, which you can use to adjust the length and angle of the line. Press the Delete key to delete it.

After you have edited the bells-used chart, enter the notation into the following staves normally. The measures numbering begins in the measure after the bells-used chart. The Handbells template contains a number of special symbols in the Articulation Selection dialog box specifically designed for handbell notation (such as "LV," "SK," "+," and several others). Also, use available expressions in the Expression Selection dialog box for other indications ("Mallets," "vib.," etc.). In the Expression Selection dialog box, duplicate existing expressions and edit them to retain consistency when adding new expressions to the library.

Tremolos

Tremolo markings indicate a rapid succession of notes, usually on two different pitches (Figure 12.10). The speed at which tremolos can be added drastically improved with the introduction of the Easy Tremolos plug-in in Finale 2002.

Figure 12.10
Easily create tremolos
such as these with the
Easy Tremolos plug-in.

To create a tremolo:

1. Enter the two notes so they equal the full duration of the tremolo. For example, for a half note tremolo, enter two quarter notes (one after the other in the same layer).

2. Choose the Mass Edit Tool.

3. Highlight the measure containing the notes you would like to convert to a tremolo. If you need to select part of a measure, from the Edit menu, choose Select Partial Measures, then highlight the desired region.

4. From the Plug-ins menu, choose TGTools > Easy Tremolos. The Easy Tremolos dialog box appears, as shown in Figure 12.11.

Figure 12.11
Use the Easy Tremolos
dialog box to specify the
visual appearance of the
resulting tremolo.

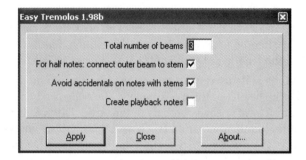

5. In the text box, enter the total number of beams. Check for half notes: Connect outer beam to stem if you want the eighth note beam to extend to the stem (like the half note tremolo in Figure 12.11). If you check Include Playback Notes, Finale will enter hidden notes in layer four for playback.

6. Click Apply. The notes in the selected region convert to tremolo markings.

Feel free to adjust settings in the Easy Tremolos dialog box and apply them to the same selected region. The figure will update accordingly.

TIP
If you add or delete notes in the same measure as a tremolo created with the Easy Tremolos plug-in, beaming may be lost on the tremolo. If this happens, simply run the plug-in on the region again to restore beaming.

Harmonics

Harmonics are notes manipulated to sound at a higher partial (in the harmonic series) of the fundamental pitch, and are most common in string notation. They are usually notated with a regular note on the fundamental pitch, and the secondary note above on the same stem (Figure 12.12). These have become far easier to create with the introduction of the Easy Harmonics plug-in in Finale 2002. This plug-in is designed to generate string harmonics from an interval of a third or fourth.

Figure 12.12
Use the Easy Harmonics
plug-in to easily create
harmonics.

To create a harmonic:

1. Enter the fundamental pitch, and the interval required for the desired harmonic on the same beat and in the same layer. Enter an interval of either a perfect fourth, major third, or minor third (intervals of a fourth will sound two octaves higher, an interval of a major third will sound two octaves and a major third higher, an interval of a minor third will sound two octaves and a fifth higher than the fundamental).

2. Choose the Mass Edit Tool.

3. Highlight the measure containing the notes. If you need to select part of a measure, from the Edit menu choose Select Partial Measures, then highlight the desired region.

4. From the Plug-ins menu, choose TGTools > Easy Harmonics. The Easy Harmonics dialog box appears, as shown in Figure 12.13.

Figure 12.13
Use the Easy Harmonics dialog box to specify the interval to look for.

5. Select the interval of the notes you want to convert to harmonics.

6. Click Apply. The notes in the selected region convert to harmonics. Play back the region to hear the resulting harmonic pitch.

Cadenzas

Cadenzas are solo passages with no barlines, and are usually notated with smaller than normal noteheads. There are several ways to create a cadenza passage in Finale. The most widely agreed upon method is to alter the Time Signature of a single measure (preserving the music spacing), enter the notes, and then use the Mass Edit Tool to reduce the note size.

To create a cadenza:

1. Click the Time Signature tool, then double-click the measure into which you want to enter the cadenza. The Time Signature dialog box appears.

2. Change the Time Signature to accommodate the number of notes you want to enter in the cadenza passage. For example, if your cadenza is 48 eighth notes, define a Time Signature of 48/8. (Here, you could also use a Time Signature with a larger beam grouping like 24/4 or 12/2 so that not every single eighth note is flagged).

3. Click the Options/More Choices button to expand the dialog box.

CHAPTER 12

4. Check Use a Different Time Signature for Display.

5. Set the Time Signature at the bottom to whatever you want to use for the display. For example, if the Time Signature for the measure previous to the cadenza is 3/4, define 3/4 here so there is no time change indicated on the cadenza measure.

6. In the Measure Region section, choose Measure _ Through _ and enter the measure number for the cadenza in both entry fields (to define this time change for the cadenza measure only).

8. Click OK to return to the score.

9. Enter the notation into the measure.

10. Click the Mass Edit Tool, then click the cadenza measure to highlight it.

11. From the Mass Edit menu, choose Change > Note Size. Enter 75 and click OK.

Orchestration Tools

Whether you are composing a piece from scratch or copying from an existing handwritten score, Finale can be used as an excellent orchestration tool. Play an excerpt of music into one staff and explode it into many, or reduce large scores into a grand, or single staff. You can even check for notes outside of an instrument's range, or tell Finale to search for occurrences of parallel motion in your score. Use the following techniques to save time while orchestrating.

Explode Music

While creating a score with several staves, you may want to enter many chord voicings into a single staff at once with Speedy Entry or HyperScribe, and then separate each voice into its own staff. To do this, use the Mass Edit Tool's Explode Music utility. This utility basically takes each note from chords entered in a single staff and delegates them into new staves, or into existing staves in the score. The result is an independent line of music in each staff consisting of a note from each original chord (Figure 12.14).

Figure 12.14
Explode each note of a chord into its own staff with the Explode Music utility.

Here is a quick demonstration showing how to explode chords in one staff into independent voices on several staves.

1. Open a new default document (File > New > Default Document).

2. Enter a number of four-note chords into the first few measures (in a single layer). If you are using a MIDI keyboard, use Speedy Entry or HyperScribe to quickly enter the chords.

3. Choose the Mass Edit Tool.

4. Click just to the left of the staff to highlight the entire staff.

5. From the Mass Edit menu, choose Utilities > Explode Music. The Explode Music dialog box appears, as shown in Figure 12.15.

Figure 12.15
Choose the number of new staves to create and where to put the extra notes while exploding music in the Explode Music dialog box.

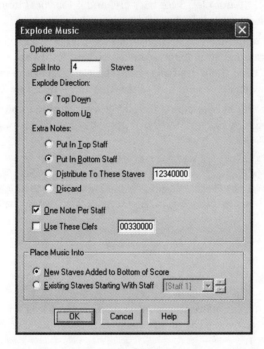

6. We will want to create four new staves, so for Split Into, enter "4" (if it isn't there already). For Place Music Into, select New Staves Added to Bottom of Score.

7. Click OK. Finale adds four new staves to the score, with each voice in its own staff.

Now, make any additional edits to the new staves. Use the Staff tool to edit their transposition, staff name, or clef in the Staff Attributes (see chapter 2). You can use the Explode Music utility to explode music into up to eight staves.

Here are some ways to customize the results generated by exploding music while in the Explode Music dialog box:

▶ If some of your chords contain more notes than others, either the top or bottom notes in chords will be isolated. If you want Finale to group the top notes in each chord together into the first new staff and then process down through each successive note, for Explode Direction, choose Top Down. If you want Finale to group the bottom notes in each chord together into the first new staff and then process up through each successive note, for Explode Direction, choose Bottom Up.

▶ Assign a clef to each new staff in the Use These Clefs text box. Each number represents the clef for each successive staff created. Use 0 for treble clef, 1 for alto clef, 2 for tenor clef, 3 for bass clef and 4 for vocal tenor clef (assuming you haven't changed the default clef definitions).

▶ If there are more notes in a chord than the number of staves you create, there will be extra notes to manage. You can choose to discard or select a staff for these notes from the Extra Notes radio buttons. Enter the order of staves to place each successive extra note into in the Distribute to These Staves text box.

▶ If your score already contains the staves you want to explode to, choose them from the Existing Staves Starting With Staff drop-down/popup menu.

TIP
To isolate a specific layer for explosion, from the View menu, choose Show Active Layer Only, then choose the layer you want to explode.

Implode Music

You can also squeeze music from many staves into one with the Mass Edit Tool's Implode Music utility. This utility takes notes from a region of selected staves and stacks them within a single staff, as shown in Figure 12.16.

Figure 12.16
Use the Implode Music utility to consolidate notes in many staves into a single staff.

Original

After
Exploding

To implode notes from many staves into one:

1. Start with any document containing several staves, and a single line of music on two or more staves.

2. Choose the Mass Edit Tool.

3. Highlight the region of measures you want to consolidate into a single staff.

4. From the Mass Edit menu, choose Utilities > Implode Music. The Implode Music dialog box appears, as shown in Figure 12.17.

Figure 12.17
Choose a destination for the notes you want to implode and edit their quantization in the Implode Music dialog box.

5. Here, choose whether you want to place the resulting notes in the top staff of the selected region or into a new staff added to the bottom of the score. Click the Quant Settings button to open the Quantization Settings dialog box (Figure 4.3), where you can choose the smallest note value, and other parameters for your results. See chapter 4 for more information on Quantization.

6. Click OK. You return to the score. All notes from the selected region now appear in one staff.

The Piano Reduction Plug-in

The Implode Music utility works well for consolidating regions of the score into a single staff, but if you want to generate a complete piano part for all, or certain staves of a score, use the Piano Reduction plug-in. This plug-in will take notes, articulations, and note expressions from selected staves and place them into a grand staff (Figure 12.18).

CHAPTER 12

Figure 12.18
Generate a piano
reduction automatically
with the Piano
Reduction plug-in.

To generate a piano reduction automatically with the Piano Reduction plug-in:

1. Start with any document containing several staves with music.

2. From the Plug-ins menu, choose Piano Reduction. The Piano Reduction dialog box appears, as shown in Figure 12.19.

Figure 12.19
Select staves to include
and a split point for
your piano reduction in
the Piano Reduction
dialog box.

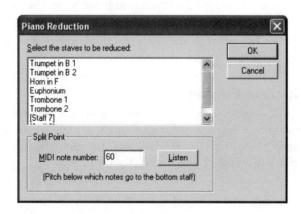

3. Here, highlight the staves you want to include in your reduction. Hold down the Shift key and click to select consecutive staves. Hold down the Ctrl/Command key and click to select nonconsecutive staves. For Split Point, choose the lowest note you want to include on the right-hand staff of your piano reduction (60 = middle C).

4. Click OK. It may take a while for Finale to generate the reduction. When it's
    done, your reduction appears in a new grand staff added to the bottom of
    your score.

You will most likely need to edit the results of the generated piano reduction. Finale will
sometimes need to shorten a note if it finds a shorter one on the same beat of a different staff.
When this happens, try entering the note in a different layer.

Check Range Plug-in

While orchestrating, arranging, or composing, you may want to check over a region of your work
to ensure all notes are within a playable range for the instrument. You can check for notes out of
range, change them, or delete them with the Check Range plug-in.

To check a region of your score for notes out of range for an instrument, do the following:

1. To check range for the whole score, move to step 2. To check range for a staff or
    staves, click the Mass Edit Tool, then click to the left of the staff (Shift-click to
    the left of additional staves you want to check to select them).

2. From the Plug-ins menu, choose Check Range. The Check Range dialog box
    appears, as shown in Figure 12.20.

Figure 12.20
Check your score for
notes out of an
instrument's range with
the Check Range dialog
box.

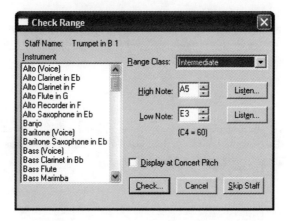

3. Look after Staff Name: at the top to see the staff you are currently checking. In
    the Instrument section, choose the instrument you are using for the current staff.
    Notice the High Note and Low Note fields update as you move between
    instruments. For Range Class, choose the skill level for the instrument range.
    You can also adjust the high and low pitches by using the up and down arrows,
    or by entering your own pitch manually.

CHAPTER 12

    4.   Click Check. If Finale finds any notes out of range, the Note Out of Range dialog box appears, as shown in Figure 12.21.

Figure 12.21
Erase or change out-of-range notes in the Note Out of Range dialog box.

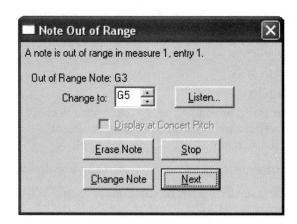

    5.   Click Erase Note to remove the note from the score. Click Change Note to change the note to the pitch specified in the Change To: field. Click Stop to return to the score.

If you are using an external MIDI device, like a MIDI keyboard, click the Listen button while checking the range (in either of the range-checking dialog boxes) to specify the pitch by simply playing a note on your external MIDI device.

TIP
To transpose any selected region of music, choose the Mass Edit Tool, highlight the region, then from the Mass Edit menu, choose Transpose.

Find Parallel Motion

If you are composing or arranging a score, and need to observe classical rules of voice leading, try running the Find Parallel Motion plug-in to find all occurrences of parallel motion in your score.

To check for parallel fifths or octaves:

    1.   Choose the Mass Edit Tool.

    2.   Select a region of your score you want to check for parallel motion, or press Ctrl/Command-A to Select All.

3. From the Plug-ins menu, choose Find Parallel Motion. The Find Parallel Motion dialog box appears, as shown in Figure 12.22.

Figure 12.22
Use the Find Parallel Motion dialog box to find occurrences of parallel fifths and octaves in your score

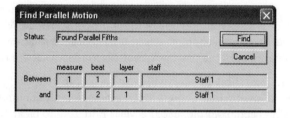

4. Click Find. Finale will search for parallel fifths and octaves in all staves, layers, and voices. Finale reports the measure, beat, layer, and staff in the two rows at the bottom of this dialog box.

5. Click Find again to move to the next occurrence or click Cancel to return to the score.

TIP

If you are using this plug-in to quickly analyze a score for parallelism in a music theory homework assignment, be sure to learn the rules of parallel motion in traditional voice leading in case Finale isn't available in an upcoming exam.

Creative Tools

Many composers and arrangers prefer to use Finale throughout the process of writing an original score. Among the advantages of composing with Finale are the numerous plug-ins and other features designed to offer ideas and spark creativity. There are ten "Composer's Assistant" plug-ins available that are specifically designed to help generate musical ideas. These tools won't write a piece for you, but they will analyze existing music and offer suggestions for chords, rhythms, and voicing. If you are looking to generate harmony for a melodic passage, Finale can offer a large number of suggestions for up to six parts with the Band-in-a-Box Auto Harmonizer plug-in. You can even create an entire jazz accompaniment for any melody with the MiBAC Jazz Rhythm Section Generator plug-in. Finally, if you are composing serial music, or in a related genre, you can easily rearrange notes by inversion or retrograde with the Canonic Utilities. Use any of the following utilities to generate thousands of musical possibilities to choose from while creating a score.

CHAPTER 12

Composer's Assistant Plug-ins

The ten Composer's Assistant plug-ins use principles of music theory to generate possibilities for modulation, voicing, and rhythm. In general, you will enter a series of notes or chords, run one of the plug-ins on the desired region, and Finale will place results in a new staff or staves added to the bottom of the score. After running one of these plug-ins, use the Mass Edit Tool to copy chosen results into your score (see chapters 2 and 9 for more information on the Mass Edit Tool). After running these plug-ins, use the playback controls to play back the results for review.

In this section, you will learn how to effectively use each of the ten Composer's Assistant plug-ins. To prepare for the following instructions, open a new default document (File > New > Default Document). After each example, use the Mass Edit Tool to clear all entries, and the Staff tool to delete the extra staves. Or, you can also open a new default document for each example. Though many of the following examples begin with notes in the first measure, you can run any of these plug-ins at any measure of your score. Make sure to always enter notes in layer one, voice one.

Chord Morphing

The Chord Morphing plug-in basically takes two chords and offers suggestions for intermediate chords you can use to modulate between them. You can choose from three methods of morphing to vary your results. Here, we'll use the Chord Morphing plug-in to find suggestions for modulating between two higher tertian (big) chords.

1. Enter two chords into the first measure of your score in layer one, as shown in Figure 12.23.

Figure 12.23
Find possible ways to modulate between chords such as this one with the Composer's Assistant Chord Morphing plug-in.

2. Click the Mass Edit Tool, then highlight the first measure.
3. From the Plug-ins menu, choose Composer's Assistant > Chord Morphing. The Chord Morphing dialog box appears, as shown in Figure 12.24.

Figure 12.24
Choose from three possible morphing methods in the Chord Morphing dialog box.

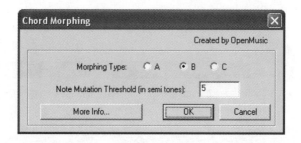

4. Here, choose the type of morphing method you want to use. Each type processes removal, mutation, and addition of notes in a different order. Each type will offer slightly different results. Choose A to tell Finale to mutate, remove, and then add notes. Choose B to tell Finale to remove, mutate, and then add the notes. Choose C to tell Finale to remove, add, and then mutate.

5. Click OK. Finale adds a staff to your score containing the generated chords. Each one appears as a whole note in duration (Figure 12.25). There is a marking entered above each original chord as a note expression. Now, you can use the Mass Edit Tool to edit the duration of the notes and add copy to your score, or undo your changes (Ctrl/Command-Z) and try one of the remaining two morphing methods.

Figure 12.25
Chord morphing results with type B.

Chord Realization

The Chord Realization plug-in can be a very useful tool if you are creating an SATB (Soprano, Alto, Tenor, Bass) arrangement. It takes a chord entered in a single staff and generates four-part realizations on that chord in root position, first, and second inversion. You can then choose from a variety of suggestions for four-part voicing. In the following example, we'll use the Chord Realization plug-in to generate voicing options for chords.

1. Enter the chords from Figure 12.23 again into the first measure of a scratch document.

2. Click the Mass Edit Tool, then highlight the first measure.

CHAPTER 12

3. From the Plug-ins menu, choose Composer's Assistant > Chord Realization. The Chord Realization dialog box appears, as shown in Figure 12.26.

Figure 12.26
Use the Chord Realization dialog box to generate voicing options for a chord.

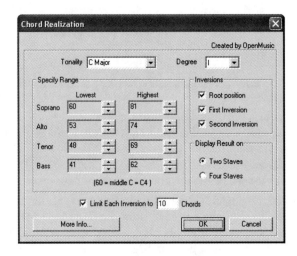

4. For Tonality, choose the key of the piece. Finale will transpose your results into any (major) key you specify. Also, specify the root scale degree of the chord by choosing from the Degree drop-down/popup menu. In this dialog box, you can also specify the range for each part, and limit the number of generated inversions and number of staves produced (two or four).

5. Click OK. Finale adds two staves to your score containing the generated realization. Each one appears a whole note in duration (Figure 12.27). Now, you can use the Mass Edit Tool to edit the duration of the notes and add copy to your score, or undo your changes (Ctrl/Command-Z).

Figure 12.27
Chord realization results using settings in Figure 12.26 and the entries from Figure 12.23.

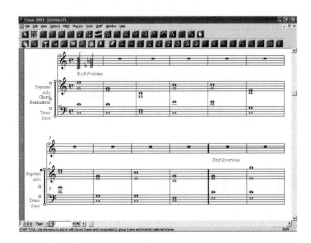

Chord Reordering

The Chord Reordering plug-in simply reorders the sequence of chords randomly, or by number of common notes. Voicing and staff position remain the same. To reorder chords using the Chord Reordering plug-in:

1. Enter several chords into a staff.

2. Click the Mass Edit Tool, then highlight the region containing the chords.

3. From the Plug-ins menu, choose Composer's Assistant > Chord Reordering. The Chord Reordering dialog box appears, as shown in Figure 12.28.

Figure 12.28
Reorder chords randomly or by number of common notes with the Chord Reordering dialog box.

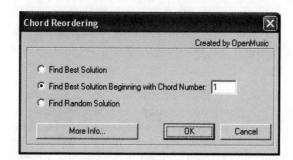

4. Choose Find Best Solution to tell Finale to order the chords based on the number of common notes. Finale will rearrange the chords with the maximum number of similar notes between adjacent chords. This can result in a smooth, yet somewhat unspectacular, harmonic progression. To specify the first chord in the reordered region, enter the sequential number of the chord after Find Best Solution Beginning with Chord Number. Select Find Random solution to tell Finale to reorder the chords randomly.

5. Click OK. Finale adds a staff to your score containing the reordered chords.

Chord Splitting

While orchestrating large chords, it is common practice to separate consonant pitches from the chord into subsets and give each subset to a particular instrumental section. In large ensembles, this technique can give the chord a smoother sound. The Chord Splitting plug-in extracts consonant notes from a chord (based on the harmonics of an implied fundamental pitch) and places them together in measures of a new staff below the score. Each of these subsets of the original chord can then be used in a unique instrumental section to achieve a blended overall sound. To generate subsets from a large chord:

1. Enter a large chord into the first measure of a scratch document.

2. Click the Mass Edit Tool, then highlight the first measure.

3. From the Plug-ins menu, choose Composer's Assistant > Chord Splitting. The Chord Splitting dialog box appears, as shown in Figure 12.29.

CHAPTER 12

Figure 12.29
Use the Chord Splitting dialog box to extract harmonic pitches from a chord to delegate to an instrumental section of your score.

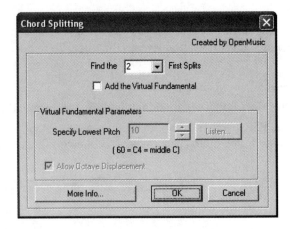

4. Finale will separate pitches from the chord in groups of one to three notes. At the top of this box, click the drop-down arrow and choose the number of times you want Finale to split the chord. Enter a higher number for larger chords. Also, check Add Virtual Fundamental if you want to add the virtual fundamental into the results (we'll talk more about virtual fundamental later).

5. Click OK. Finale creates a new staff for each split chord. Look to the staff with the most even number notes in each measure for the best results. Then, you can copy these suggestions to instrumental sections with the Mass Edit Tool.

Common Tone Transposition

Finale can offer several chord ideas by generating a list of chords that share at least one common pitch with the original. To tell Finale to create several new chords containing at least one common tone:

1. Enter a chord into the first measure of a scratch document.

2. Click the Mass Edit Tool, then highlight the first measure.

3. From the Plug-ins menu, choose Composer's Assistant > Common Tone Transposition. The Common Tone Transposition dialog box appears, as shown in Figure 12.30.

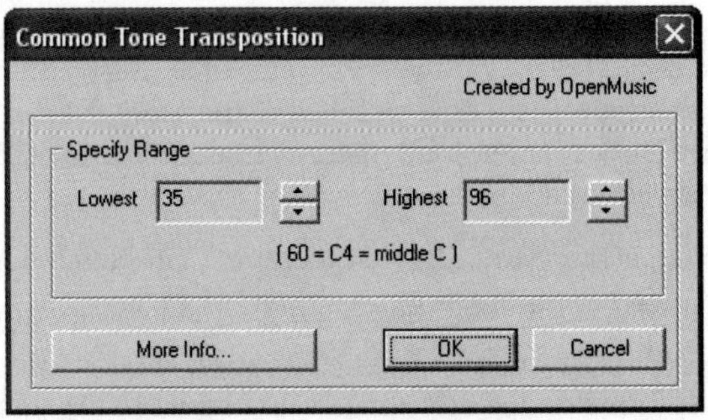

Figure 12.30
Generate a list of chords containing at least one common tone with the Common Tone Transposition dialog box.

4. Choose a highest and lowest MIDI pitch for the generated chords.

5. Click OK. Finale creates a new staff and places a list of chord ideas as whole notes in each measure, each with at least one note in common with the original chord.

Frequency Modulation Chord Generator

This plug is used to generate increasingly complex chords from two pitches. Finale uses the method of frequency modulation, popular in keyboard synthesizers, to do this. To create a list of chords with the Frequency Modulation Chord Generator:

1. Enter two notes on different pitches in the first measure of a scratch document.

2. Click the Mass Edit Tool, then highlight the first measure.

3. From the Plug-ins menu, choose Composer's Assistant > Frequency Modulation Chord Generator. The Frequency Modulation Chord Generator dialog box appears, as shown in Figure 12.31.

Figure 12.31
Use the Frequency
Modulation Chord
Generator to create
chord ideas rich in
texture and complexity.

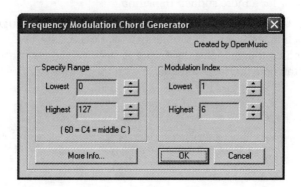

4. Since the results may exceed a useful range, choose a highest and lowest pitch for your results in the Specify Range section. You can then specify the number of results and number of notes in each chord in the Modulation Index section. The number of resulting chords will equal one greater than the highest modulation index minus the lowest.

5. Click OK. Finale creates a new staff including a list of chord ideas as whole notes in each measure. After using the Frequency Modulation Chord Generator, try using the Chord Morphing plug-in to generate additional chord ideas, or the Chord Splitting plug-in to separate each chord into harmonic subsets.

Melodic Morphing

Use the Melodic Morphing plug-in to generate a transition between two melodies. To do this:

1. Begin a scratch document with two empty staves.

2. Enter a simple melody in the top staff and one in the bottom.

3. Click the Mass Edit Tool, then highlight the measures in both staves.

4. From the Plug-ins menu, choose Composer's Assistant > Melodic Morphing. The Melodic Morphing dialog box appears, as shown in Figure 12.32.

CHAPTER 12

Figure 12.32
Generate a transition
between two melodies
with the Melodic
Morphing dialog box.

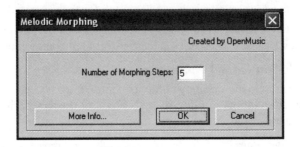

5. The results of this plug-in will begin with the first original melody, followed by the plug-in's transition, and end with the second original melody. The length of Finale's generated transition depends on the value you enter in the Number of Morphing Steps field. Enter a high number for a subtle transition, or a lower number for a more sudden transition.

6. Click OK. Finale creates a new staff including the first original melody, transition, and second original melody. Finale disregards rhythm while morphing the melodies (its output is steady sixteenth notes), so you will have to edit the note durations manually with the Simple or Speedy Entry tool.

TIP

After running the Melodic Morphing plug-in, you will probably see a number of repeated sixteenth notes. To merge all repeated notes into single notes of larger durations, use the Tie Common Notes plug-in, and then retranscribe the region with the Mass Edit Tool (Mass Edit menu > Retranscribe). Note that retranscribing looks at your quantization settings when deciding on notated rhythms.

Rhythm Generator

You can quickly create a percussion part for your score using the Rhythm Generator plug-in. With this plug-in, you can define beat patterns for notes entered into up to six new staves at the bottom of your score. To create a rhythm section with the Rhythm Generator plug-in:

1. From the Plug-ins menu, choose Composer's Assistant > Rhythm Generator (no selection is necessary). The Rhythm Generator dialog box appears, as shown in Figure 12.33.

Figure 12.33
Generate a complex
rhythm section easily
with the Rhythm
Generator dialog box.

2. Each row in this dialog box represents a new staff that you can add to your score. Check the box on the left for each new staff you want to add to your rhythm section. Define up to three rhythmic patterns from the Sieve drop-down/popup menus for each staff. Each measure is separated into sixteenth notes. Choose 1 from a Sieve drop-down popup menu to enter straight sixteenth notes. Choose 2 for a sieve to enter a note on every other sixteenth note pulse. Choose 3 for a sieve to enter a note on every third sixteenth note pulse, and so on. You can specify up to three rhythmic patterns (sieves) for each staff. Under the instrument column, choose a MIDI instrument for each staff you define.

TIP
After specifying an instrument for a staff in the Rhythm Generator plug-in, you will need to assign the same instrument to the staff in the Instrument List (see chapter 2).

3. Click OK. Finale creates the new staves with the specified rhythms and adds them to the bottom of the score. Use the Staff Attributes to change the clef of these staves to a percussion clef and make other percussion-specific changes (staff lines, notation style, etc.).

TIP
Apply a percussion map to staves created with the Rhythm Generator plug-in to assign a staff position for each part. See chapter 8 for information on creating percussion maps.

Tie Common Notes

This plug-in is straightforward enough. It looks for consecutive notes on the same pitch and ties them together automatically. To tie all consecutive common notes:

CHAPTER 12

1. Click the Mass Edit Tool, then highlight a region of measures containing consecutive notes on the same pitch.

2. From the Plug-ins menu, choose Composer's Assistant > Tie Common Notes. The Tie Common Notes dialog box appears.

3. Click OK. Finale creates ties between the common notes.

After using the Tie Common Notes plug-in, convert tied notes into single notes of a larger duration with the Mass Edit Tool's Retranscribe feature. Select the region with the Mass Edit Tool, and then, from the Mass Edit menu, choose Retranscribe.

Virtual Fundamental Generator

Any collection of pitches you enter as a chord will best fit the partials in the harmonic series of a particular fundamental pitch. The Virtual Fundamental Generator plug-in analyzes pitches in a chord, generates the most appropriate fundamental pitch, and places it in a new staff added to the bottom of the score. This pitch is basically an implied "root" of the chord. To generate a virtual fundamental for a chord:

1. Enter one or more chords into the staff of a scratch document.

2. Click the Mass Edit Tool, then highlight the first measure.

3. From the Plug-ins menu, choose Composer's Assistant > Virtual Fundamental Generator. The Virtual Fundamental Generator dialog box appears, as shown in Figure 12.34.

Figure 12.34
Create the virtual fundamental (or "implied root") for a chord with the Virtual Fundamental Generator dialog box.

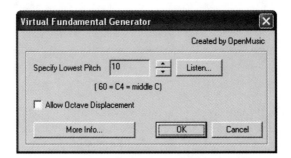

4. Since the virtual fundamental may be well below the usable range, specify the lowest pitch (as a MIDI note number) in the Specify Lowest Pitch field. If the virtual fundamental is below the note you specify, Finale will raise it an octave (or more, if necessary) as long as Allow Octave Displacement is checked. If Allow Octave Displacement is not checked, and the virtual fundamental is lower than the specified lowest pitch, the plug-in will return nothing for that chord.

5. Click OK. Finale creates a new staff including a virtual fundamental for each chord in the highlighted region.

Band-in-a-Box Auto Harmonizing

As questionable as it sounds, Finale can actually create a viable harmonic solution for up to six parts from any given melody. By choosing from an extensive collection of harmonization options, you can usually find one that works well. In practice, it is best to use the Auto Harmonizing plug-in for a basic harmonic outline, and then edit the voice leading, spelling, and texture to your own taste. Use the following instructions to easily create a four-part saxophone arrangement from a simple melody.

1. Let's start by creating a new document. From the File menu, choose New > Document with Setup Wizard. Click Next to move to page 2. Here, choose the Woodwinds category and add a Soprano, Alto, Tenor, and Baritone saxophone. Click Next, Next and Finish to create the new document with four saxophones.

2. Enter a simple melody with chord symbols like the example in Figure 12.35.

Figure 12.35
To prepare for running the Band-in-a-Box Auto Harmonizing plug-in, enter a melody with chord symbols.

3. Choose the Mass Edit Tool and click the left of the top staff to highlight the entire staff.

4. From the Plug-ins menu, choose Band-in-a-Box Auto Harmonizing. The Band-in-a-Box Auto Harmonizing dialog box appears, as shown in Figure 12.36.

Figure 12.36
Choose the type of harmonization you want to apply and where you want to place the generated notes in the Band-in-a-Box Harmonizing dialog box.

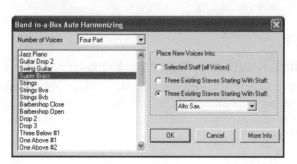

5. Here, choose the number of parts and the type of harmonization. For this example, I used four parts and the "Super Brass" type of harmonization. In the Place New Voices Into section, choose the staves into which you want Finale to place the harmonization. For this example, I chose the Three Existing Staves, starting with the Alto Sax staff.

6. Click OK. Finale generates the harmonization and places the resulting notes into the subsequent staves (Figure 12.37).

Figure 12.37
Band-in-a-Box Auto Harmonizing results (to view and hear this example, open the file "Auto Harmonizer Example" located in the Music Examples folder on the companion CD-ROM).

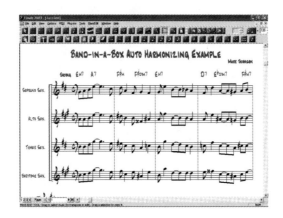

After auto harmonizing, you may need to edit the enharmonic spelling of certain notes. Also, use the Simple Entry tool to change any pitches to customize the harmonization to get the sound you're after. Press Ctrl/Command-Z to undo the harmonization and try one of the other harmonizing options available in the Band-in-a-Box Auto Harmonizing dialog box.

TIP
To give your score a handwritten look (like the score in figures 12.34 and 12.36, for example), choose the Jazz Font option on page 4 of the Document Setup Wizard.

The MiBAC Jazz Rhythm Generator Plug-in

If you are creating a jazz chart, try using the MiBAC Jazz Rhythm Generator plug-in to create a piano, bass and drum accompaniment for any melody. You can even choose from four accompaniment styles: Ballad, Swing, Beebop, or Bassa Nova. To create a rhythm section for any melody:

1. You can start by simply using the Staff tool to delete the lower three staves from the previous section. Or, start a new default document (File menu > New >

Default document) and enter a melody with chord symbols. Before running this plug-in, your staff should look something like the example in Figure 12.38.

Figure 12.38
To prepare for running the MiBAC Jazz Rhythm Generator plug-in, enter a melody with chord symbols.

2. Choose the Mass Edit Tool and click the left of the staff to highlight the entire staff.

3. From the Plug-ins menu, choose MiBAC Jazz Rhythm Generator. The MiBAC Jazz Rhythm Generator dialog box appears, as shown in Figure 12.39.

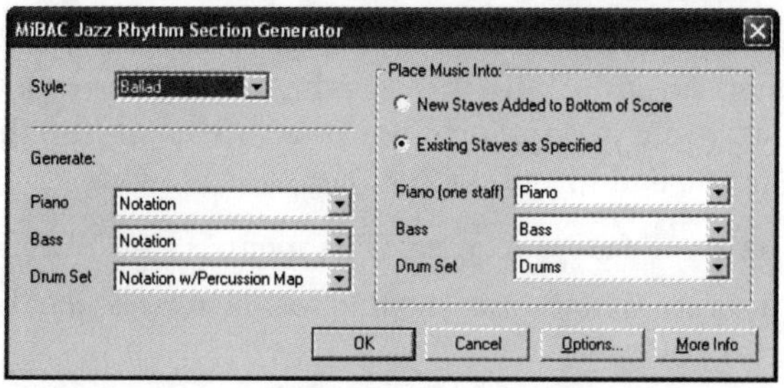

Figure 12.39
Choose the style, staves, and customize the appearance of items in the generated staves in the MiBAC Jazz Rhythm Section Generator dialog box.

4. Here, click the Style drop-down/popup menu and choose a style for your accompaniment. For this example, let's use Ballad. In the Generate section, choose the staves on which you want to place chord symbols. You will probably want to choose the Percussion Map setting for the generated drum part. In the Place Music Into section, for this example, choose New Staves Added to Bottom of Score. In the future, you may want to use this section to tell Finale to place the results into existing staves in your score.

5. Click the Options button to open the Scale Volume dialog box, where you can adjust the balance of your accompaniment. Click OK to return to the MiBAC dialog box.

6. Click OK. Finale generates the accompaniment in a piano, bass, and drum staff added to the bottom of the score (Figure 12.40).

Figure 12.40
MiBAC Jazz Rhythm Section Generator results (to view and hear this example, open the file "MiBAC Example" located in the Music Examples folder on the companion CD-ROM).

Like the Band-in-a-Box Auto Harmonizing plug-in, you may need to adjust the enharmonic spelling and notation of your results as you see fit. See chapter 4 for information on adding chords, and chapter 8 for information on defining a percussion map to a staff.

Inversions/Retrogrades, etc. The Canonic Utilities

The Canonic Utilities plug-in is particularly useful if you are composing serial music. Invert or retrograde a portion of music easily with this plug-in. You can also add or remove accidentals and transpose the region while performing these tasks. To invert (flip the music upside-down), or retrograde (flip the music end to end), or both, do the following:

1. Open a new default document (File menu > New > Default Document).
2. Enter a series of notes into the first few measures like those shown in Figure 12.41, for example.

Figure 12.41
Invert or retrograde any passage such as this one with the Canonic Utilities plug-in.

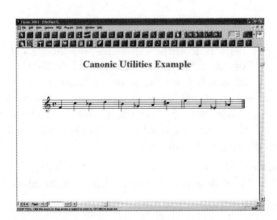

3. Choose the Mass Edit Tool and highlight the region containing the notes you want to manipulate.

4. From the Plug-ins menu, choose Canonic Utilities. The Canonic Utilities dialog box appears, as shown in Figure 12.42.

Figure 12.42
Choose the type of inversion or retrograde you want to apply to the selected region, as well as a transposition, in the Canonic Utilities dialog box.

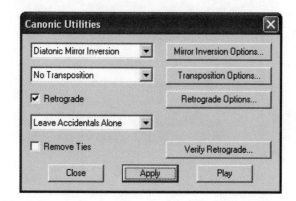

5. Here, choose the type of inversion from the drop-down menu at the top. For this example, let's select Diatonic Mirror Inversion. Click the Retrograde checkbox if you would also like to retrograde the selection (as in this example). You can also make additional settings for mirror inversions, transposition, and retrogrades by clicking the corresponding buttons on the right. Click Verify Retrograde to check the selection for invalid entries. You will not be able to retrograde music containing slurs, note expressions, or mirrored measures.

6. Click OK. Finale calculates the inversion and/or retrograde and adjusts the notes accordingly (Figure 12.43.)

Figure 12.43
Canonic Utilities results with both diatonic mirror inversion and retrograde applied.

You can also use the Canonic Utilities plug-in to show or hide accidentals on all notes, or to remove all ties.

13

Customizing Finale, Scanning, and Tricks for Music Educators

From its conception, Finale was designed to give you nearly unlimited control over the workings of the program. If there is something about the way Finale works that you don't like, you can probably customize it. For example, tell Finale to always open a new lead sheet on startup, or nudge four pixels instead of one. You can even remove tools you don't use from certain palettes to save space, or modify Finale's overall appearance.

Scanning in music notation software is a popular feature. Some purchase Finale for the sole purpose of transferring sheet music to a digital format. In this chapter, you will learn how to use Finale to produce the industry's best results while converting scanned files without having to purchase a separate scanning program. You will also learn techniques for cleaning up files after conversion,

If you are a music educator, use one of Finale's education templates to create examples, worksheets, and quizzes. Also, create customized technique-building exercises for any sized ensemble in minutes with the Exercise Wizard.

Here's a summary of what you will learn in this chapter:

▶ How to create custom documents.
▶ How to customize Finale.
▶ How to work with scanned files.
▶ Tricks for music educators.

Creating Custom Documents

Avoid the redundancy of adding the same libraries and making the same document settings for each new project. Do this by modifying the default file or creating your own Finale templates.

Customize the Default File

As you have seen, whenever you open a new default file (File menu > New > Default Document), Finale creates a single-staff, twenty-one-measure document. This document is Finale's standard template, called the Maestro Font Default. It contains default libraries for articulations, expressions, chord suffixes, and other items, as well as default settings for all items in the Document Options dialog box (Options > Document Options). If you want to use your own custom articulations, expressions, or document settings for the majority of your projects, add these elements to the Maestro Font Default file.

To customize the Maestro Font Default file:

1. From the File menu, choose New > Default Document. A new untitled "default" document appears.

2. Now, load any libraries you intend to use often (File menu > Open Library). Then, you can look in the appropriate selection window (articulation, expression, etc.) and delete any of the items you do not intend to use.

3. Program all metatools you want to include. Remember, metatools are always saved with the document.

4. If there is a particular layout you have in mind for the majority of your new documents, adjust the page format for score. From the Options menu, choose Page Format > Score to open the Page Format for Score dialog box, where you can make these layout settings. After changing the Page Format for Score dialog, redefine your pages. (Page Layout tool > Page Layout menu > Redefine pages > All Pages.)

5. If you have a particular music font you want to use for the majority of your documents, choose a new music font. From the Options menu, choose Set Default Music Font to open the Font dialog box, where you can make this setting. If you have a particular text font you wish to use with lyrics, text blocks, staff names, or text expressions, go to the Options menu, choose Document options, then choose Fonts. Make the necessary changes. When you're finished, click OK to return to the score.

6. If you want to change the default settings for any other notational items (font, beaming, noteheads, stem connections, repeats, ties, etc.), define these in the Document Options dialog box. From the Options menu, choose Document Options to open the Document Options dialog box. Choose the category on the left, make settings on the active page, click Apply to apply your settings, then do the same for any other category you want to edit. Click OK when you are finished to return to the score. If these settings already exist in another document, save and open the Document Options library to transfer all document settings to this document.

7. Remove any items you do not plan to use, such as articulations, shapes, expressions, custom Smart Shapes. This will help to reduce the size of your document and prevent any potential problems. To further clean the file, choose Remove Deleted Items from the Options menu > Data Check submenu.

8. After you have made all adjustments to your document, from the File menu, choose Save As. The Save As window appears.

9. On Windows, from the Save As Type drop-down menu, choose Coda Template File [*.FTM] (Mac users, skip ahead to step 8).

10. Name the file "Maestro Font Default" (on Windows, this should also have the extension .FTM).

11. Save the file to your Finale/Component Files folder (or, in versions previous to Finale 2003, save to the Finale folder).

12. Click Save. A warning should appear that the file exists, would you like to replace it? Confirm yes, you do want to replace it.

13. Now, open a new default document. The libraries, page format, and document settings you specified now exist in this or any future new default document.

Reset or Transport All Document Settings

You just learned how to specify a collection of document settings for future new files by modifying the Maestro Font Default file. You may want to apply a collection of document options to an existing file, or reset all document options to revert back to the default settings.

To revert all document options back to the default settings:

1. From the File menu, choose Open Library. The Open Library/Open File window appears.

2. Navigate to the Finale/Libraries folder.

3. Double-click the Document Options library. Or, choose a customized Document Options library you have saved. Finale's Document Options revert to default settings (or, your own customized default settings).

Some items will not change after loading the Document Options library. Certain changes to the document options apply only to future items entered in the score, and not existing items. For example, open the Document Options dialog box (Options menu > Document Options). Click the Fonts category. Notice the items marked with an asterisk (*). Changes to these will not apply after you return to the score. To change these items, use the Swap One Font for Another feature (Options > Data check), the Change Fonts plug-in (Plug-ins menu > Change Fonts), or Change Chord Suffix Fonts (select the Chord tool, then, from the Chord menu, choose Change Chord Suffix Fonts).

Creating Your Own Templates

As you have seen, Finale contains a variety of template files you can use as a starting point for working on a specific type of project (File menu > New > Document from Template). When you open a template file, Finale opens a copy of the template as an untitled document, so you won't have to worry about overwriting it. To create your own custom template:

1. Open any file. You might want to begin with a new default document, document with the Setup Wizard, or an existing template file.

2. Edit or load any desired libraries, edit the Page Format for Score, or make any other document-specific settings (such as the ones suggested above for customizing the Maestro Font Default).

3. From the File menu, choose Save As. The Save As window appears.

4. Navigate to the Finale/Templates folder (if you want to store this template along with the other Finale templates—any location will work fine).

5. On Windows, from the Save As Type drop-down menu, choose Coda Template File [*.FTM]. On Macintosh, a template is a regular Coda Notation file.

6. Replace "Untitled" with the desired template name. You should now see your file name, followed by the .FTM extension on Windows or a .MUS extension on Mac.

7. Click Save.

8. Now, any time you want to use this template, from the File menu, choose New > Document From Template. Then, double-click the file you created. A copy of the file will open as a new untitled document.

Customizing Finale

In addition to the basic program options described in chapter 2, there are a number of other ways to customize the way Finale works, both from within the Program Options dialog box and by using other tools Finale provides.

Customizing Finale via the Program Options

Use the Program Options dialog box to customize a variety of default program settings that you probably have been using without even knowing it. For example, you can tell Finale to open all new files in Scroll View at any view percentage, to use a different startup action (instead of starting the Setup Wizard every time), or use the arrow keys to nudge five pixels instead of one. As of Finale 2003, these, and many other program settings, are conveniently located in the Program Options dialog box.

Options for Opening New Documents

The New page of the Document Options dialog box allows you to customize settings for new or newly opened documents. From the Options menu, choose Document Options and select New from the list on the left. The New page of the Program Options dialog box appears, as shown in Figure 13.1.

Figure 13.1
Use the New page of the Program Options dialog box to specify a default file and the default view for all documents you open, including new documents.

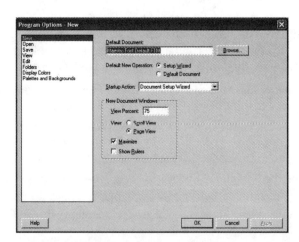

Here are some ways to specify the way Finale treats new documents from the New page of the Program Options dialog box:

▶ In the Default Document text box, specify any template file to use for your default document in place of the Maestro Font Default file. On Windows, click the Browse button to open a Windows Explorer window, where you can navigate to the desired file. This is the file Finale will use when you open a new default document (File menu > New > Default Document).

▶ For Default New Operation, specify the result of opening a file using the Ctrl/Command-N keyboard shortcut by choosing Setup Wizard or Default Document.

▶ By default, every time you start Finale, you see the first page of the Document Setup Wizard. You may want to tell Finale to open a new default file, template, or other file during startup instead. If this is the case, from the Startup Action drop-down/popup menu, choose the type of file you want to use whenever you start Finale. If you choose New Document from Template, at startup you will be prompted to choose a file from the Templates folder (as specified in the Templates field on the Folders page). If you choose Open Document, at startup you will be prompted to choose a file from your Music folder (as specified on the Music field of the Folders page).

▶ In the New Document Windows section, choose the view percentage and view (Page or Scroll View) to use for all documents you open or create.

The Open page of the Document Options dialog box allows you to customize the way Finale treats new and existing documents while opening them. Click the Open category in the Document Options dialog box to display the Open options. Here, you can tell Finale to automatically convert text (upper ASCII characters) while opening files cross-platform, and make settings for opening documents created in earlier versions. You will probably want to leave these default settings alone. If you are using Windows, however, enter a value for Number Of Recent Files In File Menu to specify the number of recently opened files to make readily available at the bottom of the File menu.

TIP

For information on using Finale's AutoSave and Backup features on the Save page of the Program Options dialog box, see chapter 1.

View Options

Use the View page of the Program Options dialog box to customize the appearance of certain items. In the Program Options dialog box, choose the View category from the list on the left. The View page appears, as shown in Figure 13.2.

Figure 13.2
Make settings for the
appearance of certain
items in the View page
of the Program Options
dialog box.

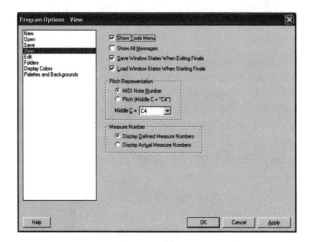

Here are some ways to edit Finale's appearance in the View page of the Program Options dialog
box:

▶ Uncheck Show Tools menu to remove the Tools menu from the list of menus
atop your screen. You might want to do this if you always select tools from
palettes and are just plain sick and tired of looking at that darned Tools menu.

▶ Check Show All Messages to tell Finale to show all dialog boxes in which you
have already checked Do Not Show Again. This brings back items that
automatically open (like the Tip of the Day, Do you want to View the QuickStart
Videos?, etc.).

▶ On Windows, check Save Windows States while Exiting Finale to tell Finale to
save your palette configuration for the next Finale session. If you check this,
make sure to also check Load Windows States when Starting Finale to load the
previous palette configuration. This option is not available on Mac.

▶ For Pitch Representation, you can tell Finale to display pitches as MIDI Note
Numbers (C=60) or Pitches (C=C4). This representation of pitch crops up in a
variety of places. For example, choose the HyperScribe tool, and then, from the
HyperScribe menu, choose Record Mode > Split Into Two Staves. The split point
representation (as "60" or "C4" by default) will depend on this setting.

▶ If you are defining measure number regions, you may want to tell Finale to
display the actual measure numbers beginning from the "real" measure one. To
do this, after Measure Numbers, choose Display Actual Measure Numbers.
Choose Display Defined Measure Numbers to go back to displaying measure
regions, as defined in the Measure Number dialog box.

Undo Options, Dragging, and Nudging

You can adjust Finale's default Undo settings as well as settings for dragging and nudging in the Edit page of the Program Options dialog box. Choose the Edit category from the list on the left of the Program Options dialog box to see the Edit page, as shown in Figure 13.3.

Figure 13.3
Customize Finale's
Undo Settings and
settings for dragging and
nudging on the Edit
page of the Program
Options dialog box.

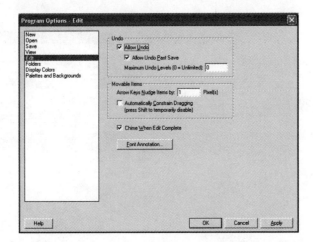

Here are some ways to edit Finale's treatment of Undo, dragging, and nudging in the Edit page of the Program Options:

▶ Finale records just about everything you do in your open file(s) in case you want to undo something (Ctrl/Command-Z). You will probably want to keep Undo on all the time, so you can quickly undo any unwanted changes while working on the score. Check Allow Undo Past Save to tell Finale to keep a record of your work so it is available after you save. To redo an undo, press Ctrl/Command-Y; note that undos will not work after you close and reopen the file.

▶ Finale can record an unlimited number of edits as you work on your score, in case you want to undo them later. To tell Finale to do this, for Maximum Number of Undo Levels, enter "0."

▶ In the Movable Items section, specify the number of pixels to nudge an item each time you press an arrow key.

▶ Check Automatically Constrain Dragging to tell Finale to always constrain to horizontal or vertical dragging (then, press Shift to drag normally at any time).

▶ Finale will chime to notify you when it is finished processing a major operation. Uncheck Chime When Edit Complete to disable this feature.

Customize Placement of Finale files on your Computer

We have touched on the Folders page of the Program Options a few times already. This page can be used to manage the placement of files used by Finale, or those you create. Choose Folders in the Program Options dialog box from the list on the left to display the Folders page, as shown in Figure 13.4.

Figure 13.4
Designate a folder for files used by Finale and those you create on the Folders page of the Program Options dialog box.

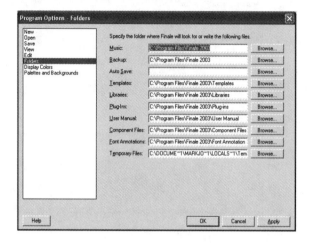

Use this page as a reference if you are looking for a specific file type used by Finale on your system. Or, select a folder to use for any of these file types by clicking the Browse button and choosing a path. For example, if you select the Finale 2003/Templates folder for Templates, Finale will open this folder when you choose New Document from Template under the File menu.

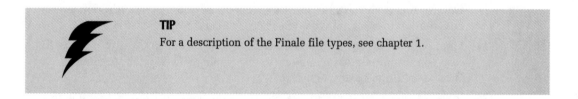

TIP
For a description of the Finale file types, see chapter 1.

Customize Finale's Display Colors

You can customize the color associated with any item, or turn off all display colors, in the Display Colors page of the Program Options dialog box. Choose Display Colors from the list on the left. You can also open this page from the View menu (View > Select Display Colors). The Display Colors options appear, as shown in Figure 13.5.

Figure 13.5
Specify a color for any item, or turn off display colors altogether on the Display Colors page of the Program Options dialog box.

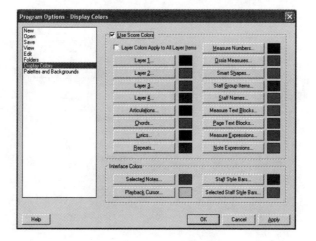

Click the item you want to customize to open the Colors dialog box, where you can choose a new color for the item. Check Layer Color Apply to All Layer Items if you want all articulations, note expressions, or other note-attached items to match the color of the layer to which they are attached. Uncheck Use Score Colors to tell Finale to only use black and white for display in the score.

TIP

To print the display colors on a color printer as they appear on-screen, check Print Display Colors in the Print dialog box.

Customize Finale's General Appearance

Finale's graphic interface was overhauled in Finale 2003. Changes include all new tool palettes and backgrounds. These improvements are purely cosmetic and were designed to give Finale a more desirable appearance. You can change the style to use for both palettes and backgrounds in the Palettes and Backgrounds page of the Program Options dialog box, as well as make other palette settings. Choose Palettes and Backgrounds from the list on the left to display the Palettes and Backgrounds page, as shown in Figure 13.6. Here, you can customize the general appearance of Finale.

Figure 13.6
Choose a style for
your palettes and
backgrounds on
the Palettes and
Backgrounds page of
the Program Options
dialog box.

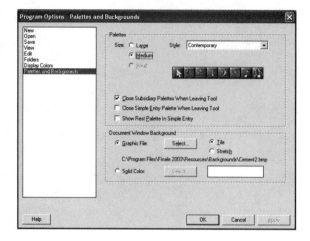

Here are some ways to customize the graphic style of tool palettes and the background on the Palettes and Backgrounds page of the Program Options dialog box.

▶ Click the Palettes drop-down/popup menu to choose from the seven available palette styles. Choose Traditional if you want to revert back to the palettes as they existed in Finale 2k2 (you can save some screen real estate this way).

▶ Check Close Subsidiary Palettes When Leaving Tool if you want Finale to automatically remove palettes not associated with the selected tool. For example, with this option checked, Finale will display only the Smart Shape Palette when the Smart Shape tool is selected. The following two checkboxes allow you to make specific palette settings for the Simple Entry tool palettes.

▶ In the Document Window Background section, you can set a color or graphic file to appear behind the page while working with Finale in Page View. Click the Select button to open one of Finale's background graphics, or navigate to your own graphic file to set it as the background. On Windows, you can set any Bitmap graphic as your background. On Mac, you can set any PICT graphic as your background.

▶ Choose Solid Color and click the Select button to the right to open the Colors dialog box, where you can select a solid color for your background.

Customize the Tool Palettes

If there are some tools you do not use at all, you may want to hide them from the tool palette to save space on your screen. You can do this with the Main Tool Palette, any of the secondary palettes, or the menu toolbars. Since this functionality is closely tied to the operating system, it works differently on Macintosh than on Windows.

TIP
To display any tool palette, select it from the Window menu.

To customize your tool palettes on Windows:

1. From the View menu, choose Customize Tool Palettes, then choose the palette you want to modify. The Customize Toolbar dialog box appears, as shown in Figure 13.7.

Figure 13.7
Remove items from any palette using the Customize Toolbar dialog box.

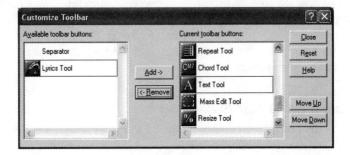

2. Choose any of the icons on the right and click the Remove button to remove it from the palette. After removing a palette icon, select it from the list on the left and click Add to place it back into the palette.

3. Select a palette icon on the left and click the Move Up or Move Down button to change the order of the palette icons. Click Reset at any time to restore the palette back to the default settings.

4. Click Close to return to the score. The modified palette appears on your screen. To change another palette, select it from the Customize Palette submenu of the View menu.

To customize your tool palettes on Macintosh:

1. While holding down the Shift key, click and drag an icon in the Main Tool Palette to move it to any location in the palette. You can do this with any Finale tool palette, but your changes to the Main Tool Palette can be retained from session to session if you program a tool set. Changes to the tool reordering on subsidiary palettes are lost when Finale is quit.

2. If you intend to resize the palette to hide certain icons, move the ones you want to keep to the left side of the palette. Click one of the icons you want to remain visible before resizing the palette. This way, Finale won't change the arrangement of icons as you resize.

3. Click and drag the Resize box at the lower right corner of the palette to change the size and number of visible tools (Figure 13.8).

Figure 13.8
Use the Resize box on the lower right of any tool palette to change its shape and number of visible tools.

Resize box

On Macintosh, you can also save the Main Tool Palette configuration to use at any time. First, Shift-click and drag the tool icons to the desired configuration. Then, hold down the Option key, and from the View menu, choose Program Tool Set > Tool Set 1. Then, to choose this palette configuration at any time, from the View menu, choose Set Tool Set > Tool Set 1. You can program up to three tool sets. Choose Master Tool Set from the Select Tool Set submenu to use Finale's default palette settings.

Menu Shortcuts (Windows only)

On Windows, you can map any menu selection to a keystroke using the Menu Shortcuts plug-in. This way, you can quickly access the dialog boxes you use often, or easily activate and deactivate parameters.

To program a keystroke to any menu item:

1. From the Plug-ins menu, choose TGTools > Menu Shortcuts. The Menu Shortcuts dialog box appears, as shown in Figure 13.9.

Figure 13.9
Use the Menu Shortcuts dialog box to program keystrokes to any menu item for easy access.

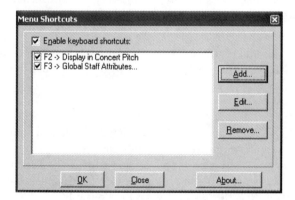

2. Check Enable Keyboard Shortcuts. In this example, we'll program two menu shortcuts—one to toggle the Display in Concert Pitch setting, and one to open the Global Staff Attributes dialog box.
3. Click the Add button to open the Key Assignment dialog box, where you can specify the key and menu item for your menu shortcut (Figure 13.10).

Figure 13.10
Choose the keystroke and menu item for your menu shortcut in the Key Assignment dialog box.

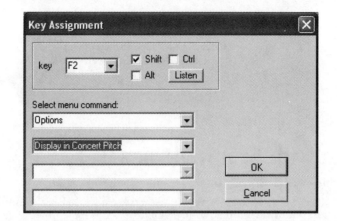

4. Click the Key drop-down menu and choose the keystroke you want to use. For this example, choose the F2 key (in the future, you can select a modifier for any keystroke by checking Ctrl, Alt or Shift on the right for more options).

5. Under Select Menu Command, choose the menu from the first drop-down menu and the submenus in the following dropdown menus. You may need to use all four tiers for some menu items. For this example, choose Options from the top drop-down menu and Display in Concert Pitch from the second.

6. Click OK to return to the Menu Shortcuts dialog box.

7. Now, let's add another menu shortcut that opens a dialog box. Click the Add button again to open the Key Assignments dialog box.

8. Now, click the Key drop-down menu and choose the F3 key.

9. Under Select Menu Command, choose Plug-ins from the top drop-down menu and Global Staff Attributes from the second.

10. Click OK twice to return to the score.

11. Now, to demonstrate these menu shortcuts at work, from the File menu, choose New > Document with Setup Wizard. Move to page 2 and add any transposing instrument (Horn in F, for example). Then, click Next, Next and Finish to open the new score. You might also want to enter some notes.

12. Press the F2 key. Your score displays in concert pitch. Press the F2 key again to display the score normally. Now, pressing the F2 key does the same thing as choosing Display in Concert Pitch from the Options menu.

13. Press the F3 key. The Global Staff Attributes appears. Now, pressing the F3 key does the same thing as choosing Global Staff Attributes from the Plug-ins menu.

Program as many keyboard shortcuts as you like to creatively improve efficiency while working on any project. For example, try assigning the F keys to Simple Entry Note durations (Simple menu > Simple Edit Commands), so you can use keystrokes for note durations with Select Notes on Entry activated under the Simple menu. The shortcuts you program will be available whenever you use Finale. To turn Menu Shortcuts off, uncheck Enable Keyboard Shortcuts in the Menu Shortcuts dialog box.

CHAPTER 13

TIP

For more options for keyboard shortcuts on Windows or Macintosh, you might investigate Quickeys. Visit <www.quickeys.com> for more info.

Working with Scanned Files

Scanning in Finale has drastically improved since its introduction to the File menu (MIDIScan) in Finale 2001. In the past, this particular feature was a tech support nightmare, as scanning technology overall really wasn't ready for primetime score recognition. Though there are still a number of limitations and problems with translating a scanned page of sheet music into Finale, you can produce far greater results with SmartScore Lite, included in Finale 2003, than in previous versions. In this section, you will learn tricks for getting the best possible results while translating a page (or pages) of sheet music into a Finale document.

Scanning Sheet Music

First, you will need to scan the sheet music using a scanner and compatible scanning software. Most flatbed scanners will do the trick. Do not try to use a hand scanner while scanning music intended for Finale. For best results, the goal is to create the cleanest possible black and white graphic image of the page. Here are some guidelines to follow while scanning a piece of sheet music. Consult your scanning program's user manual if you have trouble making any of these settings:

▶ Make sure the original document is sixteen staves or less.

▶ Do not expect quality results while translating handwritten scores, or poor-quality printed manuscripts. The cleaner the piece looks on the page, the better Finale will be able to translate it.

▶ Make sure the original document is aligned square with the plate of the scanner.

▶ Set the scanning resolution to 300 dpi.

▶ SmartScore Lite accepts TIFF and Bitmap files. Always scan in "Black and White" or "Line Art" (not color or grayscale). This also might be the "FAX" setting, depending on your scanning software (1-bit per pixel in any case). Some scanners save TIFF files specific to their product line. If you find your scanning software is producing nonstandard TIFF files, try using a black and white Bitmap file instead. Open the image in another graphics program, then save it in standard (black and white) TIFF or Bitmap format.

▶ Save as an uncompressed TIFF file (without LZW compression).

Scan each page and save it to a convenient place on your computer. Save each page as a separate file. You might try using a naming convention that relates to the page number (mypiece1.tif, mypiece2.tif, etc.). After you have scanned and saved the music, open Finale. It's now time to translate the score into a Finale document.

NOTE
You may have problems opening TIFF graphics saved directly from your computer (a screenshot taken from another notation program, for example). The SmartScore Lite scanning recognition software expects to see fine inconsistencies in lines and shapes that occur while scanning a printed page. Try printing the document, then scanning the printout to prepare a TIFF graphic for Finale.

CHAPTER 13

Importing a Scanned TIFF File

After launching Finale 2003, from the File menu, choose SmartScore Lite. The SmartScore Lite dialog box appears, as shown in Figure 13.11.

Figure 13.11
Add scanned files and prepare for scanning recognition in the SmartScore Lite dialog box.

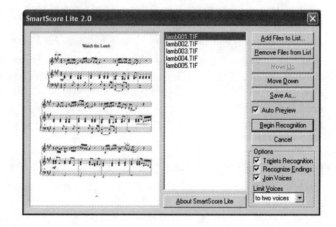

Here, click the Add Files to List button, then navigate to the folder containing your scanned files. Highlight the files you want to translate, and click Open. The files you selected now appear listed in the middle of the SmartScore Lite dialog box. Click a file name to see a preview of the file in the preview window on the left.

SmartScore Lite will translate each scanned image as a new page of the same Finale document if you recognize several files at once. Rearrange the file/page order by clicking the Move Up and Move Down buttons on the right to reposition the selected file. In the Options section of the SmartScore Lite dialog box, you can tell Finale to ignore or translate triplets and repeat endings. Uncheck these to edit/create them in the score after recognition. Check Join Voices to tell Finale to join independent voices into one layer. From the Limit Voices drop-down/popup menu, choose the number of voices you want Finale to recognize (try choosing the number of independent voices that exist in any one staff of the original document). Click Begin Recognition. Finale translates each file and opens the resulting document.

The raw results you get immediately after translation will depend on the image quality and complexity of the original sheet music. You may find somewhat of a mess after translating a staff with many voices and complex rhythms. Use the Simple or Speedy Entry tool to edit any basic notation errors after translation (see chapters 2 and 3 for information on editing with Simple and Speedy Entry). Here are some tricks for editing scanned files opened with SmartScore Lite:

▶ After translation, all staves will be set for independent Key Signatures. To turn independent Key Signatures off, click the Staff tool, doubleclick the staff, and then, under Independent Elements, uncheck Key Signature. Now, any key changes you make will apply to all staves as they would normally.

▶ Use the Document Options dialog box (Options > Document Options) to change anything from clefs, to Time Signatures, to beaming on a document-wide basis.

▶ Use the Selection tool to reposition items throughout the score as necessary.

▶ Use the Edit Page Margins and Edit System margins dialog box to update system and page margins, or drag them around manually (see chapter 11). Note the page margins are positioned directly over the page edge, so you will probably want to adjust them. If you want to edit the overall layout of your score, use the Page Format for Score dialog box (Options menu > Page Format > Score). Then, redefine pages (Page Layout > Redefine Pages > All Pages).

▶ You may find a variety of other changes necessary, for which you can find help throughout this book. If your results are poor (due to file complexity or image quality of the original score), evaluate the time necessary to fix the scanned score compared to entering the music from scratch with the Speedy Entry tool or any of the other entry methods.

Using SharpEye Scanning with Finale (Windows Only)

If you are interested in another scanning option, try using SharpEye scanning software to convert a scanned image into XML format, which can then be imported into Finale with the Dolet MusicXML Import plug-in. Some report this method produces the most accurate results. In addition, this method retains lyrics from the original sheet music, which is not supported in the scanning options included with Finale.

First, if you do not own SharpEye, download and install the SharpEye demo from their website at <www.visiv.co.uk/dload.htm> (you can find instructions for how to do this on the site). If you do not have an Internet connection, copy the SharpEye installer directly from the SharpEye folder on the *Finale Power!* companion CD-ROM to your desktop. Close all programs running on your computer and doubleclick the installer. When installation is finished, you are ready to continue. You will be able to use the SharpEye demo for thirty days without restriction. After that, you will need to register the software to use it.

To import scanned sheet music into Finale using SharpEye:

1. Scan your sheet music and save each page as an uncompressed, black and white, TIFF or Bitmap file. If you have any trouble scanning the file and saving the image, see the instruction manual that came with your scanner and/or scanning software.

2. Open SharpEye (Start > Programs > Visiv > SharpEye).

3. If your sheet music contains more than one page, from the Read menu, choose Batch Process. The Setup batch window appears. If you want to open a single page, from the File menu, choose Open Image, navigate to the image file and double-click to open it. Then, from the Read menu, choose Read to convert the file to SharpEye format. When conversion is finished, skip ahead to step 9.

4. Click Add Files. Now, navigate to the folder containing your scanned images. Drag, or Ctrl-click, to highlight the ones you want.

5. Click Open. The selected files now appear in the Setup batch window.

6. Click the Browse button, and choose a location for the processed files. For now, choose your desktop, and click OK.

7. Click Start batch. SharpEye starts converting the images into SharpEye files. This may take some time, depending on the size and complexity of the scanned images.

8. When conversion is complete, navigate to the desktop. Double-click the first page so it opens in SharpEye. Then, go back to your desktop and double-click the second page. Choose Append to add it to the end of the SharpEye score. Do this for each remaining page.

9. Now, you can do some basic editing to optimize the file for Finale import. Many errors can be corrected in either SharpEye or Finale, but it is important to check that the Time Signatures, Key Signatures, and clefs are correct before exporting from SharpEye (to ensure that rhythmic durations and pitches translate properly).

10. After you have edited the score, from the File menu, choose MusicXML > Save. Name the file, and save it to your desktop.

11. Open Finale and cancel out of the Setup Wizard if it appears.

12. From the File menu, choose New > Default document.

13. From the Plug-ins menu, choose MusicXML Import. If you do not see this option (and are using Finale 2000 or better), install the Dolet plug-in from the Finale-Power companion CD-ROM (you will find instructions for how to do this on the CD).

14. Click the Browse button, navigate to the desktop, and double-click the MusicXML you saved from SharpEye.

15. Click OK. The MusicXML file opens into a Finale document.

Tricks for Music Educators

Finale can make an excellent addition to a music educator's toolbox. Use Finale to create examples, quizzes, worksheets, or even custom exercises for warm-ups for your ensemble. Whether you are a music theory instructor or a band director, in this section you will learn how to effectively benefit from some of Finale's educational features.

Finale's Educational Templates

Finale 2003 offers several templates designed specifically for use in music-oriented classes for worksheets or quizzes. To use one of these, from the File menu, choose New > Document From Template. Then, open the Education Templates folder. Here, you will find seven educational templates.

Two- and Four-Measure Examples

Finale's two- and four-measure templates can be used to create musical examples with descriptions or questions for music theory (Figure 13.12).

Figure 13.12
Use Finale's two- and four-measure example templates for music theory examples or questions.

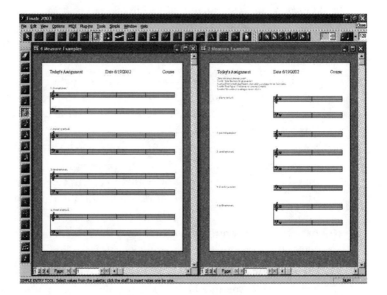

These documents are specialized in many ways. Courtesy key, clef, and time changes have been turned off, so you won't see extra material at the end of your examples if you decide to change one of these items. The final barline has been removed, the page layout altered, and other minor modifications have been made. The "2 Measure Examples" file offers some suggestions for managing these files in an existing text block. To delete this text block, use the Text (or Selection) tool. Here are some suggestions for creating musical examples or questions:

▶ There are two staves per system in both of these documents. Some staves in the two-measure example document have been hidden with a Staff Style. To hide, or show any region of measures, click the Staff tool. Blue lines appear above all hidden staves. To display the staff, drag-enclose the blue line to highlight the hidden measures (they overlap the subsequent system). Then, press Backspace/Clear to clear Staff Styles. Now, the two systems overlap. Click the Page Layout tool, and then, from the Page Layout menu, check Avoid Margin Collision. Click and drag the overlapping system slightly to snap the systems to a more acceptable layout, then make fine adjustments accordingly.

▶   To insert a measure in an example, click the Measure tool. Click a measure to highlight it, then, from the Measure menu, choose Insert. Finale will insert a measure to the left of the highlighted one. To move a measure from system to system, highlight it with the Mass Edit Tool and press the up or down arrow buttons on your keyboard. To add a measure to the end of your document, double-click the Measure tool (pages added will appear in the same format as the first page by default).

▶   For the two-measure document, use the Page Layout tool to increase the overall width of the example. Click the Page Layout tool, then click one of the system handles on the left. Press Ctrl/Command-A to select them all. Now, all of the left system margins will move in uniform.

▶   Use the Text tool to edit any of the title information or the questions (double-click the handle to view the editing frame). The questions in both documents are measure-attached text blocks, so they will reposition along with measures as you readjust them (in this case, the measure closest in proximity).

▶   Use Staff Styles to change in selected measures the clef, transposition, number of staff lines, or any other staff attribute (see chapters 7 and 8).

You can also use the "Full System, No Barlines" template to create musical examples or questions.

TIP

E-mail your students a worksheet or musical example. They can open and make basic changes with Finale NotePad, Finale's free notation software available for download, at www.codamusic.com.

Kodály/Solfège Templates

Finale offers two templates designed for teaching rhythm and sight singing in the Kodály method. With these templates, create stick notation and easily place solfège indications beneath the staff with preset articulation metatools. Here is an example created with the "Kodály 1" template.

Figure 13.13
Use Finale's two Kodály templates to create solfège and stick notation for instruction in the Kodály method.

To create a score like the example above:

1. From the File menu, choose New > Document from Template. Then, open the Education Templates folder and double-click the file "Kodály 1". The document appears in the Finale window.

2. Click the Time Signature tool to change the meter of the document. Click the Key Signature tool to change the key. The key change will not be visible in the score.

3. You can specify a moveable do by choosing a moveable do clef. Click the Staff tool and double-click the lower staff. In the Staff Attributes dialog box, click the Select button to the right of the clef display. Choose a moveable do clef from this list to coordinate with the Key Signature you chose. Note: If you are using Windows, and do not see the moveable do clefs, update to Finale 2003a.

4. Click OK back to the score.

5. Enter your notation into the lower staff.

6. Click the Mass Edit Tool, then click the left of the lower staff so it is highlighted.

7. Click and drag the highlighted region into the top (hidden) staff. Your notes convert to stems and beams to indicate rhythm.

8. Click to the left of the top staff so it is highlighted.

9. From the Plug-ins menu, choose Note Beam and Rest Editing > Single Pitch.

10. Enter "G4" and click OK. All of your stems and beams are aligned in the top staff.

11. Click the Articulation tool.

12. Now, move your cursor under the first stem in the top staff (so a small note

appears on the cursor). On your QWERTY keyboard, hold down the first letter of the solfège syllable (D=Do, R=Re, etc.) and click. The letter appears below the stem. Repeat this for all other stems in the top staff.

13. If you would like to hide barlines, click the Staff tool, doubleclick the staff, uncheck Barlines and click OK. To hide an individual barline, click the Measure tool, doubleclick the measure, in the Measure Attributes, Barline row, choose Invisible and click OK.

14. If you want the noteheads on the solfège staff to appear as shapes, click the Staff tool and double-click the lower staff. Next to Notation Style, click the drop-down menu and choose Note Shapes. Click OK to return to the score.

Manuscript Paper

You can print a page of manuscript paper from Finale containing staff lines only. To do this, open the "Blank Manuscript" template. From the File menu, choose New > Document from Template. Then, open the Education Templates folder and double-click the file "Manuscript Paper". A page appears with blank staves and some text. Use the Text tool (or Selection tool) to delete any unwanted text. Use the Page Layout tool to adjust the system spacing. Then, print this document to produce a sheet of blank manuscript paper.

The Exercise Wizard

If you are a music educator responsible for directing an instrumental ensemble, use Finale as a professional tool for enhancing your students' warm-up routine with customized technique-building exercises. The Exercise Wizard was added in Finale 2002 and has become a popular tool among educators for enhancing their rehearsal sessions. Create scales, arpeggios and twisters, with custom articulations, in any key, transposed for any instrument. Best of all, this can be done in minutes (you can usually create a customized lesson faster than you can print the parts). You can see an example of a part generated by the Exercise Wizard in Figure 13.14.

Figure 13.14
Create customized lessons, such as this one, orchestrated for any ensemble with any number of performers.

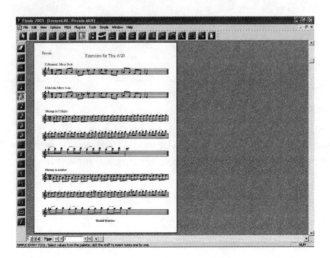

A lesson can contain several different exercises, occurring sequentially on the page (Figure 13.14). You can print or save the lesson for a single part, or any combination of instruments (with any number of copies of a part for multiple persons in a section). Here, you will learn how to easily create, save, and print custom lessons.

There are two types of files you can produce with the Exercise Wizard:

▶   The first is a lesson file (.LSN). This is basically a text file containing all of the settings you have made in an Exercise Wizard session. You can open a lesson file to launch the Exercise Wizard automatically, and edit a collection of settings you have already made.

▶   The second type of file is the actual notation file (.MUS). Instead of printing directly from the Exercise Wizard, you can save a standard Finale file for each instrumental part to be viewed on screen or stored and printed at a later time.

Exercise Wizard - Page 1

From the File menu, choose New > Exercise Wizard. Page 1 of the Exercise Wizard appears, as shown in Figure 13.15.

Figure 13.15
Specify a title and the page size for your exercises on page 1 of the Exercise Wizard.

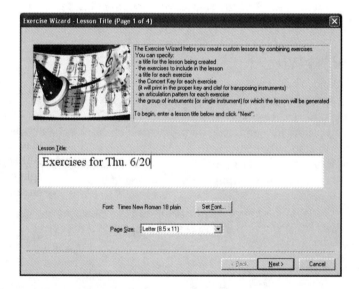

First, click the set font button and choose a font for the lesson title. Then, enter the lesson title in the text box (this title will appear at the top of the printed page). From the Page Size drop-down menu, choose a page size for your exercises. Then, click the Next button to move to page 2.

Exercise Wizard - Page 2

On page 2, choose from hundreds of available exercises (Figure 13.16).

Figure 13.16
Choose the type of
exercises you want to
include on page 2 of the
Exercise Wizard.

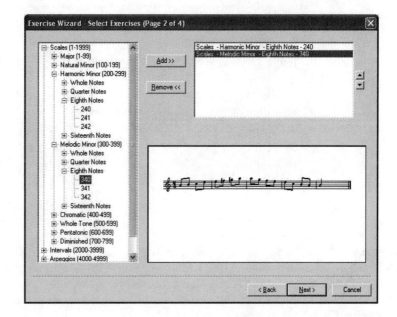

CHAPTER 13

Click the plus sign (+) to the left of any category to view and choose from items in the subcategories. First, choose the melodic structure, then scale type, interval, and note duration. The actual exercises will appear as a number (1-5571). Click a number to see an example of the exercise in the preview window on the lower right. Double-click the exercise number (or click Add) to add the exercise to the lesson. Add as many exercises as you like. Select one of the exercises you have added and use the up and down arrows to the right of the list to change the order of the exercises as you want them to appear on the page. When you have finished adding and arranging your exercises, click Next to move to page 3.

Exercise Wizard - Page 3

Here, you can enter an exercise title, concert key, and articulation pattern for each exercise (Figure 13.17).

Figure 13.17
On page 3 of the
Exercise Wizard, specify
a title, concert key, and
articulation pattern for
each exercise.

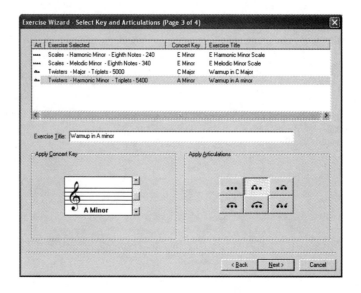

First, click the exercise you want to edit from the list at the top. Then, after Exercise Title, type a
title for the selected exercise (the title will appear above the first measure of each exercise, as
shown in Figure 13.14). In the Apply Concert Key section, use the up and down arrows in the
scroll bar to modify the concert key. Under Apply Articulations, select an articulation pattern for
the exercise. Click Next to move on to page 4.

Exercise Wizard - Page 4

Here, choose the instruments you want to include in your lesson, number of instruments for
each part, and range (Figure 13.18).

Figure 13.18
On page 4 of the
Exercise Wizard, create
an ensemble, then print
or save your lesson.

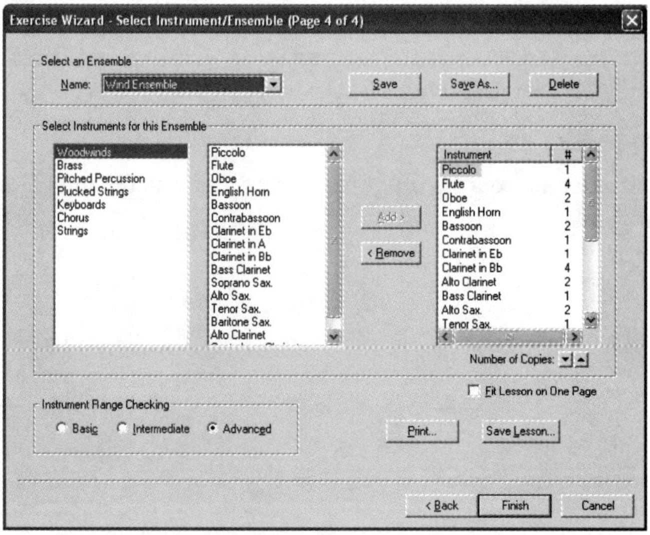

First, in the Select an Ensemble section, choose the instrumental ensemble that most closely matches the one you are instructing. Notice the instruments in the list on the right of your selection. This is the master list of instruments from which you will be generating parts. Use the following methods to edit the instruments in your ensemble:

▶ Click to select an instrument you want to remove from the list on the right, and click the Remove button to clear it from the list.

▶ To add an instrument, choose the instrument type from the list on the far left, then double-click the desired instrument from the second column. Notice that the instrument appears in your ensemble list on the right.

▶ To add or remove the number of copies per part, click one of the instruments in your ensemble to select it. Then, click the up and down arrows for Number of Copies. Notice the number to the right of the instrument changes to reflect the number of copies for that part.

After you have defined an ensemble, you might want to save it for the next time you create a custom set of exercises. To do this, in the Select an Ensemble section, click Save As. The Save Ensemble dialog box appears. Type a new name for your ensemble and click OK. Now, the next time you create a lesson, this ensemble will be available from the Name drop-down/popup menu.

Under Instrument Range Checking, choose a skill level for your ensemble. If the range of an exercise is too high or low, Finale will transpose it an octave so all notes fit within a playable range for the selected skill level.

Check Fit Lesson on One Page to tell Finale to manipulate the page layout to fit the lesson on a single page. Finale will make adjustments up to a certain point, but will still create more than one page if the layout becomes unreasonable.

Click Print to open the Print dialog box, where you can immediately send the lesson to the printer. Finale will place the exercises in the order specified on each page, and also print the number of parts chosen for each instrument. Click Save Lesson to open the Save Lesson As dialog box, where you can save the current configuration of settings for future use (choose Lesson File), or save the lesson files as standard Finale files to your computer (choose Notation File). Choose Both to save the lesson configuration and Finale files.

Click Finish to exit the Setup Wizard. If you have made changes to the current lesson, Finale will ask you if you want to save the lesson before returning to the score.

NOTE

When you are ready to come back and edit a lesson you have already created, open it just as you would a standard Finale file. Finale will automatically launch the Exercise Wizard, where you can make changes to the lesson.

14
Playback and the MIDI Tool

Finale is basically an advanced music-oriented graphics program that plays the graphic back for you. Though not designed to be a full-blown MIDI sequencer, it does have a wide range of playback capabilities you can use to review your work, and generate a quality MIDI performance. Each staff can be defined as a MIDI track with its own channel, timbre, and performance data. You can use your computer's internal sounds, or an external MIDI device (such as a MIDI keyboard or sound module) for playback. You can choose the device to use for playback in the MIDI Setup dialog box (see chapter 1 for details).

In this section, you will learn how to use Finale's playback features to spot-check any beat on the fly, play back from any measure, or specify swing playback—even isolate specific staves or layers for playback. You will also learn how to define a variety of playback effects to your score using expressions including volume, pitch bends, tempo, and MIDI controller data. For even more control over playback, we will cover how to use the MIDI tool to manipulate MIDI data for a single note or for any selected region.

Here's a summary of what you will learn in this chapter:

▶ General playback techniques.
▶ How to use the Instrument List.
▶ How to define playback with expressions.
▶ How to use the MIDI tool.
▶ How to define other markings for playback.

General Playback Techniques

You have a great deal of control over the region of playback while working on a score. You can play back an entire document from the beginning, easily start playback at any measure, or drag your mouse over a region to deliberately listen for specific chords (scrubbing playback). For any of these methods, you can isolate any number of staves and/or layers using the Instrument List, or even specify a staff or the full score for playback on the spot while scrubbing. In this section, you will learn how to make the most of Finale's playback versatility to spot-check a score in progress, or generate a quality MIDI performance.

CHAPTER 14

Playback Controls

You can use the Playback Controls to manage the basics for playing back your score. If you do not see the Playback Controls on your screen, from the Window menu, choose Playback Controls. They appear on your screen, as shown in Figure 14.1.

Figure 14.1
Start, pause, stop, record, or specify the measure to start playback with the Playback Controls.

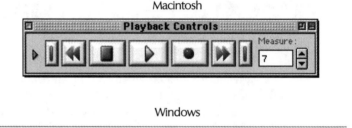

Macintosh

Windows

To use the Playback Controls:

▶ Click the Play button to begin playback at the measure specified in the counter box. Playback will start at measure 1 by default. To use the counter on Windows, click the Playback Settings icon (the speaker) on the right side of the Playback Controls. Then, under Always Start At, choose Current Counter Setting and click OK. On Macintosh, click the arrow on the left side of the Playback Controls to expand the settings. After Play From, choose the lower radio button. Now, on Mac or Win, enter a measure number in the counter box to specify a start point for playback.

▶ Click the square Stop button to stop playback.

▶ Click the Pause button (two vertical bars) to pause playback. Then, use the Fast Forward (left arrow) and Rewind (right arrow) buttons to advance to a specific measure. Click the Play button again to resume playback.

▶ Click the single bar on the left to move to the beginning of the piece for playback. Click the single bar on the right to move to the end of the piece.

▶ You can click the Record button to automatically select the HyperScribe tool and begin recording into the first measure of the staff specified for recording in the Instrument List. While recording into your score, you won't need to use the Record button. Instead, just the select HyperScribe tool and click the measure you want to record into (see chapter 4 for more information on HyperScribe).

▶ You can choose a tempo for playback in the Playback Controls. On Windows, click the Duration icon (quarter note with arrows). On Macintosh, click the arrow on the left side of the Playback Controls to expand the settings. Click the Note Duration icon you want to use for the main beat. Then, enter the number of beats per minute in the text box to the right. Note that tempo markings defined for playback in your score will override this setting.

You can make a number of other settings for playback in the Playback Settings dialog box (Win)/expanded Playback Controls (Mac). On Mac, click the arrow on the left to expand the playback controls, or on Win, click the Playback Settings (speaker) icon, as shown in Figure 14.1. You will now see additional playback settings, as shown in Figure 14.2. Use these settings to adjust the start point for playback, change the base key velocity, or set swing playback.

Figure 14.2
Use the Playback
Settings(Win)/expanded
Playback Controls(Mac)
to make a variety of
settings for playback.

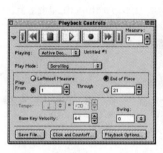
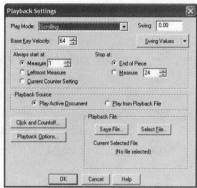

Here are some common ways to manage playback with these settings:

▶ For Play mode, you can choose between three types of playback: non-scrolling, Non-scrolling (pre-scan music), and scrolling. You will probably want to choose scrolling. With this setting, Finale first scans the music for changes and then plays back with a scrolling bar. To save time, you could choose non-scrolling. With this setting, Finale does not scan the music before playback. Choose Non-scrolling (pre-scan music) to tell Finale to scan for changes and playback without a scrolling bar.

▶ In the Always Start At (Mac: Play From) section, choose Leftmost Measure to tell Finale to always begin playback at the left-most measure displayed on your screen when clicking the Play button in the Playback Controls.

▶ The Base Key Velocity is basically the default dynamic level. This can be set anywhere from 0 (silent) to 127 (loudest). This is set at 64 by default to give you the optimal amount of contrast as you enter dynamic expressions and MIDI data that adjust the key velocity throughout the piece.

▶ Setting swing playback in Finale 2003 is as easy as choosing the type of swing playback you want from the Swing Values (Mac: Swing) option. Click the arrow to choose Light, Standard, Heavy, or Dotted Eighth, Sixteenth from the menu to set swing playback. This setting applies to the entire document. To remove swing from playback, click the same option and choose None from the menu.

Defining Regions for Playback Faster

Though the playback controls can be adequate for general playback, if you really want more speed while reviewing a score in progress, you may want to begin playback at a specific measure on the page, or play back a specific staff of your score. Following are some ways to quickly isolate specific playback regions.

Spacebar-click Playback

Here are ways to easily specify a particular measure for playback using the spacebar-click method. After starting playback with the following methods, click anywhere in the score to stop playback.

> ▶ On Macintosh, with the Playback Controls open, press the spacebar to begin playback at the measure specified in the counter box. To play back all staves from a certain measure when the Playback Controls are not open, hold down the spacebar and click the desired measure.

> ▶ To play back starting at any visible measure, hold down the spacebar and click the desired measure (with the Playback Controls closed on Mac).

> ▶ To play back the contents of a single staff starting at any visible measure, Shift-spacebar-click the staff in the desired measure.

> ▶ If you are using a staff set, spacebar-click on a staff to play back the visible staves.

> ▶ If you are using a staff set, spacebar-click between two staves to play back all visible and hidden staves (see chapter 7 for more information on creating staff sets in Scroll View).

> ▶ To begin playback starting with measure one, spacebar-click the left of the staff

Scrubbing Playback

Listen to notes in your score as you drag by using the scrubbing playback feature. This is the fastest way to play back a small portion of your score for review. On Macintosh, close the Playback Controls to use scrubbing playback.

> ▶ Ctrl-spacebar-click (Mac: Option-spacebar-Click) and drag over a region of music to hear music in all staves while dragging.

> ▶ Shift-Ctrl-spacebar-click (Mac: Shift-Option-spacebar-click) and drag over a staff to hear music in that staff only.

NOTE

On Macintosh, scrubbing playback will work only if you are playing back through an external MIDI device (it will not work with Internal Speaker Playback selected from the MIDI menu).

Recorded vs. Notated Playback

If you recorded a performance into Finale with HyperScribe, you may notice Finale plays the score back as you performed it, including all of the subtleties that go along with your recorded performance. This performance data includes key velocities, note durations, and start times for each note. You can tell Finale to play back a score as recorded, or precisely as it appears in the notation in the Playback Options dialog box. From the Options menu, choose Playback Options. The Playback Options dialog box appears, as shown in Figure 14.3.

Figure 14.3
Tell Finale to play back a score as recorded or as notated in the Playback Options dialog box.

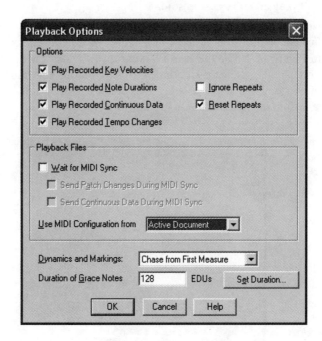

To tell Finale to play the score as notated (without the nuances of your recorded performance), in the Options section, uncheck all four Play Recorded Key Velocities and Play Recorded Note Durations checkboxes. Then, click OK to return to the score and play back the document to review your changes.

Using the Instrument List

In chapter 2, you learned how to assign a General MIDI instrument to a staff for playback. There are a variety of other ways to customize playback by editing the Instrument List. You can tell Finale to mute certain staves, or even layers within a staff. To demonstrate this, open a score with several staves. Or, begin a new document with the Setup Wizard (New > Document with Setup Wizard). Move to page 2 and add several different instruments. Click Next, Next, and Finish to open the document. Now, use the following steps to explore the options available in the Instrument List. Note that you can play back at any time, even with the Instrument List open.

1. From the Window menu, choose Instrument List. Then, make sure View by Staves is selected in the lower left corner.

2. Notice the column labeled "P". This is the "Play" column. To remove a staff from playback, click its box under the P column to clear it. Now, during playback, the staff will remain silent.

3. Designate a solo staff under the "S" column. To designate a solo staff (and mute

all other staves), click its box under the S column. Now, only the solo staff will play during playback. Feel free to choose as many solo staves as you like. Finale will play all staves set to solo.

4. Now, click the arrow to the left of a staff name to expand Display More Options for that staff. You now see options for layers, expressions and chords, as shown in Figure 14.4. Use the P and S columns to mute or solo any layer within a staff. You can also mute or solo the staff's expressions and chord symbols here. Note that even when you solo a layer, expressions, or chords in a staff, all other staves and their elements become muted.

Figure 14.4
Mute or solo layers, expressions, and chord symbols in the Instrument List.

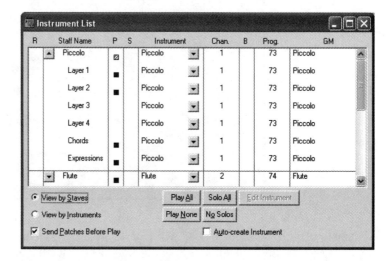

5. Click the Play All button or Solo All button to set every staff to play or solo. Click the Play None, or No Solos button to remove all play or solo settings.

Creating Non-General MIDI Instruments

If you are using an external MIDI device, you can use any sound from that device by creating a new instrument in the Instrument List. To create a non-General MIDI instrument for playback:

1. From the Window menu, choose Instrument List (if it isn't visible already). Then, make sure View by Staves is selected in the lower left corner.

2. Under the Instrument column, click the drop-down/popup menu for an instrument and choose New Instrument (at the top of the list). The Instrument Definition dialog box appears, as shown in Figure 14.5.

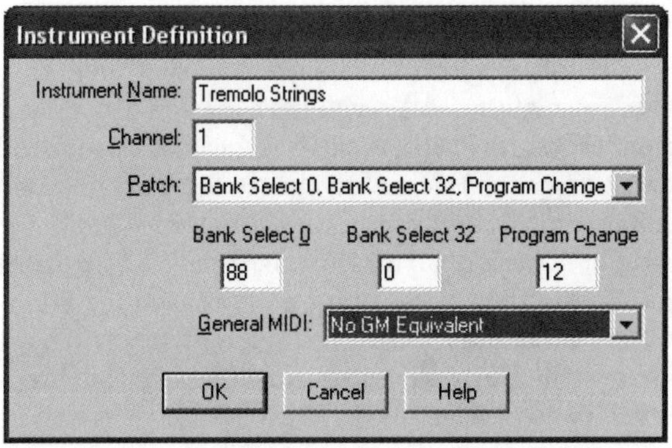

Figure 14.5
Define a non-General
MIDI instrument in the
Instrument Definition
dialog box.

Instrument Definition   ☒

Instrument <u>N</u>ame: │Tremolo Strings   │

<u>C</u>hannel: │1   │

<u>P</u>atch: │Bank Select 0, Bank Select 32, Program Change│▼│

Bank Select <u>0</u>   Bank Select 32   Program C<u>h</u>ange
│88   │   │0   │   │12   │

<u>G</u>eneral MIDI: │No GM Equivalent   │▼│

            │ OK │   │ Cancel │   │ Help │

3. In the Name text box, enter the name of the instrument as it appears on your external MIDI device (for reference in the future).

4. In the Channel text box, enter a channel not yet used by any other instruments assigned to staves in the current document.

5. For Patch, choose Bank Select 0, Bank Select 32, Program Change.

6. Under Bank Select 0, enter the primary bank number for the desired instrument. Consult the user manual for your external MIDI device to find this number. Look for one of the bank numbers labeled MSB (Most Significant Byte).

7. Under Bank Select 32, enter the secondary bank number. For the bank you want to use, this will be the LSB (Least Significant Byte) number. If the bank does not have another associated bank number, you can leave this text box empty.

8. Under Program Change, enter the instrument's number. Because some MIDI devices begin numbering at 0 instead of 1, you will need to enter the number of the instrument plus 1 (if you want to access instrument number 11 on your keyboard, for example, enter 12 in the Program Change box) to get the correct sound.

9. Click OK, then play back the document for review. Finale will send the playback data to the external MIDI device for the instrument selected.

NOTE
Make sure the external MIDI device you want to use for playback is properly installed on your computer (and on Macintosh, properly configured in FreeMIDI or OMS) and chosen as your output device in Finale's MIDI Setup dialog box. If you are using a software synthesizer, choose the driver for the synthesizer in the MIDI Setup dialog box. Follow the same steps as above for defining non-General MIDI sounds on a software synth.

CHAPTER 14

Instrument Libraries

After you have created a number of instruments, you can save them in a library to be used in any other document. This is especially useful if you have created a number of non-General MIDI instruments for a particular external MIDI device. You can save and load an instrument library just like any other library. From the File menu, choose Save Library. Choose Instruments, and click OK. Name the library and save it to your Finale/Libraries folder (or another convenient location). Then, to load the library in any document, from the File menu, choose Open Library. Navigate to the Finale/Libraries folder (or wherever you saved the library) and doubleclick the library file to open it. Now, all of the instruments in the library will appear in the Instruments drop-down/popup menu in the Instrument List. Note that after loading an instrument library into a document, you will still have to select the instruments for each staff in the Instrument List.

Defining Playback with Expressions

You may already have noticed that dynamic expressions apply to playback in the score. These expressions are already set to change the MIDI key velocity. You can define a variety of playback effects in your score with expressions, including tempo, playback instrument, sustain, ritardandi, and accellerandi. If you want, you can even apply a playback effect to your score without displaying an expression marking. You can edit the playback effect of any existing expression, or define your own playback effect. In this section, you will learn a variety of ways to edit the MIDI performance of your score using the Expression tool.

NOTE

For specific information on creating, assigning, and editing expressions, see chapter 3.

Dynamics

You can easily edit the dynamic level of your score by assigning key velocity to an expression. To assign key velocity to an expression:

1. Click the Expression tool.
2. Double-click above a measure to open the Expression Selection dialog box.
3. Click to select an existing expression, and click the Edit button. Or, to create your own new expression, click the Create button. The Text Expression Designer dialog box appears.
4. Edit the text box as necessary. Then, click the Playback Options (Show Playback Options on Macintosh) button to expand the dialog box (if it isn't expanded already).
5. Under Playback Options, for Type, choose Key Velocity.
6. For Effect, enter the new key velocity (0-127) 0=silent, 127=loudest.

7. Click OK, Select, and OK to return to the score. Play back the region for review. Finale will use this key velocity for the staff until it reaches another key velocity change.

TIP

To scale the dynamic range, you can also add a crescendo or decrescendo hairpin, and then use the TGTools Smart Playback plug-in. Look under "The TGTools Smart Playback Plug-in" later in this chapter for details.

Sustain

If you want to give your playback the same type of effect as a sustain pedal, assign Sustain Pedal MIDI data to an expression and add it to your score. You can then use metatools to easily assign pedal-on (℗.) and pedal-off (✲) symbols to your score.

To create sustain pedal expressions and define them for playback:

1. First, create a pedal-on expression. Click the Expression tool, then hold down the Shift key and press P (we'll assign a pedal-on expression as a metatool to the P key). The Expression Selection dialog box appears.

2. Click Create to open the Text Expression Designer dialog box.

3. Click Set Font.

4. In the Font dialog box, for Font, choose Maestro and Size, 24. Click OK to return to the Text Expression Designer.

5. Click in the text box and type Alt-0161 (Win), or Option-Shift-8 (Mac). On Windows, be sure to use the Num Pad.

6. Click the Playback Options (Show Playback Options on Macintosh) button to expand the dialog box (if it isn't expanded already).

7. Under Playback options, for Type, choose Controller.

8. Click the drop-down/popup menu on the right and choose Sustain Pedal.

9. For Set to Value, enter "127".

10. Click OK, then Select. You return to the score.

11. Now, create a pedal-off expression. Hold down the Shift key and press O (we'll assign a pedal-off expression as a metatool to the O key). The Expression Selection dialog box appears.

12. Click Create to open the Text Expression Designer dialog box.

13. Click Set Font.

14. In the Font dialog box, for Font, choose Maestro and Size, 24. Click OK to return to the Text Expression Designer.

15. Click in the text box and type an * (asterisk).

16. Under Playback Options, for Type, choose Controller.

17. Click the drop-down/popup menu on the right and choose Sustain Pedal.

18. For Set to Value, enter "0".

19. Click OK, then Select. You return to the score.

20. Now, hold down the P key and click below a staff to place a pedal-on symbol that applies to playback.

21. Hold down the O key and click below the same staff to place a pedal-off symbol that applies to playback.

Setting a Tempo

You may want to enter text indicating the tempo and also define it for playback (allegro, for example). To do this:

1. Click the Expression tool.

2. Double-click above a measure to open the Expression Selection dialog box.

3. Click to select an existing expression and click the Edit button. Or, to create your own new expression, click the Create button. The Text Expression Designer dialog box appears.

4. Edit the text box as necessary. Then, click the Playback Options/Show Playback Options button to expand the dialog box (if it isn't expanded already).

5. Under Playback Options, for Type, choose Tempo.

6. Click the drop-down/popup menu to the right and choose the main beat.

7. For Set to Value, enter the number of beats per minute.

8. Click OK, Select, and OK to return to the score. Now, your score will adjust the playback upon reaching this expression. Create another tempo expression if you want to change back to the original or to a different tempo.

TIP

To define a tempo at the beginning of your piece, highlight the first measure with the Mass Edit Tool and use the Create Tempo Marking plug-in (under the Plug-ins menu). You can use this plug-in to define tempo for any selected measure. This is the easiest way to create a tempo marking with a "♩=" indication.

Ritardandi and Accelerandi

You can define gradual tempo changes for playback by editing the playback characteristics of a text expression.

In this example, you'll learn how to create a ritardando marking as an expression, and define it for playback. You can apply the same principles to create an accelerando.

NOTE

Before going through the following steps, you might want to try using the JW Tempo plug-in to define gradual tempo changes. With this plug-in, all you need to do is select a region, then define an opening and closing tempo for the region. The JW Tempo plug-in is located on the companion CD-ROM.

1. With the Expression tool selected, double-click the score where you would like to begin the ritardando. The Expression Selection dialog box appears.
2. Scroll down and click the *"Rit."* marking to select it.
3. Click Edit. The Text Expression Designer appears.
4. Click the Playback Options button to expand the dialog box (if it isn't expanded already).
5. Under Playback Options, for Type, choose Tempo. Then, choose the main beat from the drop-down/popup menu to the right.
6. After Effect, choose Execute Shape, then click the Select button to the right. The Executable Shape Selection dialog box appears.
7. Click to select line number 6 (the line slanting downward—for an accelerando, you would choose a line slanting upward).
8. Click Duplicate, then click Edit. The Executable Shape Designer dialog box appears, as shown in Figure 14.6.

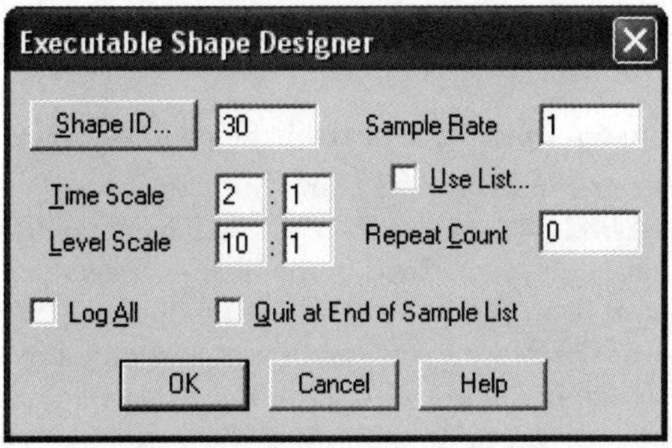

Figure 14.6
Edit the duration and degree of an executable shape in the Executable Shape Designer dialog box.

Executable Shape Designer

Shape ID...   30   Sample Rate 1

Time Scale   2 : 1   ☐ Use List...
Level Scale 10 : 1   Repeat Count 0

☐ Log All   ☐ Quit at End of Sample List

OK   Cancel   Help

9. Click the Shape ID button to open the Shape Designer dialog box. This is where you will define the basic duration and degree of your tempo change.
10. From the Shape Designer menu, choose Rulers and Grid. The Rulers and Grid dialog box appears.
11. Choose Eighth Notes. Then, for Grid Marks Every, enter "4".
12. The Shape Designer window should now contain grid markers (Figure 14.7).

CHAPTER 14

Each horizontal grid marker (from left to right) equals four eighth notes, or a half note's duration. In our example, the line extends over four grid markers horizontally, so the ritardando is defined to last for two measures in 4/4 time. Each vertical grid marker (from top to bottom) equals one beat per minute. Since our line slopes down over two markers, the tempo will slow down two beats per minute from the original tempo over the course of the tempo change. In the future, use the Selection tool to adjust the slope and length of the line as needed. For now, we'll multiply the duration and number of beats per minute of the tempo change.

Figure 14.7
Use the Shape Designer dialog box to define the basic duration and degree of your tempo change.

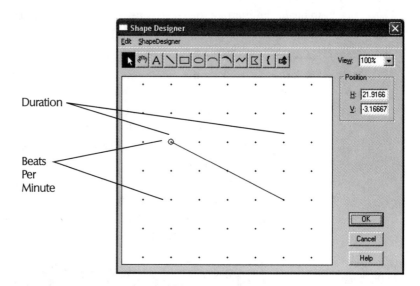

13. Click OK to return to the Executable Shape Designer.

14. Now, you can edit the duration and number of beats per minute in the Time Scale and Level Scale text boxes. You will be entering a ratio that adjusts the executable shape you defined in the Shape Designer. For Time Scale, enter 2:1 (as shown in Figure 14.6). A ratio of 2:1 tells Finale to multiply the duration by 2, in this case increasing the duration to four measures. For Level Scale, enter 10:1 (as shown in Figure 14.6). A ratio of 10:1 tells Finale to multiply the number of beats per minute by 10, in this case increasing the tempo change to 20 beats per minute. In the future, use any desired ratio to edit the executable shape you have defined in the Shape Designer.

15. Click OK, Select, OK, Select, and OK to return to the score. The "*Rit.*" marking appears. Play back your score to review your tempo change. To resume a specific tempo at any point in your score, follow the previous instructions under "Setting a Tempo."

Changing a Staff's Playback Instrument Mid-Score

Parts sometimes call for an instrumentalist to switch instruments during the piece. If this is the case, you may want to apply this instrument change to playback of your Finale document. You can change the playback instrument for a staff at any point by adding an expression defined to change the MIDI instrument. To do this:

1. Click the Expression tool.
2. Double-click above the measure you want to change the playback instrument. The Expression Selection dialog box appears.
3. Click Create. The Text Expression Designer dialog box appears.
4. In the text box, enter text that tells the performer to switch instruments ("to saxophone," for example).
5. Click the Playback Options button to expand the dialog box (if it isn't expanded already).
6. Under Playback Options, for Type, choose Patch. Several new parameters appear.
7. Choose the new instrument just as you would in the Instrument Definition dialog box. If you want to specify a General MIDI instrument, simply click the drop-down/popup menu for GM: and select the instrument. To define a non-General MIDI instrument, enter the appropriate Bank Select and Program Change numbers below (see the instructions above under "Creating Non-General MIDI Instruments" for details on how to do this).
8. Click OK, Select, and OK to return to the score. Finale will now change to the specified instrument during playback upon reaching the added expression.

Using the MIDI Tool

The MIDI tool is a powerful way to manipulate playback in Finale. Set, scale, add, change percent, or randomize the key velocity and duration of notes for any selected region, or number of selected notes. Or, apply continuous data to a region. Use the MIDI tool window for a visual display of the MIDI data as you make fine changes to the playback. We won't be able to cover every feature of the MIDI tool, but the following instructions include concepts you can use as a foundation for exploring the thousands of possibilities for creating a custom MIDI performance.

Key Velocity, Note Durations, and Continuous Data

The MIDI tool's framework is split into three sections: key velocity (how hard a key is struck as if it were played on a MIDI keyboard), note durations, and continuous data. Click the MIDI tool, then choose the MIDI menu. Whenever you are using the MIDI tool, you can choose which type of MIDI data you want to edit from the three items at the top of this menu. Key velocity and note durations are somewhat self-explanatory. Continuous data encompasses everything from pitch bends and patch changes to over one hundred types of MIDI controller data, including sustain, panning, volume, and many others. You can manipulate key velocity, note durations, and continuous data in several ways, as shown lower in the MIDI menu (Set to, Scale, Add, Percent Alter, etc.).

Here are general steps you can take to edit MIDI data for a region of your score.

Key Velocity (With Crescendo Example)

For this example, we'll scale the key velocity over two measures of eighth notes to create a crescendo effect. To prepare for these steps, open a new default document, and add eighth notes into the first two measures.

1. Click the MIDI tool.
2. Drag-select the first two measures so they are highlighted.
3. From the MIDI Tool menu, make sure Key Velocities is selected.
4. From the MIDI Tool menu, choose Scale. The Scale dialog box appears, as shown in Figure 14.8.

Figure 14.8
Specify the opening and closing values for MIDI data applied to a selected region in the (Key Velocity) Scale dialog box.

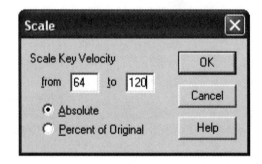

5. In the first text box, enter the key velocity for the first note in the region. Try 64. In the second text box, enter the value for the final note in the region. Try 120. These values can be anywhere from 0 to 127. In this case, 0 is silent, 127 is very loud.
6. Click OK.

Play the region back. Notice the crescendo effect. You just told Finale to evenly scale the key velocities for the selected region. Now, if you wanted to set all notes in the selected region to the same key velocity, from the MIDI Tool menu, choose Set To. To change by percent, choose Percent Alter (note that using Percent Alter after the previous example will retain the crescendo). Use any of the available menu items in the second menu section to manipulate the key velocity of the selected region as you wish.

TIP
To remove all MIDI playback data from a region, select the region with the MIDI tool and press Backspace/Clear.

Note Durations (with Start Time Example)

You can alter the start and/or stop times for any region of notes with the MIDI tool as well. For this example, enter two measures of quarter notes into your scratch document. Let's say you want notes in the second of these measures to anticipate the beat by a sixteenth note. To do this with the MIDI tool:

1. Click the MIDI tool.

2. Drag-select the second of the two measures of quarter notes.

3. From the MIDI Tool menu, choose Note Durations.

4. From the MIDI Tool menu, choose Add. The Add dialog box appears, as shown in Figure 14.9.

Figure 14.9
Edit the start and/or
stop times for a region
of notes in the (Note
Duration) Add dialog
box.

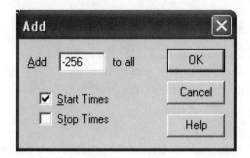

5. Enter –256 in the text box. This setting is in EDUs. There are 1024 EDUs in a quarter note, so 256 EDUs equals a sixteenth. It's negative because we want the notes to play prior to their original placement. Any time you edit note durations in the MIDI tool by entering a value, you will be using EDUs.

6. Click OK.

Play the region back. Notice the second measure of quarter notes anticipates the beat by a sixteenth note. You can use the same basic procedure to change the start time, stop time, or overall duration of notes for a selected region.

Continuous Data (with Continuous Crescendo Example)

Continuous data is somewhat different than key velocity and note duration data. Continuous data applies not only to the MIDI Note On and Note Off signals, but also to the entire duration of sustained pitches. For example, to enforce a crescendo or pitch bend on a single sustained pitch, you would need to apply continuous data to the region.

To prepare for the following steps, start a new document with the Setup Wizard. Click Next to move to page 2. Choose any sustaining instrument (like Trumpet in C). Click Next, Next, and Finish to open the document. Enter a whole note in the first measure. Use the following steps to apply a crescendo to the whole note.

1. Click the MIDI tool.

2.   Click Measure One to select it.

3.   From the MIDI Tool menu, choose Continuous Data. The View Continuous Data dialog box appears, as shown in Figure 14.10.

Figure 14.10
Choose the type of continuous data you want to apply to your score in the View Continuous Data dialog box.

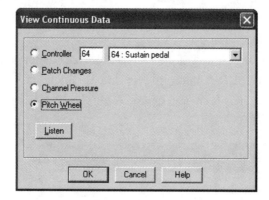

4.   From the Controller drop-down/popup menu, choose Controller 7, Volume.

5.   Click OK.

6.   Click to highlight the first measure.

7.   From the MIDI Tool menu, choose Scale. The Scale dialog box appears.

8.   Scale Continuous Data from 40 to 120 in increments of 1.

9.   Click OK.

Play the region back and notice the change in volume. To see a graphical representation of this continuous data, double-click the measure to open the MIDI Tool window.

TIP

You can apply continuous volume data to regions of your score containing hairpins automatically with the Smart Playback plug-in. See "Hairpins" under "The TGTools Smart Playback Plug-in" later in this chapter.

The MIDI Tool (Split) Window

Instead of editing your MIDI data directly in the score, you can use a separate window to view and edit MIDI data. When you double-click any measure with the MIDI tool selected, the MIDI Tool window will appear. This window takes up the top half of the screen on Windows, and opens as a moveable window on Macintosh (Figure 14.11).

Figure 14.11
View MIDI data applied
to a region of your
score, or edit MIDI data,
in the MIDI Tool
window.

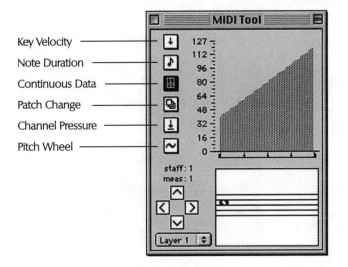

Key Velocity

Note Duration

Continuous Data

Patch Change

Channel Pressure

Pitch Wheel

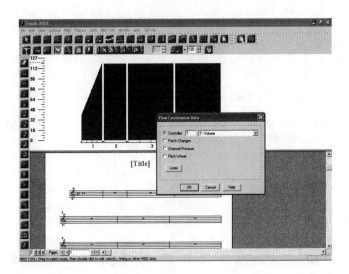

The shaded (Mac), or black (Win) area indicates continuous data applied to the measures. You
can use the MIDI Tool window to view or edit key velocities, note durations, or continuous data.

Macintosh: Editing MIDI Data in the MIDI Window

In your scratch document, enter four quarter notes into a measure. Then, choose the MIDI tool
and double-click the measure containing the four quarter notes to open the MIDI Tool window.
To edit the MIDI data for this region, first choose the type of MIDI data from the icons on the left
(Figure 14.11), or choose from the MIDI menu. If you choose Continuous Data, choose the type
of continuous data from the View Continuous Data dialog box, and click OK. Then, click and
drag in the MIDI display portion (upper right) to select the region you want to edit, as shown in
Figure 14.12. The selected region will be highlighted in blue.

Figure 14.12
Click and drag in the
MIDI display portion of
the MIDI Tool window
to select the region you
want to edit.

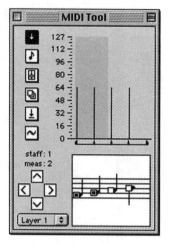

If you want to highlight more than one region, Shift-click and drag. If you are editing key velocities or note durations, you can also highlight the handles to select individual notes in the measure display portion at the bottom (Shift-click to select nonconsecutive notes). Now, from the MIDI Tool menu, choose the type of modification (Set to, Scale, Add, etc.). Enter the desired value and click OK. The MIDI display portion of the MIDI Tool window updates to display your changes.

To navigate in the MIDI Tool window:

▶ Use the arrows to the left of the measure display portion to navigate to the desired measure. Click the left arrow to move back a measure, the right arrow to move forward a measure, the up arrow to move up a staff, and the down arrow to move down a staff. Notice the Staff and Measure indicator above the arrows indicates the exact measure you are currently viewing.

▶ Click the Layer Select popup menu in the lower left to choose the layer you want to edit.

▶ From the MIDI Tool menu, choose Show Selected Notes to isolate the selected notes in the MIDI display portion of the MIDI Tool window.

To play back the region without leaving the MIDI Tool window, from the MIDI menu, choose Play.

Windows: Editing MIDI Data in the MIDI Split Window

In your scratch document, enter four quarter notes into a measure. Move to Scroll View (Scroll View tends to be more convenient while using the MIDI Split window, though both views will work). Choose the MIDI tool and double-click the measure containing the four quarter notes to open the MIDI Tool Split window. It will appear on the top half of your screen, and display MIDI data for several measures. To edit the MIDI data for this region, first choose the type of MIDI data from the MIDI Tool menu (Figure 14.13).

Figure 14.13
Click and drag to enclose the notes or region you want to edit in the MIDI Tool Split window.

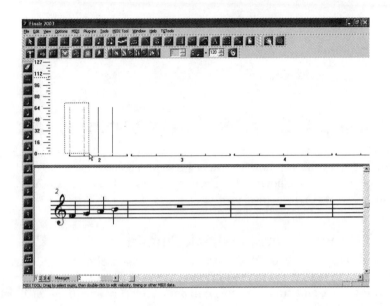

If you want to highlight more than one region, Shift-click and drag. If you are editing key velocities or note durations, you can also highlight the handles to select individual notes in the staff below the Split window (Shift-click to select nonconsecutive notes). Now, from the MIDI Tool menu, choose the type of modification (Set to, Scale, Add, etc.). Enter the desired value, and click OK. The MIDI display portion of the MIDI Tool window updates to display your changes.

To navigate in the MIDI Tool Split window:

▶ Use the scroll bar on the bottom to move horizontally through your score. Use the scroll bar on the right to move up or down between staves.

▶ Use the Layer Select buttons on the lower left of your screen as you would normally to switch layers.

▶ From the MIDI Tool menu, choose Show Selected Notes to isolate the selected notes in the MIDI Tool Split window.

To play back the region without leaving the MIDI Tool window, from the MIDI menu, choose Play.

Copy MIDI Data

You can copy MIDI data from one region and apply it to any other region of your score with the MIDI tool. This feature works just like drag-copying with the Mass Edit Tool. To copy MIDI data:

1. Click the MIDI tool.

2. Highlight a region of your score containing MIDI data you want to copy.

3. Click and drag the highlighted region to the destination region. If the destination region is out of view, Ctrl/Option-Shift-click the first measure of the destination region. The Copy MIDI Data (Mac: Copy) dialog box appears.

4.   Enter the number of times you want to copy the MIDI data. For example, if you are copying a single measure, and want to apply the same MIDI data to the next five measures, enter "5" here.

5.   Click OK.

Defining Other Markings for Playback

There are a number of common markings you may want to define for playback. In past versions of Finale, many of the following examples required advanced work with the MIDI tool or Expression tool. Now, however, defining playback is far easier for several items thanks to the TGTools Smart Playback plug-in.

The TGTools Smart Playback Plug-in

Introduced in Finale 2002, the Smart Playback plug-in eliminates the drudgery of defining trills, glissandi, and hairpins with the MIDI tool. Now, you can simply set your parameters in the Smart Playback plug-in, and Finale will adjust the corresponding MIDI data, or add hidden playback notes for you accordingly. Use these examples as a guide to easily define trills, glissandi, and hairpins for playback. The Smart Playback dialog box is modeless, so you will always be able to apply the current settings without leaving the dialog box.

To prepare for this section, open a new default document (File > New > Default Document). Use this as a scratch document while going through the following steps.

NOTE

The following are features included with Finale 2002 and 2003. For more playback capabilities, try using the full version of TGTools. You can find the TGTools demo on the companion CD-ROM.

Glissandi

When you define a glissando for playback with the Smart Playback plug-in, Finale creates continuous data (pitch bend) that increases the pitch of the starting note a certain number of times per quarter note until reaching the destination note. The successive pitch changes are so frequent that the playback gives the effect of a glissando. To define glissandi for playback using the Smart Playback plug-in:

1.   Enter two notes on different pitches into the first measure of your scratch document. Then, click the Smart Shape tool and choose the Glissando tool from the Smart Shape Palette. Doubleclick the first note to extend a gliss to the second. Your first measure should look something like the example shown in Figure 14.14.

Figure 14.14
Use the Smart Playback
plug-in to define a
glissando such as this
one for playback.

2. Choose the Mass Edit Tool.

3. Highlight the first measure.

4. From the Plug-ins menu, choose TGTools > Smart Playback. The Smart Playback
   dialog box appears, as shown in Figure 14.15

Figure 14.15
Set parameters for trills,
glissandi, and hairpin
playback in the Smart
Playback dialog box.

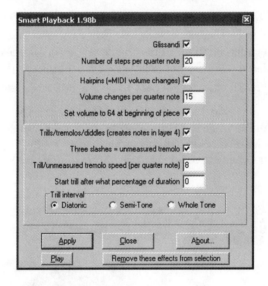

5. In the Smart Playback dialog box, make sure Glissandi is checked. For now,
   leave Number of steps per quarter note at 20 (an indistinguishable distance
   between note changes at most tempos). You can decrease this value in the future
   for a more jagged glissando (for Piano, perhaps) or increase this value for a finer
   transition at extremely slow tempos.

6. Click Apply. You shouldn't see any changes to your notation. Play the region
   back to review the glissando.

Hairpins

When you define a hairpin for playback, Finale creates continuous data scaling the volume
(controller #7) at the degree you specify. To define hairpins for playback using the Smart
Playback plug-in:

1. Enter a passage of eighth notes into the first two measures of your scratch document. Then, click the Smart Shape tool and use the Crescendo and Decrescendo tools in the Smart Shape Palette to create a crescendo under measure one and a decrescendo under measure two, as shown in Figure 14.16.

Figure 14.16
Define crescendo and decrescendo hairpins such as these for playback using the Smart Playback plug-in.

2. Choose the Mass Edit Tool.
3. Highlight the first two measures.
4. From the Plug-ins menu, choose TGTools > Smart Playback. The Smart Playback dialog box appears, as shown in Figure 0.1
5. Check Hairpins (= MIDI volume changes). Leave Volume changes per quarter note at 15 and leave Set volume to 64 at beginning of piece checked.
6. Click Apply. Play the region back to review the crescendo and decrescendo.

To see the continuous data you have created, click the MIDI tool. From the MIDI menu, choose Continuous Data, set Controller Data to "Volume: 7" and click OK. Doubleclick one of the measures. This opens the MIDI window with the volume data visible (Figure 14.17). Click and drag to highlight the region, then choose one of the editing options under the MIDI Tool menu to adjust the controller data.

Figure 14.17
Use the MIDI tool to edit controller data defined by the Smart Playback plug-in.

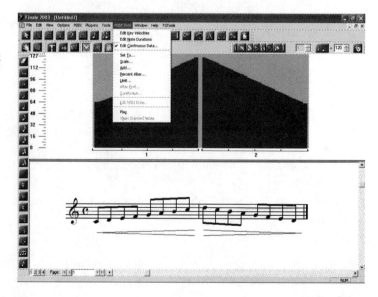

NOTE
When you choose Set volume to 64 at the beginning of a piece while defining a hairpin for playback, you may notice the document sounds quieter during playback. To restore the original volume while keeping the defined hairpin playback, try setting the Base Key Velocity to 127 in the Playback Settings (Win: click the Playback Settings icon in the Playback Controls. Mac: Expand the Playback Controls).

Trills and Drum Rolls

To define trills for playback using the Smart Playback plug-in:

1. In your scratch document, enter two whole notes in consecutive measures.

2. Enter a trill articulation over the first one and a trill Smart Shape over the second, as shown in Figure 14.18 (the Smart Playback plug-in will generate a sounding trill from either of these markings). Of course, in the future, add a trill articulation or Smart Shape to any note before using this plug-in.

Figure 14.18
Before defining trills for playback, enter either a trill articulation or trill Smart Shape over the desired notes.

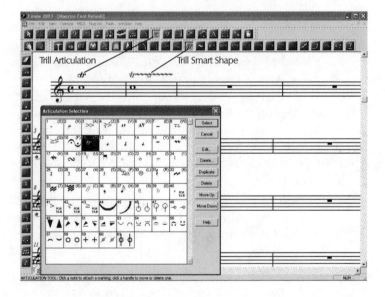

3. Choose the Mass Edit Tool.

4. Highlight the measures containing the notes with trill markings.

5. From the Plug-ins menu, choose TGTools > Smart Playback. The Smart Playback dialog box appears, as shown in Figure 14.15.

6. Now, define your trill in the lower section of options in this dialog box. For now, leave the trill checkboxes and text boxes alone (the defaults will work fine). In the future, use these parameters to adjust the frequency of your trill and the

presence of unmeasured tremolos. Under Trill Interval, choose the interval of the trill. The setting you choose will produce a trill alternating either one semi-tone higher or one whole tone higher with the original pitch.

7.   Click Apply. You shouldn't see any changes to your notation. Play the region back to review the playback you defined.

You can also use the trill settings in the Smart Playback dialog box to generate repeated pitches (for drum rolls, for example). For this example, let's start a new percussion staff. From the File menu, choose New > Document with Setup Wizard. Click Next, add a Snare Drum staff, then click Next, Next, and Finish to open a new snare drum document. Here is how to notate and define drum rolls for playback.

1.   In your scratch document, enter notes with subdivision markings like those shown in Figure 14.19.

Figure 14.19
Generate playback of drum rolls with the Smart Playback plug-in.

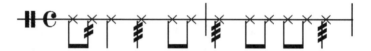

2.   Choose the Mass Edit Tool and highlight the region.

3.   From the Plug-ins menu, choose TGTools > Smart Playback. The Smart Playback dialog box appears, as shown in Figure 14.15.

4.   In this example, there are three "unmeasured tremolos," each entered on a quarter note. Make sure Three slashes = unmeasured tremolo is checked. Then, after Trill/unmeasured tremolo speed, enter the number of strikes per quarter note (a higher number = tighter roll). In the text box next to Start trill after what percentage of duration, enter 0 (since we want each roll to begin immediately).

5.   Click Apply.

6.   Play the region back to review the playback you defined. You will hear the subdivision indicated by the number of slashes, and notes with three slashes subdivided according to your settings for unmeasured tremolo.

Fermatas

Defining a fermata for playback can be done by creating two tempo expressions, one to slow the tempo for the held note and then a hidden one to return to the original tempo. To prepare for the following steps, enter four quarter notes into a measure. We'll add a fermata on the third beat and define it for playback.

1.   Click the Expression tool and double-click on the third quarter note in the measure. The Expression Selection dialog box appears.

2.   Make sure Note Expression is selected at the bottom of this dialog box.

3.   Click Create to open the Text Expression Designer dialog box.

4.   Click Set Font. The Font dialog box appears.

5. For Font, choose Maestro. For size, choose 22.

6. Click OK to return to the Text Expression Designer.

7. In the text box, type "U" (capitol U).

8. Click the Playback Options/Show Playback Options button to expand the dialog box (if it isn't expanded already).

9. Under Playback Options, for Type, click the drop-down/popup menu and choose Tempo.

10. For Set to Value, choose a slower tempo. For example, if the tempo of your piece is quarter=96 beats per minute, enter "48" to decrease the tempo by half (doubling the duration of the note).

11. Click OK, Select, then OK to return to your score. The fermata should appear above the note.

12. Now, we need to create an expression attached to the next note that tells Finale to return to the original tempo. Double-click on the note directly following the held note to open the Expression Selection dialog box.

13. Click Create to open the Text Expression Designer. Make sure the expanded Playback section is visible (note that it is not necessary to enter anything in the text field in the upper left corner).

14. Under Playback Options, for Type, click the drop-down/popup menu and choose Tempo.

15. For Set to Value, choose the original tempo. For example, if the tempo of your piece is quarter=96 beats per minute, enter "96".

16. Click OK, Select, and OK to return to the score.

17. Play back the region for review. Notice the scroll bar slows at the tempo change and then returns to the original speed after the held note. To increase the duration of the held note, rightclick the handle of the fermata and choose Edit Text Expression Definition. Then, decrease the number of beats per minute in the Set to Value text box.

Rolled Chords

In piano music, it is common to see a wavy line next to a chord telling the performer to "roll," or play each note of the chord in rapid succession, beginning with the lowest written note. In Finale, you can create a rolled chord marking and define it for playback with the Articulation tool.

To create rolled chord marking and define it for playback:

1. Enter a tall chord in a scratch Finale document with the Simple or Speedy Entry tool.

2. Click the Articulation tool.

3. Click the bottom note of a chord to open the Articulation Selection dialog box.

4. Click to highlight the Rolled Chord articulation (number 31 by default).

5. Click Edit to open the Articulation Designer dialog box.

6. In the Playback Effect section, notice Change Attack is selected and the setting for Bottom Note Value is –256. These settings tell Finale to play the bottom note of the chord 256 EDUs prior to the beat, followed by the remaining notes in ascending order. The top note will sound directly on the beat (since Top Note Value is set to 0). If you want to begin the roll on the beat, set the Bottom Note Value to 0 and the Top Note Value to 256. To increase the overall duration of the roll, set the number for Bottom Note Value to less than –256 if the roll starts before the beat, or set the number for Top Note Value to greater than 256 if the roll starts on the beat.

7. Click OK and Select to return to the score. Click the top handle and drag to position the articulation. Click and drag the lower handle up or down to change the length of the roll marking.

TIP

Use the "R" metatool to quickly enter a rolled chord. With the Articulation tool selected, simply hold down R and click the chord.

Slurs

You can produce a slur effect for playback by increasing the note durations within the slur so they overlap slightly. You can do this by using the MIDI tool.

To create a slur effect for playback:

1. Enter a passage of eighth notes on different pitches into a scratch document.

2. Click the MIDI tool (on Windows, from the Window menu, make sure Advanced Tools Palette is checked, then choose the MIDI tool in the Advanced Tools Palette).

3. Click and drag to highlight the region of music.

4. From the MIDI Tool menu, choose Edit Note Durations.

5. From the MIDI Tool menu, choose Percent Alter. The Percent Alteration dialog box appears.

6. Enter "105". This tells Finale to increase the duration of the selected notes by 5%. Depending on the tempo, this value may need to be lower or higher.

7. Click OK and play back the region. The notes now slightly overlap, giving a slurred effect to the playback.

15

Integrating Finale With the Web and Other Programs

Finale files are extremely versatile. Share any Finale file with the world by posting it to your website or on the Finale Showcase, where visitors can view and listen to your score. E-mail a Finale file to anyone. The recipient can open it in NotePad—Finale's free, downloadable counterpart. Or, save your Finale file as a MIDI file to edit in a MIDI sequencer. These are just a few examples of Finale's ability to transfer your music into other formats. With the help of third-party programs and plug-ins, you can even perform more tasks, such as converting a Finale file to a WAV file to burn onto a CD, or save in MusicXML format to transfer to other music programs, or even earlier versions of Finale.

Here's a summary of what you will learn in this chapter:

▶ How to share files online.
▶ How to transfer music between programs.
▶ How to supplement Finale with third-party plug-ins.

Sharing Files Online

There are several ways to post a Finale file to the web. You can save your Finale file in HTML format and post it to a site. If you do this, visitors can open the file in the Finale Viewer, where they can play back, transpose, or even print your file depending on the security level you set. If you want to share your sheet music over the web without playback capabilities, you can also convert a Finale file into PDF format with the help of Adobe's Distiller software. Finally, you can simply post a file in Finale format for others to open in Finale. Visitors who don't own Finale can always download a free, basic version of Finale, called Finale NotePad, which is capable of opening any Finale file. In this section, you will learn how use the above methods to integrate Finale with the web.

Saving a Finale File as a Web Page

Post a Finale file to the web in three steps: Prepare the file for use with the Finale Viewer, save the file as a web page with your own custom settings, and post the .htm and .mus file to your website, or to the Finale Showcase.

Here are some tips for preparing a Finale file for the Finale Viewer:

▶ Adjust the page layout and general appearance just as you would any Finale file before printing. Note that all colored items (expressions, text blocks, etc.) will appear black and white in the Finale Viewer.

▶ Make sure the score plays back as you want it to. See chapter 14 for information on editing playback.

▶ Windows: Click the Playback Settings button in the Playback Controls to open the Playback Settings dialog box. Under Always Start At, choose Measure "1". Mac: Click the arrow on the left side of the Playback Controls to expand the lower section. For Play From, choose measure "1".

▶ To ensure your music will be visible on all machines, use the Maestro music font. From the Options menu, choose Set Default Music Font. Choose Maestro, and set the size to 24. Then, click OK to return to the score. Note that any text or music in an uncommon font will not display properly on any machine that does not have that font installed. See chapter 9 for information on changing fonts.

▶ Graphics will not display in the Finale viewer. Use the Graphics tool to delete any graphics you have placed in your document. If necessary, create new expressions to include any vital information that was in the form of a placed graphic.

After you have made final preparations to the file, save it as a web page. From the File menu, choose Save Special > Save as Web Page. The Web Page Options dialog box appears, as shown in Figure 15.1.

Figure 15.1
Edit the viewer's options for playback, printing, and other items in the Web Page Options dialog box.

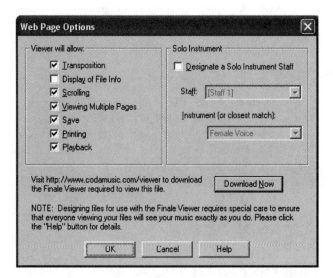

Under the Viewer will Allow section, check all items you want Finale Viewer to allow. For example, if you do not want to allow those who view your file to print it, uncheck Print. Do the same for any of the other options. If you decide to give those who view your file the ability to transpose, and your file contains a solo instrument, check Designate a Solo Instrument Staff, and choose the solo staff and instrument to allow users to transpose the solo and accompaniment independently (for example, if someone wants to play your solo line on a B flat clarinet instead of flute).

CAUTION

Even if you uncheck Save in the Web Page Options dialog box, it is still possible for someone to download your .mus file. If you would like to ensure the most security, but still allow users to view and play back your file, simply post a portion of your piece to the website (like the first few pages) instead of the whole thing.

After you have made your settings, click OK to open the Save As dialog box. Name the file, choose a destination and click OK. Finale will save two files; one with the extension .mus (the Finale file), and one with the extension .htm (web page file). Now, you can post these files to your website. Create a link to the .htm file. Always keep both the .htm and .mus files in the same folder when posting them to your site, since the viewer references the .mus file.

If you want to post your file on the web, but do not have your own website, you can easily post to Coda's "Finale Showcase" website. Finale Showcase is hosted by Coda, and contains a collection of Finale files created by users who want to publish their scores online. To upload your file to the Finale Showcase, from the File menu, choose Post at Finale Showcase. A browser will open and you will be routed to the Finale Showcase website. Login or create a personal account and follow instructions for posting a file.

To view the Finale Showcase, go to Coda's website at <www.makemusic.com> and click the Showcase button in the upper right corner of the page.

The Finale Viewer

Whether you post a Finale file to the Finale Showcase, or to your own website, visitors will always need to have the Finale Viewer (also called SmartMusic Viewer) plug-in installed to view the file. Installing the Finale Viewer plug-in is easy.

To download and install the Finale Viewer:

1. Open your browser and visit Coda's website <www.makemusic.com>
2. Click the Showcase button on the upper right corner of the page. The Finale Showcase website appears.
3. Click Download the Finale (or SmartMusic) Viewer.
4. Choose Windows or Macintosh depending on the platform you are using. Then, continue to follow instructions on the site to download the Viewer.
5. Save the file to your desktop.
6. Close any programs you have running.

7. Unzip/unstuff the file as necessary and doubleclick the installer icon. Then, follow the instructions to finish installation.

8. Restart your computer. Now, go to Coda's website, go to the Finale Showcase and click a file to view it. The file will open in the Finale (SmartMusic) Viewer.

Here is an example of a Finale file as it appears in the Finale (SmartMusic) Viewer (Figure 15.2).

Figure 15.2
A Finale file as seen in the Finale Viewer opened from the Finale Showcase website.

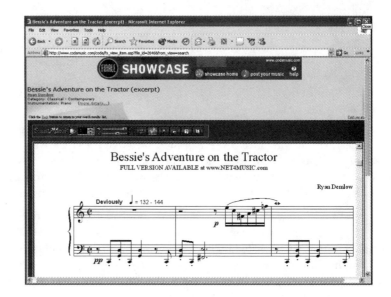

Finale NotePad

You may want to transfer a Finale file over your website or by e-mail, with the intention of allowing those who receive the file full access to print, save, or even make minor changes to the file. You may be a music educator sending a musical example or homework to your students. If this is the case, recipients of the file may not own Finale (or the most recent version of Finale). That's OK. Tell them to download Finale NotePad.

Finale NotePad is Coda Music's baby notation product. It offers a considerable amount of power considering the price (free). Here are some of NotePad's features:

▶ Open, save, and print any Finale file. That includes any file created in any version of Finale, Finale Allegro, Finale PrintMusic! or Finale NotePad. You can also create a new file from scratch with up to eight staves (File menu > New).

▶ Simple Entry. Edit or create notation.

▶ Transpose to any key.

▶ Add basic elements to your score, including articulations, expressions, lyrics, text blocks, slurs, and hairpins.

▶ Save as a Web Page or as a SmartMusic Accompaniment.

To download Finale Notepad, visit Coda's website at <www.makemusic.com>. There is a link on their home page that will direct you to the NotePad download page (you can't miss it).

NOTE

If you are using Finale for Macintosh, and you intend to e-mail a file, make sure to check Append File Extension in the Save As dialog box. This way, the file will open on Finale for Windows.

Saving as a PDF file

The PDF file format is great for transferring files over the web or by e-mail. Unlike saving as a web page, where others can open your music in the Finale Viewer, PDF files are opened using the Acrobat Reader (available for free at Adobe's website <www.adobe.com>). The Acrobat Reader is also installed with Finale and used to view the Finale User Manual. What exactly is a PDF file? Here's some text from their website that sums it up nicely:

"Adobe® Portable Document Format (PDF) is the open de facto standard for electronic document distribution worldwide. Adobe PDF is a universal file format that preserves all the fonts, formatting, graphics, and color of any source document, regardless of the application and platform used to create it. Adobe PDF files are compact and can be shared, viewed, navigated, and printed exactly as intended by anyone with free Adobe Acrobat® Reader® software. You can convert any document to Adobe PDF using Adobe Acrobat 5.0 software." (see <www.adobe.com/products/acrobat/adobepdf.html>).

To save a Finale file in PDF format:

1. First, set up the Adobe Distiller as a printer. See your Adobe Acrobat instruction manual for instructions on how to do this.
2. Then, from the File menu, choose Print. On Mac, if the Page Setup dialog box appears, click OK. On Windows, click the Setup button.
3. Click the Printer/Name drop-down/popup menu and choose the Adobe Distiller. Win: Then, click OK to return to the Print dialog box.
4. Mac: For Destination, choose File. Win: Check Print to File.
5. Click Print/OK.
6. The Save As dialog box appears. Name the file, choose a destination and click Save to save the PDF file.

If you like, you can also generate a PostScript file to be converted to a PDF later. To do this, from the File menu, choose Compile PostScript Listing. The Compile PostScript Listing dialog box appears. Make any necessary changes to page size and format and click Compile. In the Compile/Save PostScript File As dialog box, name the file, choose a destination and click Save. Now, to convert the .PS file to a PDF, simply drag it into the Adobe Distiller icon.

Transferring Music Between Programs

You may want to take a file you have created in a MIDI sequencer (such as Cakewalk or Cubase) and open it in Finale to generate sheet music. You can do this by saving and opening a MIDI file, or even copy excerpts of music back and forth between these programs using the MIDI clipboard. In this section, you will learn how to do this. We'll also explain a method for opening new Finale files in earlier versions (back to Finale 2000) and how to convert a Finale file into WAV format to be converted into an MP3 or burned to a CD.

MIDI Files

If you want to use another music program to open a Finale file, you could save it from Finale as a MIDI file. To do this, click the File menu and choose Save As. On Windows, for Files of Type, choose MIDI File; on Macintosh, click the Standard MIDI File radio button, then enter a file name and click Save. You will then see the Export MIDI File Options dialog box, as shown in Figure 15.3.

Figure 15.3
The Export MIDI File
Options dialog box

You will probably want to choose Type-1, which will designate your staves into tracks. This is by far the most common MIDI file format. If you want to place all of your music into one track, choose Type-0. Click OK to save as a MIDI file.

If you want to open a file from another program, such as a MIDI sequencer, first save the file in Standard MIDI format from the sequencer. Then, in Finale, choose the File menu and then Open. For Files of Type, choose MIDI File, then double-click the MIDI file and you will see the Import MIDI File Options dialog box, as shown in Figure 15.4.

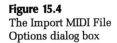

Figure 15.4
The Import MIDI File
Options dialog box

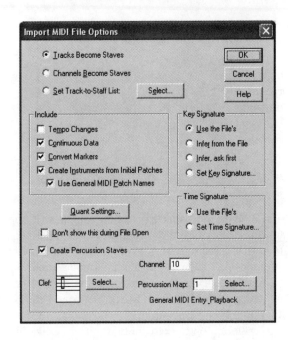

In this dialog box, you can tell Finale how to interpret the MIDI file. Make any desired changes and click OK to open the MIDI file into a Finale document.

Copying Music Between Programs with the MIDI Clipboard

Like copying music from measure to measure in Finale, you can also move selected regions of music between documents in other programs that support the MIDI clipboard. The other program could be any MIDI sequencer, or any program with MIDI editing capabilities. To move music (MIDI data) from Finale to another program, do the following:

1. Open Finale and the other MIDI program.
2. In Finale, click the Mass Edit Tool.
3. Highlight a region of music.
4. From the Edit menu, choose Export MIDI to Clipboard.
5. Move to the other MIDI program with the file you want to work with open.
6. Select a region of one of the MIDI tracks (or equivalent). See documentation of the MIDI application for more details (precise instructions for selecting a region vary between programs).
7. Press Ctrl-V to paste MIDI data into the selected region.

Similar steps can be used to copy MIDI data from another MIDI program to Finale. In the other MIDI program, select a region of a MIDI track and press Ctrl-C. Then, in Finale, highlight a region of measures with the Mass Edit Tool. From the Edit menu, choose Import from MIDI Clipboard. You will see the Import MIDI Data from Clipboard dialog box, as shown in Figure 15.5.

Figure 15.5
Customize Finale's
interpretation of MIDI
data in the Import MIDI
Data from Clipboard
dialog box.

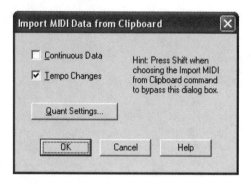

While copying MIDI data between programs, the results you get will depend on the quantization settings in the program of the destination document. In Finale, click the Quant Settings button in the Import MIDI Data from Clipboard dialog box to choose the smallest note value and make other settings for the imported MIDI data (refer back to chapter 4 for more information about quantization in Finale). Click OK back to the score to see the MIDI data as notes in a Finale staff. Hold down the Shift key while choosing Import MIDI Data from Clipboard from the Edit menu to bypass the Import MIDI Data from Clipboard dialog box. Consult the user manual for the other MIDI program for information on how to configure its quantization settings.

In addition to copying notes from other MIDI programs, you can copy MIDI data such as volume changes and pitch bends. Make sure the source region in the other MIDI editing program doesn't contain MIDI note data, then copy and import the MIDI information into the desired region in Finale. There is more information on Finale's MIDI capabilities in chapter 14.

TIP

While attempting to review results from copying MIDI data between programs, you may find that playback in Finale or the other MIDI program may not work if they are both open at the same time. Close both programs (make sure to save any files you want to keep), then open the program you want to play back with first.

Backwards Compatibility and MusicXML (Windows Only)

Many programs, such as Microsoft Word, allow you to save documents so that they are compatible with earlier versions of their software. For example, you can save a document from Microsoft Word 2000 in Word 97 format. Then, you can open the file on a different computer that has only Word 97. This makes the program "backwards compatible." Finale does not support backwards compatibility, so files created in Finale 2003 cannot be opened directly in Finale 2002 or any earlier version of Finale. There are always too many new features in Finale that control placement of slurs, articulations, and other items, that did not exist in earlier versions. Therefore, older versions of Finale would not be able to read this information, and many items would be misplaced in translation.

NOTE

Though files created in newer versions of Finale cannot be opened in any older version, the latest version of Finale will open any Finale file created in all earlier versions.

In the past, the best way to transfer documents to earlier versions was by saving and opening a MIDI file. This method is unacceptable most of the time, because all text and formatting gets lost while generating the MIDI file. Today, a new universal music file format has been developed called MusicXML. Unlike MIDI files, the MusicXML format does retain text and musical symbols. You can use the Recordare's Dolet plug-in to export and import files in MusicXML format. The full version of their Dolet plug-in is compatible with Finale versions back to Finale 2000. Therefore, you can use this plug-in to export a MusicXML file, then use the Dolet plug-in to import the file in Finale 2002, 2001 or 2000. A 30-day, full-featured demo version of the Dolet plug-in has been included on the Finale Power! CD-ROM for your convenience.

To transfer a file backwards to an older Finale version (back to Finale 2000):

1. First, run the Dolet installer located on the *Finale Power!* companion CD-ROM. When prompted, choose to install to the Finale folder containing the older version of Finale. Then, install this plug-in to all versions of Finale you plan to transfer documents between. Finale 2003 already contains the MusicXML plug-in, so you will not have to install the Dolet plug-in if you are exporting your file from Finale 2003.

2. Open the Finale file you want to export.

3. From the Plug-ins menu, choose MusicXML Export. The Dolet MusicXML Exporter dialog box appears, as shown in Figure 15.6.

Figure 15.6
Specify a path for your MusicXML file in the Dolet Light MusicXML Exporter dialog box.

4. Click the Browse button to choose a destination. The Save MusicXML window appears. Choose a path for your file here (like the desktop, for simplicity), and enter a name for your file. Click Save to return to the MusicXML Exporter dialog box.

5. Click OK to generate the MusicXML file.

6. Now, open the older version of Finale.

7. Make sure a new default document is open. If not, open a new default document (File > New > Default Document). If you used a template to create the original file, you could also open the template before importing for the most accurate layout in the translated file.

8. From the Plug-ins menu, choose MusicXML Import. The Dolet MusicXML Importer dialog box appears, as shown in Figure 15.7. This is the plug-in we installed earlier. If you do not see the MusicXML Import option under the Plug-ins menu, run the Dolet installer again and be sure to specify the folder containing the older version of Finale.

Figure 15.7
Specify a path for your MusicXML file in the Dolet Light MusicXML Importer dialog box

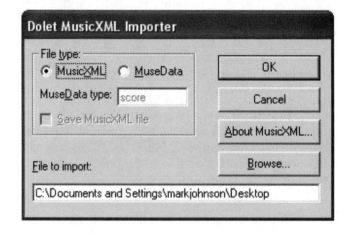

9. In the File Type section, make sure MusicXML is checked.

10. Click the Browse button, then navigate to your desktop (or wherever you saved the file).

11. Doubleclick the XML file to return to the Dolet MusicXML Importer dialog box. The path to the file should now appear in the File to Import text field.

12. Click OK. After some processing, the MusicXML file opens into the Finale document.

After importing the MusicXML file, you will need to make some changes, since the music is essentially dropped into the empty Finale document.

Here are some suggestions for editing files imported from MusicXML:

▶ From the File menu, choose File Info. Here, enter the title, composer, copyright, and description. Then, use text inserts to put this info into your document. Select the Text tool, double-click on your file and choose from the Text menu, Inserts > Title, etc.

▶ Use the Page Layout tool to edit the layout of the document (see chapters 2 and 11 for more information on laying out the page)

▶ If you have more than one staff in your document, you may have to respace your staves. Click the Staff tool, and then, from the Staff tool, choose Respace Staves. Enter a percentage or value to revert your staff spacing back to that of the original document.

▶ You will find that your score reverts to the default fonts. To specify a new music font, from the Options menu, choose Set Default Music Font. Then, to change other fonts, from the Options menu, choose Document Options and select Fonts.

TIP

If your original score was in the Jazz font, start by opening the Jazz Font Default file before importing from MusicXML. From the File menu, choose New > Document from Template. Double-click the file "Jazz Font Default.FTM" found in your Component Files folder.

Saving as a Wave File on Windows

If you'd like to burn a Finale file onto a CD to be played in a normal audio CD player, you'll need to first convert them into wave files. Finale does not currently have the ability to save as wave files. However, Finale can save MIDI files, and there are several programs that can convert these MIDI files to wave format. Save your Finale file as a MIDI file (see "MIDI Files" above), then use a MIDI-to-wave converter program to create the wave file. One free program that does this is Winamp. A full-featured trial version of Winamp is available for free from their website (www.winamp.com). Follow these instructions to download Winamp and use it to create a wave file.

(2004 Save Special Audio)

To convert a Finale file into wave format (note: the following instructions require an Internet connection):

1. Save your Finale file as a MIDI file. See the above instructions under "MIDI Files" for more information on how to do this. For now, save the MIDI file to the desktop.

2. Next, download and install Winamp 2.80 and the MIDI plug-in: Go to <www.winamp.com>. Under the picture for Winamp 2.80, click Download Winamp. Across from "Choose a Version," click the button for "Full" and underneath that click "Begin Download." In a few seconds, the "File Download" dialog box will appear. Choose "Save this program to disk" and click OK. Next, specify in the "Save In" box that you want the file saved to your desktop (to make it easy to find). Then, click Save.

3. Now, download the MIDI plug-in: Go to <www.blorp.com/~peter/>. On the left side, click MIDI Plug-in. Then, click the word "download" in "Newest version: v2.63 – Download (100k)". Choose to save this program to disk as well. Click OK. For Save In, choose Desktop, and click Save. When finished, click Close. Now, exit out of all programs so that only your desktop is visible.

4. Doubleclick the file called winamp280_full.exe (on some computers, the .exe extension will be hidden). If you agree to Winamp's license agreement, click Next. Leave everything checked except "AOL Icon (new installs only)" and "AOL Icon (upgrades)" (unless you want these).

5. Click Next. Let it install to the default directory (C:\Program Files\Winamp).

6. Click Next. Then, Uncheck everything except "Add Start menu icons." Choose the type of Internet connection you have.

7. Click Next. The User Information dialog box appears. If you want Winamp to send you information, you may enter your e-mail address here and check the desired options.

8. Click Next and then Run Winamp. If your speakers are turned on, you'll now hear a colorful sound byte.

9. Exit Winamp. Now, back on your desktop, double-click the in_midi.exe file. If you agree to the license agreement, click I Agree. Click Yes when asked if you want to run Winamp. In the future, you can run Winamp by going to Start > Programs (or All Programs) > Winamp > Winamp.

10. In Winamp, press ctrl+p (or click the top left corner and choose Options > Preferences). Underneath Plugins, choose Input. Then, on the right side highlight "Winamp2 MIDI plug-in v2.63b [in MIDI dll]."

11. Click Continue.

12. Click the Direct Music tab, then uncheck "Disable DirectMusic Support."

13. Click OK, and then close.

14. Exit Winamp.

15. Start Winamp again (Start > Programs (or All Programs) > Winamp > Winamp).Go back to the preferences (ctrl+p). Highlight "Winamp2 MIDI plug-in v2.63b [in MIDI dll]" and click Configure. Go to the Device tab and change the Device to "DM / Microsoft Synthesizer." Now, click the Output tab and check "Play through Winamp's Output System." Also, check "Write wave files to:" and click the button directly underneath (c:\).

16. Next, select a folder for your wave files. For simplicity, choose the desktop for now. Click OK, click OK again, and then Close. Only the normal Winamp screen should now be visible. Then, press l (lowercase letter L), or click the top left corner and go to Play > File. Browse on your computer (the desktop) to find the MIDI file that you saved from Finale. When you find it, highlight it and click Open. Winamp will now play your file, and at the same time it will create a wave file from it and place it in the folder you specified.

Now that you have your wave file, you can burn it onto a CD. Follow the instructions that came with your CD-writing software to do this.

It might be necessary to have a recent version of DirectX installed for this procedure to work. If you find that Winamp isn't running after enabling DirectMusic, try downloading and installing the latest version of DirectX from Microsoft's website <www.microsoft.com/directx>. Download and install the most recent version of DirectX for your operating system.

Saving as an AIFF File on Macintosh

If you'd like to burn a Finale file onto a CD on a Macintosh computer to be played in a normal audio CD player, you'll need to first convert them into AIFF files. Finale does not currently have the ability to save as AIFF files. However, Finale can save MIDI files, and there are several programs that can convert these MIDI files to AIFF format. Save your Finale file as a MIDI file (see "MIDI Files" above), then use a MIDI-to-AIFF converter program to create the wave file. One program that does this is Ultra Recorder. A full-featured trial version of Ultra Recorder is available for free from members.aol.com/ejc3. Follow these instructions to download Ultra Recorder and use it to create an AIFF file.

To convert a Finale file into AIFF format (note: the following instructions require an Internet connection):

1. Save your Finale file as a MIDI file. See the above instructions under "MIDI Files" for more information on how to do this. For now, save the MIDI file to the desktop.

2. Proceed to the the Ultra Recorder website and download the Ultra Recorder Installer.

3. Install Ultra Recorder.

4. Start Ultra Recorder.

5. Click Convert File.

6. Choose your MIDI file.

7. From the list of options, choose Standard AIFF.

Saving a Finale File as a SmartMusic Accompaniment

The SmartMusic Studio (previously called Vivace) intelligent accompaniment system is another product developed by Coda. It can accompany brass, woodwind, and vocal performers while responding to tempo changes and start/stop signals from a foot pedal. There is currently a library of over 20,000 accompaniments that are all available via subscription (see www.smartmusic.com for details). As of Finale 2002, you can add to their library by creating your own intelligent accompaniments with Finale.

NOTE
To use SmartMusic Studio accompaniments created from Finale, you need to first subscribe to SmartMusic Studio at www.smartmusic.com.

Here are the basics for saving a Finale file as a SmartMusic accompaniment:

1. Open or create a Finale file containing a solo instrument staff and accompaniment staves.

2. From the File menu, choose Save Special > SmartMusic Accompaniment (then click OK to bypass the SmartMusic Studio splash screen if it appears). The SmartMusic Accompaniment Options dialog box appears, as shown in Figure 15.8.

Figure 15.8
Designate solo and
accompaniment staves
for your accompaniment
file in the SmartMusic
Accompaniment
Options dialog box.

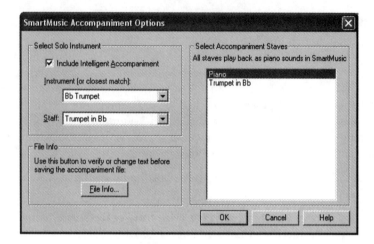

3. In the Select Solo Instrument section, check Include Intelligent Accompaniment
    if you want the file to respond to tempo changes during the performance (you
    might want to uncheck this for jazz accompaniments). For Instrument (or closest
    match), click the drop-down/popup menu to select the instrument you intend to
    use for the solo. If the instrument you want to use is not in the list, choose one
    with the same transposition as the desired instrument. For Staff, click the drop-
    down/popup menu to select the staff containing the solo part from your Finale
    document.

4. In the Select Accompaniment Staves section, choose all of the staves you want
    to hear in the accompaniment part. Shift-click and drag to select multiple staves,
    or Ctrl/Command-click to select nonconsecutive staves.

5. If you want to change the title, composer, and copyright, click the File Info
    button to open the File Info dialog box, where you can make these changes.
    Click OK to return to the SmartMusic Accompaniment Options dialog box.

6. Click OK to open the Save SmartMusic Export File As dialog box. Here, name
    the file and choose a destination.

7. Click Save. You have now saved the file as a SmartMusic Accompaniment. It
    will have the extension .smp and can now be opened in SmartMusic Studio. For
    information on opening files in SmartMusic Studio, see the SmartMusic User
    Manual.

For more information, including detailed information on preparing a Finale file for SmartMusic,
go to the Index of the Finale User Manual and go to SmartMusic Accompaniment Options
dialog box. Then, click the link To Prepare a File for SmartMusic Studio.

NOTE

Finale files saved as SmartMusic accompaniments will always use a piano sound for playback in SmartMusic Studio.

Supplement Finale with Third-Party plug-ins

Finale offers anyone with programming experience in C or C++ (and their own development tools) the ability to create Finale plug-ins. In this way, code-savvy users can produce their own Finale "features" for use in their work. A number of third-party plug-in developers have created a large amount of helpful utilities, and even sell their plug-ins to users anxious to get the very most out of Finale. Many professional engravers rely on third- party plug-ins in their Finale work, and any Finale user can benefit from them. In this section, you will learn where to find available third-party plug-ins and how to incorporate them into your Finale repertoire.

If you are a programmer interested in Finale plug-in development, you can download the Plug-in Development Kit (PDK) from Coda's download page (visit www.makemusic.com, and then click Downloads to run a search). Note that Coda's technical support department specializes in the Finale program itself, and does not answer questions specific to plug-in development. Visit the PDK Users Forum, also available from Coda's website, to interact with other plug-in developers.

TGTools

The TGTools plug-in set is a collection of supplemental plug-ins created by third-party plug-in developer Tobias Giesen. You already have seen a limited version of his plug-ins under Finale's Plug-ins menu (Plug-ins > TGTools). These have been included with the Finale package since version 2002. The full version of TGTools offers many additional features, including utilities for expression management, music spacing, lyrics, playback, and more (over sixty commands total). To purchase TGTools, or to download a demo version, visit <www.tgtools.de>. The full-featured, 30-day demo also has been included on the *Finale Power!* companion CD-ROM. If you haven't installed this demo, do so now. You can find specific installation instructions in chapter 1 under "The Companion CD-ROM" (or look to the TGTools website for installation instructions if you have downloaded TGTools). In this section, we'll give a brief overview of TGTools and explore some ways to incorporate them into your Finale work. For complete information on TGTools, download the manual PDF available at <www.tgtools.de>.

After you have installed TGTools, you will see a new menu item at the top of your screen. Under this menu, you can find all of the TGTools utilities (Figure 15.9).

Figure 15.9
After installation, you
will see a the TGTools
menu on the top of your
screen, where you can
access all of the
TGTools plug-ins.

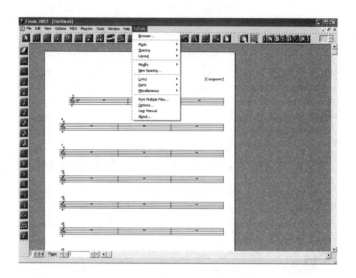

You can use TGTools to manipulate entries, selected regions, or your entire document. Most
commands will require selection of a region of measures with the Mass Edit Tool. To select
partial measures, from the Edit menu, choose Select Partial Measures. Feel free to experiment
with the TGTools commands. Any change to your score can be undone by pressing
Ctrl/Command-Z.

Expression Browser (Windows only)

You may have noticed that new expressions in Finale always appear at the bottom of the
Expression Selection window. While adding many expressions to the list, you may find yourself
struggling to find each expression, even if you have reordered them manually. For more control
over your expressions, use the TGTools Browser for Text Expressions plug-in. From the TGTools
menu, choose Browser. The Browser for Text Expressions dialog box appears, as shown in
Figure 15.10.

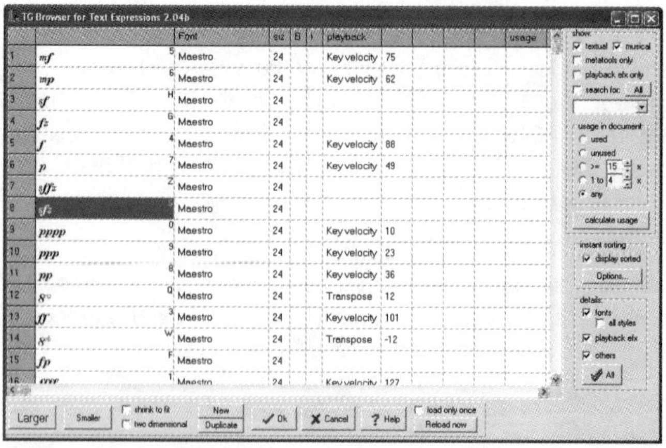

Figure 15.10
Manage text expressions
easily with the TGTools
Browser for Text
Expressions.

Notice all of your expressions, and their attributes (font, size, playback, etc.) appear neatly within the window with assigned metatools on the right side of each box. Click Larger in the lower left to zoom in on the list, or Smaller to zoom out.

Here are some ways to manage text expressions in the TGTools Browser for Text Expressions:

▶ To edit any item, click the box and type your new text. Click again to activate the editing cursor or drop-down/popup menu. Make your changes, then click outside the box. Use the font character maps (Help menu > User Manual) to find the keystroke for any characters in Finale music fonts.

▶ In the Show section to the right, you can specify certain types of expressions to display in the window by checking the desired options. To search for an expression, click Search For and enter the search text in the text field beneath. The window updates automatically.

▶ Sort your expressions. In the Instant Sorting section, click the Options button to open the Text Expression Sorter, where you can choose a priority for ordering based on family, size, and style.

▶ Click the New button at the bottom to create a new expression, or the Duplicate button to duplicate the selected expression.

Double-click, or click the X in the upper right corner, to close the expression browser. Any changes will be reflected in the Expression Selection dialog box.

Select Text Expression (Macintosh)
On Macintosh, the Select Text Expression feature is used in place of the Expression Browser. This is a good way to manage metatool assignments for your text expressions. From the TGTools menu, choose Select Text Expression. The Select text Expression dialog box appears, containing all text expressions and their metatool assignments. To assign a metatool, type the key you want to assign so it appears in the Assign to key text box. Then, click the text expression on the left. You return to your score with the expression clicked assigned to the key you entered.

Smart Explosion of Multi-part Staves
Often, while creating a score, several parts in an instrumental section are entered on a single staff to minimize the number of staves necessary in the system. This works well for the full score, but such staves can be confusing to the performers while reading the extracted part. You can use the Smart Explosion of Extracted Parts plug-in to "explode" a staff containing multiple voices into two or more independent parts. This plug-in will even recognize keywords such as "tutti" or "a2" to intelligently place the correct notes into the generated staves (Figure 15.11).

CHAPTER 15

Figure 15.11
Use the Smart
Explosion of Multi-part
Staves plug-in to
generate two or more
parts from a single staff .

Original Multi-part Staff

After Running Smart Explosion of Multi-part Staves

To explode a multi-part staff into two or more parts, each on its own staff:

1. Open any document containing a staff containing multiple parts. The staff can display the voices in the form of different layers, the same layer or using voice 2.

2. From the Options menu, choose Program Options and select the View category. Make sure Show Defined Measure Numbers is selected. Click OK to return to the score.

3. From the View menu, make sure Show Active Layer Only is turned off.

4. Select the Mass Edit Tool, and click to the left of the staff to highlight it (or select any region of the staff you would like to explode).

5. From the TGTools menu, choose Parts > Smart Explosion of Multi-part Staves. The Smart Explosion of Multi-part Staves dialog box appears, as shown in Figure 15.12.

Figure 15.12
Choose from a number
of settings for your
exploded parts in the
Smart Explosion of
Multi-part Staves dialog
box.

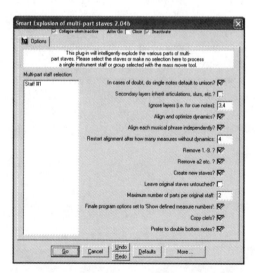

6. Most of the time, the default settings here will work fine. Make sure Finale's Program Option, "Show defined measure numbers," is checked (Options > Program Options > View).

7. Click Go. A dialog appears telling you not to touch the mouse or keyboard while the plug-in is working. Click OK and wait until things settle down. When a dialog pops up, click OK.

Your parts are now neatly separated into individual staves. To undo these changes, you'll have to undo several times (from the View menu, choose Undo/Redo lists, select "TG Smart explosion of multi-part staves" and everything above, then click OK). You can find more detailed information regarding exploding parts and even entire groups at once in the TGTools User Manual PDF (available at www.tgtools.de).

Add/Remove Space in Measure

While editing your spacing, you may want to adjust the amount of space before the first note in a measure or after the last note. To add or remove space at the beginning or end of a measure, use the Add/Remove Space in Measure plug-in. Click the Mass Edit Tool and select a measure or a region of measures. Then, from the TGTools menu, choose Spacing > Add/remove space in measure. The Add/remove space in measure dialog box appears, as shown in Figure 15.13.

Figure 15.13
Specify the amount of space to leave the beginning or end of a measure with the Add/remove space in measure dialog box

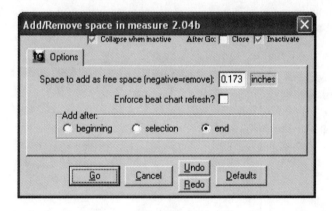

In the "add after" section, choose beginning to add/remove space before the first note of the measure. Choose Selection to add/remove space after the selection. Choose End to add/remove space after the last note (Figure 15.14). After Space to add as free space, enter the amount of space (a negative number here removes space). Click the measurement unit box to the right to select the desired measurement unit. Check Enforce beat chart refresh to ensure that the change is visible immediately. Click Go to apply your changes.

Figure 15.14
Results from increasing the space at the end of the measure using the TGTools Add/remove space in measure plug-in.

Before

After adding free space to the end

Convert Measure-Attached Expressions to Note-Attached

For a number of reasons, you may need to convert measure-attached expressions to note-attached. For example, if you are copying between documents (where measure-attached expressions will be left out of the destination region). You can use the TGTools Expressions plug-in to convert measure-attached expressions to note-attached. Click the Mass Edit Tool and select a measure or a region of measures containing the measure-attached expressions you want to convert. Then, from the TGTools menu, choose Modify > Expressions. The TGTools Expressions dialog box appears, as shown in Figure 15.15.

Figure 15.15
Use the TGTools Expressions dialog box to convert measure-attached expressions to note-attached.

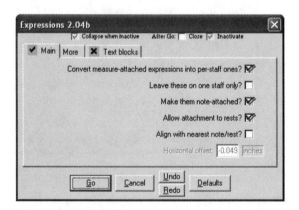

Here, check Make them note-attached. Also, for best results, check Allow attachment to rests, and Align with nearest note/rest. If you want to isolate expressions above or below the staff, you can do so by clicking the More tab. Click Go. All measure-attached expressions in the region convert to note-attached and align to the nearest note or rest. Now, you will be able to copy these expressions across two open Finale documents.

NOTE

For information on cleaning up music after a HyperScribe section, and for breaking beams intelligently, visit <www.tgtools.de> and download the TGTools QuickStart Video. Also, download the TGTools User Manual PDF for complete TGTools instructions at this site.

The Patterson Plug-in Collection

Robert Patterson is a third-party plug-in developer whose work appears both in supplemental plug-ins you can download from his website (www.robertgpatterson.com), and within the Finale program itself. Patterson Beams is also one of Robert's creations, and has shipped with Finale since version 2002 (you can find more information on Patterson Beams in chapter 10). The plug-ins offered at his website are free of charge for thirty days, and can be activated with a single, modest registration fee. You can also find the evaluation version of his plug-in collection on the *Finale Power!* companion CD-ROM. You can find detailed instructions for installing the plug-in collection from the web, or in the Read Me file located on the companion CD-ROM.

You can find a complete description of all plug-ins included in the Patterson Collection in the User Help section of the Patterson Plug-in collection website. I recommend reading the user help for each plug-in before putting it to use, as you will find a wealth of valuable information (see www.robertgpatterson.com/.fininfo/finmain.html and click the User Help link).

Beam Over Barlines

The somewhat complicated procedure for extending beams over barlines (as shown in chapter 10) has always been a complaint of Finale users. The need for a simple way to do this has been addressed by Patterson's Beam Over Barlines plug-in. Before going through the following steps, make sure the plug-in file "BmOvrBar" (Win: with the extension .fxt) exists in your Finale/plug-ins folder.

The following steps are a simple demonstration of how to use the Beam Over Barlines plug-in. To prepare for these steps, start a new default document (File > New > Default Document). Then, change the Time Signature to 2/4 and enter eighth notes into the first three measures.

To extend beams over barlines using the Beam Over Barlines plug-in:

1. Choose the Mass Edit Tool.
2. Highlight the first three measures of the scratch document you have prepared.
3. From the Plug-ins menu, choose Beam Over Barlines. The Beam Over Barlines dialog box appears, as shown in Figure 15.16.

Figure 15.16
Customize settings for
beams over barlines in
the Beam Over Barlines
dialog box.

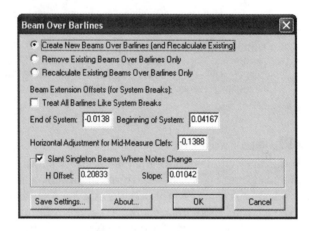

4. For now, we'll use the default settings. Click OK. You return to the score with beams extending over the first and second barline.

NOTE

The Beam Over Barlines plug-in works by adding extra notes at the end of measures, and hiding the first note(s) in the subsequent measure. To edit these notes, activate the Speedy frame on the first of the two measures, and use the right arrow key to advance beyond the right end of the speedy frame.

Mass Copy

You may have noticed that you cannot copy items attached to notes (expressions, articulations, Smart Shapes, etc.) without copying the notes themselves if Select Partial Measures is turned on (under the Edit menu). The Patterson Mass Copy plug-in is basically a new way to copy items without having to copy the notes to which they are attached. This plug-in will copy such items to and from partial measures.

Before going through the following steps, make sure the plug-in file "MassCopy" (Win: with the extension .fxt) exists in your Finale/plug-ins folder. If you would like to copy to and from partial measures, from the Edit menu, choose Select Partial Measures.

Here is the basic procedure for using the Mass Copy plug-in:

1. Choose the Mass Edit Tool.
2. Highlight the region containing note-attached items (or measure-attached Smart Shapes) you want to copy.
3. From the Plug-ins menu, choose Mass Copy. The Mass Copy dialog box appears, as shown in Figure 15.17.

Figure 15.17
Choose the items you
want to copy in the
Mass Copy dialog box.

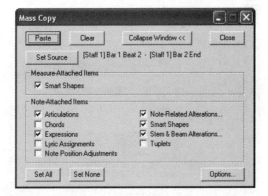

4. Click Set Source. Any time you click Set Source, the highlighted region will be set as the source region (the precise region is indicated to the right of this button). If a region is selected upon invoking the Mass Copy dialog box, the highlighted region will be selected automatically.

5. Check the items you want to copy from the selected region.

6. Highlight the destination region and click Paste. Items from the source region appear in the highlighted destination region, provided there is a corresponding entry available for the note-attached item.

NOTE
The Mass Copy plug-in will copy items only within a single document.

Staff Sets

In chapter 7, we explained how to define specific staves for viewing in Scroll View using Staff Sets. The Patterson Staff Sets plug-in expands this concept to offer additional features for staff viewing, including defining a view percentage for each Staff Set. With this plug-in, you can also save settings for each Staff Set you define, allowing you to define an unlimited number of Staff Sets (instead of the eight offered in Finale proper).

Before going through the following steps, make sure the plug-in file "StaffSet" (Win: with the extension .fxt) exists in your Finale/plug-ins folder.

To define Staff Sets with the Patterson Staff Sets plug-in:

1. Move to Scroll View (View > Scroll View).

2. From the Plug-ins menu, choose Staff Sets. The Staff Sets dialog box appears, as shown in Figure 15.18.

Figure 15.18
Define staves to include in a Staff Set and a desired view percentage in the Staff Sets dialog box.

3. Select the staves you want to include in the Staff Set. Ctrl/Command-click the desired staves.

4. Check Set View Percentage, and choose a desired view percentage. If you would like to use a view percentage other than the ones available, you will need to use a macro program to define the custom percentage (see the User Help for the Staff Sets plug-in accessible from www.robertgpatterson.com for additional info).

5. For Use Finale Staff Set, choose the Staff Set (1-8) you want to define. Note that you can define several Staff Sets for each Finale Staff Set by choosing the Save Settings option (see the User Help website for details).

6. Click OK. You return to the score with the selected staves isolated on the screen.

Staff Sets you define in the Staff Sets plug-in will be accessible from the View menu (View > Select Staff Set). To view all staves, from the View menu, choose Select Staff Sets and choose All Staves.

JW Plug-ins

There are a number of freeware plug-ins available online created by Jari Williamsson. These include JW Tempo for easily defining gradual tempo changes, JW Search and Replace, JW Playback, and several others. Jari has posted a collection of links to sites containing his own and other available third-party plug-ins. Visit <www.finaletips.nu> and click the Plug-ins link on the left. This site is also a good resource for helpful Finale productivity tips. The following are descriptions of some JW plug-ins, where to get them, and how to use them.

JW Tempo

The JW Tempo plug-in offers an easy solution for defining accelerandi and ritardandi. This plug-in is freeware available for download at <www.jwmusic.nu/freeplugins/index.html>. Download the file from this site, and copy the enclosed file "jwtempo2000.fxt" into your Finale/Plug-ins folder. Then, launch Finale.

To define accellerandi and ritardandi with the JW Tempo plug-in.

1.   Select the Mass Edit Tool.

2.   Select the region of measures to which you want to apply a gradual tempo change.

3.   From the Plug-ins menu, choose JW Tempo. The JW Tempo dialog box appears, as shown in Figure15.19.

Figure 15.19
Define the opening and closing tempo for the selected region in the JW Tempo dialog box.

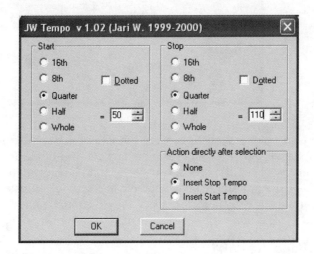

4.   In the Start section, enter the original tempo of the region. Select the main beat from the radio buttons (check Dotted if necessary). Then, enter the number of beats per minute in the text box (or use the up and down arrows). You can enter any value between 20 and 600 beats per minute.

5.   In the Stop section, enter the number of beats per minute you want to define for the tempo at the end of the region.

6.   Under Action directly after selection, choose Insert Stop Tempo if you want to continue using the tempo reached at the end of the selection. Choose Start Tempo if you want to revert to the tempo at the beginning of the selected region.

7.   Click OK. Your tempo changes gradually from the "Start" to the "Stop" tempo over the course of the selected region.

JW Search and Replace - Text

If you are working on a large score, and want to find and change every occurrence of a specific text expression, text block, lyric, or any other text, try the JW Search and Replace plug-in. This plug-in is also freeware available for download at <www.jwmusic.nu/freeplugins/index.html>. Download the file from this site, and copy the enclosed file "jwsearchreplace2000" into your

Finale/Plug-ins folder. Then, launch Finale. To use this plug-in, no selection is necessary. From the plug-ins menu, choose JW S&R - Text. The JW Search and Replace dialog box appears, as shown in Figure 15.20.

Figure 15.20
Enter the text to find, and its replacement, in the JW Search and Replace dialog box.

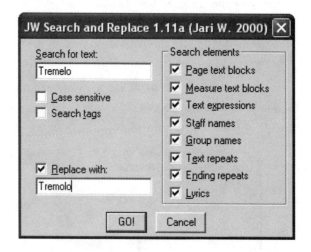

Under Search for text:, enter any existing text in the score you want to find. Then, to use the replace feature, check Replace with, and enter the text you would like to enter in its place. Under Search elements, check all types of text you want to include in the search. Click OK. A Search Results dialog box appears, showing you the location of first instance of matching text. Click Yes to find and replace the next instance, or Yes to All to find and replace all instances. Click OK to return to the score.

JW Playback (Windows only)

You can easily specify staves, groups, selected measures, or even Staff Sets for playback while reviewing your score by using the JW Playback plug-in. This plug-in is also freeware available for download at <www.jwmusic.nu/freeplugins/index.html>. Download the file from this site, and copy the enclosed file "jwplayback2000" into your Finale/Plug-ins folder. Then, launch Finale and open a document you want to play back. This plug-in is most beneficial in scores with many staves. To use this plug-in, no selection is necessary. From the Plug-ins menu, choose JW Playback. The JW Playback dialog box appears, as shown in Figure 15.21.

Figure 15.21
Choose specific staves, staff sets, selected regions, and other parameters for playback region in the JW Playback dialog box.

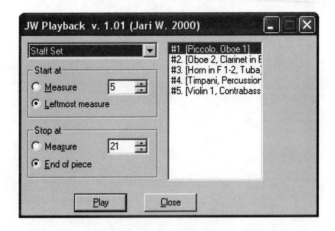

Click the drop-down menu at the top to select a region of staves. To select any combination of staves for playback, choose Specific Staves, then click any number of staves on the right. Under Start at, choose the measure to start playback. Under Stop at, choose a measure to stop playback. Click Play to begin playback. Click at any time to stop playback.

Forza

The Forza plug-in set, which is currently in its development stages (as of the production of this book), will offer a variety of plug-ins designed to enhance Finale's interface by offering alternatives for navigation, such as fully customizable popup menus for easy access of any Finale feature. There also will be features for editing and managing rehearsal figures, text blocks, and MIDI data. Visit <www.jwmusic.nu/forza> for a description of the Forza plug-in set, and for the latest news regarding this work in progress.

Index

Note: Italicized page numbers refer to figures and Tip, Note, and Caution boxes.

INDEX

customizing, 146, 202, 204
entering tablature, 194
fret numbers, 196, 207, 208
hammer-ons and pull-offs,
    201, 207
lowest fret settings, 203
nonchromatic fretboards, 205
number of strings, 203
picking indicators, 202
setting up a staff, 194
slash and rhythmic, 179–83
specifying pitches for open
    strings, 204–5
staff attribute settings, 203
stems and beams, 202, 203–4
string tuning, 202
tablature, 194–204. *See also*
    TAB staff
tremolos, 141, 200–201
.FTM (template files, Coda), 20–21

G

general appearance, customizing,
    337–38
Generate Names From option, 277,
    289
Giesen, Tobias, 4
glissandi, 131, 143, 145, 201,
    374–75
Global Staff Attributes, 287
Graphic Attributes dialog box,
    278–79
graphics, 276
    editing, 278–79
    entering as expressions,
        279–80
    exporting, 276–77
    file formats, 276–77
    importing, 278
    missing, *279*
    previewing, 277
    scaling, 279
    storing, *279*
Grid Line Settings section, 240
Grid Line Style drop-down/popup
    menu, 241
grids, 240–41
Group Attributes dialog box, *165*
groups
    adding to staves, 164–65
    brackets, 158, 164, 172
    deleting, 166
    in optimized systems, 172
    settings on a global basis, 176
    of staves for instrumental
        families, 164

Groups field, 288
guides, 241–42
guitar
    creating parts with TAB,
        205–8
    notation and tablature. *See*
        fretted instrument notation
    templates, 205
    tremolos, 141
Guitar Bend, 144, 199

H

hairpins
    aligning, 140, 242–43
    automatic generation between
        expressions, 141
    crescendos and decrescendos,
        138–41
    defining for playback, 375–77
    horizontal, 139
    line thickness and opening
        width, 139
    placement, 139
    playback, 140
    system breaks, 140–41
half notes, EDUs for, *16*
half note triplets, EDUs for, *16*
hammer-ons and pull-offs, 201, 207
Hand Grabber tool, 15–16
handbells, 302–3
handles, 13
harmonics, 179, 304–5
Help button, on dialog boxes, 5
Help menu, 3
Hide Numbers option, 271
Hide Staff Staff Style, 283
hiding
    brackets and text, 151
    clefs, 113–14
    Key Signatures, 119–20
    layers of notation, 183
    measure numbers, 34
    notes, 183, 192–93
    palettes, 10
    portions of a staff, 183
    Time Signatures, 31, 125
Horizontal text box, 266
.HTM files (Web files), 21–22
HyperScribe, 81–89
    Auto-Dynamic Placement
        plug-in, 89
    overview, 81, 82–87
    playback, 88–89
    recording into two staves at
        once, 87–88

Transcription Mode, 23
using with MIDI guitar, 88

I

icons, page layout, 43–44
Ignore Printer Margins for N-up
    option, 292
Illustrator files, 277
Illustrator Options dialog box, *277*
Implode Music utility, 308–9
importing
    graphics, 278
    plug-in for, 4–5
    scanned TIFF files, 343–44
Include TIFF Review option, 277
Independent Elements section, 221
independent lines of music,
    creating, 177
inkjet printers, 277
inserting measures, 30–31
Installation and Tutorials manual, 2
installing
    Finale, 6–8
    TGTools demo, 3–4
Instrument List, 359–62
instrumental families, groups of
    staves for, 164
isorhythmic notation, 128–29
Items to Snap to Grid dialog box,
    240, 241

J

Jazz font, 232
Jump to Next Measure option, 253
JW Booklet plug-in, *293*
JW Playback plug-in, 406–7
JW plug-ins, 4, 404–7
JW Search and Replace plug-in,
    405–6
JW Tempo plug-in, 405

K

key changes, adding double
    barlines, 163
key of C, 264
Key Signatures, 116–21, 212–13
    changing, 31, 116–18, *218*
    displaying or hiding, 119–20
    entering, 116–18
    metatools, 117
    nonstandard, 120–21
    outgoing, 120
    and percussion staves, 188
    selecting default font for, 118

INDEX

INDEX

![MUSKA & LIPMAN Publishing logo]

We want to hear from you.

We are interested in your ideas and comments. When you provide us the feedback, we'll add you to our monthly announcement list if you wish so you can hear about new books. We won't sell or share your personal information with anyone.

Tell us what you think of this book—what you like and what you don't like or what you would like to see changed.

Let us know what other books you would like to see from Muska & Lipman. You are a valuable resource for us.

Visit our Web site to submit your feedback:

http://www.muskalipman.com/feedback.html

Or send us a letter with your feedback at:
Muska & Lipman Publishing
P.O. Box 8225
Cincinnati, Ohio 45208-8225